The Evolution of the Nigerian State

Ibadan History Series

Published by Northwestern University Press
Christian Missions in Nigeria 1841–1891
by J. F. A. Ajayi
The Zulu Aftermath
by J. D. Omer-Cooper

Published by Humanities Press
The Missionary Impact on Modern Nigeria 1842–1914
by E. A. Ayandele
Britain and the Congo Question 1885–1913
by S. J. S. Cookey
The Sokoto Caliphate
by Murray Last
Benin and the Europeans 1485–1897
by A. F. C. Ryder
Niger Delta Rivalry
by Obaro Ikime
The International Boundaries of Nigeria
by J. C. Anene
Revolution and Power Politics in Yorubaland 1840–1893
by S. A. Akintoye
Power and Diplomacy in Northern Nigeria 1804–1906
by R. A. Adeleye
The Segu Tukulor Empire
by B. O. Oloruntimehin
The Warrant Chiefs
by A. E. Afigbo

In preparation
The New Oyo Empire
by J. A. Atanda
The Malagasy and the Europeans
by P. M. Mutibwa

For further details of the books in this series please consult the publisher.

Ibadan History Series
General Editor J. F. A. Ajayi, Ph.D.

The Evolution of the Nigerian State

The Southern Phase, 1898–1914

T. N. Tamuno, Ph.D.
Department of History, University of Ibadan

Humanities Press

First published
in the United States of America 1972
by Humanities Press Inc.
303 Park Avenue South
New York, N.Y. 10010

© T. N. Tamuno 1972
SBN 391 00232 5

Printed in Great Britain

To my children

Contents

		Page
Abbreviations		xi
Preface		xiii

1 **The Critical Century** 1
 The diplomatic, constitutional and political factors –
 Social ferment – Economic strains and stresses – The
 rôle of the British government in the protectorates

2 **Control through Coercion** 23
 The military and police establishments – Punitive
 expeditions and patrols – The Aro expedition – The
 Ekumeku disturbances – Territories acquired by
 conquest – The Coercion Ordinances – The paradox of
 the Pax Britannica

3 **Control through Diplomacy and Usage** 64
 The problem of jurisdiction in the Lagos Protectorate –
 The judicial agreements in Yorubaland – MacGregor
 and Egba politics – Government attitude towards the
 EUG since 1907

4 **The Mild Autocracy** 95
 The new rulers – Checks by British public opinion –
 The rôle of the British Parliament – The rôle of the
 Colonial Office – The man-on-the-spot and his
 environment – The Newspaper Ordinance, 1903 – The
 Seditious Offences Ordinance, 1909

Contents

5   The Executive and Legislative Councils   122
Unofficial representation on the Executive Council – The rôle of the Legislative Council

6   Law, Justice and Ministerial Duties   148
Blending the old and the new – The structure and rôle of the British Judiciary – African tribunals in the Protectorate of Southern Nigeria – The era of Native Councils in Yorubaland

7   Direct and Indirect Administration   184
The central administration – Educated Africans and the Civil Service – The relevance of anthropological data to administration – The rôle of the Eleko and White Cap chiefs of Lagos – Government attitude towards the chiefs of the protectorate – Oyo-Ibadan relations – Tributary relationships – Policy towards unpopular chiefs

8   Internal Boundaries and Amalgamation   222
The internal boundary questions – Gradual amalgamation

9   Development and Structural Changes in the Economy   246
The inter-dependence of administration and development – Imperial economic objectives and administrative means – Egerton's advantages – Structural changes in the economy: (i) Sylvan and agricultural produce. (ii) Trade. (iii) Exchange. (iv) Distribution problems. (v) Transportation. (vi) The balance sheet

10   Social Obligations and Performance   287
Formal social obligations – The liquor controversy – Public health and sanitation – Public education – Land policy

Contents

11	Labour and Domestic Slavery *Factors in the regulation of labour – Forced labour problems – Domestic slavery*	317
12	Conclusion	339
	Appendices	353
	Bibliography	402
	Index	409

Maps
1 Areas under firm administration in Southern Nigeria, June, 1909   61
2 Outline map of Southern Nigeria, 1909   207
3 Railways completed and projected in Nigeria, 1920   226
4 Nigeria, January 1911   241
5 Railway plans for Nigeria, 1905   259

Plates

Appearing between pp. 112–113
1 Overami of Benin
2 Sir Henry McCallum
3 H. L. Galway and the Chiefs of Bonny, 1896

Appearing between pp. 144–145
4 Sir Ralph Moor
5 Sir William MacGregor
6 The Rt Rev. James Johnson
7 Dr Obadiah Johnson

Appearing between pp. 272 273
8 C. A. Sapara-Williams
9 Henry Carr
10 Herbert Macaulay
11 Sir Walter Egerton

Appearing between pp. 304–305
12 Political and military staff in Southern Nigeria, 1910
13 John Holt
14 The Rt Rev. Isaac Oluwole

Contents

Acknowledgements

The publishers are grateful to the British Library of Political and Economic Science for permission to reproduce extracts from the copyright material of the following: E. D. Morel for Private Papers (unpublished); A. Boyle for *Trenchard*, A. Kirk-Green (editor) for *The Principles of Native Administration in Nigeria*, and the author for Appendix F of *West Africa*. We are also grateful to John Holt and Company for permission to reproduce Plate 13.

Abbreviations

A.P.S.	Aborigines Protection Society
A.S.A.P.S.	Anti-Slavery and Aborigines Protection Society
C.M.S.	Church Missionary Society
C.O.	Colonial Office
E.U.G.	Egba United Government
F.O.	Foreign Office
H.C.	House of Commons
H.L.	House of Lords
J.A.S.	Journal of the African Society
J.H.S.N.	Journal of the Historical Society of Nigeria
M.P.	Member of Parliament
MP	Minute Paper
N.R.L.T.U.C.	Native Races and Liquor Traffic United Committee
O.A.G.	Officer Administering the Government
P.R.C.I.	Proceedings of the Royal Colonial Institute
S.M.A.	Société des Missions Africaines (Catholic Society of African Missions)
S.P.	Sessional Paper
W.A.F.F.	West African Frontier Force

Preface

This book makes a further contribution to Nigeria's administrative history. It emphasises the southern aspects of the evolution of the Nigerian state during the period 1898-1914. The territory covered in detail includes the Lagos Colony and Protectorate as well as the Protectorate of Southern Nigeria both before and after the 1906 amalgamation. Except where qualified in the text, the expression 'Southern Nigeria' is to be taken in this wider sense.

There are several ways in which the present study supplements the works of Nigerian and non-Nigerian scholars in this field. In particular, I. F. Nicolson's *The administration of Nigeria, 1900-1960*, published in 1969, dealt mainly with official 'men, methods and myths'. Despite the wide coverage of developments in Southern and Northern Nigeria till 1918, this otherwise valuable work failed to provide any sustained discussion of the impact of the British policies and measures on Nigerians. It again did not trace the responses of Nigerians to the important constitutional, diplomatic, political, economic and social developments which they witnessed during this period.

Though the late J. C. Anene's useful *Southern Nigeria in transition, 1885-1906*, published in 1966, sought to discuss the reactions of the people of 'Southern Nigeria' to colonialism, his analysis did not go far enough. By excluding Lagos Colony and the vast Lagos Protectorate, Anene missed the opportunity of discussing their unique problems. He therefore ignored a comparative analysis of the complicated but historically important and interesting developments in that vital part of Southern Nigeria. On balance, Anene focused more on general developments during the nineteenth century rather than on those of the early twentieth. Concerning the time-span for issues such as amalgamation, Native House Rule and others dealt with in the

Preface

work, 1914 and not 1906 provides the more logical cut-off point. Besides, the new sources of information available since Anene's book was published in 1966 call for a fresh approach to Southern Nigerian history with particular reference to developments during the crucial period, 1898–1914.

The developments in Southern Nigeria between 1898 and 1914 marked important stages in the evolution of the Nigerian state. The period begins with the recommendations made by the Niger Committee in August 1898 for the amalgamation of the 'Niger territories' or 'Districts' and ends with the further implementation of these proposals in January 1914. The British intervention in the government and politics of Southern Nigeria resulted in the creation of the Nigerian state which the controlling power desired as a political condition for its economic and humanitarian interests. The need for centralisation of authority and the pooling of economic resources so impressed the British government that from 1898, it planned and later executed in stages the amalgamation of the 'Niger Districts' then under its jurisdiction. With the expansion and consolidation of alien rule, political and economic power steadily passed from the Africans to the British authorities, who accordingly enlarged the scope of the 'protectorates' under them. By 1914, most of the various communities south of the Niger-Benue valley had been compelled by British officials to dissolve their pre-colonial sovereign powers in the newly-emergent Nigerian state. The processes through which a common political entity, a central authority and a co-ordinated economic and fiscal system developed in Southern Nigeria until the 1914 amalgamation therefore constitute major themes in this work.

In the end, a common central authority emerged and Lagos became the capital of an enlarged and well-defined political entity. Correspondingly, the need for securing economic co-ordination and interdependence assumed greater urgency and significance while the export-import figures rose steadily and encouragingly for Britain. The firm economic and political foundations laid in Southern Nigeria during this period were further developed from January 1914 when the Nigerian state was born as a British dependency.

While emphasising the evolution of the Nigerian state, the present work lays considerable stress on the close relationship between administration and development, particularly in the context of Southern Nigerian history between 1898 and 1914. It further shows the interaction of commerce, government, humanitarianism and politics in a sizeable West African dependent territory during the same period. The need to raise sufficient revenue for administration and limited welfare frequently provided a vital link between various political and economic measures.

Problems of administration and development at the town and village levels as well as those of the centre have received appropriate emphasis in this book. Administration and development in Southern Nigeria provided a means to an end: the satisfaction of Britain's self-interest measured in political, economic and humanitarian terms. There was the other related end in view: the well-being of the Africans under British rule. When the African interpretation of their welfare differed from Britain's, however, violent conflicts and non-violent protests resulted.

It is not enough to discuss the opposition or other reactions of townsmen and villagers to the establishment and consolidation of British political and economic control over them. It is equally important to ascertain simultaneously the mainsprings of the official policies and measures which provoked the varied responses. Due emphasis is given to the examination of the double standards adopted by the British government in handling the administrative issues which affected Lagos Colony and Protectorate on the one hand and the Protectorate of Southern Nigeria on the other. Throughout the analysis the changing constitutional angle is given the emphasis lacking in the other major works already cited.

The other problem—of public relations between the new rulers and those under their authority—is given sufficient emphasis here. There is a sustained analysis of the relationship between the British government and its principal 'men-on-the-spot'— Sir Ralph Moor, Sir Henry McCallum, Sir William MacGregor, Sir Walter Egerton, Sir Frederick (later Lord) Lugard and their deputies—and that between the controlling authority and the indigenous inhabitants.

The material for this study is taken from sources in Nigeria and the United Kingdom. In Nigeria, the Ibadan and Enugu branches of the National Archives and the *Africana* section of the University of Ibadan Library were very useful. But by far the bulk of the information came from the Public Record Office, the Colonial Office Library and the British Museum, all in London;

Preface

Senate House Library, the Institute of Historical Research, the Institute of Commonwealth Studies, the School of Oriental and African Studies, the E. D. Morel Private Papers at the British Library of Political and Economic Science, London School of Economics and Political Science, all at the University of London; the Private Papers of Joseph Chamberlain at Birmingham University Library; the Private Papers of Lord Salisbury (3rd Marquess) at Christ Church Library, Oxford University; and the Private Papers of Lord Lugard and the Anti-Slavery and Aborigines Protection Society Private Papers, at Rhodes House Library, Oxford.

This work has developed from my Ph.D. thesis submitted to London University in October 1962. At the thesis stage, Dr K. O. Dike, the late Dr J. C. Anene, and Dr I. M. Cumpston, my supervisor at Birkbeck College, University of London, gave invaluable help and encouragement. Dr Cumpston, in particular, was very thorough and considerate in her supervision. In preparing this expanded and revised work for publication, I have gained from the criticisms and suggestions of Professor J. F. A. Ajayi, Professor J. E. Flint, Dr J. A. Ballard and others. But I am entirely responsible for any fault. Mr A. M. Fagbenro of NISER, University of Ibadan, took infinite pains in typing the final draft.

Lastly, I am grateful for the financial assistance which directly and indirectly has helped me in preparing this work for publication. A post-graduate scholarship awarded by the University of Ibadan during the 1959–60 academic session and an Inter-University Council Fellowship between 1960 and 1962 enabled me to undertake and complete my Ph.D. thesis. A study-leave allowed me by the University of Ibadan from August to December 1969 gave me the opportunity of using new sources in the United Kingdom besides affording me more time to revise the thesis for publication. But neither the University of Ibadan nor the Inter-University Council is responsible for the views expressed in this book.

Tekena N. Tamuno

Department of History,
University of Ibadan,
Ibadan,
Nigeria.
August 1970

1 The Critical Century

THE DIPLOMATIC, CONSTITUTIONAL AND POLITICAL FACTORS

For Southern Nigeria the nineteenth century was critical in several respects. At the beginning, its states and communities enjoyed undisputed control over their external and internal affairs. The middle of the century brought serious challenges to the sovereignty of most of these communities, particularly those along the coast. Towards the turn of the century, their control over both external and internal affairs was either lost or severely curtailed. Too late they learnt that sovereignty was indivisible.

Complex constitutional adjustments and diplomatic changes followed the shift of responsibility. These changes were closely connected with the early stages of the long process of state formation—the evolution of the modern Nigerian state.

There is no intention here to chart in detail the long and tortuous course of these diplomatic and constitutional changes. It is sufficient to indicate briefly the major internal and external factors which influenced developments.

Politically, serious internal dissensions within the various states and communities threatened their stability and integrity and exposed them to external dangers. For example, the decline and collapse of the old Oyo Empire and the resultant long period of warfare among the various successor-states weakened the Yoruba communities until peace was restored under British auspices in 1893.[1] Such wars continued to agitate the Yoruba hinterland for nearly half a century, even when new political

[1] For details see Ajayi, J. F. A. and Smith, R. S. *Yoruba Warfare in the Nineteenth Century*, Cambridge 1964; Biobaku, S. O.: *The Egba and Their Neighbours*, Oxford 1957; Akintoye, S. A.: *The Ekiti Parapo and the Kiriji War* (Ph.D. thesis), Ibadan 1966; Awe, B. A.: *The Rise of Ibadan as a Yoruba power in the Nineteenth Century* (D.Phil. thesis) Oxford 1964; Atanda, J. A. *The New Oyo Empire: a study of British indirect rule in Oyo Province, 1894–1934* (Ph.D. thesis), Ibadan 1967.

threats to their integrity arose after the first British consul for the Bights of Benin and Biafra had been appointed in 1849. They remained unabated even in 1861 when Britain annexed Lagos and began to expand her influence into Yorubaland. In 1893 when the warring Yoruba states made peace, they were too exhausted to resist the more effective fire-power of the British-controlled troops already established in Lagos.

Neither the Ijebu's stubborn resistance of 1891–92 nor the defiance of the Alafin of Oyo which led to the bombardment of his domains by British troops in 1895 proved that the long period of wars had not seriously affected the Yoruba ability to take up arms in defence of their rights. The Ijebu steadfastness in defending their economic and other rights and the resultant British punitive expedition of 1892[1] came shortly before the long period of warfare in Yorubaland was formally concluded in 1893. As far as the Ijebu were concerned, the 1892 episode was the external aspect of an otherwise internal war in which they sought to safeguard their commercial, social and political rights.

The neighbouring Egbas, equally concerned over their rights in the Yoruba hinterland, at first resisted just as fiercely as the Ijebu the advance from Lagos of European influences. They had been intelligent enough not to try armed combat with the British-controlled troops after the disastrous British siege of Ikorodu in April 1865, and now understood clearly the military message of the Ijebu expedition of 1892. War-weary and internally weak from the long struggles between the war-lords and the Alakes,[2] the Egbas, as will be shown later, preferred a diplomatic solution to the British threats against their independence.

Both in duration and intensity, the 1895 attack on the Alafin's palace[3] represented a smaller episode than the Ijebu expedition. The police action of 1895 at Oyo merely confirmed what had been apparent to careful observers since the 1830s – the military incapacity and exhaustion of the Alafins who for six decades had relied first on Ijaiye and later on Ibadan to defend New Oyo

---

[1] For the details see Aderibigbe, A. A. B.: *The Expansion of the Lagos Protectorate, 1863–1900* (Ph.D. Thesis) London 1959; Ayantuga, O. O.: *Ijebu and its Neighbours, 1851–1914* (Ph.D. thesis) London 1965.
[2] Biobaku, *op. cit.*, pp. 98–9.
[3] Atanda, *op. cit.*, p. 123; Ayandele, E. A.: *The Missionary Impact on Modern Nigeria, 1842–1914*, London 1966, p. 167.

against the disaffected Yoruba warriors and jihadists under Fulani leadership at Ilorin.

The long and bitter struggle between the Yorubas and the jihadists of Northern Nigeria on one hand and the Yoruba states *inter se* on the other, left unresolved the controversial question of Ilorin. It was lost by the Yorubas to the Fulani-dominated political system centring on Sokoto-Gwandu during the first two decades of the nineteenth century. The British settlement in 1894 which confirmed the loss of Ilorin to the Yorubas left considerable bitterness on both sides of the demarcation line.[1]

War exhaustion and problems of internal security compelled the Egbado Yorubas to surrender their independence to Britain in the 1880s. Sandwiched between two aggressive antagonists – the Dahomians and the Egbas – and unable to unite for defence against their common foes, the militarily weak Egbado sought and later secured British protection.[2] From the 1880s, when the Egbado spoke of 'independence', they were refuting continued Egba claims to their territory rather than reclaiming the sovereignty they had surrendered. In the same context, the British government in Lagos opposed the Egba demand for the Egbado territory of Ilaro.[3]

Also disastrous for Yorubaland in the long run was the continuation of serious dynastic feuds in Lagos. The long contest for power between Kosoko and Akitoye of Lagos exhausted the major combatants to the extent that the British consul, John Beecroft, cast his decision in favour of the anti-slavery candidate in 1852. But Akitoye, who was enthroned in January 1853, died mysteriously – presumably from poison – a few months later.[4] His rival, Kosoko, continued to adopt a divisive rôle in Yoruba politics first during his temporary exile in nearby Epe and later at Lagos from 1862 until his death in 1872. Anti-British during the 1840s and 1850s, Kosoko became a loyalist in his later years.[5] He was always a serious threat to Dosunmu[6] who had succeeded

---

[1] Adeleye, R. A.: *The Overthrow of the Sokoto Caliphate, 1879–1903* (Ph.D. thesis), Ibadan 1967, p. 272.
[2] Folayan, K.: *Egbado and Yoruba-Aja Power Politics, 1832–1894* (M.A. Dissertation) Ibadan 1967, Chapters 3 and 5 and pp. 195–6.
[3] C.S.O. 7/1/2, Legislative Council Debates, 24 August 1891.
[4] Losi J. B.: *History of Lagos*, Lagos 1967, pp. 29–39.
[5] *Ibid.*, pp. 41–3.
[6] Usually spelt as Docemo in several official documents instead of the Nigerian version – Dosunmu.

Akitoye in 1853, and his tactics suited admirably the interests of the pro-annexation British consuls, European merchants and Christian missionaries. The annexation of Lagos in August 1861 came as the logical conclusion to the long drawn-out drama in which the rival kings of Lagos, British consuls and European commercial and humanitarian interests had all taken part.

In the neighbouring kingdom of Benin, Oba Ovonramwen (Overami) who had begun his rule in 1888 faced serious domestic and external difficulties. However, in 1889 he successfully reasserted his control over Akure and six years later executed three Edo chiefs who had defied him. Before he had consolidated his authority, his tributary subjects in Agbor showed signs of restlessness and a desire to secede from Benin. At the same time the Oba was trying to resist British attempts to extend their influence and authority in Benin; so he failed to crush the Agbor revolt in 1896.[1]

Such Itsekiri leaders as Chief Omadoghoghone Numa (Dogho) saw in the collapse of the Benin kingdom a golden opportunity to escape from the trade restrictions previously imposed by the rulers of Benin. Dogho therefore substantially assisted the British expedition against Benin in 1897.[2] Personal ambition and hatred of Nana, the Itsekiri merchant-leader, also influenced Dogho's loyalty to Britain from 1894 to 1932.[3] Before the British overthrew Nana in 1894, the Itsekiri had failed to settle the serious feuds between their various chiefs, particularly those affecting the Nana and Dogho families, during the long interregnum which began in 1848.[4] Here again, the internal divisions of Itsekiriland were exploited by the British authorities in the Oil Rivers (Niger Coast) Protectorate in the 1880s and 1890s.

In Bonny, bitter local inter-House feuds over commercial and political matters played into the hands of some European merchants and British consuls eager to exploit the weakness of the city-state. The failure of Oko Jumbo, the Head of the Manilla Pepple House, and JaJa, the Head of the rival Annie Pepple

---

[1] Igbafe, P. A.: *Benin under British Administration, 1897–1938* (Ph..D thesis) Ibadan 1967, pp. 57–8.

[2] Ikime, O.: *Niger Delta Rivalry: Itsekiri-Urhobo relations and the European presence, 1884*–1936, London 1969, p. 187.

[3] *Ibid.*, pp. 186–7.

[4] Ikime, O.: *Merchant prince of the Niger Delta.* (*The rise and fall of Nana Olomu last Governor of the Benin River*), London 1968, pp. 8–94.

The Critical Century

House, to control events led to the bitter civil war of 1869,[1] which further weakened Bonny. Jaja and his supporters left the fast-declining Bonny to found the new settlement at Opobo which, with the support of friendly British consuls and European traders during the 1870s, flourished commercially and politically before JaJa's conflict with the British consuls in the 1880s.

The Amakiri dynasty of the Kalabari Ijos of the Niger Delta encountered similar decline in power, prestige and authority in the 1870s and 1880s from the rivalries of over-mighty and ambitious House Heads. Shortly before leaving their Elem Kalabari site near the Bonny estuary for more convenient settlements inland, the King of Kalabari clashed with Chief Will Braide and the members of the Barboy House who eventually left their kith and kin to establish a new homeland at Bakana. Similar defections led to the withdrawal of Chief Bob-Manuel and his followers to Abonnema. Consequently, the Amakiri dynasty obtained the support of relatively few Kalabaris first at Degema and later at Buguma.[2] Thus, the Kalabari and the people of Bonny and Opobo became politically too weak to avoid steady British consular encroachment upon their sovereignty.

In Old Calabar, after the death in 1858 of King Eyo of Creek Town and of King Duke of Duke Town in 1897, their people lost power and control over their own affairs to European missionaries and traders and British consular officials. The internal conflicts of the various Ibibio-Efik communities took a sharper turn in the last quarter of the nineteenth century when the predominantly Christian Henshaw Town broke away from Duke Town which had been reluctant to give the Presbyterian missionaries wholehearted support.[3]

Internal divisions and jealousies of the various communities precluded concerted action against the influence of European traders, Christian missionaries and British consular authorities. It was not so much that the British officials adopted a policy of divide and rule as that they reaped the benefit of these internal dissensions.

[1] Dike, K. O.: *Trade and politics in the Niger Delta, 1830–1885*, Oxford 1956, pp. 150, 219–20; Anene, J. C.: *Southern Nigeria in transition, 1885–1906*, Cambridge 1966, p. 42.
[2] Jones, G. I.: *The trading states of the Oil Rivers*, London 1963, pp. 150–5; 207; Anene, *op. cit.*, p. 46.
[3] Nair, K. K.: *Politics and society in Old Calabar, 1841–1906* (Ph.D. Thesis) Ibadan 1967, Abstract and p. 361; Jones, *op. cit.*, p. 85.

External factors influencing social, economic and other factors of Southern Nigerian history had various effects on the people, differing from place to place. Much also depended on the complex adjustments made to accommodate some of the pre-colonial institutions and practices in the values represented by the new order, which included British humanitarian interests, Christian missionaries, European traders, British authorities, and some loyal and co-operative Africans.

SOCIAL FERMENT

After the imperial Acts of 1807 and 1833 relating to the abolition of the slave trade and slavery, the various activities of the humanitarians and consular officials threatened the social, economic and political institutions of several communities in Southern Nigeria. Quite seriously threatened was the form of mobile currency and reservoir of labour represented by slaves at a time when the means of transportation and modern banking facilities were either lacking or sadly inadequate. The basis of law enforcement which allowed slavery as part of the traditional penal code of several communities in Southern Nigeria was equally menaced by the British humanitarian interests seeking to abolish this institution.

In their eagerness to abolish the slave trade in Southern Nigeria (and elsewhere in West Africa), the humanitarians hardly realised the confusion, misapprehension, suspicion and distrust engendered by their otherwise salutary attitude. To the British, traffic in human beings after 1807 was both 'uncivilised' and illegal. As the century went on, a strong feeling developed that the slave trade, as an aspect of piracy, stood condemned in international and municipal law. This change in moral tone over the slave trade at first seemed incomprehensible to generations of people in Southern Nigeria who within a relatively short period were presented with two different concepts of right and wrong. Their scepticism about the correctness of such conflicting standards persisted into the early twentieth century.

In the British attempts to abolish the slave trade and slavery in Southern Nigeria, there were two separate but historically inter-related processes. One was the replacement of the foreign export trade in slaves by the export of palm produce. The other stemmed from the enlargement of the coastal trading 'Houses' so as to transport more palm produce and other trade goods from the inland districts, to meet increasing export demands. Both processes were considerably influenced by the Christian missionary opposition to slavery, the operations of the preventive squadron and the general attitude of the British authorities. In the post-abolitionist Southern Nigeria, the growing pains of the new structure, though it was geared in some respects to the pre-colonial social and political systems, came near to shattering them. Consequently, the society became weak in the face of foreign pressure.

The abolitionist doctrine of the British humanitarians worsened the cleavages between masters and former slaves and threatened other institutions directly and indirectly connected with slavery, for example the system of plantation slavery among the Ibibio-Efik communities and the House system of several Niger Delta communities.

The message of hope and freedom conveyed by the imperial Act of 1833 which was disseminated by British consuls in the Bights of Benin and Biafra since 1849 and Christian missionaries from the 1840s caught the imagination of the plantation slaves employed by Ibibio-Efik masters for the legitimate commerce in palm produce. They conceived and carried out a bloody insurrection against their masters in 1851.[1]

In the end, the British consul became the peace-maker, not the *Ekpe* (*Egbo*) lodge which in pre-colonial times had dealt with such matters. The significance of the struggle of the Order of Bloodmen for equal opportunity and social justice was clear to the Ibibio-Efik masters and office-holders of 'Grand Egbo'. As part of the peace-pact, the British consul forbade such pre-colonial practices as human sacrifices for which slaves had been preferred.[2] This represented a severe loss of sovereignty to the Ibibio-Efik authorities.

In the Niger Delta city-states where the institution of slavery affected the membership of the age-old House system, there was further cause for alarm. In those Delta States whose commercial and political fortunes centred on trade and fishing, free

---
[1] Dike, *op. cit.*, p. 157. Some free men took part in this disturbance to protect their own rights against authoritarianism.
[2] *Ibid.*, p. 158. During the nineteenth century, European observers mistakenly referred to the *Ekpe* Society (the Leopard Society) as *Egbo* (Ghost).

and servile members of Houses were of great value as sources of man-power for the ceremonial gigs of the chiefs, the war-canoes of the Houses and other purposes.

The House system of the Niger Delta states, including those of the Ibibio-Efik, allowed free and servile members to share certain obligations and benefits. Although, among the Ibibio-Efik, membership of the higher grades of such secret cults as the *Ekpe* society was closed to slaves,[1] they could participate freely in the other social and economic activities of their various communities. Persons of servile status could even by sheer ability and demonstrable success become Househeads. JaJa of Opobo belonged to that category, eventually becoming king (*Amanyanabo*). Under the House system of the Niger Delta Ijos, the House head was chosen democratically by all the members irrespective of servile origins. The position of the House head often went to males of proven ability, sagacity and influence. To the members of the House, the House head became a common 'father' who dealt with the social, economic and political problems of those under him.

At the higher level, the House head represented the views of his people in the Council of Chiefs which discussed the affairs of the community with the king. He was responsible for the general welfare of the members of his House. His permission was required for their marriages. He authorised the use of House funds for trading and mutual assistance. Such expenditure was necessary for the burial of the dead, the maintenance of dependent children and the upkeep of needy persons.

The House fund, which originally developed from the contributions in kind of the members, later benefited from the customs dues paid by European traders in the Oil Rivers.[2] As the custodian of the House fund, the House head wielded considerable influence. He was, however, responsible to the members for its proper use. The various contributions which traders, farmers and fishermen made to their House funds constituted a social security investment, if not for themselves at least for their dependents. Under responsible leadership and with satisfactory co-operation, the House system provided group solidarity for free and servile

---

[1] *Calprof.* 2/688, *The Efiks.* Anonymous document with no dates in the National Archives, Ibadan.

[2] Newns, A. F. F. P.: *Re-organisation report on the Kalabari clan,* 1947, p. 28.

members. Besides their contributions to the House fund, the members provided labour to meet the needs of the House head and others within the same system. They worked the House land together but owned other property privately.

The House system so far described was *par excellence* the institution of such coastal ethnic groups as the Ijos, Efiks and the Itsekiri of Sapele and Warri. It was alien to the people of the hinterland. Though not a nineteenth-century product, the House-system had clearly become a firmly rooted institution among the people of several Niger Delta city-states by the beginning of the century. It was threatened by the expansion of British administrative control over parts of Southern Nigeria. The chiefs and people of the Niger Delta city-states therefore expressed strong reservations when Claude MacDonald, on the Foreign Office's instructions, consulted them in 1889 on the type of administration which they would like established in place of extending to them the control of the Royal Niger Company chartered in 1886. So vital to their well-being was the House-system that the chiefs urged MacDonald to reserve to them, among other things, the right to retain domestic slaves in accordance with customary law and practice.[1] From 1891 when MacDonald became Commissioner and Consul-General in the Oil Rivers (later Niger Coast) Protectorate, he at first treated domestic slavery 'with moderation, patience, and commonsense'.[2]

Later MacDonald and Ralph Moor, who succeeded him from 1896, adopted measures which aroused the anxieties of the chiefs and nearly jeopardised the guarantees which they had sought and obtained in 1889. MacDonald and Moor faced the dilemma of carrying out the chiefs' wishes and meeting the imperial obligation to guarantee freedom to former slaves. Consequently, in special cases, both MacDonald and Moor issued 'free papers' to domestic slaves who testified to continuous neglect or ill-treatment. Such papers sought to protect the holders and serve as guarantees of absolute freedom in disposing of their private property despite the restrictions imposed under the House system. Convinced, however, of the inadequacy of the existing administrative arrangements, MacDonald and Moor limited the practice of issuing free papers to the Old Calabar district where

[1] FO. 84/1940, MacDonald to F.O., 12 June 1889, enclosures. They also wanted their rights to land and polygamy reserved to them.
[2] FO. 2/85, MacDonald to F.O., 17 December 1895.

the control of the newly-established government was strongest. For similar reasons, the Foreign Office refused to approve, outside the Old Calabar district, 'a system which is at present beyond the power of the Protectorate authorities to enforce'.[1]

In the Ibo hinterland, the British anti-slavery campaign threatened the social, economic and political institutions associated with the Long JuJu (*Chuku Ibinokpabi*) and other Ibo oracles. Aro agents, who were also important middlemen traders between the Ibo producers of palm oil and kernels in the hinterland and the Niger Delta traders along the coast, cleverly manipulated their oracle to serve the needs of slave-dealers,[2] as the Niger Coast Protectorate authorities knew.

The Aro were unwilling to allow the British authorities, European traders and missionaries to penetrate the Ibo heartland,[3] realising that this would put an end both to their monopoly of trade in the Ibo hinterland and to their lucrative exploitation of the Long JuJu for slaves from the ranks of the votaries who consulted their shrine in such disputed cases as murder, witchcraft and poisoning.[4]

While the British authorities between 1893 and 1897 tried to deal with opposition from such African chiefs as Nana of the Itsekiri and Overami (Ovonramwen) of Benin, the Aros allied with the Ikwes and Quas to check government penetration into the hinterland through fear of losing their trade monopoly in potash, guns, powder and slaves.[5]

The danger of a government attack against the Aros increased between February and March 1899 when British authorities rescued 136 refugees, the remnants of a party of about 800 people from Aboh and Aseh who had gone to consult the Long JuJu.[6] A later chapter will explain why the punitive expedition which

[1] FO. 2/85, Moor to F.O., 25 December 1895; FO. 2/99, F.O. to Moor, 18 February 1896.

[2] Anene, J. C., *op. cit.*, 3. 224; Smith, S. R.: *The Ibo people* (*A study of the religion and customs of a tribe in the southern provinces of Nigeria*), (vol. 1, Ph.D. thesis) Cambridge 1929, pp. 135-6.

[3] C. 7596, London, 1895, pp. 33-43; CO. 444/2, Moor to C.O., 9 September 1899; CO. 520/14, Moor to C.O., 24 April 1902, enclosure.

[4] Ottenberg, S.: 'Ibo oracles and intergroup relations'. *South Western Journal of Anthropology*, vol. 14, 1958, p. 303.

[5] CO. 444/2, Moor to C.O., 9 September 1899, and enclosures.

[6] *Ibid.*

The Critical Century

Moor recommended against the Aros in June 1899 did not take place until 1901, and will indicate its results.

No less socially and politically menacing was the evangelism of the Christian missionaries who emphasised monotheism, monogamy, individualism and Western European education. So long as the African rulers of the Southern Nigerian states and communities wielded political power, they were able to control the activities of Christian missionaries in their midst. Before the nineteenth century, the Edo and Itsekiri, for example, showed that in welcoming Christian missionaries, they alone had the political control without which such missions could hardly succeed.[1]

The Egba chiefs and people similarly demonstrated their authority by expelling in 1867 the Christian missionaries who threatened their way of life.[2] By 1880 when they returned, they did so with Egba approval.[3] The Presbyterian missionaries invited to Creek Town and Duke Town by the Ibibio-Efik chiefs and people in 1846 subsequently threatened the peace and stability of the city-states there. Before his death in 1858, King Eyo of Creek Town tried to control the missionaries' activities.[4]

The problem of checking the over-zealous Christian missionaries became more complex as the African chiefs lost power and authority. Correspondingly, the increased number of evangelical establishments gained more and more protection from the British authorities in the Bights of Benin and Biafra.

Between 1841 and 1891 five major Christian missions operated in several parts of Southern Nigeria. These included the Anglicans (C.M.S.), the Wesleyan Methodists, the United Presbyterians of Scotland, the Southern Baptists of the United States of America and the members of the Catholic Society of African Missions (S.M.A.).[5]

The disruptive influences of the expanding evangelical efforts

---

[1] Ryder, A. F. C.: 'Missionary activities in the Kingdom of Warri to the early nineteenth century', *J.H.S.N.*, vol. 2, no. 1, December 1960, pp.1-24; Ryder, A. F. C.: 'The Benin Missions', *J.H.S.N.*, vol. 2, no. 2, December 1961, pp. 231-57.
[2] Biobaku, *op. cit.*, pp. 83-4; Ajayi, J. F. A.: *Christian missions in Nigeria 1841-1891*, London 1965, p. xv; Ayandele, *op. cit.*, pp. 14-15.
[3] CO. 147-166, MacGregor to C.O., Conf. 25 July 1903, enclosure.
[4] Nair, *op. cit.*, abstract.
[5] Ajayi, J. F. A.: *Christian missions in Nigeria, 1841-1891*, London 1965, pp. xiii-xv.

showed themselves in divisions among heathens and Christian missionary converts. In such communities as the Nembe-Ijos, the new Christian mission established at Ogbolomabiri in 1867 seriously complicated the political tensions which resulted in the civil war between them and their heathen Bassambiri kith and kin.[1]

When the Christian missionaries combined with the government in this common desire to spread Western European 'civilisation' in Southern Nigeria, the cultural identity and political stability of the African communities suffered adversely. Not only were the people's pre-colonial religious beliefs and practices in danger, the links between pre-colonial religion and administration began to show signs of snapping. Such pre-colonial practices as secret cults, trials by ordeal, infanticide and human sacrifices and the like offended both the Christian missionaries and the British authorities so much that the latter actively tried to suppress them through punitive expeditions and other forms of coercion.

Among the Western Ibos of the Asaba hinterland a difficult period began in 1888 when the officials of the Royal Niger Company pressed for the abolition of human sacrifices. So did the S.M.A. missionaries, whose evangelism in the Lower Niger began in 1884. The Ibos were so incensed that they channelled their opposition to the new 'civilising' forces through the *Ekumeku* secret society with effective lodges in Issele-Uku and elsewhere. By offering to protect the S.M.A. missionaries, the Royal Niger Company involved itself in active interference with the internal religious and social life of the Ibos of the Asaba hinterland. The Ibos there later observed that their sovereignty suffered gradual erosion from 1886 as a result of the charter granted the Royal Niger Company[2] to include their homesteads in the territories administered by the company. Unable to safeguard even their autonomy after 1886, the Ibos of the Asaba hinterland between 1893 and 1898 used their *Ekumeku* lodges to attack the missionary outposts in their midst. Consequently, the Royal Niger Company sent units of its constabulary in January and July 1898 to punish Ibusa, Issele-Uku and other centres of the *Ekumeku*-organised dissidence.[3]

[1] Jones, *op. cit.*, p. 85.
[2] For the details see, Flint, J. E., *Sir George Goldie and the making of Nigeria*, London 1960.
[3] Ayandele, *op .cit.*, p. 114; Anene, *op. cit.*, pp. 240–2.

The Critical Century

ECONOMIC STRAINS AND STRESSES

During the nineteenth century, a different kind of combination – between trade and the British flag – emerged. Here also, the cumulative results of such a combination were to have an adverse effect on the external and internal relations of the various states and communities of Southern Nigeria. The close relationship between trade and politics is already familiar, particularly in the nineteenth-century history of the Niger Delta city-states.[1] Equally important were the beginnings of major economic changes in both the coastal and hinterland areas.

For convenience, the nature of the major economic changes which occurred in the areas close to the coastal belt before 1900 will be briefly examined under production, trade, exchange, distribution network, and transportation.[2] At the beginning of the nineteenth century, African producers and African entrepreneurs exercised an important control over the economic aspects of their various communities. Towards the end of the century, they were no longer the major determinants of change in such matters. An economic crisis with serious political implications occurred. While the chiefs and people of Southern Nigeria wielded political power they were able to defend their economic rights. Such problems became more complicated as the economic changes assumed greater proportions. Africans discovered that the commercial attractiveness of their areas increased the dangers of interference with their economic, social and political institutions.

During the nineteenth century, and well up to the first half of the twentieth century, the people of Southern Nigeria were primarily agriculturists, despite interests in such occupations as weaving, smithery, fishing and pottery. Blessed with a profusion of the oil palm (*Elaeis Guineensis*) in the wet belts of the coastline and in the evergreen forests along the larger streams of the hinterland, the people were satisfied with the results of natural regeneration. As a protected tree,[3] the oil palm in several

---

[1] Dike, *op. cit.*
[2] Some of these guide-lines have been suggested by Szereszewski, R. in his *Structural changes in the economy of Ghana, 1891–1911*, London 1965.
[3] The Yoruba regarded the *Ope-Ifa* variety as a sacred tree. Similarly, the *Ogedudin* (King palm tree) species was considered sacred by the Edos.

13

communities was seldom destroyed while people cleared the land for cultivation. Used properly, the oil palm in Southern Nigeria had a life of 100–200 years and so provided the people with a permanent economic asset.

The most significant economic development in Southern Nigeria since 1807 was the transition from the pre-colonial emphasis on subsistence agriculture to an increasing concentration on production for sale. Without radical changes in technology the people of Southern Nigeria were able to produce a marketable surplus in palm produce. By adapting the pre-colonial techniques of oil and kernel extraction, they succeeded in meeting the needs of an export economy based largely on palm produce.

During the nineteenth century, trade was local as well as international. Specialising in foodstuffs and handicrafts, the people met in their local markets at the appointed times and places. Climatic differences encouraged regional specialisation and this in turn compelled economic interdependence in local trade. The Ijebu cloth weavers, the Hausa horse traders and leather workers, the Nupe blacksmiths, the Ijo fishermen, the Aro slave brokers, the Ife and Benin bronze specialists and other suppliers of goods and services met the commercial needs of Nigerians in pre-colonial times. Caravan trade routes utilised the Niger, Benue, Cross, Ogun and other rivers and the several bush paths. In turn, these land-and-river routes were connected through Kano, Bornu and other towns with the trans-Saharan routes which linked the southern markets along the coast with the Mediterranean ports of North Africa.[1] In Southern Nigeria, local markets took place along the banks of the River Niger south of Idah and others elsewhere for traffic in ivory, slaves, cotton goods, beads and so on. These and other markets provided commercial opportunities for traders from Northern Nigeria, Yorubaland, the Cross River estuary, the Niger Delta, Edoland and Iboland. For some of these traders, language constituted no serious problems as they were able to use Hausa for business transactions. The exchange problem was tackled through barter and the use of cowries.[2]

For details, see CSO. 12/26/3, File 3081/1907. The species were differentiated by the size, colour, number and hardness of the nuts.

[1] Ifemesia, C. C.: *British enterprise on the Niger, 1830–1896* (Ph.D. thesis) London 1959, pp. 13–25.

[2] *Ibid.* Cowries were imported from East Africa.

Southern Nigeria exported mainly palm produce, and imported cotton goods, liquor, hardware, fire-arms and ammunition.

Before 1880, the exchange was through barter, credit, manillas, cowries, brass rods, copper wires and Spanish dollars. Then, Spanish dollars were demonitised and the other forms of currency were gradually displaced from the 1890s by British silver coins.[1] This was understandable, as the other currencies suffered from price fluctuations and proved too bulky for transportation in inland trading centres.[2]

No sooner had the people of Southern Nigeria adjusted themselves sufficiently to these currency changes than modern European commercial banks began to appear in Lagos. The African Banking Corporation, the first bank established in Lagos in 1891, failed, but its successor in 1894 attained remarkable success and permanence.[3] Operating from Lagos, the Bank of British West Africa, established in 1894, monopolised the supply of British silver coins, until 1911.[4] Till then, the Bank of British West Africa became an important factor in stimulating that transition from barter to an economy increasingly based on British currency.[5]

The distribution network for imports and exports passed through the markets along the coast to others in the hinterland of Southern Nigeria. During much of the nineteenth century the European traders were content to confine themselves to their 'factories' along the coast, leaving the hinterland free for their African agents and middlemen, Consequently, Lagos wholesale and retail traders, Ijebu and Egba middlemen in the Yoruba hinterland, Itsekiri middlemen along the Benin River, Niger Delta middlemen in the Oil Rivers, Efik middlemen along the Cross River, and Aro middlemen in Iboland formed the major links in the chain of supply and distribution during this period. African middlemen obviously opposed any radical disturbance

[1] Hopkins, A. G.: *An Economic History of Lagos, 1880–1914*, (Ph.D. thesis) London 1964, pp. 53–4.
[2] *The Nigerian Times*, 26 April 1910. Of these the most popular were cowries. But 2,000 cowries amounted to 6d. – 2s. 6d. in parts of British-controlled West Africa.
[3] Hopkins, *op. cit.*, pp. 206–15.
[4] Loynes, J. B.: *The West African Currency Board, 1912–1962*, London 1962, p. 9.
[5] Newlyn, W. T. and Rowan, D. C.: *Money and Banking in British Colonial Africa*, Oxford 1954, p. 26.

of the existing pattern of the export–import trade whereby they would be displaced in favour of European merchants. Any alignment between European traders and the British consular staff to achieve such a radical change in commercial relationships led, as will be seen later, to intense opposition with serious military and political results.

Transportation also changed significantly during the nineteenth century. The discovery by the Lander brothers of the outlet of the Niger in 1830 and its subsequent exploitation by various steamship companies[1] revolutionised trade along this important highway and its several tributaries. The advent of steamships into West African trade helped to reduce freight rates, shortened the length of voyages and generally increased the volume of commerce.[2] Inland areas distant from the Niger estuary, however, continued to rely on the pre-colonial forms of transportation. In the areas with criss-crossing creeks and other waterways, dug-out canoes became convenient. Along the several bush-paths, head porterage was common.

The revolutionary impact of the railway and its feeder roads came much later. Although the construction of the Lagos Railway began in 1896 it was not open to public traffic until 1901.

By themselves, these changes in the economy raised the problem of group or individual adjustment. That such changes were serious enough was undoubted. Yet, for most people in the inland regions they did not prove catastrophic.

THE RÔLE OF THE BRITISH GOVERNMENT IN THE PROTECTORATES

Greater danger came, not from the effects of the combination between the impersonal forces of supply and demand, but from the collaboration between the British authorities, European merchants and Christian missionaries. The British goals of developing legitimate commerce and encouraging Western European civilisation met part of the needs of European traders and Christian missionaries. Both these two groups of Europeans in Southern Nigeria looked to the British government to protect them and their various activities from the opposition of the people of Southern Nigeria. From the 1880s, when the British

[1] Ifemesia, *op. cit.*, p. 28. [2] Hopkins, *op. cit.*, pp. 18 and 318.

government concluded treaties of protection, friendship and commerce with the coastal chiefs and people, another major crisis developed over the meaning of, and obligations under, a protectorate in this part of West Africa.

Problems of that kind assumed serious proportions following the conclusion by the British consuls of several protectorate treaties[1] adopted by the chiefs with 'x-marks' on the eve of the Berlin West African Conference, 1884-85. Their number increased after the Brussels Conference of 1889-90 under which Britain assumed more extended international obligations to make the control over her protectorates in West Africa effective.[2] Under the treaties of the 1880s and 1890s the chiefs and people of the Oil Rivers (later Niger Coast)[3] Protectorate accepted British protection, gave up relations with foreign powers except with the sanction of the British Crown and agreed to protect Christian missionaries and European traders in their midst. In some cases, the chiefs also undertook to promote free legitimate commerce. The chiefs again agreed to assist the British authorities in the execution of their duties and be guided by their advice in judicial administration, commercial development, matters affecting peace, order and good government and the 'general progress of civilisation'.[4] How far the chiefs and people understood these provisions is doubtful.

The British government tried to give its own interpretation of these treaties whenever controversies arose in conflicts between its officers in the newly-acquired protectorate and the chiefs and people. During the JaJa episode of the 1880s, Lord Rosebery, the Foreign Secretary, informed the King of Opobo that 'a principal object' of the protectorate was 'the promotion of the welfare of the natives of all those territories taken as a whole by ensuring the peaceful development of trade and by facilitating their intercourse with Europeans.'[5] Between 1884 and 1898[6] the British

[1] Copies in FO. 93/6/10.
[2] C. 6048, London 1890. Ratified by Britain in 1892.
[3] In 1893, the Oil Rivers Protectorate became known as the Niger Coast Protectorate.
[4] *Report by the Resumed Nigeria Constitutional Conference, 1958*, Lagos 1958, p 37.
[5] FO. 84/1828, Quoted in a memorandum of 27 August 1887 submitted by Consul E. Hewett on JaJa's closing of markets to Europeans. Lord Rosebery's letter was dated 16 June 1886. See also Anene, *op. cit.*, pp. 62-7.
[6] In November 1898, R. L. Antrobus of the Colonial Office admitted

interpretation of a protectorate in Africa changed significantly. Britain at first felt content to control only the 'foreign' relations of her protected peoples. She later came to control their internal affairs as well.

Before 1895, Britain distinguished between her obligations in 'annexations' and 'protectorates'. Britain then showed more interest in safeguarding the interests of her subjects and others who 'properly enjoyed' her protection than in the firm control of the internal affairs of Africans. Important landmarks in the development of the legal doctrine concerning the meaning of a British protectorate in Africa will now be briefly explained. Developments of this kind help to throw more light on the escalation from the 1880s of violent conflict between Britain, the protecting power, and the Africans under her jurisdiction in parts of Southern Nigeria.

In an attempt to indicate the degree of British obligations in territories overseas, Lord Chancellor Selborne, in January 1885, distinguished between 'annexations' and 'protectorates'. To him, an 'annexation' meant 'the direct assumption of territorial sovereignty' whereas a 'protectorate' recognised 'the right of the aboriginal, or other actual inhabitants, to their own country, with no further assumption of territorial rights than is necessary to maintain the paramount authority, and discharge the duties of the Protecting Power.'[1] The Lord Chancellor, however, failed to explain the meaning of 'paramount authority' and 'duties'.

In a memorandum of November 1888, H. Jenkyns, one of the Law Officers of the Crown, explained that 'the object of declaring a protectorate' was 'to avoid the assumption of jurisdiction over the internal government of the people who had been prevented from having direct relations with any European power.'[2] In a further memorandum also dated November 1888, Jenkyns admitted that the extent of the 'internal sovereignty' which the Crown could exercise in a protectorate differed from place to place. For example, 'where there are merely native tribes, the

---

that the old distinctions between colonies and protectorates had gone. See CO. 446/4, MP. 25517.

[1] FO. 84/1819, Note by the Lord Chancellor (Selborne) on the Law Officers' report on the third basis (of the Berlin West African Conference), 3 January 1885.

[2] FO. 97/562, Note on 'British Protectorates' by H. Jenkyns, 16 November 1888.

The Critical Century

chiefs of which have tribal but no territorial authority, the amount of internal sovereignty acquired by the protection is much larger than where there is a semi-civilised government, with a sultan or other ruler exercising control.'[1] It will be helpful, at a later stage, to refer to Jenkyns' rider on the degree of British interference with the autonomy of protected persons so as to understand the double standards adopted by the British authorities in the Lagos and Oil Rivers (Niger Coast) Protectorate since the 1890s.

C. P. Ilbert, another Law Officer of the Crown, agreed with Jenkyns. In January 1889, Ilbert observed that by a protectorate 'What we do mean is not to upset the native chief, or to displace native customs or institutions in their application to his subjects, but to assert authority over all foreigners within his gates, and to exercise that authority by British officers and in accordance with British laws. The exercise of such 'partial sovereignty', Ilbert continued, constituted 'a convenient half-way house between complete annexation and complete abstinence from interference. . . .'[2]

These legal distinctions, undoubtedly quite abstract, the Foreign Office sought to maintain in its Instructions to Claude MacDonald in April 1891 when it appointed him the first Commissioner and Consul-General of the re-organised administration of the Oil Rivers Protectorate. In these Instructions[3] the Foreign Office advised MacDonald that his aim 'should be, by developing legitimate trade, to relinquish inhuman and barbarous customs, and by gradually abolishing slavery, to pave the way for placing the territories over which Her Majesty's protection is and may be extended, directly under British rule.'

The same Instructions, however, stated that, concerning means: 'It is not advisable that you should interfere unduly with tribal government: the chiefs should continue to rule their own subjects and to administer justice to them: but you should keep a constant watch so as to prevent injustice and check abuses, making the chiefs understand that their powers will be forfeited by mis-government.' Furthermore, the Foreign Office warned MacDonald: 'You should be careful . . . not to arouse discontent by attempting too abrupt reform. You will take under your

[1] Ibid., memorandum dated 26 November 1888.
[2] FO. 97/562, Confidential memorandum by C. P. Ilbert on 'Indian and African Protectorates', 24 January 1889.
[3] FO. 84/2110, F.O. to MacDonald, 18 April 1891.

19

immediate control the inter-tribal and foreign relations of the native chiefs.'

In practice, neither MacDonald nor his successor Moor kept strictly to the terms of the April 1891 Instructions. Generally, the more they interfered with the internal affairs of the people of the Oil Rivers Protectorate, the firmer their control over administration became.

Several opportunities for interference occurred in the British re-organisation of Native Councils of Chiefs, in their attempts to encourage legitimate commerce and break down the opposition of African middlemen and in their efforts to discourage human sacrifices and similar practices. MacDonald and Moor as well as their predecessors, E. Hewett and H. Johnston, from 1884, became so involved in African affairs that they exercised the power of deporting African rulers for offences which did not come under the rubric of 'external relations.'

The British consuls as well as other officers of the Crown soon saw the futility of making abstract legal distinctions between protectorates and annexations. Meanwhile, the Law Officers of the Crown had by 1895 begun to admit that in the past decade the British distinctions between protectorates and annexations had been academic.[1] In January 1895 they endorsed the view:

> The existence of a Protectorate in an uncivilised country carries with it a right on the part of the Protecting Power to exercise within that country such authority and jurisdiction, in short, such of the attributes of sovereignty as are required for the due discharge of the duties of a Protector both for the purpose not only of protecting the natives from the subjects of civilised Powers, and such subjects from the natives and from each other, but also for protecting the natives from the grosser forms of ill-treatment and oppression by their Rulers, as from the raids of slave-dealers and marauders.[2]

This wider interpretation allowed so much flexibility that the British authorities in the Niger Coast Protectorate had plenty of freedom of action, particularly from 1895. Charges of breaking protectorate treaty obligations and generally opposing British rule provided convenient excuses for punishing or deporting the

[1] CO. 96/263, MP.2865, Law Officers to Ripon, 14 February 1895.
[2] CSO. 1/10/5, Anderson to MacDonald, 14 March 1895, enclosure: C.O. to Sir B. Griffith 'January 1895'.

The Critical Century

dissenting chiefs. In that category belonged the JaJa (1887), Nana (1894) and Overami (1897) episodes.[1]

The punitive expedition against Benin in 1897 and the deportation of Overami in the same year gave Commissioner and Consul-General Moor the opportunity to propound his own views on the new repository of power and authority in the Niger Coast Protectorate. Shortly before he pronounced the deportation sentence at Benin City, Moor informed Overami and the other chiefs in September 1897: 'Now this is the white man's country. There is only one king in the country and that is the white man; the only person therefore to whom service need be shown is the white man . . .'.[2]

The events which preceded the deportation of JaJa of Opobo, Nana of Itsekiri-land, Overami of Benin and others indicated that directly and indirectly these African leaders were charged with contravening treaty obligations or with challenging the general authority of the protective power. The chiefs concerned denied these charges but paid the penalty of deportation. Despite reservations, the Foreign Office approved the action of their consular officers on-the-spot.

As the African leaders thus punished never had the benefit of defence counsel during their trials by political officers, the legality of such proceedings was not tested before British courts of law. In 1958 when the question of the value of the legal and moral aspects of the nineteenth-century protectorate treaties concluded between the British Crown and the Oil Rivers chiefs came up during the Nigeria Constitutional Conference, the Secretary of State for the Colonies adopted a curiously interesting line of argument. Speaking on behalf of the British government as advised by the Law Officers of the Crown, Secretary of State A. Lennox-Boyd (later Lord Boyd) affirmed that 'these Treaties did not create obligations that could be enforced either under international law or municipal law . . . '. The government admitted only 'moral obligations' to 'secure justice and fair dealing on the matters mentioned in the treaties'.[3]

Granted that the protectorate treaties of the 1880s and 1890s in the Oil Rivers Protectorate imposed only 'moral obligations'

---

[1] For the details see: Anene, *op. cit*, pp 87–90; Ikime, O.: *Merchant Prince of the Niger Delta*, pp. 147–73; Igbafe, *op. cit.*, pp. 53–100.
[2] FO. 2/123, Moor to F.O., 18 October 1897, enclosure.
[3] *Report by the Resumed Nigeria Constitutional Conference*, 1958, p. 38.

on the parties, how far were the alleged infringements by Africans offences punishable by deportation and other means? If those compacts imposed only 'moral obligations' since the 1880s, why were they not regarded as such when punitive expeditions and patrols took place against the people accused of infringing them? Moral obligations alone, as interpreted by Africans during the 1880s and 1890s, did not render the JaJas, Nanas and Overamis culpable. It is unrealistic to adopt or expect only one absolute standard – the British standard – of morality in trade, politics, government and religion. The chiefs and people who opposed such consular officers as Hewett, Johnston, MacDonald and Moor adopted the mores of their people in such matters but suffered the penalty of punitive expeditions, patrols, fines and deportation. Hence, it is difficult to excuse the deportations of the anti-Christian mission King Ibanichuka of Okrika in 1896, the deposition in the same year of King Koko who defended the political and commercial rights of the Nembe-Brass people when threatened by the Royal Niger Company, the suppression in 1898 of the local freemasonry of 'Konka' at Ohumbella[1] and similar acts adopted by the British authorities in this part of Southern Nigeria during the 1880s and 1890s under the cover of the protectorate treaties and obligations.

The long-term results of the severe penalties imposed for the alleged breaches of treaty obligations in the Oil Rivers Protectorate seriously affected the pre-colonial monarchical institutions of the Niger Delta, the neighbouring Benin kingdom and the Ibibio-Efik city-states. Moor's dictum of 'There is only one king in the country and that is the white man' again made him unwilling to encourage rival African kingships during his tenure of office from 1896 to 1903.

Generally, Moor encouraged the establishment of Native Councils of Chiefs with members chosen for their loyalty, not because of kingly status. In Nembe (1896) and Kalabari (1897) Moor showed his willingness to remove from such councils the kings who opposed the new administration. That clearly became the fate of King Koko in Nembe and King Amakiri in Kalabari.[2]

Deaths frequently relieved Moor of the embarrassment of

[1] FO. 2/100, Moor to F.O., 9 April 1896, enclosure; FO. 2/101, Moor to F.O., 24 June 1896; FO. 2/179, Gallwey to F.O., 2 June 1898; Alagoa, E. J.: *The Small Brave City-state*, Ibadan 1964, pp. 115 and 118.

[2] Alagoa, *op. cit.*, pp 115–18; Anene, *op. cit.*, p. 203.

having to administer through African kings. For example, after the death of King Duke of Duke Town in 1897 that city-state had no successor for a long time.[1] After King Koko's death at Nembe in 1898 no new *amanyanabos* were installed until the era of King Oguara at Bassambiri (installed 1924) and King Ockiya at Ogbolomabiri (1926).[2] King Amakiri IV, sacked by Moor from the Native Council of the Kalabari in 1897, died about 1900[3] and for the next decade there was no record of a crowned successor. After the death in exile of King Ibanichuka of Okrika about 1896 no successor was crowned until April 1964. Until Overami's death in exile in 1914, the people of Benin were without an approved Oba.[4] The long interregnum in Itsekiri-land continued from 1848 until 1936.[5]

The Benin and Okrika cases raised special difficulties. Until Overami's death in 1914, the people of Benin could not select for government approval a new Oba. Fortunately for the people of Benin, Overami died after Moor had retired from service in Southern Nigeria in October 1903. First, Moor's 1897 speech at Benin City showed that he had no desire to have black kings there under the new order. Second, in a disputed succession involving such contestants as the pro-government Obaseki who was not descended from the Benin royal line and the legitimate claimant Aguobasimi from the Overami line, a wrong choice by Moor would have severely rocked the foundations of monarchy there. That, however, was not a speculative problem. The position in Benin became quite serious in 1914, when Obaseki, who from 1897 had been the leading supporter of the government there, became an active contender for the office of Oba against the legitimate successor, Aguobasimi. Edo traditions, however, prevailed and Aguobasimi was crowned in 1914 as Eweka II of Benin.[6]

In Okrika, the deportation of Ibanichuka to Degema in 1896 raised another problem. The Niger Coast Protectorate did not officially gazette the king's death in exile about 1896. His former subjects, however, knew the circumstances of Ibanichuka's misfortune in trying to escape from exile. Considering the hatred and

[1] Nair, *op. cit.*, p. 361. [2] Alagoa, *op. cit.*, p. 119.
[3] Jones, *op. cit.*, p. 26. [4] Igbafe, *op. cit.*, pp. 205–11.
[5] Ikime, *Merchant prince of the Niger Delta*, pp. 8 and 16.
[6] Igbafe, *op. cit.*, pp. 167–8; Egharevba, J.: *A Short History of Benin*, Ibadan 1960, pp. 62–3, 95.

mistrust engendered by his compulsory exile in 1896, the people of Okrika made no official report on his death.[1] Consequently, they could not appoint another crowned successor at the time.

Despite such special cases, Moor deliberately played down the status and role of African monarchs till he retired in 1903. Moor produced a rider to his theories in the 1897 speech at Benin City in 1902 when he secured the passage of Native Council Rules at Old Calabar, under which new Ibibio-Efik monarchs could no longer use the high title of *Edidem*. In its place, they were required to adopt the least important title of *Obong*.[2] Moor's objective, from 1896 to 1903, was to avoid any African institution of kingship which directly and indirectly had the effect of competing with the British Crown.

While the rôle of African kings was deliberately de-emphasised from the last two decades of the nineteenth century in the Oil Rivers Protectorate, a new leadership of loyal African chiefs and educated élite emerged in some of the communities. As political agents and vice-presidents of the newly-established Native Councils, these co-operative Africans[3] assumed power and authority during the good pleasure of the British political staff. From the 1890s, the government stressed working through such loyal members of the Native Councils rather than on the exercise of power and authority through African monarchs. In the coastal communities of the Oil Rivers Protectorate there was a remarkable departure from the pre-colonial system of government based on *amanyanabos* (owners of the land) to the protectorate practice of administration through *amadabos* (executive heads).

In the light of these developments, it is possible to explain the anxiety of Legislative Councillor H. Buowari Brown (Rivers Province) during the 1950 General Conference on the review of the Nigeria Constitution at Ibadan. In holding the British government mainly responsible for the accelerated decline of the insti-

[1] Based on oral evidence obtained at Okrika. The people suspected homicide.
[2] Nair, *op. cit.*, pp. 358–61. In the descending order of status and preference, the pre-colonial monarchical titles of the Ibibio-Efik were *Etinyin*, *Edidem* and *Obong*.
[3] These included Joseph Alagoa of Nembe, Daniel Oju Kalio of Okrika, Dogho Numa of the Itsekiri, Coco Otu Bassey of the Upper Cross river, Obaseki, Ineh, Osula and Oshodi of the Benin District, Magnus Duke, Eyo Eyo Ita, Joseph Henshaw, Richard Henshaw and David Henshaw of the Ibibio-Efik communities.

tution of kingship in parts of Eastern Nigeria, Buowari Brown asked:[1]

We are now looked upon as people of the East having no chiefs at all. We have Obas in the West and Emirs in the North but no chiefs at all in the East. Was it originally so? Was it ever so and what has been the cause?

Neither the late nineteenth century nor the early twentieth could be regarded as a propitious era for the institution of kingship in parts of Southern Nigeria. Gone were the awe and majesty of the monarchs of Onitsha, the Asaba hinterland, the Benin kingdom, the Niger Delta and Ibibio-Efik city-states. They had been replaced, as Moor aptly acknowledged, by the British Crown. In these areas, Jenkyns' rider, in his further memorandum of November 1888, applied to the disadvantage of the African kings of small territories.

It is not necessary here to extend the scope of the present inquiry to Northern Nigeria as Buowari Brown's searching question demands but the position in Yorubaland deserves immediate attention. In view of the British assessment of the value of treaties and agreements, the rulers of Ijebu-Ode and Oyo in 1892 and 1895 respectively committed no less serious offences than JaJa (1887), Nana (1894), Ibanichuka (1896) and Overami (1897). Despite the similarity of punitive expeditions and police actions against such monarchs, those of Ijebu-Ode and Oyo were left safely on their thrones.

Only smaller Yoruba rulers were deported or threatened with deportation. In 1891, the Lagos government deported and detained at Lagos Asada Awopa, the Egbado King of Addo for allegedly interfering with the liberty of British subjects, violating British territory and stopping trade between the colony, Addo, Badagry and Ajiliti.[2] The Rev. James Johnson and C. J. George, the two Nigerian unofficial members of the Legislative Council, strongly opposed the deportation and questioned its legality. The government later responded favourably not to James Johnson and George but to the White Cap Chiefs and other dignitaries of Lagos who showed much interest in the case. These chiefs, together with the war chiefs of Lagos, promptly paid the £75

---

[1] *Proceedings of the General Conference on review of the Constitution, January* 1950, Lagos 1950, p. 163.
[2] CSO. 7/1/2, Legislative Council Debates, 14 March 1891.

fine imposed on the Addo King and gave security of £500 for his future good behaviour. The government therefore released Asada Awopa and allowed him to return to his throne in Addo after his brief detention at Lagos.[1]

The Nigerian unofficial members of the Legislative Council failed to save another minor Yoruba 'headman' from deportation in 1892. Abaku, the 'headman' of the Ijebu town of Mushin, was accused by the government of prohibiting trade between Mushin and Ejirin market. The Rev. James Johnson opposed the deportation as the alleged offence was not 'political' but was overruled by the other members of the Legislative Council.[2]

Acting Governor G. C. Denton had in 1898 also 'unjustly' deposed Bale Asani of Epe. Though the offence was not recorded, the government in 1904 regretted its earlier action.[3]

Compared with the Oil Rivers Protectorate, the Lagos Protectorate had a short list of deported African rulers during the 1880s and 1890s. Under such administrators as G. T. Carter[4] and G. C. Denton,[5] with navy, army and police backgrounds, there was a marked tendency to adopt coercion in the government's dealings with the chiefs and people of Yorubaland in the decade following the Brussels conference, 1889–90.

H. E. McCallum[6] and W. MacGregor,[7] their successors from the late 1890s, however, preferred diplomacy. Despite his Royal Military Academy experience, McCallum had had a long career in the Far East which prepared him to respect the chiefs of Yorubaland when he became Governor there between 1897 and 1898. MacGregor, with a longer Far Eastern experience as an administrator, was a doctor by profession, not a soldier, and, even more than McCallum, had a special fondness for the chiefs of Yorubaland.

[1] *Ibid.* CSO. 7/1/2, Legislative Council Debates, 27 May 1891.
[2] CSO. 7/1/2, Legislative Council Debates, 3 October 1892.
[3] CO. 147/169, Moseley to C.O., 13 February 1904.
[4] Entered the Navy (1864); Governor of Lagos, 1890–96.
[5] Capt., 57th Regiment, 1878; Chief of Police, St Vincent, 1880; Colonial Secretary, Lagos, 1888 and Deputy Governor on several occasions till 1900.
[6] Attended the Royal Military Academy, Woolwich; Colonial Engineer and Surveyor-General, Straits Settlements, 1884–1897; Governor, Lagos 1897–99.
[7] Chief Medical Officer, Fiji, 1875; Administrator, British New Guinea; 1888; Lieutenant-Governor, British New Guinea, 1895; Governor, Lagos, 1899–1904. Born, 20 October 1846; died 3 July 1919.

The Critical Century

MacGregor's earlier experience in the Far East had an important effect on his attitude to administration in Lagos between 1899 and 1904. In Fiji, MacGregor had encountered the powerful influence of Arthur Gordon (later Lord Stanmore) whom he described in March 1899 as 'my principal teacher in all that I know with regard to administration'.[1] The policy and practice of indirect administration through local chiefs, adopted by Gordon in Fiji, MacGregor later adapted to suit the needs of the Lagos Protectorate.

Macgregor assumed the Lagos administration at a time when the British control of the Lagos Protectorate was at its crucial stage. In his desire for a tactful exercise of British influence and authority in that protectorate, Chamberlain in July 1898 wanted as Governor of Lagos a man 'whose personality is sympathetic to the natives and whose influence will keep the peace and settle disputes at the outset which may lead to war'.[2] These qualities MacGregor possessed in full measure.

In choosing the administrators of the Oil Rivers Protectorate the Foreign Office did not exercise as much caution as the Colonial Office later demonstrated in finding and using persons of MacGregor's kind. Instead, all three administrators – E. H. Hewett,[3] C. M. MacDonald and[4] R. D. R. Moor[5] – who were involved with deportation crises in the Oil Rivers Protectorate had military backgrounds. Before his consular appointment, Hewett had had military experience in the Royal Bucks King's Own Militia and the East Kent Militia during the 1850s. MacDonald combined combat service in Africa with his record as the Military Attaché to the British Agency at Cairo between 1882 and 1887. Moor, his deputy and successor as Commissioner and Consul-General,

[1] MacGregor, W.: 'British New Guinea', *P.R.C.I.*, 30, 1898–99, p. 269.
[2] CO. 147/132, McCallum to Chamberlain, 5 May 1898, minute by J.C.
[3] Served in the Royal Bucks King's Own Militia, 1854–55 and in the East Kent Militia, 1859–60; Consul in the Bight of Biafra (later Oil Rivers Protectorate) 1880–88.
[4] Entered 74th Highlanders, 1872; Major (Brevet), 1882; Served as a volunteer with the 42nd Highlanders in the Egyptian and Suakin expeditions (1882, 1884); Military Attaché to the British Agency in Cairo, 1882–87. Commissioner and Consul-General, Oil Rivers (Niger Coast) Protectorate, 1891–96.
[5] Acting Commissioner and Consul-General, Oil Rivers (Niger Coast) Protectorate, 1892–95; Commissioner and Consul-General, 1896–99; High Commissioner, Southern Nigeria, 1900–3. Born, 31 July 1860; died 13 September 1909.

had been a former District Inspector at the Royal Irish Constabulary depot in Dublin which he had joined in 1882. From 1891, Moor headed the first semi-military establishment under the MacDonald administration in the Oil Rivers Protectorate.

Such differences in the backgrounds and aptitudes of the senior British administrative staff, important in themselves, were only partly responsible for the paucity of punitive expeditions and deportations of chiefs in the Lagos Protectorate in the last two decades of the nineteenth century. The presence and activities of Nigerian unofficial members of Yoruba origin in the Legislative Council of Lagos since 1872 provided only a partially successful legitimate vent for redressing public grievances against government actions in the colony and protectorate. The Oil Rivers Protectorate then lacked such a forum.

The people of Lagos Colony and Protectorate also had a vocal press run by African proprietors and editors since the 1880s.[1] About the same time, the people of the Oil Rivers Protectorate had only the limited circulation newspapers run by missionaries at Old Calabar.[2] The Lagos press reported and criticised government actions in both territories but such comments had little effect on the policies and practices pursued by Moor and his predecessors.

The presence of more educated Africans in Lagos and their readiness to recall the treaties, agreements and pledges made between the British Crown and the chiefs of Yorubaland during the 1880s and 1890s constituted a salutary check on some of the Governors in their relations with the people of the Lagos Protectorate. A brief examination of the nature of these nineteenth-century treaties, agreements and pledges will not only help to answer part of the provocative question asked by Buowari Brown but also indicate some of the jurisdictional problems in the Lagos Protectorate which continued until 1914.

The chiefs and people who sought to limit the expansion of British jurisdiction appealed to treaties, agreements, declarations and undertakings. Of these, the Colonial Office paid special attention to the treaties, but Africans made no such distinctions. Between 1886 and 1893, the British Crown entered into several treaties with the people of the Lagos Protectorate. The treaty of

[1] Omu, F. I. A.: *The Nigerian Newspaper Press, 1859–1937*. (Ph.D. thesis) Ibadan 1965, pp. 1–44.

[2] For details see Chapter 2 of the present work.

peace, friendship and commerce between the various Yoruba chiefs in June 1886[1] marked the British-inspired attempt to end the Yoruba wars. The other treaty with the King and chiefs of Ife in May 1888 recognised the 'independence' of the kingdom of Ife which paid 'tribute to no other power'.[2] The strict construction of Ife's 'independence' was in relation to the other Yoruba states.

Of great significance was the treaty of friendship and commerce with the Egbas in January 1893.[3] The Egba authorities insisted on the British Crown's agreeing that the 'independence' of the Egba territory would 'be fully recognised' as long as the treaty was faithfully observed by the Egbas. In constitutional terms, that section of the treaty provided the key to the intricate relations between the Lagos government and the Egba United Government (EUG) until 1914.

In a further treaty of peace and friendship in February 1893,[4] the British Crown recognised the Alafin of Oyo as the 'Head of Yorubaland' and allowed him 'a yearly present' of £100. There was, however, no attempt in this treaty to spell out the geographical and political meaning of 'Yorubaland'.[5] The exact limits of the Alafin's overlordship before and after 1893 became the subject of later controversy.[6]

With the other Yoruba states, the British Crown concluded agreements. In that group lay the agreement of January 1892[7] between the Crown and the Awujale and chiefs of Ijebu for free and open roads passing through their territory. The government obtained the right of appointing an officer at Ijebu-Ode to enforce the terms of the agreement. So long as its provisions were faithfully observed, the government agreed to give the Awujale 'a yearly present' of £500, that is, five times the sum allowed the

[1] CSO. 5/1/13. The Treaty of peace, friendship and commerce between various Yoruba chiefs, 4 June 1886. The signatories – with the usual x-mark – represented Oyo, Ibadan, Ilesha, Otun, Ijero, Ido, Ife, Modakeke and Ijebu.
[2] CSO. 5/1/15, Dated 22 May 1888.
[3] CSO. 5/1/18, Dated 18 January 1893.
[4] CSO. 5/1/19, Dated 3 February 1893.
[5] In its earlier use, the term referred to the Oyo people, but it was later expanded to include those who adopted Yoruba as their language. Not all Yorubas were under the Old Oyo Empire controlled by the Alafin.
[6] For a detailed treatment of various aspects of this controversy, see Atanda, *op. cit*. [7] CSO. 5/2/5, Dated 21 January 1892.

Alafin. The reason for this differential treatment was that open roads through Ijebu territory were, during the 1890s, of greater importance to Lagos than those in Oyo.

The 1892 agreement between the British Crown and Ijebu-Ode was remarkable for the absence of the usual 'x-marks' found in such documents. In effect, the British Crown made an agreement with the representative chiefs of *Agunrin, Ogboni, Pampa* and *Parakoyi* status. These same representatives

> declared that it was contrary to the custom of their country to make their marks or touch paper but that they in the name of the Awujale and people of Jebu and on their behalf agreed to all the terms of the agreement and undertook to carry them out and declared that they were authorised to do so. The said representatives further signified their acceptance of the terms by taking the country oath on kolas and water.[1]

It can be argued that by such tactics the Ijebu representatives sought to avoid contracting a valid treaty. Despite their scruples, the 1892 concessions paved the way for more concessions in 1908, when the Ijebu chiefs agreed to give up more powers and authority to the government through their new Judicial Agreement. This time they abandoned their former scruples and put their 'x-marks' on the document.[2] In the provisions of the 1892 agreement and the results of the punitive expedition of the same year, Ijebu pre-colonial institutions and values suffered a dramatic change, the signs of which persisted much longer. In external affairs, if not also in internal matters, the Ijebu, like the other Yoruba communities, gradually lost much of their pre-colonial control.

The Ibadan agreement of August 1893,[3] like the Egba treaty of the same year, showed the unwillingness, at first, of the chiefs and people to surrender control over their internal affairs. Later, the people of Ibadan retained their power to administer such dependent towns as Iwo, Ede, Oshogbo, Ikirun, Ogbomosho, Ejigbo and Isein (Iseyin). At the same time, they recognised the Alafin of Oyo as 'the King and Head of Yoruba Land'. The most controversial aspect of the Ibadan agreement however, arose from the British desire to appoint an officer to enforce its provisions. The Ibadan chiefs and people regarded this as an affront to their

[1] *Ibid.* [2] CSO. 5/2/24, Dated 11 November 1908.
[3] CSO. 5/2/6, Dated 15 August 1893.

autonomy in such matters as land and domestic slavery. When, however, Acting Governor Denton pledged[1] not to interfere with these and other matters of local concern through the British Resident, the chiefs and people of Ibadan withdrew their objections. The conclusion of this agreement marked, as B. A. Awe correctly observed, the end of Ibadan as the 'town of warriors'.[2]

No comparable vehement objection to the appointment of a British representative at Shagamu followed the agreement of August 1894[3] between the British Crown and the king and people of Ijebu-Remo. For accepting British protection, the Akarigbo of Ijebu-Remo received a yearly stipend of £100.

The declarations and undertakings made with other Yoruba states did not command much official comment during the nineteenth century and subsequently. At the Kiji-Mesi battlefield in September 1886[4] the people of Ife undertook to abolish human sacrifices. In the declaration of May 1888,[5] the chiefs and people of Igbessa ratified and confirmed their protection by the British Crown and pledged themselves to abolish human sacrifices. In another declaration of August 1891[6] the king and people of Addo agreed to abolish slave-dealing and human sacrifices.

This short list of the treaties, agreements and pledges made by various parties in Yorubaland in the last two decades of the nineteenth century demonstrated some of the constitutional obstacles against further expansion of British authority and jurisdiction in the Lagos Protectorate. But in the Oil Rivers Protectorate, such treaties and agreements became convenient pretexts for maximising the degree of British control at the expense of the chiefs and people.

However, much depended on how the obligations conferred by those treaties and agreements were interpreted by the government and the governed, and also on the type of reaction offered by the aggrieved persons under the newly-established protectorates in Lagos and the Oil Rivers. Unlike the Yorubas of the Lagos Protectorate, the people of the Oil Rivers Protectorate were not war-weary from the 1880s when the scramble for Africa

[1] Awe, *op. cit.*, p. 328.
[2] *Ibid.*, p. 329.
[3] CSO. 5/2/8, Dated 4 August 1894.
[4] CSO. 5/9/5. Dated 23 September 1886.
[5] CSO. 5/9/15. Dated 15 May 1888.
[6] CSO. 5/9/20. Dated 8 August 1891.

The Evolution of the Nigerian State

entered its eventful stage. The willingness to take up arms in defence of their sovereignty was then more readily demonstrated by the people of the Oil Rivers Protectorate than those of the Lagos Protectorate where Africans increasingly developed the strategy and tactics of less violent protests. That trend continued unabated until January 1914.

The status of the chiefs of the Lagos Protectorate again impressed such administrators as H. McCallum and W. MacGregor much more than that of the traditional authorities in the Oil Rivers Protectorate administered by C. MacDonald and R. Moor. Besides the differences in the attitudes of the administrative hierarchy, there developed a remarkable contrast in the style of controlling the external and internal affairs of the people in both British protectorates during the nineteenth century and subsequently. Issues connected with the establishment and consolidation of British power and authority in other parts of Southern Nigeria from 1900 will now be discussed.

2 Control through Coercion

THE MILITARY AND POLICE ESTABLISHMENTS

In several parts of Southern Nigeria the protectorate established, expanded and consolidated between 1900 and 1913 was backed by force. In the Protectorate of Southern Nigeria[1] as in the Lagos Colony and Protectorate troops and police were either actively used in punitive expeditions, patrols and escorts or maintained as a threat. These forces became notorious for their reign of terror. In their rôle as part of the executive branch of the new government, they competed with the law enforcement agencies of the old order.

The area and population of Southern Nigeria and the difficult terrain, however, limited the effectiveness of control through troops and the police. In a territory of about eight million people and 80,000 square miles[2] with dense tropical forest, difficult means of transportation and communications, inadequate anthropological information and intelligence reports, aggressive administration did not always pay rich dividends. On the whole, however, the governments of the Protectorate of Southern Nigeria and the Colony and Protectorate of Lagos were satisfied with their military and police forces, which had developed from the nineteenth-century constabularies.

Before the establishment in 1898 of the West African Frontier Force (WAFF), both Lagos (from the 1880s) and the Niger Coast Protectorate (from 1894) had their own constabularies. The Lagos Constabulary became the Hausa Force during the 1890s, which

---

[1] Between January 1900 and April 1906, the former Niger Coast Protectorate became known as the Protectorate of Southern Nigeria which included parts of the territory formerly administered by the Royal Niger Company from Idah to the Akassa outlet of the Niger.
[2] CO. 592/9. *Report on the Southern Nigeria Census*, 1911. The actual census figures were: population – 7,858,689; area – 79,880 square miles.

33

in 1900 numbered 855 under an Inspector-General. In November 1901, this military force became the Lagos Battalion WAFF, comprising 543 rank and file commanded by a major.[1] The Lagos Battalion later became one of the WAFF's Regiments.

The Niger Coast Protectorate Constabulary, in January 1900, became the 3rd Niger Battalion and subsequently the Southern Nigeria Regiment, WAFF. Between 1901 and 1905, this force, over a thousand strong, came under the command of Lt. Col. A. F. Montanaro of the Royal Garrison Artillery.[2]

The civil police of the Protectorate of Southern Nigeria, which in 1900 comprised the Niger Coast Protectorate Court Messengers and forty men taken over from the Royal Niger Company, was reorganised by Moor in 1902 after the 1901–2 Aro Field Operation to comprise an inspector, two assistant inspectors and 304 other ranks.[3]

From 1896, Lagos had a distinct civil police organisation. Headed by a commissioner, the force increased from 398 in 1900 to 448 in 1902.[4] On the other hand, the strength of the military force decreased between 1900 and 1901.

These increases and decreases reflected the pacific method of establishing and maintaining British administrative control. In the larger, more populous and more difficult to control Protectorate of Southern Nigeria, the military and police forces went on increasing in response to the enlargement of the area under firm administration.

The military and police arrangements changed when both territories were amalgamated. From 17 May 1906, the new military force – the Southern Nigeria Regiment, WAFF – had 61 officers, a paymaster who was also quarter-master, an intelligence officer, 34 British NCOs and 1,883 privates. The headquarters of the regiment and the second battalion were at Lagos and the first battalion at Calabar.[5] Lt.Col. H. C. Moorhouse of the Royal

---

[1] CO. 151/38, *Lagos Blue Book*, 1900; CO. 151/40, *Lagos Blue Book*, 1902.

[2] *Colonial Reports Annual*, Southern Nigeria, 1899–1900, 1901, 1903. Montanaro gave up the command of this Regiment on 3 August 1905.

[3] CO. 520/1, Moot to C.O. 27 January 1900. *Colonial Reports, Annual*, Southern Nigeria, 1901, 1903. CO. 588/1, The Police Proclamation, No. 4 of 1902.

[4] CO. 151/38, *Lagos Blue Book*, 1900. CO. 151/40, *Lagos Blue Book*, 1902.

[5] CO. 592/3, *Annual report, Southern Nigeria Regiment*, 1906. From May 1904 Old Calabar became known as Calabar.

Control through Coercion

Artillery commanded the regiment. He was succeeded in 1908 by Brevet-Major H. M. (later Lord) Trenchard of the Royal Scots Fusiliers. The two police forces were similarly amalgamated. At the end of 1906, the new Southern Nigeria police force, commanded by an inspector-general, had 1,052 men out of an authorised establishment of 1,084.[1]

PUNITIVE EXPEDITIONS AND PATROLS

Before and after the amalgamation, there were many punitive expeditions and patrols in the Protectorate of Southern Nigeria (called the Eastern and Central Provinces from May 1906). Excluding the major expedition against the Aros from 1901 to 1902, twelve other 'field operations' – punitive expeditions and patrols – took place between 7 July 1902 and June 1903.[2]

After Moor's retirement in October 1903, a 'pacification' programme[3] became a yearly occurrence during the dry season (November–February). By this means, his successor, Walter Egerton,[4] expanded and consolidated the area under British control. Between October 1904 and June 1905, Egerton recommended eight 'field operations',[5] during which 'jujus' and secret societies which competed with the official law courts were destroyed or suppressed.[6]

---

[1] CO. 592/3, *Annual report, Police Force*, 1906. For details on police developments see Tamuno, T. N., *The police in modern Nigeria, 1861–1965*, Ibadan 1970.

[2] CO. 520/20, Probyn to C.O., 21 August 1903.

[3] Eight others followed from October 1904 to June 1905 and 3 more during the dry season of 1905–6. For the annual pacification programmes see: CO. 520/31, Egerton to CO., 22 July 1905; CO. 520/36, Egerton to C.O., conf. 9 June 1907; CO. 520/56, Egerton to C.O., 10 July 1907; CO. 520/65, Egerton to C.O., 8 September 1908; CO. 520/81, Egerton to C.O., 11 September 1909; CO. 520/82, Egerton to C.O., 2 October 1909; CO. 520/91, Egerton to C.O., conf. 29 January 1910; CO. 520/103, Egerton to C.O., conf. 17 May 1911.

[4] W. Egerton, (1858–1947), Cadet, Straits Settlements, 1880; Magistrate, Singapore, 1881; 1st Magistrate, Penang, 1897; British Resident, Malay Peninsula, 1902; High Commissioner, Southern Nigeria; 1903–4; Governor, Lagos; 1904–6; Governor, Southern Nigeria, 1906–12.

[5] CO. 520/31, Egerton to C.O., 22 July 1905.

[6] CO. 520/26, Egerton to C.O., conf. 11 October 1904, enclosures.

Egerton asked the political staff who accompanied these patrols to bear in mind that their purpose was 'to effect such a change in the feelings and attitude of the natives as will facilitate the future administration of such areas by District Officers with the ordinary Civil Staff without danger to themselves'.[1] At such times, these officers explained the government's policy requirements to the people, assuring them that the government did not intend to interfere with their institutions as long as they were 'not inconsistent with good government'.[2]

The Colonial Office believed that 'punitive expeditions' decreased after the Aro Field Force whereas 'organised patrols or displays of military force' in the 'more lawless and unsettled districts' of the Protectorate of Southern Nigeria increased.[3] The Colonial Office never doubted the necessity for these operations. It maintained that, far from being 'unprofitable' as the Aborigines Protection Society (APS) contended, patrols had 'been very successful in rapidly effecting the establishment of good government . . .'.[4]

THE ARO EXPEDITION

The Aro Field Force of 1901–2 tackled a special problem. In authorising this expedition, the government complained that the Aros, through their Long JuJu at Ibun, had enriched themselves by fines and fees collected from consultants or by selling these devotees in default of payment.[5]

The influence which the Aros exercised in blocking British penetration into the Ibo hinterland was compared by R. L. Antrobus of the Colonial Office with that of the Ashantis of the Gold Coast (later Ghana).[6] Though equally intelligent, the Aros lacked the military might and organisation of the Ashantis. Their alleged military prowess turned out to be a myth, which was exploded by the punitive expedition organised against them between 1901 and 1902.

[1] *Ibid.*
[2] CO. 520/26, Egerton to C.O., conf. 11 October 1904, enclosure.
[3] CO. 147/178, C.O. to APS., 7 February 1905.
[4] *Ibid.*
[5] *Colonial reports, annual*, Southern Nigeria, 1902.
[6] CO. 444/2, Moor to C.O., 9 September 1899, minute by RLA.

Control through Coercion

Several factors delayed this expedition. In June 1899 Moor had expected the WAFF to spare at least 400 men to send against the Ikwes and the Inokun branch of the Aros who were harassing traders along the Cross River.[1] F. D. Lugard, then in charge of the WAFF, could not release the men before arrangements were completed for the revocation of the Royal Niger Company's charter and the subsequent reorganisation of the troops.[2] Moor postponed the expedition to January 1900,[3] but then became too busy with the new administration of the Protectorate of Southern Nigeria, after the transfer of more territories from the Royal Niger Company.[4] Then the Ashanti war broke out early in 1900, and Secretary of State J. Chamberlain advised Moor not to press the Aro expedition until the position 'elsewhere' – the Gold Coast and South Africa – had improved.[5] Eventually, the Colonial Office sanctioned the punitive expedition for the dry season of 1901–2 'at the time which suits us best' lest 'the Aros may force our hands and compel us to engage in a punitive expedition at some most inconvenient time'.[6]

Having received this approval, Moor reiterated the principal aims of the Aro expedition. The abolition of slave-dealing was the most important. The others included the destruction of the Long JuJu, the opening up of the Aro territory to 'civilisation', the inducement of the people to engage in legitimate trade, the introduction of cash currency to replace slaves, brass rods and manillas, and the establishment of a labour market in lieu of slavery.[7]

The Aro expedition, which engaged a total of 1,745 officers and men, began on 15 November 1901 and ended on 23 March 1902. Lt.Col. A. F. Montanaro led the entire Aro Field Force which comprised a regiment from Northern Nigeria, a battalion from Lagos, 14 special service officers from England and troops in the Protectorate of Southern Nigeria. For political advice 28 members

---

[1] CO. 444/1, Moor to C.O., 14 June 1899. In August 1899, the protectorate had a Constabulary of only 550 rank and file. See CO. 444/2, Moor to C.O., 24 August 1899.
[2] CO. 444/4, F. D. Lugard to C.O., 20 November 1899. C.O. 444/1, Moor to C.O., 14 June 1899, and minutes by R.L.A. and E.W.
[3] CO. 444/2, Moor to C.O., 9 September 1899.
[4] CO. 520/1, Moor to C.O., 24 January 1900.
[5] CO. 520/6, Moor to C.O., 5 June 1900, minute by J.C.
[6] CO. 520/8, Moor to C.O., 25 June 1901, minute by R.L.A.
[7] CO. 520-10, Moor to C.O., 24 November 1901, enclosure.

of the protectorate's administrative staff accompanied the troops.[1]

Militarily, the campaign was remarkable for the use of converging columns which caused Aro-Chuku, the Aro capital, to fall to government troops on 24 December 1901. The troops took the capital and destroyed the Long JuJu with little resistance.[2]

The whole operation demonstrated that the Aros were not a fighting group. In refusing Moor's recommendation for a gratuity to the officers and men engaged in the Aro Field Force, the Colonial Office stressed that unlike the 'exceptionally arduous' Sierra Leone expedition (1898) and the Ashanti campaign (1900) where troops suffered 'special exposure, privation and hardships', the conditions of the Aro operations had not been fulfilled 'to the same extent'.[3] C. Strachey, of the Colonial Office, regarded the employment of the contingents and special service officers brought from outside the protectorate as the only aspect of the Aro Field Force which made it 'exceptional' and brought it 'outside the category of ordinary punitive measures carried out by local forces'.[4]

During the same operations, the troops arrested Okori Torti, the ringleader, and other chiefs accused of murdering some 400 men, women and children at Obegu on 21 November 1901. Moor considered bringing to justice those responsible for this massacre 'another object and duty' of the Aro Field Force.[5]

Special military tribunals were set up for the trials of alleged Aro war criminals, sitting between 22 January and 11 March 1902. The charges brought against the accused, mostly chiefs and people of Ikorana, Ogwe, Umolu and Isuigu, included the withholding of information on roads, failure to provide guides, complicity in the Obegu massacre and the concealment of guns. Those found guilty were detained in prison by the government pending the Colonial Office's confirmation of their punishment.[6]

[1] CO. 520/14, Moor to C.O., 17 April 1902, enclosures.

[2] About 25,000 'war guns' (rifles and cap guns) were captured or surrendered. The casualites sustained by the Field Force numbered 13 Europeans wounded, 27 African troops killed and 140 wounded, 70 others died from disease. No figures of enemy casualties were reported by Montanaro.

[3] CO. 520/14, C.O. to Moor, 27 May 1902.

[4] CO. 520/14, Moor to CO., 5 April 1902, minute by C.S.

[5] CO. 520/14, Moor to CO., 17 April 1902, enclosures. Obegu in the Akwete district was a town friendly to the government.

[6] CO. 520/13, Moor to C.O., 15 February 1902; CO. 520/13, Moor to C.O., 16 March 1902; CO. 520/14, Moor to C.O., 4 April 1902.

J. S. Risley of the legal section of the Colonial Office maintained that the persons tried and found guilty were not amenable to the jurisdiction of 'a British military court'. H. B. Cox, also of the Colonial Office, agreed with Risley that the men had been 'illegally tried'.[1] Acting on the Colonial Office's advice, Moor discharged all the prisoners except those implicated in the Obegu massacre, whom, for political reasons, he deported to Old Calabar.[2]

Politically, the Aro expedition had considerable significance. As soon as the troops had completed their assignment, Moor stepped in to deal with the various problems of the people in the 6,000 square miles of territory brought under control at an estimated cost of £55,000. In his various meetings with the chiefs and people of the newly-acquired territory, Moor discussed the abolition of slavery, punishment for homicide, the removal of tolls, the encouragement of legitimate trade, the adoption of the Native House Rule Proclamation, 1901[3] and the establishment of Native Councils. At the end of these discussions, he established in Iboland new district headquarters at Owerri and Bende and sub-district headquarters at Aro-Chuku. Protectorate forces garrisoned all three new stations.[4] The Aro expedition marked the biggest single effort made by the government to bring much of the Ibo hinterland under its control.

Later developments showed that the Aro Field Force did not completely destroy the Long JuJu in 1901. By 1913, the Colonial Office feared that it had been revived.[5] Probably it had merely gone underground, thus avoiding a second punitive expedition.

Agbala, another Ibo oracle worked by the itinerant Awka blacksmiths, met a similar fate in 1904 when it was listed for destruction by government troops.[6] The government was satisfied that its mission was successful, but in 1921, it once more

[1] CO. 520/13, Moor to C.O., 15 February 1902, minutes by J.S.R. and H.B.C.
[2] CO. 520/14, C.O. to Moor, conf. 16 May 1902; CO. 520/15, Moor to C.O., conf. 2 August 1902; CO. 520/15, Moor to C.O., conf. 26 October 1902.
[3] This proclamation will be discussed in chapter 11.
[4] CO. 520/14, Moor to C.O., 18 April 1902, enclosure; CO. 520/14, Moor to C.O., 12 April 1902; CO. 520/14, Moor to C.O., 7 May 1902.
[5] CSO. 1/20/55, C.O. to Lugard, 6 January 1913.
[6] CO. 520/26. Egerton to C.O., conf. 11 October 1904, enclosures.

became aware of the criminal activities of *Agbala* agents, two of whom were executed for murder.[1]

THE EKUMEKU DISTURBANCES

Other Ibos, in the Asaba hinterland, found their *Ekumeku* Society lodges a convenient way of dealing with their local problems although the society was disapproved of by the government. It will be recalled that since the 1890s the Ibos of the Asaba hinterland had reacted through the *Ekumeku* Society against the combined threats of Christian missionary enterprises and increasing government control. By their repeated protests against such activities, the Ibos of the Asaba hinterland became a nuisance to Christian missionaries and the protectorate staff. Because of the political agitation in Ugwashi-Uku, Onitsha-Olona and Ezi in the Asaba hinterland in 1902, Father Humbert, a Roman Catholic missionary, confidently predicted that an 'anti-European' rising, like the Indian Mutiny, was imminent. He attributed the unrest there to the political activities of the *Ekumeku* (the League of the Silent Ones) and the *Otuchichi*, a similar secret society.[2]

The disturbance he feared eventually took place between 1903 and 1904. Native court houses and mission stations in the Asaba hinterland suffered destruction or looting by the members of the *Ekumeku* Society who normally operated at night. Among the worst hit were the Native Court houses at Onitisha-Olona, Ezi, Onitsha-Uku and Idumaje-Ugboko. The *Ekumeku* members murdered or maltreated the chiefs and missionary converts who had been friendly to the government, released criminals from the government lock-ups, closed markets and stopped trade.[3]

Captain Ian Hogg, in charge of the expeditionary force against the disaffected areas, believed that the *Ekumeku* Society constituted an 'Anti-European Club'.[4] W. E. B. Copland-Crowford, the Commissioner in charge of the disturbed areas, supported

[1] Ottenberg, S.: 'Ibo oracles and intergroup relations', *South Western Journal of Anthrolopogy*, 14, 1958, p. 308; Smith S. R.: *The Ibo People*, vol. 1 (Ph.D. thesis) Cambridge 1929, pp. 144-5.

[2] *Calprof.* 10/3/4, Fosbery to the High Commissioner, Southern Nigeria, 2 September 1902.

[3] CO. 520/24, Egerton to C.O., 7 May 1904, enclosure. CO. 520/24, Fosbery to C.O., 9 February 1904.

[4] CO. 520/24, Egerton to C.O., 7 May 1904, enclosure.

Control through Coercion

him, and charged the *Ekumekus* with seeking to seize power in the Asaba hinterland.[1] Copland-Crawford further maintained that during a large meeting at Onitsha-Olona, before the disturbances, a leading *Ekumeku* cultist had been elected 'judge or District Commissioner' who maintained his own 'court messengers' to serve 'summonses' on the persons to appear before the 'Ekumeku Court'.[2] Both Copland-Crawford and Hogg, however, mistook the course of the *Ekumeku* disturbance for its cause. The *Ekumeku* and the Ibos they represented had nothing against European missionaries and government authorities as long as they did not interfere with their customary practices.

The British political staff brought new concepts of law and justice, while the European Christian missionaries, with the protection of the government, spread new ideas of morality and ethics. The *Ekumeku* society, therefore, attacked Ibo chiefs and people who had collaborated with the government and the Christian missions to the utter disregard of the old institutions and practices.

The government visited the disturbed areas of the Asaba hinterland with a punitive expedition, arrested and later tried about 300 *Ekumekus*. Copland-Crawford felt satisfied that the expedition had had a 'reassuring effect' over an extended area including the Kwale territory, another disturbed part of the protectorate.[3]

The *Ekumeku* disturbances revealed a need for a proclamation for 'facilitating the suppression of secret societies dangerous to the maintenance of peace and good government'.[4] In November 1905 Egerton passed the Unlawful Societies Proclamation,[5] which defined unlawful societies and provided for the punishment of their members.

This proclamation (later an ordinance) did not, however, prevent a further *Ekumeku* disturbance in the Asaba hinterland between 1909 and 1910. The *Ekumeku* members exploited the

[1] CO. 520/24, Egerton to C.O., 20 May 1904, enclosure.
[2] *Ibid.*
[3] CO. 520/24, Egerton to C.O., 20 May 1904, enclosure.
[4] CO. 520/26, Egerton to Lyttelton, 6 December 1904. Gaining from his experience in the Far East, Egerton gave Attorney-General J. Winkfield a copy of the Straits Settlement Ordinance, No. 1 of 1889, which was adapted to serve the needs of Southern Nigeria in dealing with unlawful societies.
[5] CO. 588/1, No. 16 of 1905.

41

political unrest caused by the chieftaincy dispute between Nzekwe and Okonjor over the headship of Ugwashi-Uku, thereby taking the opportunity of running their branch 'clubs' or lodges.[1] The government dispatched troops who broke up the *Ekumeku* 'town clubs' at Issele-Uku, Idimo-boro, Idimugi-Unu, Onitsha-Uku and Ugbodo. The *Ekumeku* members caught were later tried and imprisoned by the government.[2]

The establishment of a permanent government station in the Asaba hinterland, quite independent of the senior District Commissioner at Onitsha, helped to check further open confrontations between the government and the *Ekumeku* Society. That administrative reform became by far the most important political lesson learnt from the *Ekumeku* disturbances of 1909–10.[3] The *Ekumeku* and other movements which centred on secret cults can be compared in extent and violence with such post-1914 disturbances as the Women's Riots (1929–30), with the exception that the latter had more publicity.

TERRITORIES ACQUIRED BY CONQUESTS

Through punitive expeditions and patrols much of Iboland and other parts of the protectorate became 'conquered territory'. Shortly before the 1914 amalgamation, the senior political and intelligence officers of Southern Nigeria recalled the methods which they and their predecessors had adopted in bringing territories there under government control. Provincial Commissioner H. Bedwell first defined his terms. The expression 'conquered territory' could have at least two meanings. In its restricted sense, the term applied wherever force was used 'to enter a country and to establish a government station'. In a more general sense, Bedwell extended it to 'the use of force for any reason whatever'.[4] In this sense, Bedwell maintained 'that practically the whole of the Central and Eastern Provinces, with the exception of port towns, have been either taken or settled by force of arms'.[5]

[1] CO. 592/7, *Annual report on the Central Province*, 1909.
[2] CO. 520/107, Egerton to C.O., conf. 30 November 1911 and enclosure.
[3] CO. 520/93, Egerton to C.O., conf. 19 April 1910; CO. 520/93, Egerton to C.O., conf. 17 May 1910 enclosure; CO. 520/94, Thorburn to C.O., conf. 16 June 1910.
[4] African (West) No. 1005.   [5] *Ibid.*

Control through Coercion

While adopting a similar view, Provincial Commissioner Lt. Col. H. C. Moorhouse considered that Calabar, Bonny, Opobo, Degema, Brass, Forcados and Warri could not 'fairly be described as having been occupied by conquest'.[1] Major W. H. Beverley, the Intelligence Officer, qualified that opinion by indicating that a 'small area' north of the Brass district had been brought under control during the Sabagreia expedition of 1903 besides the earlier punitive expedition of 1895 when the people of Nembe and Brass suffered punishment for their raid on the Akassa depot of the Royal Niger Company.[2] Moorhouse made similar qualifications for the Degema, Warri and Opobo districts. He noted that Isiokpo, in the north-eastern part of Degema district, came in the category of an area 'occupied by conquest'. In the Warri district, he recalled that the Urhobo villages in the north had been 'dealt with' by the Asaba hinterland expedition of 1904. He also noted that the Kwa (Qua) Ibo area in the northern part of the Opobo district and the Ogoni territory in the west had been 'visited' by 'expeditions and patrols'.[3]

Both Moorhouse and Bedwell put in a special category Idah, Akassa, Onitsha, Asaba, and Aboh, the districts taken over from the Royal Niger Company in 1900. They believed that the Royal Niger Company had forcefully occupied them before their transfer to the Protectorate of Southern Nigeria.[4] Using Moorhouse's list of territories 'occupied by conquest', clearly some of these territories transferred to Southern Nigeria did not escape punitive expeditions and patrols. Moorhouse's list included:[5]

1. Benin, Ifon, Ishan or Ubiaja, and Idah, West of the Niger (Benin City Expedition, 1897 and Ishan Expedition, 1901).
2. Eket (Oron Expedition, 1901).
3. Aro-Chuku, Ikot-Ekpene, Itu, Uyo, Abak, Aba, Owerri and Bende (Aro expedition, 1901–2).
4. Ahoada (Sabagreia Expedition, 1903).
5. Afikpo, Obubra, Ikom, Abakiliki (Ezza Patrol, 1903; and the German Boundary Expedition, 1904).
6. Asaba, Agbor, Kwale, Aboh, Sapele (Asaba Hinterland Expedition, 1904).

[1] *Ibid.* Dated 17 February 1913.   [2] *Ibid.*, Dated 11 March 1913.
[3] *Ibid.*, Dated 17 February 1913.
[4] *Ibid.* Confidential letters of 17 February 1913 and 28 February 1913.
[5] *Ibid.*, Dated 17 February 1913. Moorhouse made reservations about the correctness of the dates of these expeditions.

7. Awka, Onitsha, Idah, east of the Niger (Onitsha Hinterland Expedition, 1904–5).
8. Udi, Okigwi (Niger-Cross River Expedition, 1908).
9. Okwoga, Ogoja, Obudu (Northern Hinterland Expedition, 1908–9).

Using the term 'conquered territory' in a restricted sense, Bedwell had a shorter list, including the districts of Aba, Abak, Abakiliki, Afikpo, Ahoada, Aro-Chuku, Bende, Eket, Ikom (Okuni), Ikot-Ekpene, Obubra, Obudu, Ogoja, Owerri, Okigwi, Orlu and Uyo.[1]

The rate of progress made by British officials and government troops in expanding the area under firm administrative control can be assessed differently. In the non-Yoruba-speaking parts of Southern Nigeria, the area of territories successively brought under control through the use of punitive expeditions and patrols between 1903 and June 1909 showed:[2]

Year	Square Miles
1904	911
1905	3,133
1906	1,331
1908	2,703
1909	7,834
Total	15,912

There were other territories considered 'open' by the British authorities in 1903 but which subsequently required revisiting with troops till 1906.[3]

Year	Square Miles
1904	694
1905	2,006
1906	154
Total	2,854

[1] *Ibid.*, Dated 28 February 1913.
[2] CO. 520/93. Information on map drawn by the Intelligence Department, Southern Nigeria, and signed by Lt.Col. H. C. Moorhouse and Capt. W. H. Beverley on 17 June 1909. The total area of Southern Nigeria then was 77,260 square miles.   [3] *Ibid.*

Control through Coercion

THE COERCION ORDINANCES

Having consolidated their control over more districts in the hinterland of the Protectorate of Southern Nigeria, the British authorities soon discovered that the new areas required special attention. As most of these areas had been forcibly acquired, the people found it extremely difficult to adjust readily to the new administration.

To deal with instances of unrest, Egerton's administration, with the Colonial Office's approval, passed three sets of special ordinances between February and June 1912. This series of coercive legislation – the Collective Punishment, Unsettled Districts, and Peace Preservation Ordinances – operated only in the Central and Eastern Provinces (formerly called the Protectorate of Southern Nigeria).[1]

In certain cases, the government found it difficult to distinguish between individual and collective responsibility. Attorney-General A. R. Pennington maintained that through the Collective Punishment Ordinance (1912) the government legalised 'what in practice has always been done in the Central and Eastern Provinces' where such offences as murder represented 'practically the crimes of the whole village or community'.[2] By this ordinance fines were imposed on towns, villages and other communities for homicide and other crimes necessitating the use of soldiers and police. On such occasions, the government would conduct an inquiry before imposing a collective fine. The same law disallowed appeals 'by suit or otherwise' when an order had been made under this ordinance. The Governor would, however, report immediately to the Secretary of State for the Colonies on the causes and course of the actions taken.

The administrative convenience of this form of justice became clear in May 1912 when the government applied it to the disturbed areas of Owerri and Okigwi districts. Provincial Commissioner H. Bedwell reported that the 'truculent' Oguta people had

[1] CO. 588/4, The Collective Punishment Ordinance, (No. 67, 1912), Dated 8 February 1912. CO. 588/4, The Unsettled Districts Ordinance (No. 15) of 1912, dated 4 June 1912; CO. 588/4, The Peace Preservation Ordinance (No. 14 of 1912), dated 4 June 1912. CO. 588/4, The Peace Preservation (Amendment) Ordinance (No. 31 of 1912), dated 27 September 1912.

[2] CSO. 1/19/47, Egerton to C.O., 24 February 1912, enclosure.

45

refused to carry government luggage and clean roads with compulsory labour. He further accused them of murdering people suspected of witchcraft, though the 'Warrant Chiefs' of the area denied the charge. As fines were not effective, Bedwell instructed the District Commissioner at Oguta 'to sit down in the town with an escort at the expense of the town until such time as the people come to their senses . . .'.[1]

In the newly and forcibly acquired districts, the government encountered another type of problem which resulted partly from the activities of African lawyers in disputes over land and partly from arbitrary actions and decisions of the political staff. The government charged persons 'of undesirable character and reputation' with the responsibility of causing serious troubles in those districts. Through the Unsettled Districts Ordinance, explained Attorney-General Pennington, the government sought to get rid of such persons.[2] The Colonial Office indicated that it particularly wanted to prohibit from those districts such 'aliens' as the 'black lawyer' and the 'Lagos agitator'.[3]

The Unsettled Districts Ordinance made it possible for parts of the Eastern and Central Provinces to be declared 'Unsettled Districts'. Thereafter, the government had power and authority to prohibit any person or persons, being 'non-natives' or 'aliens', from entering or re-entering the district. The penalties for a breach of the Unsettled Districts Ordinance included a fine, imprisonment or both, Offenders could also be deported, paying the expense of their deportation to a place determined by the Governor with the approval of the Secretary of State.

The Peace Preservation Ordinance provided a machinery 'for the better preservation of the public peace in those parts of the protectorate which are not under absolute control'.[4] By failing to define 'absolute control' the government was able to interpret this ordinance flexibly so as to strengthen its authority. Attorney-General Penington explained that the Peace Preservation Ordinance was partly inspired by legislation for the Gold Coast. The other part, section four, came from the Irish Coercion Acts. In his view, 'it was under a similar section that Parnell and William O'Brien and certain others were imprisoned . . .'. He hoped that

---

[1] CSO. 1/19/50, Cameron to C.O., 23 July 1912, enclosures.
[2] CSO. 1/19/49, James to C.O., 19 June 1912, enclosure.
[3] CO. 520/103, Egerton to C.O., conf. 17 May 1911, minute by J.A.
[4] CO. 588/4, Ordinance No. 15 of 1912, preamble.

Control through Coercion

the ordinance would provide 'a means of preventing disturbances and possible bloodshed, and avert the various hardships which are the natural outcome of expeditions that cannot be helped'.[1] Egerton concurred.

Under the Peace Preservation Ordinance, the Governor had power and authority to declare any part of the Eastern and Central Provinces 'a disturbed district'. In emergencies, the Provincial Commissioner could make this declaration, provided he reported immediately to the Governor for confirmation or otherwise. Following such a declaration, the people could be searched and arrested with or without warrants for possessing arms and ammunition. In the case of a 'rebellion, civil commotion, or riot', fines would be imposed and imprisonments made. The cost of stationing 'additional' troops or police would be paid by the inhabitants. The Peace Preservation Ordinance gave District Commissioners and other commissioned officers – civil, military or naval – immunity from liability for criminal or civil actions, except by or with the consent of the Attorney-General.

These three Coercive Ordinances helped to maintain or restore law and order in parts of the Eastern and Central Provinces. At the same time, they demonstrated the forceful occupation of these parts. Through the new emphasis on 'conquered territory' and coercive legislation, the administration became more and more direct, despite the existence of Native Councils comprising loyalist warrant-holding chiefs. In considerably changed circumstances, the conflicts between the people and the new government resulted in bloody encounters which involved the frequent use of troops and police.

THE PARADOX OF THE PAX BRITANNICA

A régime clearly based on force provided enough ammunition for its critics. The central issue was whether these operations could be justified under the *Pax Britannica*. The long and bitter controversy showed that punitive expeditions, patrols and coercion generally constituted the paradox of the *Pax Britannica*. Such measures were not the goal of British control over Southern Nigeria, only a means to an end. What, then, was the goal? E. D. Morel, the former clerk with the West African shipping line of

[1] CO. 592/11, Legislative Council Debates, 8 February 1912.

Elder, Dempster and Company Limited, who subsequently became a member of the West African section of the Liverpool Chamber of Commerce, outlined the goal expected by the European traders.

> What are we in West Africa for? What do we hope to do there? ... Commerce took us to West Africa; commerce keeps and will keep us in West Africa. It is the *fons et origo* of our presence in West Africa. The day that it ceases to be so, West Africa ceases to be of use to the Empire.[1]

In 1889, P. H. Ezechiel, then a second-class clerk at the Colonial Office, explained that the 'main *raison d'être* of our West African Colonies' lay in 'trade (and the development of the native)'.[2] Joseph Chamberlain, Secretary of State for the Colonies from 1895 to 1903, defined the goal and indicated the means. In August 1895 he had told the House of Commons that 'expeditions punitive or otherwise' provided 'the only system of civilising and practically of developing the trade of Africa'.[3] Again in March 1897, he publicly declared:

> We feel now that our rule over these territories [in Africa] can only be justified if we can show that it adds to the happiness and prosperity of the people.[4]

Chamberlain then further explained that in establishing the *Pax Britannica*

> ... there has been bloodshed, there has been loss of life among the native populations ... You cannot have omelettes without breaking eggs; you cannot destroy the practices of barbarism, of slavery, of superstition which for centuries have desolated the interior of Africa, without the use of force ...[5]

Unofficial opinion, however, queried this idea of breaking African 'eggs' in order to make a British 'omelette'. In his address before the African section of the Liverpool Chamber of Commerce on 9 September 1901, E. W. Blyden, the educated negro

[1] E. D. Morel, *Affairs of West Africa*, London 1902, p. 21.
[2] CO. 147/141, Denton to C.O., 16 February 1899, minute by P.H.E.J. Chamberlain saw this minute but made no comments.
[3] H.C. Deb. 4s. 36, 22 August 1895, 641.
[4] *P.R.C.I.*, vol. 28, 1896–7, London, Annual dinner speech, 31 March 1897, pp. 236–7.
[5] *Ibid.*

and former Honorary Secretary to the Lagos Native Advisory Board during the 1890s, urged an end to the use of 'maxim guns and martini rifles'. He endorsed instead 'the only war that the natives gladly welcome . . . the war against poison-bearing mosquitoes'.[1]

Among the Liverpool merchants with significant interests in West Africa, John Holt became the strongest critic of the punitive expeditions. Writing to E. D. Morel in May 1901, he observed:

> Wherever there are soldiers there must be war, particularly if you have helpless people to slay in order to get your ends quickly. Moor is at his work again killing people in order to make them humane and civilised. I like that old Lagos Governor [W. MacGregor]. He at all events is a man of peace, and he is making use of the natives. The other fellows are deporting the best men of the country and embroiling it in continuous warfare as a consequence. When peace is honoured by Chamberlain the country will make progress and the butchers be relegated to a back seat. At present they are taking all the honours thanks to a deluded people drunk with sham imperialism.[2]

Holt disliked Governors with military backgrounds, blaming their professional training for their readiness to resort to force. He preferred 'men of peace and patience' like William MacGregor of Lagos,[3] who, said Holt, had 'no bloodstains on his hands to answer for'.[4] Condemning 'military Governors', Holt observed:

> The murdering rascals, when shall we get rid of them? We are as barbarous as the natives in spite of our veneer of Christianity and civilisation. We must get these military Governors away attending to their regiments. They are quite out of place and altogether unnecessary as Governors. We want men of peace and patience.[5]

Holt deplored such punitive expeditions as those launched

---

[1] *West Africa*, 12 October 1901, p. 1194; Blyden, E. W.: *West Africa before Europe*, London 1905, pp. 35–6.
[2] E.D.M.P. F/S, J. Holt to Morel, 6 May 1901.
[3] E.D.M.P. F/S, Holt to Morel, 13 December 1902.
[4] E.D.M.P. F/S, Holt to Morel, 23 April 1901.
[5] E.D.M.P. F/S, Holt to Morel, 13 December 1902.

against the Binis and the Aros as 'sad specimens' of the *Pax Britannica*.[1] He demanded control through 'peaceful penetration'.[2] He dismissed the idea that the goal of the British authorities in Southern Nigeria lay in commercial exploitation alone, believing instead that they aimed at 'taxation and punitive expeditions'.[3] If Holt confused the goals with some of the means, he laid the blame for punitive expeditions on the incapacity, arrogance and wickedness of the British authorities.[4] Writing of punitive expeditions under the Moor and Egerton administrations, Holt disclosed:

> I consider that the punitive expeditions of Southern Nigeria since the establishment of our government in that district have been a disgrace to our country. They have been the outcome of imaginations and injustice, and want of recognition of native rights, and the ideas that govern native actions. They want to establish civilisation by force instead of persuasion by argument and example. Conversion by force is no doubt a much quicker operation, but there is nothing to boast of in it or to be proud of. At the same time it suits these young men to have a fling at the natives. There is little risk in the matter, and the glory is sure to be recognised by those who are parties to the system of promoting them for bloodshed.[5]

The views of mercantile interests on punitive expeditions appeared in a leader in *West Africa* in October 1901. The merchants decried this practice as 'a wrong policy' in that

> commercially, it is not practical to shoot your customer. Politically, it is not practical in a country like West Africa to destroy the native form of society, break the power of the chiefs . . . Financially, it is not practical, for it means the piling up of debts . . . and the ultimate impoverishment of the country.[6]

The attitude of European commercial interests in West Africa was nearly always guided by short-term considerations. They dis-

---

[1] *E.D.M.P.* F/S, Holt to Morel, 23 April 1901.
[2] *E.D.M.P.* F/S, Holt to Morel, 21 January 1906.
[3] *E.D.M.P.* F/S, Holt to Morel, 2 January 1901.
[4] *Ibid.*
[5] *E.D.M.P.* F/S, Holt to Morel, 2 August 1904.
[6] *West Africa*, 12 October 1901, p. 1184.

liked any measures that would disturb the peace and interrupt commerce. But from the 1890s the Chambers of Commerce had advocated the penetration of the hinterlands of British West Africa[1] and punitive expeditions represented some of the bloody consequences of this policy.

Alfred L. Jones, the Liverpool shipping magnate connected with Messrs Elder, Dempster, and Company Limited and other financial interests in British West Africa, had a foot in each camp. 'I always beg of our Governors', he said during a banquet in 1902, 'to be patient with the natives, but sometimes force is necessary, and it must be used . . . but let it be the very last resource, because in destroying the African native you destroy our assets there. Africa cannot be worked without him.' Even so,

> I must say that in the selection of the present Governors the Colonial Office have shown their wisdom, and we have some splendid fellows out there . . . In Sir William MacGregor, at Lagos, we have a most humane man, who sympathises with our progressive policy, and Lagos has never seen a better Governor. Sir Ralph Moor and Colonel Lugard, in Nigeria, are excellent men in the cause of the Empire.[2]

E. D. Morel, however, advocated a slow pace in the expansion of British control. Writing in 1902, he pleaded:

> The country [British West Africa] needs political rest . . . It should be our object to intermeddle as little as possible with native institutions, abide with scrupulous exactitude to both the spirit and the letter of our treaties with the chiefs; develop the native peoples along the lines of their own civilisation . . . use conciliation in preference to dictation, gold rather than the sword . . . Patience, more patience, and again patience. That should be, ought to be, the corner-stone of British policy in West Africa. It was the tortoise that won the race; not the hare.[3]

The Aborigines Protection Society (APS) also condemned punitive expeditions. In a lecture on 'Punitive Expeditions' given under the auspices of the Liverpool Peace Society on 4 October 1901, H. R. Fox-Bourne, the APS Secretary, accused

---

[1] CO. 267/397, T. H. Barker to C.O., 9 April 1892. Barker was the Secretary, Liverpool Chamber of Commerce.
[2] *West Africa*, 4 January 1902, p. 16.
[3] Morel, *op. cit.*, pp. 15–16.

the British government of adopting a policy of 'nigger-hunting'[1] generally in British West Africa and particularly in 'Nigeria'. He observed:

> The essential fact to be borne in mind is that within the past few years, and most extensively since Mr Chamberlain's policy of 'developing our West African estates' was entered upon in 1896, there have been scores of 'punitive expeditions' against troublesome native communities . . . many of them ostensibly for the suppression of slavery, human sacrifices, and other savage institutions, but all having for their real object the development of British commerce.

It is unfair to suggest that Chamberlain liked punitive expeditions *per se*. In the Protectorates of Lagos and Southern Nigeria he did not wish to go too far too fast in bringing the people under British control. For example, he showed much concern in 1899 when Acting Governor G. C. Denton of Lagos sought to impose a British Resident upon the Egbas. Fear that such an action would lead to disturbances influenced him to suggest a policy of *festina lente*.[2]

Similarly, when Moor in 1899 asked for permission to undertake the punitive expedition against the Aros, Chamberlain was not immediately convinced of the necessity for it. 'The people on the spot ought to know best', he remarked, 'but they are sometimes too much in a hurry. I am not clear that this tribe may not be brought gradually under control without war . . .' Until F. D. Lugard and G. T. Goldie, formerly of the Royal Niger Company, replied to his inquiry about the necessity of the expedition proposed by Moor, Chamberlain refused to approve it. The sanction came when Goldie also endorsed Moor's proposal.[3]

The Colonial Office invariably followed the best course suggested by the man-on-the-spot but advised him to keep the degree of fighting with the people within reasonable limits. Much therefore depended on the attitude of its men-on-the-spot.

Moor's attitude to punitive expeditions did not change since

[1] *West Africa*, 12 October 1901, p. 1195.
[2] CO. 147/141, Denton to C.O., tel., 14 January 1899, minute by J.C.
[3] CO. 444/2, Moor to C.O., 9 September 1899, minute by J.C.; CO. 444/4, Goldie to C.O., 17 November 1899, and minute by J.C.

June 1896 when he mapped out his Ten Point Programme for developing the territory under his administration. Though he emphasised 'expeditions of a peaceable nature', Moor made it quite clear that should 'peaceable means' fail, force would be necessary 'in specific cases'.[1] A year later Moor repeated that he undertook punitive expeditions only after peaceful overtures had failed.[2]

Without a clear understanding of the African viewpoint, some of Moor's senior lieutenants believed that the 'low' level of the people they dealt with justified the use of force. Some observers today may hesitate to attribute objective value to the official views on the obstacles posed by 'savagery', 'barbarism', 'uncivilised people' and so on. Though such comments would be rightly rejected outright by analysts today, yet they need discussion in that they revealed the psychological state of those who used them to rationalise the punitive expeditions and patrols they recommended or carried out. Such views illustrate the spontaneous reactions of ambitious, largely ignorant soldiers and administrators to a society which they did not understand and which stubbornly resisted the imposition of their rule. In referring to the conduct of the Aro Field Force, Lt.Col. H. L. Gallway, the senior political officer in the field, considered the methods employed 'not unduly severe' and 'as humane as could be expected under the circumstances' – the 'manners and customs' of the people concerned being 'on a par with what one could expect from the lowest scale of animal creation . . .'.[3]

On another occasion, H. Bedwell, then Acting Secretary, suggested that 'the type of native to be dealt with is of a lower scale than probably any other in British West Africa'. He further observed that among these people, 'Diplomacy' may win a point here and there, but in the person of the Administrative Officer it is often sent, unless supported by a strong escort, flying out of a town somewhat quicker than it entered it.'[4]

Some of the political and military officers, believing that the people were 'savages', maltreated them as such during some of these punitive expeditions and patrols. Brevet-Major H. M. (later Lord) Trenchard, whose military experience in Southern

[1] FO. 2/101, Moor to F.O., 14 June 1896.
[2] FO. 2/121, Moor to F.O., 6 May 1897.
[3] CO. 520/14, Moor to C.O., 18 April 1902, enclosure.
[4] *Colonial reports, annual*, Southern Nigeria, 1903.

Nigeria extended from 1903 to 1910, attested to the high-handedness of some of the officers he worked with. According to Trenchard's biographer, A. Boyle,

> Having consolidated his position, Trenchard had no inhibition about treating the precedents and standard practices of district officials strictly on their merits. When, for instance, he discovered that a batch of Ibo captives had been flogged for refusing to talk, he ordered their instant release, severely reprimanded the officer responsible, and warned all his men that he would not tolerate any maltreatment of prisoners. The paradoxical contrast between Trenchard's overbearing strength of personality and this unexpected manifestation of tenderness towards sullen captives, traditionally held to be incapable of understanding any language but that of physical violence, dumbfounded them. They coined a word for natives . . . 'Trenchard's-mustn't-touch-'ems,' they called them. And it stuck. Trenchard's attitude, in fact, was inspired by an instinctive contempt for force as an argument anywhere off a battlefield. As a method of emphasising the white man's right to rule, it seemed to him barbaric, inhuman and certain in the long run to defeat its own ends.[1]

Trenchard did not stop there. He condemned the dissolute habits of the officers and men of the Southern Nigeria Regiment who before his arrival there had found much solace in 'drinking, gambling and sexual exploits'.[2] Nor did Trenchard express satisfaction with the conduct, during the punitive expeditions and patrols, of some Aro guides who had misused their position to terrorise and blackmail their weaker neighbours as the 'harbingers of the white man's vengeance.'[3] In such incidents, the ordinary farmers and other rural folk were able to contrast British colonial justice with African justice. Though in pre-colonial times they had witnessed the havoc caused by inter-village feuds and slave-raiding malefactors, they could hardly understand the wanton destruction and robbery which occurred under what the new rulers euphemistically called the *Pax Britannica*.

The justification of punitive expeditions by African 'barbarism' was also used by Egerton to explain the military action taken after the murder at Agbor in 1906 of F. O. S. Crewe-Read, the

[1] Boyle, A.: *Trenchard*, London 1962, p. 79.   [2] *Ibid.*, p. 76.   [3] *Ibid.*, p. 78.

acting District Commissioner, who exacted too much compulsory labour from the people.¹

If by backwardness or barbarism, Gallwey, Bedwell, Egerton and other British officials referred to the practice of some Africans in taking the law into their own hands when provoked, then it was certainly seen in the areas which had suffered punitive expeditions and patrols. Such conduct, however, did not necessarily convert those who so opposed British rule into savages. Colonial 'law' was neither understood nor accepted by several Africans, and those who appeared to have taken the law into their own hands were in fact resisting the overthrow of the existing law by superior British force.

The British authorities did not sufficiently appreciate the grounds for the people's grievances. None of them found out whether the illiterate masses understood the meaning of the newly-established protectorate under which, from the 1880s, they had steadily lost control over their external and internal affairs. To most Africans, treaties of protection attested to with 'x-marks' by illiterate chiefs meant nothing.

Deprived of a legitimate vent through trustworthy representatives in a Legislative Council, the inhabitants of the Protectorate of Southern Nigeria turned to instruments mistakenly believed to give immediate redress. They, however, found that their use of guns, matchets and fire-brands only brought greater suffering. In the bloody reprisals which followed, they realised their inability to counter the superior fire-power of the government troops and police.

Unlike the people of Lagos, those in the Protectorate of Southern Nigeria lacked African-owned and African-edited mass-circulation newspapers. It is true that from 1855 the United Free Church of Scotland mission at Old Calabar had published a monthly newspaper *Unwana Efik* (The Light of Calabar) and subsequently the *Obukpon Efik* (The Horn of Efik). But these evangelical newspapers were short-lived. *The Calabar Observer*, begun by the same mission in 1902, came to an abrupt end in 1904.² Thereafter, provincial newspapers in Eastern Nigeria did not re-appear until the 1930s.³

¹ CO. 520/46, Egerton to C.O., conf. 28 May 1907.
² CO. 520/14, Moor to C.O., 6 June 1902. Part of the *Calabar Observer* was in Efik; CO. 147/167, MacGregor to C.O., 16 October 1903, minute by P.H.E. dated 23 January 1904.
³ Omu, F. I. A.: *The Nigerian Newspaper Press 1859–1937* (Ph.D.

In the political officers' relationship with the people under their control a wide gulf – a chasm, as it were – existed between two cultures. Unlike the Christian missionaries, several British political officers did not live close to the people and failed to bridge the language-gap. The use of interpreters with a poor knowledge of English offered only limited assistance.

The growing awareness of the people of the Protectorate of Southern Nigeria that they were being brought under alien control sharpened their determination to avert the loss of independence.

Savagery or backwardness as conceived by Gallway, Bedwell and others could not explain the prolonged African opposition to the British government. Did something more compelling, though less tangible, nullify the fear of the superior fire-power of the British-controlled troops and police? Otherwise, why did the people in the disturbed areas, having witnessed or heard of the destruction caused by Maxim guns, rifles, seven-pounders and the like, persist in their opposition?

The fact that government troops visited some of the patently troublesome areas more than once ought to have removed all doubts about the effectiveness of modern weapons, yet, the Asaba hinterland, one of the major disturbed areas, was the scene of four successive waves of *Ekumeku* unrest in 1898, 1902, 1903–1904, and 1909–10. Punitive expeditions and patrols followed every time. Similarly, after the major punitive expedition against the Aros from 1901 to 1902, the government believed that the Long JuJu had been completely destroyed. But in 1908, the same Aros, still described as 'detrimental to the pacification and good government' of the newly-controlled areas, were reported as having resumed their oracle.[1]

Was the behaviour of these people a result of intractability? The deeper the historian delves into the hard core of the disquiet in the Protectorate of Southern Nigeria which made punitive measures and patrols necessary, the more elusive the cause becomes. The determination of the link between 'savagery' and punitive expeditions is more a matter for the anthropologist and psycho-analyst than for the historian. The backward condition of

---

Thesis), Ibadan 1965, p. 109. These were the: *Nigerian Echo* (1933) – Aba; *Nigerian Eastern Mail* (1935) – Calabar; *African Advertiser* (1935) – Calabar.

[1] CO. 520/62, Egerton to C.O. conf. 22 June 1908, enclosure.

the people in terms of Western European standards merely aggravated the difficulties of establishing and maintaining mutual understanding and confidence between the new British rulers and those under them. In June 1896, Moor had noticed that the good faith of the British administrator was suspect. He recalled then that since the JaJa episode of 1887 when, contrary to H. Johnston's pledge of safe-conduct, the government kidnapped and banished the former king of Opobo, a 'bogey'[1] concerning the word of British officers had arisen. Moor and his successors continued to be associated with that 'bogey'.

The intensity and duration of opposition to British rule in parts of the Protectorate can be further explained by the effects of punitive expeditions and patrols. These field operations instilled fear of an authority which immediately or subsequently would explain by word and deed the aims of the new order and so the impression was left that it intended to stifle existing power and wreck the foundations of the various communities. So, despite overwhelming odds, several people mounted desperate resistance in their attempts to protect their cherished pre-colonial values and institutions. But in their reactions to the steady imposition of colonial rule, some Africans revealed a lack of consistency. The reaction of the people in the areas re-visited by punitive expeditions and patrols indicated the phenomena of waves of resistance to colonial rule followed by waves of temporary acceptance which in turn gave way to further waves of rejection.

In analysing further sources of sustained violent conflict between British authorities and communities in the Protectorate of Southern Nigeria, sufficient allowance should be made for the problem of adjustment. Given this problem of uneasy adjustment, barbarism or inadequate 'civilisation', in the Western European sense, can no longer be regarded as a valid explanation for the conflicts. The Iseyin-Okeiho disturbance of 1916 among the Oyo-Yoruba and the Egba unrest of 1918 showed that even among a comparatively cautious and otherwise peaceful people, there were limits to the degree of administrative interference and injustice which they could tolerate without resistance whatever the consequences.[2] Such situations arose when people found it

[1] FO. 2/101, Moor to F.O., 14 June 1896.
[2] Burns, A.: *History of Nigeria*, London 1958, pp. 228–9. Atanda, J.: 'The Iseyin-Okeiho rising of 1916: an example of socio-political conflict in colonial Nigeria', *JHSN*, vol. 4, no. 4, June 1969, pp. 497–514.

difficult to adjust themselves sufficiently to the new message of 'civilisation' preached by the government and the Christian missionaries.

'Civilisation' conveyed different things to different societies at different times. By 'civilisation' during the period covered by this study, the British government and the Christian missionaries involved in the affairs of Southern Nigeria entertained notions of literacy in English, a willingness to adopt peaceful means of resolving conflicts through the law courts controlled by British officers and warrant-holding African loyalists, the avoidance of customs resulting in injury or death to members of any community, and the acceptance of white rule and Western European standards of right and wrong.

On the other hand, most Africans in rural communities found nothing basically wrong with their pre-colonial institutions and moral code. Besides, reforms involved radical changes in their way of life. For example, to the disgruntled Aros, abolishing slavery did not necessarily become a humanitarian or moral issue. To them, the abolitionist stance of the British government and its representatives in Southern Nigeria meant an immediate loss of profit.

The government's 'civilising' mission directly and indirectly prolonged the period of conflict. Those in authority did not appreciate the cumulative effects of their reformist zeal. By making the pattern for the 'civilisation' of the people Western European, and not traditional, except in parts, the government compounded conflicts which were not easily resolved.

Whatever the official rationalisation, the main purpose of the series of punitive expeditions and patrols in parts of the Protectorate of Southern Nigeria was not 'civilisation'. On the contrary, these field operations sought to destroy any force or power which could possibly challenge the absolute authority of the British government.

Without sufficient anthropological data, the British government did not find it easy to discover what to preserve and what to destroy in the institutions of the people. Punitive expeditions which sought to destroy ju-jus, oracles, secret societies and ordeals made the administration appear negative and abhorrent in the eyes of the traditionalists, who rose in defence of their age-old institutions. Remove human sacrifices, infanticide, ordeals, the consultation of ju-jus, witchcraft accusations and punishments, or any other African practice 'repugnant to natural justice, equity, and good conscience', and what was left? Not 'native law and custom' as most of the indigenous inhabitants understood it. Moreover, the residue could not inspire confidence in the people. Aro society, for example, could not be the same after the Aro Field Force had desecrated the site of the Long JuJu. Aro political influence, and not only their economic power, suffered a serious blow under an administration dedicated to the abolition of slave-dealing.

It must be emphasised that indigenous institutions differ from the parts of a machine which can be removed and replaced at will. Rather, the several parts make an organic whole; remove one part and the other parts suffer. Modern medical science may permit spare-parts surgery, but spare-parts grafting in administration is a dangerous operation, particularly when attempted by men without adequate anthropological information. In either case, the element of rejection cannot be ruled out.

These factors added to the people's confusion and increased their opposition to the government. They also made more sense than the arguments based on barbarism.

Egerton also had another argument to put forward. Emphasising the economic aspects of his administration, he justified the 'field operations' for the period 1907-8 because by restoring 'law and order' they afforded 'facilities' for 'more extensive agriculture and trade'.[1]

Under Egerton's administration, and after the 1906 amalgamation, the people of Lagos feared that the policy of punitive expeditions would, for similar reasons, be extended to the Yorubas. In his Amalgamation Day Speech at Lagos, Legislative Councillor C. A. Sapara Williams publicly expressed the fears of his people.[2] In reply Egerton said he hated punitive expeditions but believed they were sometimes necessary. However, he considered them expensive, preferring to spend the sums allotted to them on 'making roads or railways or . . . otherwise increasing the prosperity and the development of the country'.[3] He tried to avoid punitive expeditions in Yorubaland, but continued till 1911 to justify annual 'pacification' programmes in the Eastern and Central Provinces of the amalgamated territories on the grounds

[1] CO. 520/65, Egerton to C.O., 8 September 1908.
[2] CO. 591/3, *Southern Nigeria Gazette*, 9 May 1906.
[3] *Ibid.*

of barbarism.[1] In fact, he found such annual 'pacification' programmes convenient because they enabled him to take only bits of territory which could be administered effectively year by year.[2]

In this analysis of punitive expeditions and patrols, it is pertinent to compare the experience of the Protectorate of Southern Nigeria with Northern Nigeria's during the same period. The expeditions against the emirates, which covered the main cities and the trade routes apart from the settled centres in northern Zaria, Kano, Katsina, Sokoto, Bida and the somewhat different case of Bornu, were relatively short-lived, tapering off after the Satiru unrest of 1906, if not much earlier. It was, however, clear that in those emirates also coercion became a means of consolidating control.

In parts of Northern Nigeria there were instances of stiff and prolonged resistance. The people of the Benue valley, particularly the Idoma and Tiv, and others who inhabited the foothills of the Bauchi Plateau and the plains and mountains of southern Adamawa witnessed punitive expeditions and patrols of the classical type until the 1930s. The Tiv provided the best example[3] of prolonged resistance and bloody reprisals in these areas.

Part of the tacit bargain which ensured the submission of the emirates lay in the British enlargement of the area under the control of the emirs, except in the case of Bida which subsequently gave constant trouble to the colonial administration. Hausa scholars and civil servants from the emirates secured jobs under the new colonial régime in areas where they would not have been able to operate continuously in the past. Hence, the subjugation of the emirates marked only the beginning of the conquest of Northern Nigeria. That conquest entailed the destruction of the major powers which could have opposed colonial authority. Outside the emirates, the method of subjugation resembled that employed in the Protectorate of Southern Nigeria.

Why was the resistance put up by the emirates relatively short-lived? First, the more open territory in the emirates facilitated the movement of troops who covered wider areas in a relatively shorter time. The forest lands of the Protectorate of Southern

[1] CO. 520/103, Egerton to C.O., conf. 30 May 1911.
[2] CO. 520/67, Egerton to C.O., conf. 2 November 1908.
[3] Dorward, D. C.: 'The development of the British colonial administration among the Tiv, 1900–1949.' *African Affairs*, **68**, no. 273, October 1969, pp. 316–33.

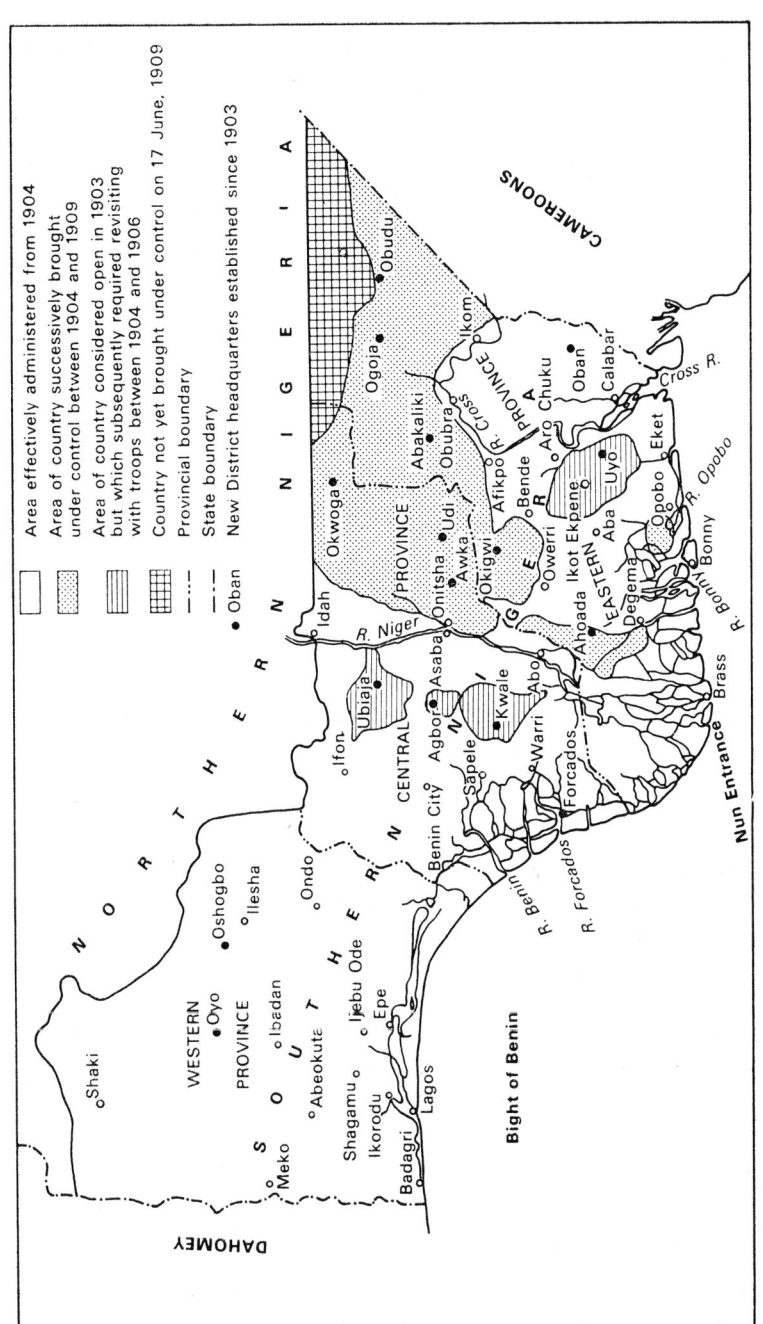

Areas under firm administration in Southern Nigeria, June 1909

The Evolution of the Nigerian State

Nigeria provided far greater logistic and commissariat problems which were only partially tackled through the practice of undertaking punitive expeditions every dry season.

Secondly, the nature of the reaction of the chiefs and people of the emirates was partly dictated by the degree of the popularity or otherwise of Fulani rule following the Sokoto jihad of 1804. But in the Protectorate of Southern Nigeria, no comparable relations and reactions on a large scale affected the situation to the same extent.

The religious factor had a different impact on the reactions to British rule in the Protectorates of Northern and Southern Nigeria. The Muslims of Northern Nigeria found in Islam a powerful international, and so supra-ethnic, magnet for the aspirations of the community of the faithful. Without a comparable unifying pre-colonial religion, the people of the Protectorate of Southern Nigeria struggled to defend their variety of religious values.

The submission of the Sultan of Sokoto, as the Commander of the Faithful, again set an example to the millions of devout Muslims who were thereby discouraged from prolonging the conflict through small-scale jihads. No such common religious leader emerged in the Protectorate of Southern Nigeria.

In the ranks of moderate members of the community of the faithful in Northern Nigeria, the main reason for their military confrontation with British forces disappeared from 1903 when Lugard guaranteed the continuation of Islam, which to them represented not only a religious faith but a way of life. Thereafter, they did not have to fight tenaciously for the preservation of other pre-colonial political and judicial institutions endowed with religious values. For example, in the Muslim areas of Northern Nigeria, religious orthodoxy frowned upon syncretism which involved the adoption of such institutions as secret cults, ordeals and the like. In Southern Nigeria, on the other hand, with their abundance of secret cults and similar institutions, which also closely affected their pre-colonial religious, political and judicial systems and values, the people received no such guarantees from the British authorities when some villages and communities capitulated to the punitive expeditions and patrols.

Not only were the states and communities of the Protectorate of Southern Nigeria smaller in their boundaries than the emirates, their rulers were less powerful. The existence of large emirates under autocratic rulers ensured that the capitulation of the chief ended the insurrection of his people. But in the Protectorate of Southern Nigeria, opposition to British rule proceeded more on a village-by-village than on a state-by-state basis.

This factor also accounted considerably for the prolongation of punitive expeditions in Southern Nigeria, and to that extent, Moor and Egerton had a much more difficult task than Lugard and MacGregor, particularly between 1900 and 1906. Egerton tried to follow the precedents set by his two immediate predecessors – Moor in the Protectorate of Southern Nigeria and MacGregor in the Colony and Protectorate of Lagos. But whereas Moor frequently adopted coercive measures, MacGregor refrained as much as possible. The patient, cautious and diplomatic MacGregor suited the needs of the war-weary and discreet Yorubas. The complementary needs of the time were best illustrated by the Rev. J. H. Samuel (later A. Edun) when, as Honorary Secretary to the Lagos Institute founded in 1901 by MacGregor, he responded to the Governor's inaugural address, the same year, with these words:

> We have had our times of war . . . Now we are enjoying our season of peace. Our present requirement is not the strong Arm, our real need is the wise Head, the Heart with large sympathies – sympathy with native idiosyncracies and the racial aspirations of a primitive people.[1]

By word and deed MacGregor showed that he preferred control through diplomacy, tact and usage. He thereby set Egerton, the lawyer-administrator, a precedent to follow in Yorubaland.

[1] CO. 147/157, MacGregor to C.O., 7 November 1901, enclosure.

3 Control through Diplomacy and Usage

THE PROBLEM OF JURISDICTION IN THE LAGOS PROTECTORATE

Jurisdictional difficulties complicated by the conflicting interpretations of the nineteenth century treaties, agreements and pledges as well as the special position of Egbaland in the Lagos Protectorate raised incalculable problems for the administrations of William MacGregor and Walter Egerton. Above all, they had to contend with the stiff opposition of the chiefs and people of the Lagos Protectorate to any further loss of their control.

The chiefs and people disregarded the tactics of such secret cults as the *Ekumeku* Society and avoided mob violence which could result in military confrontation with the officers of the new régime. They preferred non-violent procedures, such as debates in the Legislative Council, mass meetings to protest against unwanted legislation, and monster petitions to the British authorities. MacGregor and Egerton found diplomacy and usage the best way to consolidate their authority. Their influence was not confined to the immediate neighbourhood of Lagos Colony. Since 1898 the European merchants in Lagos had begun actively to establish branches in Abeokuta and Ibadan[1] – centres which eventually had much importance because of their site along or being close to the Lagos Railway.

Faced with the serious threat to their economic and political institutions, the chiefs and people of the Lagos Protectorate were compelled by the colonial administration to abandon their former technique of closing trade routes to meddlesome intruders. The disastrous failure of this form of opposition was quite obvious after the triumph of British firearms during the Ijebu expedition of 1892. The British bombardment of the Alafin's palace in 1895 emphasised the inadequacy of any pro-

[1] Hopkins, A. G.: *An Economic History of Lagos* (Ph.D. Thesis) London 1964, pp. 393–8.

Control through Diplomacy and Usage

longed armed conflict between the war-exhausted Yorubas and the well-equipped British authorities eager for the expansion of their jursidiction.

With the beginning of the construction of the Lagos Railway in 1896, the question of commercial exploitation of the rich hinterland merged with the troublesome issue of jurisdiction. The extension of the railway from Lagos through the Aro section of Egbaland to Ibadan exposed these parts of Yorubaland to increasing British influence from European traders and political officers. The opening of the 125-mile long Lagos-Ibadan section to public traffic on 4 March 1901 thereby had considerable economic and political significance. MacGregor wanted this section to be extended through other Yoruba states to the Niger and Chad basin. A limited extension began from 1905. In time there emerged a close relationship between control of the railway lands and the need for wider British jurisdiction over them.

From the government viewpoint, matters affecting Abeokuta and Ibadan assumed greater importance than those which concerned such states as Oyo, Ilesha, Ondo, Ekiti and others distant from the Lagos Railway. The political and economic issues which affected the Lagos Railway, an important administrative and strategic connecting line between Lagos and the Yoruba hinterland, subsequently had a lot of bearing on the major issue of jurisdiction. Thereafter, an atmosphere of railway politics gripped the British authorities in Lagos and the Colonial Office.

More than any other single factor, the railway compelled the government to interfere from time to time in the internal affairs of such Yoruba states as Abeokuta and Ibadan. History vindicated the stand of W. H. Mercer of the Colonial Office who understood the political significance of the Lagos Railway in the relations between the British Crown and the Egba rulers. In March 1898, Mercer had prophetically observed:

> The right given to us by the treaty of 1893 . . . will require extension in course of time, especially when the railway is opened . . . and when we are prepared to establish some form of administration steps should be taken either to proclaim a protectorate formally or to secure by another treaty the further powers required.[1]

[1] CO. 147/130, McCallum to C.O., 2 February 1898, minute by W.H.M. dated 16 March 1898.

Until the Lagos Railway reached Abeokuta in 1899, however, the Colonial Office advised Governor Henry McCallum that 'forcible interference in their affairs would not be compatible with the promised recognition of their independence'.[1] About five years later, the Colonial Office modified that advice and decided to give MacGregor, McCallum's successor,

> a very serious confidential warning as to the danger of doing anything to strengthen in the Egbas and Yorubas the idea of independence, and to ask him to seize every opportunity which he can safely take of undermining that idea.[2]

That warning seemed redundant for in May 1903 an official in the Colonial Office had impressed a similar view on Mac-Gregor. At the time, R. L. Antrobus of the Colonial Office, who had always desired the annexation of the whole of the Protectorates of Lagos and Southern Nigeria but for the obstacle of the Egba treaty, had told MacGregor

> when he was in England, that he ought to be careful not to do anything to perpetuate a state of things which is very unsatisfactory. Sooner or later the Egbas and Ibadans will have to be brought under our control, and it is better that they should be brought under it peacefully than that they should be encouraged to adopt an attitude which will end in conflict.[3]

Concern for the Lagos Railway and fear that such other Yoruba states as Ibadan, whose 'independence' was not as guaranteed by treaties or agreements as Abeokuta's, would resent a different attitude towards them by another Governor partly explained the Colonial Office's intense dislike of MacGregor's well-meaning friendliness with the 'independent' Egba United Government (EUG). The other explanation lay in the Colonial Office's increasing embarrassment over the limits of its jurisdiction in the Lagos Protectorate under MacGregor and Egerton.

Similar embarrassment had preceded MacGregor's adminis-

---

[1] CO. 147/131, C.O. to McCallum, conf. 30 March 1898.
[2] CO. 147/166, MacGegor to C.O., tel. 14 June 1903 and minute by F. G. A. B(utler). The records did not reveal whether this warning was actually given.
[3] CO. 147/168, Liverpool Chamber of Commerce to C.O., 26 May 1903, minute by R.L.A.

Control through Diplomacy and Usage

tration as a result of the British annexation of Lagos in August 1861 and the extension of British influence through further acquisitions of territory and the conclusion of protectorate treaties. By 1887, the Colonial Office sought to legalise the basis of its control. By an Order in Council of 29 December 1887 the government attempted to extend its jurisdiction to the 'divers countries on the West Coast of Africa near or adjacent to Her Majesty's said Colony of Lagos'.[1] Yet the question of jurisdiction remained unsolved.

Through 'local proclamations', the government extended its authority over a non-legal 'Protectorate of Lagos'. In March 1913, Chief Justice A. W. Osborne admitted that no legal 'Protectorate' had been declared by the British Crown until the Order in Council of 24 July 1901 which came into operation on 27 August 1901. He also agreed that the earlier Order in Council of 27 December 1899, repealed by the Order in Council of July 1901, had been a nullity as it never came into operation.[2]

The territorial limits of the 'Protectorate' declared under the Order in Council of July 1901 included Egbaland and the rest of Yorubaland. The same Order in Council authorised the Legislative Council to exercise the 'powers and jurisdiction' acquired at any time by the Crown in the Lagos Protectorate. In doing so, the legislature had to respect the treaties, agreements and pledges made on behalf of the Crown with the Yoruba chiefs and people.[3]

To rectify any misunderstandings and to remove legal 'doubts', the Foreign Jurisdiction Ordinance, 1902, which repealed that of 1890, made further provisions for the application of the laws made by the Legislative Council of Lagos to the territories within the limits of the 1901 Orcer in Council. It gave the Governor in Legislative Council authority to apply to the adjacent territories any ordinances, rules and orders in force in the Colony of Lagos as well as amend, suspend or revoke these in whole or in part.[4]

[1] *African (West) No.* 1005, Enclosure 2 in No. 6 – Confidential memorandum by Chief Justice A. W. Osborne, dated 10 March 1913.   [2] *Ibid.*
[3] CO. 147/159, Council Office to C.O., 30 July 1901, enclosure According to MacGregor's 1904 estimate, the area of Abeokuta province (Egbaland) was 6,000 – 7,000 square miles and its population about 350,000–400,000. See MacGregor's memorandum of 17 March 1904 on the Alake's visit to England in May 1904, filed with C.O. 147–170, Moseley to C.I., conf. 26 April 1904.
[4] *Lagos Government Gazette*, 18 January 1902, Ordinance No. 1 of 1902. For the legalistic and technical 'doubts' see C.O. 149/6, Legislative

In the light of these provisions, MacGregor's views on jurisdiction in December 1903 had greater force than those of the Colonial Office. He then reported that 'up to the present time it has been held that Lagos Courts possess no jurisdiction in, for example, Ibadan, Oyo, Ilesha, Ekiti, Ondo, Akure and Idanre. No jurisdiction has been established there by force; none has been ceded; and no jurisdiction has grown up by use or custom'.[1] The Colonial Office disagreed but merely pointed out the differences in the legal positions of Ibadan and Abeokuta in their relations with the government.[2]

Theoretically, a wide jurisdiction had been proclaimed over the Lagos Protectorate after 1902. But in practice, the jurisdiction exercised was limited. The extent to which the government interfered with the day-to-day administration of the various Yoruba provinces differed from place to place, according to such factors as the Governor's attitude, the influence of individual British officers and the goodwill, consent, acquiescence or sufferance of the African authorities. On balance, the government exercised its jurisdiction in the Lagos Protectorate more by sufferance, tact and diplomacy than as of right. The legal uncertainties revealed during the long controversy over jurisdiction confirmed that viewpoint.

The precise limits of the jurisdiction which the Crown had acquired, in law, in the Lagos Protectorate long remained a vexed question. Attorney-General A. R. Pennington stated in August 1909 that until the 1901 Orders in Council 'Ibadan, Oyo, Ilesha, Ondo, etc.' had been merely 'spheres of influence'.[3] What they became after 1901 was disputed for the next decade. The policy which J. Anderson (later Lord Waverley) of the Colonial Office recommended in July 1911, and which also applied even before that date, was 'to leave the jurisdiction as far as possible undefined, to pass new legislation where it is thought necessary without geographical limitation, and to administer the law everywhere as if full jurisdiction had been acquired, trusting that the native authorities will not desire or feel strong enough to raise the legal objection.' He left it, however, to the men-on-the-

---

Council Debates, 7 January 1902. The nature of these 'doubts' was explained by Attorney-General E. A. Speed.

[1] CO. 147/167, MacGregor to C.O., conf. 15 December 1903.
[2] CO. 147/169, C.O. to O.A.G. (Lagos), conf. 17 March 1904.
[3] CO. 520/83, Egerton to C.O., 16 November 1909, enclosure.

spot to decide whether they could do so where 'quasi-independent native states' existed.¹

By far the greatest obstacle to the unlimited expansion of British jurisdiction in the Protectorate of Lagos arose from the conflicting interpretations of 'treaty rights'. The tendency was to assume that the nineteenth-century treaties and agreements made between the British Crown and the chiefs and people of Yorubaland followed a common pattern, or that all of them equally guaranteed 'independence' – more correctly autonomy – to the African authorities.

The Egba treaty of January 1893 was *sui generis* and only the Ibadan agreement of August 1893 came near to guaranteeing African rights in internal affairs. Even there, the Colonial Office took pains to point out 'a real difference' between the 'formal independence' which had been 'unfortunately' conceded to Abeokuta, and that claimed by Ibadan where there had been no comparable recognition.²

Ibadan, however, was not easily discouraged. Its chiefs and people knew well that the 1893 agreement by itself did not constitute a charter which guaranteed their autonomy. They therefore gave more emphasis to Acting Governor G. C. Denton's 'pledges' in his letter of 14 August 1893 in which he had informed them that their 'rights will not be infringed by the Lagos Government . . .'³

Some officials in the Colonial Office had been critical of MacGregor's attitude towards the Yoruba provinces claiming independence, without sufficient consideration of the difficulties he had experienced over treaty rights ever since he took over in Lagos in 1899. MacGregor's critics and supporters alike found his attitude confusing. During the debate on the Native Councils Ordinance in September 1901, when the question of treaty rights and the 'independence' of the Yoruba states received much emphasis from the Nigerian unofficial members of the Legislative Council, he had reaffirmed his opinion that:

> . . . the chiefs were not politically independent. They could never be politically independent. It was never his wish to make

¹ CO. 520/102, Egerton to C.O., 29 April 1911, minute by J.A.
² CO. 147/167, MacGregor to C.O., conf. 15 December 1903 minute by P.H.E.
³ Johnson S. (ed. O. Johnson): *The History of the Yorubas*, London 1921, p. 640.

them independent in that sense, as to which there should be no mistake.¹

Over the alleged infringement of treaty rights under the Native Councils Ordinance, the pro-fairplay Aborigines Protection Society (APS) obtained an interview with MacGregor during his leave of absence in England in June 1902. They asked for his interpretation of the clause in the Egba treaty of 1893 which stipulated that 'the independence of the country should be fully recognised'.²

MacGregor then informed the APS:

> They [the Egbas] are not independent as a State, although they are held responsible for the maintenance of peace and order in their provinces, for the administration of justice . . . They are responsible authorities, but certainly not an Independent State.

Pressed further by Fox-Bourne, the spokesman for the deputation, he stated that the term 'independent' used in the Egba treaty was 'a mere phrase'.³

Such statements, particularly that made during the debates of the Legislative Council on 24 September 1901, most exposed MacGregor to criticisms by friends and opponents alike.

Critics of MacGregor's policy towards such Yoruba provinces as Abeokuta and Ibadan included such senior administrators in British West Africa as Governor M. Nathan of the Gold Coast, R. Moor of the Protectorate of Southern Nigeria and F. D. Lugard of the Protectorate of Northern Nigeria. In May 1903, R. L. Antrobus of the Colonial Office noted that both Nathan and Moor had expressed to him their fear that MacGregor was 'laying up a store of trouble for his successor, if not for himself, and possibly also for the neighbouring Governments'.⁴ Lugard painted an exaggerated picture of MacGregor as a Governor keen on 'building up little independent states'.⁵ Nor was his other

---

[1] CO. 149/6, Legislative Council Debates, 24 September 1901.
[2] *West Africa*, 19 July 1902. *The Lagos Standard*, 6 August, 13 August, 3 September, 10 September, 1902.
[3] *Ibid.*
[4] CO. 147/168, T. Barker to C.O., 26 May 1903, minute by R.L.A., dated 28 May 1903.
[5] Perham, M.: *Lugard: The Years of Authority*, London 1960, 406 and 433.

allegation that 'Independent Native Rule' in the Lagos Protectorate was 'started by MacGregor and Co. . . .'[1] true.

MacGregor had other critics – the European merchants interested in trade with Lagos Colony and Protectorate. But their criticisms were based on such issues as the railway, forestry laws and unregulated tolls.

In his own defence, MacGregor as early as December 1902 had indicated that the 'network of treaties with the different chiefs of the countries' imposed a severe restriction upon the freedom of action of his administration in Lagos. MacGregor acknowledged that he had been 'in no way responsible for those contracts' but considered it his 'duty to respect them so long as they exist'.[2]

THE JUDICIAL AGREEMENTS IN YORUBALAND

The charge that MacGregor and Egerton merely propped up 'independent' Yoruba states could not be supported by the judicial agreements of the period 1904–1908 through which Abeokuta, Ibadan, Oyo, Ife and Ijebu-Ode in turn surrendered important powers and authority over certain criminal and civil matters to the British government. Through their efforts in these respects, the Governors from 1904 claimed a wider jurisdiction in the Lagos Protectorate.

The Egba Jurisdiction Ordinance, 1904, enabled the government to extend the limits of the powers and authority vested in the Lagos Supreme Court beyond the railway areas in Egbaland. By the same arrangement MacGregor improved upon the earlier agreement of 21 February 1899 under which the Egba United Government (E.U.G.) had allowed the Lagos government to arrest and try British subjects and foreigners accused of offences committed on the railway lands in Egba territory. Again, on 17 December 1900, the E.U.G. had agreed to extend the same authority to certain other lands along the Lagos Railway.[3] The

[1] *Ibid.*, p. 452.
[2] CO .147/164, MacGregor to C.O., December 1902, MP. No. 50795. M. Perham in her *Native Administration in Nigeria*, London 1937, p. 16, recognised that limitation.
[3] CO. 147/165, MacGregor to C.O., 25 April 1903, minute by H. B. C(ox).

powers thus conferred on the Lagos government were exercisable by its Supreme Court.

Beyond the railway areas, and until the 1904 judicial agreement, the Lagos Supreme Court had no jurisdiction in Egba territory. Outside those areas, only the Egba courts were competent to try cases involving British subjects, Europeans and 'native foreigners'[1] in Egbaland. In Egbaland, as in other parts of the Lagos Protectorate, MacGregor expressed dissatisfaction with the standard of justice enforced in the tribunals of the Yoruba provinces, In particular, he noticed certain cases of 'gross oppression'. In Abeokuta and Ibadan the advent of the railway brought more European traders to settle there consequently increasing the number and complexity of the commercial and other cases dealt with by the indigenous authorities.[2]

To guard against injustice to Europeans and non-Egbas, MacGregor and Chief Justice W. Nicoll privately sounded the Alake of Abeokuta on the possibility of concluding a judicial agreement, which MacGregor hoped would lead to similar ones in the rest of the protectorate.

MacGregor began with the Alake for two principal reasons. First, of all the Yoruba states only Abeokuta's 'independence' had formal recognition in a treaty. A satisfactory judicial agreement with Abeokuta would, he hoped, be followed in the other provinces with relatively little opposition. Secondly, he enjoyed the confidence of the Alake. As MacGregor explained in December 1903, he had in the past three years prepared the Egba authorities in various ways for entering into such an agreement.[3]

In the diplomatic arrangements which followed, MacGregor, Chief Justice Nicoll, Alake Gbadebo I (1898–1920) and A. Edun,[4] the Secretary to the E.U.G., played substantial rôles. Through

---

[1] 'Native foreigners', in this special case, meant natives of British West Africa resident in Egbaland. In general, the term applied to such persons resident in other parts of the whole of Southern Nigeria.

[2] CO. 147/165, MacGregor to C.O., conf. 22 March 1903; CO. 147/173, MacGregor to C.O., 19 August 1904.

[3] CO. 147/167, MacGregor to C.O., conf. 15 December 1903.

[4] He changed his name from the Rev. J. H. Samuel to Mr. A. Edun in 1904. He was formerly a Wesleyan clergyman, but resigned from evangelical work in 1902. From 1902 to 1918 he became the Secretary to the E.U.G., and thus guided substantially the administration headed by the illiterate Alake Gbadebo. See; Ajisafe, A. K.: *History of Abeokuta*, Bungay 1924, pp. 168 and 208.

their efforts the Yoruba and English texts of the draft agreement were compared and studied before the general principles of the agreement were approved. As will be shown later, certain aspects of interpretation and procedures for implementation caused considerable anxieties to the E.U.G. after the judicial agreement had been duly signed.

Earlier on, the Alake welcomed the proposals of the Lagos government. Though he had given away substantial aspects of the E.U.G.'s control over judicial matters, Gbadebo expressed optimism that MacGregor would 'consolidate' the E.U.G. and 'maintain' its 'independence . . . in its internal administration'.[1]

The judicial agreement concluded with the Egbas, whose 'independence' had been specifically guaranteed in a treaty, was unique in British imperial history. Not even Johore, which had an analogous status of 'independence' in the Straits Settlements, had a comparable judicial agreement with the British government.[2]

As soon as the Colonial Office approved the MacGregor-Gbadebo negotiations, the judicial agreement, initialled on 13 January 1904, came before the Legislative Council which put it into effect under the Egba Jurisdiction Ordinance of 16 May 1904. The legislature vested in the Supreme Court the jurisdiction acquired.[3]

Under this agreement, the Egba authorities ceded to the British Crown for twenty years power and jurisdiction over non-Egbas in the repression and punishment of such indictable offences as murder and manslaughter, in suits of £50 or more affecting non-Egbas, in the administration and control of the property and persons of all non-Egbas and in the appointment of the president of a 'Mixed Court'. The Egba authorities also undertook to establish this Mixed Court comprising a president and two members appointed by the E.U.G. The Mixed Court had jurisdiction to try summarily and punish non-Egbas who committed non-indictable offences. Its civil jurisdiction covered disputes affecting non-Egbas over sums less than £50. The penalties it could impose were those allowed for similar offences in the District Commissioner's Court. Its decisions in such matters would be

[1] CO. 147/166, MacGregor to C.O., conf. 9 June 1903, enclosure – Alake Gbadebo to MacGregor, 3 June 1903.
[2] *Ibid.*, minute by C.S.
[3] *Lagos Government Gazette*, 21 May 1904, Ordinance No. 14 of 1904.

guided, 'so far as practicable', by the laws in force in Lagos Colony. In criminal causes where one of the members of the Mixed Court dissented from its decisions, a right of appeal was allowed.¹ The Egba authorities again granted appellate jurisdiction from the decisions of the Mixed Court in criminal cases and over civil disputes involving a sum of £5 or more.

The Egba authorities, not necessarily MacGregor, expressed the strong desire to debar barristers and solicitors from 'the Courts' vested with the exercise of the 'civil jurisdictions' ceded by this agreement. The Egbas continued to exercise authority to try other causes not covered by this agreement in their native courts.²

Although the British Railway Commissioner at Aro received no specific mention in the agreement, it was intended, as P. H. Ezechiel of the Colonial Office explained in June 1904, that he should preside over the Mixed Court.³ Chief Justice Nicoll also maintained that outside the Mixed Court, the Railway Commissioner had the 'ministerial duty' of committing for trial before the Supreme Court any persons charged with indictable offences in Egba territory.⁴ In short, he assumed the rôle of a District Commissioner in all but name.

The new courts at Abeokuta – a divisional court of the Supreme Court and the Mixed Court – were ceremonially opened on 15 June 1904.⁵ The meaning given to the term 'non-Egba' in Chief Justice Nicoll's speech evoked some unsuccessful Egba attempts, between August and September 1904, to review the general interpretation of the agreement. They considered the Chief Justice's construction of the term 'non-Egba' too broad. They also maintained that they had not vested the judicial powers granted under the agreement in the Supreme Court but only in a judge of that court. In the determination of indictable offences and other causes specified in the agreement they wanted African assessors to sit as 'Judges with the Judge' and not act as the jury as explained by the Lagos government. They further objected to the Chief Justice allowing the Railway Commissioner the right 'to hold a court' through the 'ministerial duty' assigned him.

¹ *Ibid.*, The schedule.   ² *Ibid.*
³ CO. 147/173, W. Speakman to C.O., 14 June 1904, minute by P.H.E., dated 22 June 1904.
⁴ CO. 147/171, Egerton to C.O., conf. 29 October 1904, enclosure – Nicoll's memorandum of 13 August 1904.
⁵ CO. 150/11, *Lagos Government Gazette*, 18 June 1904.

They again contended that the judicial agreement conferred 'Mixed Jurisdiction' to be exercised through a 'Higher Mixed Court' and the Mixed Court. Consisting of the Chief Justice of Lagos, two Egba judges and two assessors where necessary, the former court would deal, they said, with indictable offences whereas the latter would handle 'petty offences, etc.'[1]

Such detailed criticisms made by Ghadebo and A. Edun implied that either there had been serious errors in the English and Yoruba translations of the original draft agreement or that the E.U.G. had found major differences between the letter of the agreement and its spirit.[2] The controversy closely touched upon the means of implementing the judicial agreement.

It later became clear that Gbadebo and his advisers were not sure, when they signed the agreement, that their idea of a 'Higher Mixed Court' differed from the Lagos interpretation under which the jurisdiction acquired was subsequently vested in the Supreme Court. Had the Lagos interpretation been known in advance, Gbadebo complained in September 1904:

> it would have served to render the matter plain and unfold its meaning to myself and Council and so give us the opportunity of taking into consideration the not at all light question of the introduction into the country of a wholly European Court with all its accessories of Lawyers and technicalities and complexities of English Law and its practice and which as forming part of such Court must necessarily follow the Court wherever it is introduced. The question would involve the serious consideration whether such a system of Judicial Administration would be for the good of the people living under primitive conditions, since its operation must lead to a dislocation of the customs, institutions and traditional usages obtaining and introducing a tendency to ... promote litigation as regards land tenure, the right of succession and inheritance as also the laws and customs relating to marriage; and all of which while of vital importance, would be affected and affected seriously by the introduction and exercise of jurisdiction of a European Court in the country while the advantage afforded of the help of lawyers would naturally act as an attraction and

[1] CO. 147/171, Egerton to C.O., conf. 29 October 1904, enclosures.
[2] *Ibid.*, enclosure: Gbadebo to Moseley, 13 September 1904.

so operate to the detriment of the powers and jurisdiction of the Native Court.[1]

Replying to some of these objections in October 1904, Chief Justice Nicoll explained that the Supreme Court, not a Higher Mixed Court, would exercise jurisdiction. In criminal cases before the Supreme Court, the Attorney-General would represent the Crown and lawyers would be allowed to defend accused persons. In civil cases, however, the Supreme Court would carry out 'as far as possible' the expressed desire of the E.U.G. that lawyers be discouraged from appearing in the determination of such matters.[2] Nicoll allowed the appearance of lawyers before the Railway Commissioner whenever the latter acted in his 'ministerial capacity' as the 'investigating magistrate', but left it to the Mixed Court – in his opinion, a 'native court' with an English president – to determine whether or not lawyers would be discouraged.[3]

In this controversy, the Chief Justice of the Supreme Court actively involved himself in the negotiation of a judicial agreement with serious political implications. The Egba objections had compelled him to interpret, out of court, matters over which lawyers and other litigants could appeal to the Supreme Court and expect his verdict. Fortunately for Nicoll and the Supreme Court, he retired from Lagos before the controversy was finally resolved.[4]

MacGregor, who received copies of the Egba protests, left Lagos in 1904 without making his comments known to the Colonial Office. C. Strachey of the Colonial Office, however, admitted in December 1904 that 'at present it seems . . . the Alake's case is rather a strong one'.[5]

When Egerton succeeded MacGregor in 1904, the E.U.G. sent a strong deputation to him to express their objections to the judicial agreement. Acting on the advice that it was educated Africans in Lagos, not the Alake and Council, who had been behind the Egba protests, Egerton advised the Alake 'to withdraw his protest and to accept and loyally carry out the Agreement'.[6]

[1] *Ibid.*   [2] *Ibid.*, Memorandum dated 28 October 1904.   [3] *Ibid.*
[4] Nicoll's retirement had no connection with his involvement in the negotiation of this agreement.
[5] CO. 147/171, Egerton to C.O., conf. 29 October 1904, minute by C.S. on 12 December 1904.
[6] CO. 147/171, Egerton to C.O., conf. 29 October 1904.

For a while, the Alake and Council persisted in their protest but withdrew it in January 1905 after Egerton's assurance that he would carry out the provisions of the judicial agreement 'in its spirit and intention' without any detriment to their interests.[1]

In spite of such assurances, the existence of parallel British and African law courts in Egbaland soon revealed some of the dangers feared by the Egba authorities. In his report on the Egba province for 1905, Railway Commissioner C. Punch observed that considerable friction had arisen from the institution of new courts of law following the 1904 agreement. Its provisions conflicted with the jurisdiction previously exercised by the Ogboni chiefs, war-lords, the guild of merchants, women leaders and the association of hunters.[2] To remedy this the Ogboni Court was reorganised to include such Ogboni dignitaries as the Oluwo, Apena and Ashipa as well as the representatives of the war chiefs, traders' guild, the women leaders, the hunters and the chief priest of the Ifa oracle.[3] In the same year, the new Native Court of Appeal, comprising two educated officials of the E.U.G., began to hear appeals from the reorganised native (Ogboni) court.

Meanwhile, the government in Lagos received the approval of the Colonial Office to conclude similar judicial agreements, and did so, but without any provision for Mixed Courts, with Ibadan (8 August 1904), Oyo (16 August 1904), Ife (23 September 1904) and Ijebu-Ode (11 November 1908).[4] Officially, the judicial agreements with Abeokuta and Ibadan – the major provinces along, or close to, the Lagos Railway – were far more important than those concluded with the other Yoruba provinces. Of these, the judicial agreement with Abeokuta, where there was the greatest opposition to the exercise of British jurisdiction through usage and sufferance alone, became by far the most important.

The Oyo, Ife and Ijebu-Ode judicial agreements followed Ibadan's pattern, which differed in certain respects from the Egba judicial agreement. In March 1904, the Colonial Office directed that, unlike the Egba judicial agreement, Ibadan's

[1] CO. 147/174, Egerton to C.O., conf. 21 January 1905, enclosure.
[2] CO. 591/3, *Lagos Government Gazette Supplement*, 9 May 1906.
[3] *Ibid*. The Ifa oracle was used for divination and played a decisive rôle in cases of disputed succession to the office of Oba or paramount ruler.
[4] *Lagos Government Gazette*, 21 May, 24 September, 3 December 1904. *Southern Nigeria Government Gazette*, 17 November 1909.

The Evolution of the Nigerian State

should make no reference to ceding jurisdiction.[1] Hence, the government ensured that where the E.U.G. did 'cede and grant' powers and jurisdiction to the Crown, the Ibadan, Oyo, Ife and Ijebu-Ode authorities merely did 'agree and acknowledge' that the same powers and jurisdiction were vested in the Crown.[2]

In their significance the judicial agreements with Oyo and Ife differed from those of Abeokuta and Ibadan. Oyo did not actually require one except to confirm the agreement concluded with Ibadan since, in the opinion of the government, the Alafin as head of Yorubaland had a *shadowy* influence over Ibadan. Thus in 1904 the government repeated the diplomatic niceties adopted since 1893 in Oyo-Ibadan relations.[3] In his mistaken view that the judicial agreements with Abeokuta, Ibadan and Oyo constituted symbols of diplomatic prestige, the Oni of Ife applied to have one for his territory. The Colonial Office reluctantly obliged.[4]

The government gave no special reasons for the judicial agreement with Ijebu-Ode which, despite its closeness to Lagos, did not attract as many European mercantile establishments as Abeokuta and Ibadan, which were served by the railway. Shortly after the 1908 judicial agreement with Ijebu-Ode, the government reviewed the position there. After very protracted arguments, Attorney-General Pennington and the legal experts of the Colonial Office eventually agreed that the Ijebu-Ode judicial agreement and the ordinance which put it into effect were 'superfluous' and should be treated as such.[5] However, the agreement remained in force until Lugard abrogated it on 20 November 1914.[6]

When the Colonial Office contacted MacGregor in London over the Oni of Ife's application in 1904 for a judicial agreement, he approved it for political reasons – the high prestige of Ife in

[1] CO. 147/169, C.O. to the O.A.G. (Lagos), conf. 17 March 1904.
[2] See Appendixes G and H.
[3] CO. 147–170, Moseley to C.O., conf. 11 June 1904, minute by C.S.; CO. 147/170, Moseley to C.O., conf. 17 June 1904; CO. 147–170, Moseley to C.O., conf. 27 June 1904, minute by P.H.E.; CO. 147/170, Moseley to C.O.; 29 June 1904, minute by C.S.
[4] CO. 147/171, Moseley to C.O., conf. 8 July 1904, enclosure and minute by P.H.E.; CO. 147/171, O.A.G. (Lagos) to C.O., tel. 6 July 1904, minute by P.H.E.
[5] CO. 520/78, Thorburn to C.O., 30 April 1909, enclosures. C.O. 520/78; C.O. to Egerton, 12 July 1909.
[6] Ayantuga, O. O.: *Ijebu and its Neighbours, 1851–1914* (Ph.D. Thesis), London 1965, p. 337.

early Yoruba history – without suggesting that a similar arrangement be made with Ijebu-Ode. Instead, he advised that Ilesha and Ondo be considered for such agreements but in the other cases 'by letter'.[1]

Egerton dealt informally with the issue of further judicial agreements. He continued MacGregor's policy and practice of disallowing the reorganised native courts in such areas as Ilesha, Ekiti, Illa and Meko from inflicting death sentences or handling cases involving British subjects.[2] By 1911, the Colonial Office felt dissatisfied because Egerton showed less zeal than MacGregor in concluding more judicial agreements with the Yoruba provinces, attributing this to Egerton's preoccupation with economic development to the neglect of firmly establishing British jurisdiction.[3]

Even those judicial agreements already concluded showed certain defects which in March 1913 disturbed Chief Justice A. W. Osborne. In his view, they failed to prevent certain 'anomalies' which later became obvious. Osborne noted that as the Ibadan judicial agreement did not cover such offences as 'rape and indecent assault' a case involving a soldier, Ojo Ibadan, had to be dealt with by 'the military authorities' there. Similarly, a case of larceny brought by a European firm in Abeokuta against an Egba went before the native court because of jurisdictional difficulties. Osborne believed that the native courts could not adequately cope with such tangled juridical issues as the falsification of accounts and embezzlement.[4]

These jurisdictional defects persisted until 1913 when Chief Justice Osborne brought them to the knowledge of F. D. Lugard who was interested in increasing British administrative control throughout Yorubaland. The Ijemo disturbance[5] of August 1914 over the major issues of Edun's increasing unpopular authoritarianism, forced labour and the death under mysterious circumstances of Ponlade, the Ijemo head of the guild of hunters,

[1] CO. 147/171, Moseley to C.O., conf. 8 July 1904, minute by P.H.E.
[2] *African (West) No. 1005*, Enclosure No. 6, Lugard to C.O., 30 June 1913. Lugard's report covered practice under the Native Councils Ordinance, 1901, of Lagos.
[3] CO. 520/102, Egerton to C.O., 29 April 1911, minute by J.A.
[4] *African (West) No. 1005* Osborne to Lugard, 14 March 1913.
[5] For the details see: Folarin, A.: *The Demise of the Independence of Egbaland (The Ijemo trouble)*, Parts 1 and 2, Lagos 1916 and 1919; Ajisafe: *op. cit.*, pp. 187–95.

demonstrated the inability of the E.U.G. to restore law and order without appealing for government troops. It was not surprising that Lugard took the opportunity of tightening British control over that part of Yorubaland. Thereafter, Lugard[1] terminated the 1893 Egba treaty by a further agreement in September 1914,[2] and repealed in December 1914, with the Colonial Office's approval, all the previous judicial agreements in parts of Yorubaland.[3]

MACGREGOR AND EGBA POLITICS

Despite the special attention given to the Ijemo incident because of its occurrence during the tense moment of World War I, it recalled the usual pre-1914 link between the problem of law enforcement and public safety in Egbaland and the question of British jurisdiction in that part of the protectorate declared under the Order in Council of 1901. The earlier threats to the authority of the E.U.G. and the response which these evoked under the MacGregor and Egerton administrations dramatised the long drawn-out struggle between two opposing forces – one seeking to protect its autonomy from further encroachment and the other attempting to increase its influence, if not authority, in Egbaland whenever circumstances permitted it. Despite their official positions as representatives of those conflicting forces, MacGregor and Gbadebo established and maintained a strong personal affection for each other which, at times, even embarrassed some officials in the Colonial Office. In October 1903, the exasperated P. H. Ezechiel of the Colonial Office observed:

> We have known for some time past that Sir W. MacGregor's policy has been to exalt the native rulers of Abeokuta and Ibadan, and to treat them as friends and equals. He is said to have walked arm-in-arm with the Alake of Abeokuta along the Marina at Lagos, and it is even rumoured that he once held the regal umbrella over the Alake's head! This attitude of the

[1] W. Egerton left Lagos finally on 27 February 1912 and was on leave of absence till 18 June 1912. F. D. Lugard was appointed to succeed Egerton by the Royal Commission dated 25 March 1912 but he assumed the administration in October 1912.

[2] CSO. 5/2/25, Agreement dated 16 September 1914.

[3] CO. 583/21, Lugard to C.O., tel. 30 December 1914; CO. 583/21, C.O. to Lugard, tel. 4 January 1915.

Governor is one which must tend to make the native arrogant, and may lead to trouble in the future ... but Sir W. MacGregor will not be at Lagos much longer, and I am inclined to think it will be better only to talk over the position with Mr. Moseley (who is, however, already quite alive to the error of Sir W. MacGregor's policy) and with the new Governor [Egerton] when he is appointed.[1]

While Gbadebo remained Alake of Abeokuta (1898–1920), Adeyemi, the Alafin of Oyo (1875–1905), who was also officially recognised as the 'Head of Yorubaland' made less impact on MacGregor. Since 1899, MacGregor looked upon the illiterate but progressive and intelligent Alake Gbadebo as the exemplar of Yoruba chieftaincy and hoped that under him the E.U.G. would show 'the other provinces how to govern having an eye to the past and an eye to the future'.[2] Guided by Prince Ademola who later succeeded him as Alake, and inspired by the reformist zeal and drive of A. Edun, the Secretary to the E.U.G. Gbadebo matched MacGregor's tact, patience and diplomacy. Above all, the MacGregor-Gbadebo relationship at that level seemed more impressive than the understanding which from 1906 developed between District Commissioner W. A. Ross and the Alafins of Oyo.[3]

When MacGregor found it necessary in 1904 to advertise a progressively Yoruba monarch in England, his choice understandably fell on Gbadebo, not on Adeyemi. With some exaggeration, MacGregor stated:

> The Alafin of Oyo is traditionally and theoretically the greatest chief of the Yorubas; but in actual practice the present Alake of Abeokuta is by far the most powerful and influential, and at the same time, the most enlightened chief and ruler in Yorubaland. This is well known and recognised all over the country that whatever is done at Abeokuta is quoted elsewhere, and is held up as something to be imitated.[4]

[1] C.O. 147/166, MacGregor to C.O., 14 August 1903, minute by P.H.E., dated 8 October 1903. It is not certain whether the Colonial Office actually held such a discussion with Egerton.
[2] CO. 147/166, MacGregor to C.O., 29 August 1903, enclosure.
[3] Atanda, J. A.: *The New Oyo Empire* (Ph.D. thesis) Ibadan 1967, pp. 131–50. Ross was the District Commissioner who later became the Resident in charge of Oyo and Ibadan.
[4] MacGregor's memorandum of 17 March 1904 which the C.O. filed with CO. 147/170, Moseley to C.O., conf. 26 April 1904.

For the June 1904 visit, MacGregor desired that Gbadebo, Prince Ademola and A. Edun be granted an audience with the British Crown. Its diplomatic significance, would, he felt sure, 'be productive of much good to the Yoruba people and be of decidedly political advantage to the King's government of Lagos'.[1] MacGregor had his wish, but outside Egbaland he exaggerated the significance of the Alake's United Kingdom tour which perhaps merely represented a celebration of the Abeokuta Judicial Agreement signed in January 1904.

Despite the good relations between the E.U.G. and the Lagos government, MacGregor at times sought to correct injustice even in matters which directly or indirectly affected the prestige of the Alake. When the Oluwo of Ilawo, a member of the Egba State Council, and the Ogbonis put to death for theft one Akiode in 1901, the Lagos government immediately investigated the matter with the co-operation of the E.U.G. Following these inquiries, the Oluwo suffered a term of ten years' imprisonment as well as eviction from the Egba Council while the Ogboni chiefs concerned collectively paid a £100 fine.[2] In spite of MacGregor's good intentions, in the Oluwo case he exceeded the terms of the jurisdiction allowed the British government under the 1893 treaty.

Generally, the Egba claim to 'independence' gave MacGregor other problems. Could he decline to interfere in the internal affairs of Egbaland and allow disturbances there to cause unrest elsewhere? Would disturbances among the Egbas not endanger the section of the Lagos Railway passing through their territory? Moreover, would the threat to law and order there not affect the interests of the European traders living in Abeokuta? The need to solve these problems as well as the desire to help his friend Gbadebo whenever his authority was challenged by dissident groups provoked MacGregor's intervention in the internal affairs of the Egbas despite the 1893 treaty.

Whenever possible, MacGregor sought to allay the suspicions of Gbadebo who feared that the British government would use any pretext to annex his territory. MacGregor, however, assured Gbadebo in June 1900 that if he ruled 'justly and fairly' his administration would always support the authority of the E.U.G.[3]

[1] *Ibid.*
[2] CO. 147/156, MacGregor to C.O., 19 July 1902, enclosures.
[3] CO. 147/149, MacGregor to C.O., conf. 22 June 1900.

Disturbances in Abeokuta in 1901 and 1903 demonstrated the powerlessness of the E.U.G. to restore law and order and embarrassed the Alake by circumscribing the 'independence' which he and his people claimed. They further illustrated the mutual understanding between MacGregor and Gbadebo. The otherwise peace-loving MacGregor intervened with Lagos government troops on both occasions to support the authority of the Alake and Council.

In these attempts to strengthen the authority of the Alake, MacGregor indirectly disturbed the long-standing strong 'township' strand[1] in Egba politics. The Itori and Kemta disturbances of 1901 and 1903 showed similar elements just as the Ijemo incident did in 1914. It was significant, however, that MacGregor refused to capitalise on the internal dissensions of Egbaland to abrogate the 1893 treaty much earlier.

During the Itori 'township' crisis of May 1901, it became clear that the loyalties of the people there lay with their own chief, the Onitori, not with the Alake. The Itori explosion arose from two major factors. One was the determination of responsibility for the execution of capital sentences. Traditionally, the Alake avoided the odium associated with this and allowed the Onitori and his people to pass and carry out death sentences. The people of Itori therefore claimed that as a 'final Court of Appeal', theirs was superior to the Ake's, the Alake's quarter of Abeokuta. Again, as evidence of their political autonomy, the Onitori and his people claimed Isheri, the Abeokuta custom-house along the Ogun river, and tried to stop the collection there of tolls (*octroi*) by the E.U.G. Thus threatened, Gbadebo, with the approval of the E.U.G., appealed to MacGregor to help restore law and order in Abeokuta.[2]

MacGregor responded immediately with troops, who, however, were not used in combat. After a prompt inquiry into the trouble, MacGregor publicly declared his support for the Alake in Council as the only government which he recognised.[3] The Colonial Office congratulated him on 'the effective manner in which peace was restored on this occasion'.[4]

---

[1] Biobaku, S. O.: *The Egba and their Neighbours, 1842–72*, Oxford 1957, p. 99.
[2] CO. 147/155, MacGregor to C.O., conf. 26 May 1901, enclosure.
[3] *Ibid.*
[4] CO. 147/155, C.O. to MacGregor, conf. 8 July 1901.

The E.U.G. hardly realised how far this appeal to MacGregor had encouraged further intervention in its internal affairs. To justify his action, MacGregor informed the Colonial Office in May 1901:

> The mere fact that Abeokuta had to ask for, and obtained, assistance from this Government when that place was in difficulty and its chiefs in danger settles the fact in the native mind that Abeokuta is subject to Lagos. But I see no reason for taking any advantage from that beyond the added moral power it gives this Government in advising the Abeokuta authorities in whatever is seen to be necessary from time to time.[1]

Since the E.U.G. itself had set the precedent for inviting Lagos troops to put down an Egba disturbance, Railway Commissioner Punch at Aro took the hint and appealed over the heads of the Egba authorities to MacGregor in November 1903 when trouble began in Kemta 'township', another quarter of Abeokuta. This concerned the relations between the *Apena* of Kemta, an *Ogboni* dignitary, and the Alake and Council.[2] A woman and her daughter maltreated by the Apena's messengers sought refuge in the Alake's quarter where both women immediately had Gbadebo's protection. A scuffle arose when the Alake's orders for the aged and feeble Apena to appear before him were disobeyed and the Alake's messengers were assaulted by those of the Apena. Alarmed, the British Railway Commissioner at Aro telegraphed the Lagos government for troops. MacGregor at once set out for Abeokuta with some 230 soldiers.

During the public meeting at Abeokuta in the presence of MacGregor, the Egba chiefs settled the misunderstanding between the Alake and the Apena of Kemta. Gbadebo further authorised MacGregor to impose and announce a fine of £250 on the Kemta quarter 'to cover the expense of transporting the military to Abeokuta'. That fine, however, excluded punishment for 'sedition, etc.' which the Alake and Council reserved for their own decision. Thus ended what MacGregor later called his 'bloodless expedition'.[3]

Officials in the Colonial Office received MacGregor's initial announcement of the Kemta affair with mixed feelings. To R. L.

[1] CO. 147/155, MacGregor to C.O., conf. 26 May 1901.
[2] CO. 147/167, MacGregor to C.O., 23 November 1903, and enclosures.
[3] CO. 147/167, MacGregor to C.O., 23 November 1903, and enclosure.

Antrobus it was a 'misfortune' that the 'rising should have occurred before MacGregor's departure' from Lagos as the opportunity would have been taken 'to get rid of the "independence" which is only good for the chiefs and the educated Egbas ... while it is bad for the people generally and for the development of the country'.¹ Before MacGregor's final report on the Kemta situation reached the Colonial Office, C. Strachey commented:

> 'It will be interesting to hear some details about this little rebellion. Sir William MacGregor has always held strongly to the recognition of the independence of Abeokuta, and we are not bound to assist the Alake in any troubles with his subjects. It may not be a bad thing if he comes to look to us for support...'²

The feeling of regret and disappointment expressed by some officials in the Colonial Office continued when they obtained more detailed information on the Kemta episode. From P. H. Ezechiel's viewpoint,³ 'The rising is evidently of no importance, except that the protection afforded by the British Government on this occasion makes it a little easier to get rid of the Alake's independence when an opportunity occurs.' M. F. Ommanney, then the permanent Under-Secretary of State at the Colonial Office, added: 'The independence of the Alake, who could not quell a small local riot without our assistance, seems to be somewhat of a farce'.⁴

Neither the Colonial Office nor MacGregor's critics in general fully appreciated the significance of his friendly attitude towards the outwardly 'independent' E.U.G. By his support of the African authorities in Abeokuta, and others elsewhere, MacGregor patiently endeavoured to build for the British government a reservoir of good will. In time, MacGregor's principal instrument for effecting the changes he desired in Yorubaland was the personal influence drawn from that treasury of goodwill. It represented a diplomatic investment of great value and significance. A major result of MacGregor's personal influence with the

---

¹ CO. 147/167, MacGregor to C.O., tel. 21 November 1903, minute by R.L.A.
² *Ibid.*, minute by C.S.
³ CO. 147/167, MacGregor to C.O., 23 November 1903, minute by P.H.E.
⁴ *Ibid.*, minute by M.F.O.

Alake in Council lay in his successful negotiation of the Abeokuta Judicial Agreement which, though a revolutionary reform, evoked no critical comment from the Nigerian unofficial members of the Legislative Council.[1] His actions dovetailed into one another. Together they yielded satisfactory results. With justification MacGregor reported in December 1903[2] that he had in the past three years prepared the Egba authorities for entering into the 1904 judicial agreement. His support of them during the Itori and Kemta conflicts was one of the ways in which MacGregor won and retained the goodwill of the E.U.G.

GOVERNMENT ATTITUDE TOWARDS THE E.U.G. SINCE 1907

Egerton followed MacGregor's lead by intervening in the internal affairs of Egbaland whenever he thought it desirable. Like his predecessor's, Egerton's concern was for the E.U.G. He therefore advised the Egba authorities to grant more powers and jurisdiction to the British government.

It will be recalled that some officials in the Colonial Office had criticised MacGregor's attitude towards Gbadebo and the other Egba authorities. Though in October 1903, P. H. Ezechiel of the Colonial Office had promised to discuss this matter with Egerton, when appointed Governor, there is no record that he did so. In their relations with the E.U.G., both MacGregor and Egerton tried to promote the best interests of Britain without provoking violent opposition by the Egbas. This trend in fairly harmonious relations between Lagos and the E.U.G. had a rude shock in the stiff opposition of the Egbas to the radical reforms proposed by the British government in 1907.

Acting on the recommendation by P. V. Young, the British Commissioner at Aro, Egerton on 17 December 1907 sanctioned the following proposals for the consideration of the E.U.G. His administration offered the Alake a yearly stipend of £300; promised to spend not less than £2,000 annually on roads, drainages and sanitation in Egbaland; asked the Egba authorities to allow the British Commissioner to sit in their Council; wanted the Commissioner or other officer appointed by the Governor to preside over the Native Court in Abeokuta to try all cases

[1] CO. 149/6, Legislative Council Debates, 9 May 1904.
[2] CO. 147/167, MacGregor to C.O., conf. 15 December 1903.

brought before it and proposed that the EUG accounts should be audited by the Colonial Audit Department.[1]

Aware of the far-reaching constitutional implications of Egerton's proposals, Gbadebo invited a public meeting to discuss them in the *Ogboni* house at Itoku on 3 January 1908. Over 40 *Apenas* and *Olowus* (*Ogboni* dignitaries), war chiefs, representatives of the merchant guilds and about 300 chiefs of other ranks attended. The British Commissioner at Aro was also present. The *Apena* of Iporo, the senior *Ogboni* chief present, presided.[2]

Commissioner Young sought to impress the assembly with parallels from British practice in auditing accounts. He explained how in the United Kingdom Somerset House had exercised the responsibility for auditing the accounts of the Colonial Office, the War Office and other government departments. Reluctantly, the Egba chiefs and people agreed that their accounts be checked by the Colonial Audit Department at Lagos.

Young further assured the Egbas that the other proposals were dictated by the need to correct 'miscarriages of justice'. He denied that the government sought to 'bribe' the Alake except to show 'a small appreciation of the loyal co-operation he has always extended to the British Government'.

The Egbas, however, vehemently rejected the other proposals which reminded them of the grounds already lost since the judicial agreement of 1904. That point received special emphasis from the Molasin of Owu who observed:

> We have our Judicial Agreement with the British Government. Have we broken it? When a white man sits in the Native Court, is it any longer a Native Court?

Bolade, the Balogun of Iddo, had no doubts that the proposals meant a surrender of 'the independent internal management of the country'. Aselegbe of Oko disliked the financial inducements in the proposals which reminded him of the rôle of the paymaster as the piper calling the tune. Aselegbe asserted that when British authorities sought to 'improve and pay money, they must command'. The Jaguna of Itoko stressed:

> If the Europeans are allowed to sit in the Native Courts, it is finished. We have a Judicial Agreement for 20 years for the other Court, and now after only 4 years we are asked to accept

[1] CO. 520/61, Egerton to C.O., conf. 4 June 1908.
[2] *Ibid.*, enclosures.

a European Judge to the only remaining court left to us . . .
We want to advance in enlightenment but do not let the light
be too bright or else we shall be blinded, do not drive us too
fast or else we shall not know where we are.

The Ashipa of Erunwon summarised for the chiefs and people
assembled and recalled:

In the olden days once a case is settled at Ake, it was final. We
have entered into Judicial Agreement with the British Government. That Agreement recognises our Native Court . . . It is
the one great thing left us. We know that Court has not given
satisfaction at all times and hence the men appointed Judges
have retired and others put in their place. If these again fail to
do their duty let us do away with them and get others . . . Let
the British Government allow us to advance not too fast lest
we fall. We want progress but not such progress as shall be
fatal to us in the long run. These things in the proposals of the
Governor are distasteful to the Egbas.

The major exception came from a small group of Egbas led
by Fadayiro, the Base of Iporo. In a petition addressed to Commissioner Young, on 8 January 1908, this group accepted the
proposals with the puzzling qualification: 'We shall, however,
not be in favour of anything that will hinder the progress of the
Egba Government or its people.'

Egerton admitted that Commissioner Young had done 'excellent work' in Abeokuta but regretted that he had negotiated the
controversial proposals 'rather injudiciously'. During a subsequent visit to Abeokuta, Egerton assured Gbadebo that he had
'no intention of insisting on the acceptance of the proposals and
that they were merely put forward to facilitate the better Government of his Province and its quicker development'. To Egerton's
mind, administration and development were inseparable. He
showed less tact, however, in handling administrative matters;
his zeal for development sometimes leading to excesses and indiscretion over matters of administrative detail. Egerton's performance in Egbaland over the 1908 proposals emphasised this
basic problem of his entire administration.

C. Strachey of the Colonial Office agreed that the whole effort
made by Egerton and Young at Abeokuta seemed 'rather injudicious'. To Strachey, the offer of the £300 stipend for the

Alake and the £2,000 promised for roads constituted 'nothing more or less than a bribe, no matter what Mr. Young called it'. Strachey also considered the 'spirited attitude' of the Egbas in defending their autonomy against British attempts to encroach on their rights 'perfectly justified'.[1]

The failure of the 1908 attempt did not, however, discourage Egerton from making further proposals for the reform of the E.U.G. He very much favoured the idea of seconding British officers to that government (and occasionally to Ibadan) to undertake specialist works of a technical kind.[2] A measure of his success was evident in 1910 when Gbadebo accepted Egerton's advice to appoint a British officer, seconded from the government, to supervise police and prison matters in Abeokuta.[3] The number of British technical officers seconded to the E.U.G. later increased.

The policy and practice of seconding British officers to the E.U.G. brought its own problems. Such officers hoped to return to the Colonial Service even when they served the E.U.G. Consequently, they had 'a divided allegiance' which annoyed the E.U.G. But the British Government regarded it as much safer to supply the E.U.G. with such specialist officers than to allow the latter to employ 'Germans or others'. In 1913, the government expressed its awareness of 'a serious danger' from 'an independent Government run by foreign Europeans, situated astride of the railway'.[4] The government, however, felt satisfied so long as such British officers came under the control of the president of the Egba Financial Advisory Board. Until 1913, the British Commissioner at Aro served as president of the Egba Financial Advisory Board, but not because of his commissionership. The British government later feared that the advantages of such an arrangement would be lost if the E.U.G. eventually chose an Egba as the president.[5]

Meanwhile, the British government increased its influence in Egbaland by other means. On 31 December 1910, Gbadebo entered into another agreement with Egerton. By this agreement, the government consented to lend the E.U.G. £30,000 at the

[1] *Ibid.*, minute by C.S.
[2] CO. 520/61, Egerton to C.O., conf. 4 June 1908.
[3] CO. 520/91, Egerton to C.O., conf. 28 February 1910.
[4] *African (West) No. 1005*, Enclosure 6 in No. 6, Minute by F. D. Lugard, 23 February 1913.
[5] *Ibid.*

nominal interest of 1 per cent annually for expenditure on such public works as roads and water supply. As a *quid pro quo*, the E.U.G. allowed the British Commissioner to sit permanently on its Financial Committee or Advisory Board which would submit expenditures on public works for the Governor's approval.[1]

These arrangements seriously compromised Egba 'independence'. But according to Egerton, 'the independence of Egbaland is recognised by treaty and . . . that government is a protected independent state'. He also claimed that Gbadebo had 'generally been quite willing to accept the advice tendered to him through the government Commissioner at Abeokuta'.[2]

In securing the approval of the Legislative Council for the £30,000 loan to the E.U.G. Egerton tried to dispel the 'very great suspicion' that his administration had sought 'to grab the Abeokuta territory'. He affirmed that the British government would not take such a step so long as the E.U.G. had such 'an enlightened chief and a good administrator as the Alake'. He considered it much better 'that the Egba government should be carried on by the native administration than that the Imperial Government should be burdened with the conduct of its affairs . . .'.[3] The two Nigerian unofficial members then present, Kitoyi Ajasa and C. Sapara Williams, raised no objections.[4]

In assessing Egerton's policy towards Egba affairs, a distinction must be made between the goals and the means of attaining them. During an interview between Commissioner Young, other officials and F. D. Lugard on 23 February 1913,[5] Young disclosed that Egerton had sought to 'build up a strong independent state, financially independent and to relieve the Colonial Government of the cost of administering a large territory'.

There were, however, differences of opinion concerning his methods. Commissioner Young indicated that Egerton relied on two: the employment of British personnel in the pay and service of the E.U.G. as engineers, mechanics and the like for develop-

[1] CO. 520/101, Egerton to C.O., 10 January 1911, and enclosure. The agreement was dated 31 December 1910. The revenues of the E.U.G. between 1908 and 1910 amounted to £18,450; £16,835; and £29,377 respectively. See the dispatch cited *supra*.
[2] *Ibid.*
[3] CO. 592/11, Legislative Council Debates, 31 January 1911.
[4] *Ibid.*
[5] *African (West) No. 1005*, Enclosure 6 in No. 6, Minute by F. D. Lugard, 23 February 1913.

ment; and the offering of loans at nominal interest. A. G. Boyle, the Colonial Secretary, who also acted as Governor on several occasions during the temporary absence of Egerton and who was present during the same interview, indicated that Egerton had encouraged the employment of British technical officers in Abeokuta to convince the E.U.G. of its inability to manage its own affairs. He regarded Egerton's offer of loans to the E.U.G. as a means of involving the latter in heavy debts in order to facilitate greater control. Seen in that light, Boyle contended, Egerton's goal was 'to obtain control of rather than to render the Egba Government independent of control by these means'.

Lugard preferred a policy of vesting 'ultimate control' in the Governor who would exercise it through British officers to ensure a 'cleaner' administration of justice and promote 'a larger experience of civilisation and knowledge of administration' in Egbaland. Lugard then had no worries about the additional cost to the government in bringing Egbaland under direct control as the territory promised 'great potential wealth' which would be 'more rapidly and advantageously developed as part of the Colony ... than as a small independent State'.[1]

Clearly Lugard had notions of ending the special status of the E.U.G. from early 1913 onwards. The Ijemo incident of 1914 and the abrogation in the same year of the 1893 Egba treaty did not simply represent cause and effect. The Ijemo episode became a convenient pretext, so far as Lugard was concerned, for ending the Egba claim to independence. For over a decade MacGregor and Egerton had declined to utilise other pretexts to achieve the same result.

Egerton had a particularly favourable pretext for assuming direct control over Egbaland in August 1908 when the E.U.G. faced a serious threat of sedition,[2] far surpassing those of the earlier Itori and Kemta incidents. In August 1908 the growing resentment against the increasing influence of A. Edun, the E.U.G. Secretary, considered by several Egbas as Gbadebo's 'evil genius',[3] came to a head. Edun epitomised the growing centralisation of authority around the Alake against the strong currents of 'township' sentiments. In restoring law and order

[1] *Ibid.* In 1913 Lugard reckoned that Egbaland comprised 1,869 square miles and had a population of 265,000. See CSO. 1/19/55, Lugard to C.O., 17 January 1913.
[2] Blair, J.; *Intelligence report on Abeokuta*, 1937, p. 11.   [3] *Ibid.*

during the 1908 crisis, the Egba Police Force, inaugurated in 1904, killed the *Ifa* priest of Ikija. The E.U.G. subsequently paid the priest's bereaved family a compensation of £50, but followed that measure with a severe law to deal with sedition in Egbaland.¹

Like MacGregor, Egerton upheld the authority of the E.U.G. without sacrificing the interests of the people. He found the E.U.G.'s law of 13 August 1908 to suppress and punish 'seditious meetings' too severe. The E.U.G. law sought to impose upon persons convicted of sedition a term of seven years' imprisonment with or without a fine of £25–£100.² In objecting to its 'drastic provision', Egerton feared that it would be used as an instrument of oppression. He therefore promptly sent Acting Chief Justice E. A. Speed to Abeokuta to modify the E.U.G. law.³

After consultations with the E.U.G. and the Colonial Office, Egerton concluded a new agreement with the Egba authorities in November 1909. This extended until 4 January 1924, the Supreme Court's jurisdiction in Egbaland to the repression and punishment of sedition against the Alake in Council.⁴ By this agreement, the relations between the British Crown and the 'independent' Egba state took another step unprecedented in British imperial history. Attorney-General Pennington observed in April 1909 that under English law the offence of 'treason' could only be committed against the British Crown.⁵ Much earlier, in December 1908, Pennington had also maintained that 'the offences against the Alake and his government' were 'unknown to English law'.⁶ These legal difficulties were, however, resolved when the Legislative Council approved the 1909 agreement with the E.U.G.

Once more, the government involved a high-ranking member of the Judiciary in the negotiation of an agreement with the E.U.G. Acting Chief Justice Speed exceeded the terms of the legal assignment by involving himself and Gbadebo in matters of grave political significance. At the end of his mission in Sep-

¹ *Ibid.*
² CO.520/68, Thorburn to C.O., 18 December 1908, enclosure.
³ *Ibid.*
⁴ *Southern Nigeria Government Gazette*, 16 February 1910. Agreement dated 18 November 1909.
⁵ CO. 520/79, Thorburn to C.O., 5 May 1909, enclosure: memo. dated 21 April 1909.
⁶ CO. 520/68, Thorburn to C.O., 18 December 1908, enclosure: minute dated 9 December 1908.

tember 1908 Speed reported to Egerton the substance of what he had 'privately and informally' told Gbadebo. He had urged upon Gbadebo: 'the advisability of admitting a much larger measure of Government control over the local administration as at Ibadan and elsewhere . . . ' Speed further assured Egerton of his confidence that Gbadebo would not be 'adverse to adopting any well considered proposal in that direction when it is deemed advisable to urge it'.[1] The records did not reveal whether Egerton regretted Speed's political activities.

Although its stature, power and authority were considerably weakened by these series of negotiations and concessions, the E.U.G. tried to stress its 'independence' in other respects. During this period, the E.U.G. maintained its own 'agent' in Lagos,[2] and in 1912 succeeded in its claim to have an 'agent' in London to handle its own affairs. At the latter stage, Secretary of State L. Harcourt intervened and advised that the E.U.G. obtain its stores through the government of Southern Nigeria and the Crown Agents for the Colonies.[3]

The E.U.G. however, ably defended its conduct in appointing the small British firm of A. M. Buchanan, and not the Crown Agents, to transact its own business. The Crown Agents, the E.U.G. argued, catered for the wider interests of the British Empire but would have had no time for the orders of 'such a small Government as ours'. Fear of maladministration of its overseas transactions could not arise since its accounts were audited by the Colonial Audit Department in Lagos. The E.U.G. further pointed out that an extra check lay in the British Commissioner's membership in its Financial Advisory Board. Saddled with slender financial resources, it wanted the 'cheapest market to get the best wares'. Approaching the Crown Agents for such stores, it observed, seemed like 'having one's masters as one's servants'. The E.U.G. also drew attention to its rights under the 1893 treaty and affirmed that its commercial transactions came within the scope of its internal affairs.[4] Acting Governor F. S. James accepted the E.U.G.'s arguments and recommended the approval

[1] CO. 520/68, Thorburn to C.O., 18 December 1908, enclosure: Speed's minute dated 29 September 1908.
[2] CO. 147/170, Moseley to C.O., conf. 26 April 1904, enclosure: Gbadebo to Moseley, 22 April 1904.
[3] CSO. 1/20/47, C.O. to Egerton, 16 January 1912.
[4] CSO. 1/19/47, James to C.O., 27 March 1912, enclosures.

of its action in appointing and using its own agent in London.[1] The Colonial Office gave its consent in May 1912.[2]

In retrospect, the façade of Egba 'independence' continued until the Ijemo incident removed it in 1914. Neither diplomacy nor tact could save an 'independent' E.U.G. under Lugard who had earlier decided to end that status. The usage allowed by MacGregor and Egerton had gone too far to save the E.U.G. from complete absorption into the general administration of the rest of the protectorate. In trying to protect the E.U.G. from that fate, MacGregor and Egerton had, through the policy and practice of intervention in instalments, prepared the Egbas to accept the worst. Consequently, when the Egba shock came under Lugard's administration, it did not appear catastrophic. For the Egbas, 1914 marked the end of an era – that of claiming unrestricted control over their own internal affairs. For the rest of the people of Southern Nigeria that era had ended much earlier, bringing with it several problems of a different kind. Above all, the people there had to contend with the various issues which developed under the new, mildly autocratic régime.

[1] *Ibid.*
[2] CSO. 1/20/49, C.O. to O.A.G. (Southern Nigeria), 3 May 1912.

4 The Mild Autocracy

THE NEW RULERS

Through coercion, diplomacy and usage the British authorities established, expanded and consolidated their control over Southern Nigeria. Consequently, the people in the colony and protectorate steadily lost control over their external and internal affairs.

From 1900 to 1914, the differences between a British Crown colony and a protectorate became more and more academic. Correspondingly, the British exercise of power and authority hardly distinguished between the external and internal affairs of the people of Southern Nigeria. It soon became clear that the policy-making power in the major issues which affected the lives and property of the people of Southern Nigeria lay almost entirely in foreign hands. Under the prevailing Crown Colony system of government, there was hardly room for African 'indirect rulers' but a lot of scope for African 'indirect administrators'.

The new ruling class of major policy-makers comprised the British Governors, their deputies and permanent and parliamentary members of the Colonial Office. Some of the administrators were also British; but the Africans, particularly the chiefs, associated with the administration at a lower level were no more than executives. Only the few educated Nigerian unofficial members of the Legislative Council came close to the category of policy-makers. Even within the Legislative Council, as will be seen later, these Nigerian and other unofficial members played a limited rôle. Such developments revealed the nature of the mild autocracy which developed under the Crown colony system of government in Southern Nigeria.

At the local level, Moor and Lugard, rather than MacGregor and Egerton, were the more honest exponents of the constitutional transformation which had occurred under British rule. Both

Moor, during his Benin City speech of 1897, and Lugard at Sokoto in 1903[1] showed clearly that the major policy-making rôle lay with the British Crown, not with the African chiefs. Both emphasised who were the new *rulers* and executives and whose *orders* the chiefs should carry out even if by so doing their otherwise *African institutions* were radically transformed.

Neither Moor nor Lugard disguised the autocratic nature of British rule. At the higher level, there was considerable force in the statement made by Secretary of State L. Harcourt in June 1912 concerning the major features of the Crown Colony form of government. According to him:

> The position of the Colonial Secretary on the Crown Colony side of his Department carries with it the powers, duties, responsibilities, and anxieties of a practical and laborious despot, controlled only by the forces of nature, by his own discretion, and by the sporadic curiosity at Question Time of friends or opponents – inspired either by imagination or information – and often with the best intentions creating difficulties they wot not of, and not seldom innocently damaging the causes to which they are devoted. But even a despot under democracy is glad to have an opportunity of justification and of

[1] In part of his speech at Sokoto in 1903, Lugard stressed: '... The old treaties are dead, you have killed them. Now these are the words which I, the High Commissioner, have to say for the future. The Fulani in old times under Dan Fodio conquered this country. They took the right to rule over it, to levy taxes, to depose kings and to create kings. They in turn have by defeat lost their rule which has come into the hands of the British. All these things which I have said the Fulani by conquest took the right to do now pass to the British. Every Sultan and Emir and the principal officers of state will be appointed by the High Commissioner throughout all this country ... The Emirs and Chiefs who are appointed will rule over the people as of old time and take such taxes as are approved by the High Commissioner, but they will obey the laws of the Governor and will act in accordance with the advice of the Resident... In conclusion, I hope that you will find our rule sympathetic and that the country will prosper and be contented. You need have no fear regarding British rule ...'.
In the same speech, Lugard forbade such other African practices as slavery, mutilation and confinement as punishment and other practices. He reserved to the British Crown land ownership, mineral rights, certain categories of taxes, currency, freedom of worship, judicial appeals, the power to make war and peace, and so on. What sphere of policy-making was then left to the Emirs? For the full speech see, Kirk-Green A. H. M. (ed.): *The Principles of Native Administration in Nigeria: Selected Documents, 1900–1947*, London 1965, pp. 43–44.

The Mild Autocracy

proof that his mild autocracy is not inconsistent with benevolence, or that the machinery of legislation by ordinance or letters patent may in the circumstances of undevelopment be a not unsuitable, though temporary, substitute for more representative methods.[1]

In the exercise of his 'mild autocracy', the Secretary of State generally exposed himself to at least four related forms of checks: British public opinion outside Parliament; Parliament; the permanent staff of the Colonial Office and the man-on-the-spot. The effectiveness of each of these four broad categories of checks will now be explored.

CHECKS BY BRITISH PUBLIC OPINION

The task of critically examining British colonial policies and measures in Southern Nigeria had sporadic attention in the United Kingdom. It interested only the individuals and groups who felt concerned enough to criticise their government's policy towards Africans in general and the people of Southern Nigeria in particular. These included such humanitarian organisations as the members of the 'Third Party' led by Mary Kingsley, John Holt and E. D. Morel,[2] the Anti-Slavery Society, the Aborigines' Protection Society (A.P.S.), and from 1909 the Anti-Slavery and Aborigines Protection Society (A.S.-A.P.S.).[3] Since its foundation in March 1887 the Native Races and Liquor Traffic United Committee (N.R.-L.T.U.C.) interested itself not only in the temperance movement in the United Kingdom but also in the liquor traffic in West Africa.[4] Of these bodies only the 'Third Party' consistently tried between 1895 and 1915 to uphold the otherwise declining humanitarian zeal in the United Kingdom.[5] After Mary Kingsley's death in June 1900,[6] John Holt and E. D. Morel became its leaders. E. D. Morel, the influential journalist, seemed more tolerant of the British government's policies towards Southern Nigeria than John Holt, the business tycoon,

[1] H.C. Deb. 5s. 40, 27 June 1912, 505–6.
[2] Nworah, K. K. D.: *Humanitarian pressure groups and British attitudes to West Africa, 1895–1915*. (Ph.D. thesis) London 1966, pp. 20–32.
[3] *Ibid.*, pp. 112–21.
[4] *Ibid.*, pp. 151–2.
[5] *Ibid.*, p. 654.
[6] *E.D.M.P.*, F/8, Holt to Morel, 6 June 1900

humanist, social reformer and big Englander. As will be shown later, the nature of John Holt's business interests in Southern Nigeria coloured his brand of humanitarianism. In particular, Holt's views on the tolls controversy and the forestry laws revealed the clash of interests with the people's aspirations.

However, John Holt was intolerant of colonial despotism and the authoritarianism of the men-on-the-spot. His tirades against the Crown Colony system of government, as it operated in British West Africa, received much prominence in his frequent correspondence with E. D. Morel. For example, MacGregor's rôle during the tolls controversy in 1903, as the supporter of the claims of the Abeokuta and Ibadan provinces against those of the European mercantile interests, reminded Holt of 'the arbitrary system which we have established in our Crown Colonies'.[1] He hated the Colonial Office's attempts to 'protect their Governors at any cost';[2] condemned the 'despotic one-man power given to these Governors';[3] detested the combination of 'militarism and despotic government' as a source of 'wrong and robbery';[4] and advocated the checking of the 'arrogance and intemperate use of power' by the British authorities in Southern Nigeria.[5]

In September 1910 Holt wanted the British government 'to get rid of the fetish of trusting the man on the spot without question . . .'.[6] Much earlier, he had vehemently disapproved of the system of government which, in his view, adopted excessive legislation through proclamations and ordinances. In October 1901 Holt had informed Morel:

> I hate these eternal ordinances every one of which centres all power increasingly in the hands of a created despot. Everything omnipotent is in the hands of the Governor 'in Council'. Such a Council!![7]

The alternatives to colonial autocracy Holt indicated, but did not elaborate, in December 1908. In his view:

> They [West Africans] are not by any means ready for a representative form of government but I think it is high time a step

---

[1] E.D.M.P., F/8, Holt to Morel, 5 August 1903.
[2] E.D.M.P. F/8, Holt to Morel, 22 November 1901.
[3] E.D.M.P. F/8, Holt to Morel, 29 October 1901.
[4] E.D.M.P. F/8, Holt to Morel, 8 November 1901.
[5] E.D.M.P. F/8, Holt to Morel, 13 July 1906.
[6] E.D.M.P. F/8, Holt to Morel, 14 September 1910.
[7] E.D.M.P. F/8, Holt to Morel, 14 October 1901.

forward was taken in doing away with official majorities on every subject coming before the legislative councils and that the best of the natives should be made use of in sharing with us the responsibility of government, not as tools of our Governors or as dummies but as representatives of the ideas of the natives and in some way nominated and freely appointed by them.[1]

Such legislation as the forestry laws annoyed Holt since the Governors and High Commissioners in Southern Nigeria hardly consulted the interests of the commercial organisations – the Chambers of Commerce – in Britain with interests in that part of West Africa.[2] He admitted, however, that at other times the Colonial Office consulted the views of the Chambers of Commerce in legislation which affected their interests in West Africa.[3]

With their varied sources of grievances and protests, Holt and the other members of the United Kingdom-based humanitarian organisations were able to influence British public opinion through the press, through deputations to the Colonial Office and by lobbying sympathetic members of the British Parliament.

Their main problem, however, lay in obtaining reliable local intelligence. Few members of these humanitarian organisations visited West Africa. For a while, such organisations as the N.R.-L.T.U.C. and the A.P.S. relied on private letters and interviews with such local informants as the Rev. James Johnson, one of the Nigerian assistant bishops in the CMS diocese of Western Equatorial Africa.

These difficulties, however, improved with the formation in 1905 of the Lagos Aborigines' Protection Society under the leadership of Prince Eshugbayi Eleko, C. A. Sapara-Williams, S. H. Pearse and G. A. Williams.[4] In August 1910 there was further improvement when the reorganised Lagos Auxiliary of the A.P.S. began. From 1910, its leaders included such educated Africans as James Johnson, I. Oluwole, M. Agbebi, C. A. Sapara-Williams, C. A. da Rocha and S. H. Pearse.[5]

[1] *E.D.M.P.* F/8, Holt to Morel, 19 December 1908.
[2] *E.D.M.P.* F/8, Holt to Morel, 10 May 1902; *E.D.M.P.* F/8, Holt to Morel, 19 October 1905.
[3] *E.D.M.P.* F/8, Holt to Morel, 17 December 1908.
[4] Omu, F. I. A.: *The Nigerian Newspaper Press, 1859–1937* (Ph.D. thesis) Ibadan 1965, p. 225.
[5] Nworah, *op. cit.* pp. 222–31.

Though the Lagos Auxiliary helped the parent society in Britain with the necessary local information, there were rivalries among its leaders and disagreements between them and the United Kingdom-based A.S.-A.P.S., in particular, over British land policy.

Similar differences arose in the Chambers of Commerce based in the United Kingdom over such issues as the liquor trade, the cultivation of cotton under the auspices of the British Cotton Growing Association and the freight rates charged by British steamship companies operating in West Africa. Divisions in the ranks of those organisations which theoretically were in a strong position to influence government policies in British West Africa, left the Colonial Office free to adopt and continue the measures recommended by its men-on-the-spot.

Only in a few cases did the Colonial Office agree to share its control of policy with the Chambers of Commerce. While they maintained a solid front, it expressed willingness to consult their views on legislation proposed by its men-on-the-spot. In 1903, Secretary of State Chamberlain regretted that over the tolls question MacGregor 'had not afforded opportunity for consideration of their views in accordance with my promise that Chambers of Commerce should be consulted on questions affecting their interests'.[1] As a matter of general policy, Chamberlain and his immediate successors in the Colonial Office met the Chambers of Commerce desire for consultation through the monthly meetings they held with them to discuss matters of 'Nigerian development'. In these meetings with the West African Council of the Associated Chambers of Commerce of Manchester, Liverpool and London, the Colonial Office usually discussed the 'commercial questions' which interested those bodies.[2]

The Colonial Office, however, did not wish to go as far as the Chambers of Commerce and the interested United Kingdom-based humanitarian organisations desired in ensuring representative government in British West Africa. Not satisfied with the limited concessions made in this direction, for example in Lagos since 1872, the Manchester Chamber of Commerce in February 1902 urged the appointment of more European and African unofficial members in the Legislative Councils of British West

[1] CO. 147/166, C.O. to MacGregor, tel. 18 June 1903.
[2] HC. Deb. 4s. 163, 1 November 1906, 1325; Statement by W. S. Churchill.

Africa.¹ In 1912, the A.S.-A.P.S. made a similar proposal for the Legislative Councils of the Gold Coast and Southern Nigeria as a check against autocracy.²

Neither in 1902 nor in 1912 did the Colonial Office show any willingness to agree. It did not wish to depart from the parity of representation – three members each – enjoyed by European commercial firms and African interests in the Legislative Council at Lagos, since May 1906.³

The Colonial Office viewpoint was reiterated by C. Strachey in May 1912:

> As regards the merchants, they have at present a considerable voice in the Council, and it is by no means certain that they ought to have any more power over *administration* [sic] than they have at present. 'They' are the agents of Manchester and Liverpool firms, whose first duty is to their principals in England. I should not consider that they would be a tower of strength if advice were required on such subjects as education, 'concessions', missionary enterprise and agricultural or scientific work.⁴

Strachey correctly emphasised the problem caused by the difficult position of the agents of commercial firms with headquarters in Britain. John Holt himself had earlier admitted their dilemma: as members of the Legislative Council, they feared criticism by their employers in Britain if they misrepresented their interests in discussions with the government. They also feared government reprisals if they appeared too critical.⁵

The Colonial Office advanced different reasons for rejecting the plea for wider representation of African interests in the Legislative Council. Here again, Strachey's arguments received the support of J. Anderson and Secretary of State Harcourt:

---

[1] CO. 147/162, Manchester Chamber of Commerce to C.O., 11 February 1902.

[2] CO. 554/10, T. Buxton to C.O., 1 May 1912; CO. 554/10, T. Buxton to C.O., 3 June 1912.

[3] CO. 554/10, T. Buxton to C.O., 1 May 1912, minutes by C.S. and J.A.; CO. 554/10, T. Buxton to C.O., 3 June 1912, minute by C.S.

[4] CO. 554/10, T. Buxton to C.O., 1 May 1912, minute by C.S., dated 9 May 1912. See also minute by J.A., 10 May 1912 and CO. 554/10, T. Buxton to C.O., 3 June 1912, minute by C.S., 7 June 1912.

[5] *E.D.M.P.* F/8, Holt to Morel, 27 July 1904; *E.D.M.P.* F/8, Holt to Morel, 4 August 1904.

As to the *natives* [sic] it has been realised here for some time past that the educated native barrister at Lagos is just as much a 'foreigner' to the Efik or Ibo people and chiefs of the Central and Eastern Provinces as an Englishman is . . . The problem is, how to get the un-Europeanised native represented. He cannot be brought up to Lagos to sit at a table with gentlemen in frock coats . . . The solution is . . . rather to diminish than to extend the powers of the Lagos Legislative Council, and to continue the present policy of governing the protectorate through the Chiefs, and the Native Councils which have been established.[1]

This comment emphasised that the Colonial Office then did not attach much importance to the representative rôle of the Legislative Council.

The further interest shown by European commercial interests in securing the establishment of a separate Legislative Council for the Protectorate of Southern Nigeria from 1902 was rebuffed by Moor, whose views were approved by the Colonial Office. The Royal Instructions issued to Moor in January 1900 did not provide for Executive and Legislative Councils but vested all powers and jurisdiction in the High Commissioner.[2] Hence, Moor's administration became in Egerton's words, 'a one-man show'.[3] The High Commissioner alone assumed responsibility for everything, but was 'not bound to consult anyone' under the existing constitutional arrangement.[4] This situation in the Protectorate of Southern Nigeria irritated the representatives of European mercantile interests who wanted a say in the administration of the British West African territories.[5] In particular, the Manchester Chamber of Commerce condemned the 'somewhat autocratic powers' vested in the High Commissioner of the Protectorate of Southern Nigeria and demanded 'some sort of representative

---

[1] CO. 554/10, T. Buxton to C.O., 1 May 1912, minute by C.S., dated 9 May 1912. See also minute by J.A., 10 May 1912 and CO. 554/10, T. Buxton to C.O., 3 June 1912, minute by C.S., 7 June 1912.
[2] CO. 380/152, Royal Instructions dated 1 January 1900.
[3] CO. 520/26, Egerton to C.O., 5 November 1904.
[4] CO. 520/29, Egerton to C.O., conf. 29 January 1905, minute by R.L.A.
[5] Morel, E. D.: *Affairs of West Africa*, London 1902, p. 25; *West Africa*, 5 October 1901, p. 1156.

government'.¹ So did, shortly afterwards, the West African Trade Association.²

Moor rejected such reforms for two principal reasons. It would be difficult to obtain suitable representatives from the European mercantile and African communities, and transport difficulties made matters worse. He maintained that the European trading agents with their depots confined to the coast knew little about the affairs of the people of the hinterland. He impressed upon the Colonial Office that he could not get Africans to speak for wider groups in view of local jealousies and rivalries.³ In accepting these arguments against a separate Legislative Council, the Colonial Office requested that Moor consult the views of the African chiefs and European trading interests.⁴

Moor's second reason was the serious language difficulty. Using interpreters at council meetings would have entailed longer sessions and more confused deliberations.

The transport difficulty emphasised by Moor in 1902 continued much longer. Aware of this, the Liverpool, Manchester and London Chambers of Commerce rejected in 1905 the proposal made by the Commercial Intelligence Officer of Southern Nigeria that all European firms there establish a central Chamber of Commerce for consultation in matters relating to trade.⁵

Apart from these practical difficulties, Moor did not believe in representative government. He wished to tackle the problems of the Protectorate of Southern Nigeria single-handed and condemned the alleged active participation of educated Africans and chiefs in the administration of Lagos Colony and Protectorate under MacGregor.⁶

On balance, the question of representative government which interested the members of the 'Third Party', the A.S.-A.P.S. and the Chambers of Commerce impressed neither the Colonial

---

¹ CO. 520/16, Manchester Chamber of Commerce to C.O., 1 May 1902.
² CO. 520/15, Moor to C.O., conf. 21 September 1902, minute by R.L.A.
³ CO. 520/15, Moor to C.O., conf. 21 September 1902.
⁴ CO. 520/15, C.O. to O.A.G., conf. 25 March 1903.
⁵ CO. 520/31, Thorburn to C.O., (19) July 1905, enclosure. CO. 520/33, Liverpool Chamber of Commerce to C.O., 20 September 1905; CO. 520/33, Manchester Chamber of Commerce to C.O., 2 November 1905; CO. 520/33, London Chamber of Commerce to C.O., 7 November 1905.   ⁶ CO. 520/10, Moor to C.O., conf. 14 December 1901.

Office nor Moor, and failed to alter the general trend of Colonial Office policy towards Southern Nigeria.

THE RÔLE OF THE BRITISH PARLIAMENT

The precise amount of influence which the British Parliament exercised over the administrative policies adopted by the Colonial Office in such a dependent territory as Southern Nigeria cannot be easily determined. It was potentially an important check as the Secretary of State for the Colonies, his Parliamentary Secretary, and other officials had seats there, and the government must have been conscious that the administration of any dependency could be questioned during debates in the Commons.

In practice, a great deal depended on the Secretary of State's attitude towards public opinion in the United Kingdom whether or not it received expression in Parliament. Chamberlain, for example, showed considerable concern over the question of slave-dealing in Southern Nigeria and impressed upon Moor that public opinion in Britain rightly considered it a sensitive issue.[1]

Parliament was less concerned than the A.S.-A.P.S. and the N.R.-L.T.U.C. with domestic slavery, labour and the liquor traffic.[2] In none of these issues did the Colonial Office and the men-on-the-spot alter their approach significantly because of criticism in Parliament and the British press.

Between 1910 and 1911 the British Parliament strongly criticised supporting the colonial chaplain and church at Lagos from public funds.[3] The British government, however, upheld Egerton's action in this issue with the promise that it would con-

[1] CO. 520/1, C.O. to Moor, 23 May 1900, and enclosure.
[2] For Parliament and the liquor traffic in Southern Nigeria, see: HL. Deb. 4s. 147, 6 June 1905, 826–45; H.L. Deb. 4s. 170, 27 February 1907, 5–16; HC. Deb. 4s. 190, 24 June 1908, 1810; HC. Deb. 4s. 191, 29 June 1908, 250–1; HC. Deb. 4s. 192, 20 July 1908, 1456–8; HC. Deb. 4s. 193, 22 July 1908, 82; HC. Deb. 4s. 193, 30 July 1908, 1715–16; HC. Deb. 4s. 193, 1 August 1908, 2093; H.C. Deb. 4s. 194, 21 October 1908, 1135–9; H.C. Deb. 4s. 196, 11 November 1908, 265–6; HC. Deb. 4s. 198, 7 December 1908, 50; HC. Deb. 4s. 198, 9 December 1908, 448.
[3] HC. Deb. 5s. 15, 21 March 1910, 741–2; HC. Deb. 5s. 15, 23 March 1910, 1036–7; HC. Deb. 5s. 15, 4 April 1910, 3; HC. Deb. 5s. 17, 13 June 1910, 1017; HC. Deb. 5s. 18, 27 June 1910, 661; HC. Deb. 5s. 18, 29 June 1910, 1042, 1044, 1065–7; HC. Deb. 5s. 21, 13 February 1911, 668–9; HC. Deb. 5s. 22, 6 March 1911, 992–3.

sider appeals for financial assistance from 'other denominations' at Lagos 'in a spirit of complete impartiality'.¹

Generally, between 1900 and 1913, Parliament allowed Secretaries of State for the Colonies much freedom of action. This was not surprising in view of the larger questions which confronted the entire British Empire and the limited time available to discuss all these. Commenting on the attitude of the House of Commons Committee towards the colonial estimates for 1911, Harcourt noted:

> We ranged ... over a variety of topics with no geographical, administrative, philanthropic, or commercial relation to one another. The searchlight shifted from a cable in the West Indies to the Masai in East Africa; from a railway in Nigeria to a dusky prisoner in Ashanti. Where there was criticism or curiosity some debate took place, but the better the administration, the greater the prosperity of a Colony, the less the attention it received in this House and the less credit it acquired from the public outside.²

In Southern Nigeria, the reticence of Members of Parliament on financial questions had another cause. Unlike Northern Nigeria during this period, Southern Nigeria did not receive imperial grants-in-aid for its administration. Parliamentary interest in the details of Southern Nigeria's administration between 1900 and 1913 was therefore intermittent. Debates were provoked mostly by such questions as slavery,³ military operations,⁴ labour,⁵ the liquor traffic, the endowment of the colonial church and chaplaincy and occasionally by the prospects for cotton cultivation.

THE RÔLE OF THE COLONIAL OFFICE

The inadequate surveillance by Parliament of the administrative policies which affected Southern Nigeria left the Colonial

[1] HC. Deb. 5s. 15, 21 March 1910, 843.
[2] HC. Deb. 5s. 40. 27 June 1912, 504.
[3] HC. Deb. 4s. 80, 12 March 1900, 586.
[4] HC. Deb. 4s. 115, 20 November 1902, 12; HC. Deb. 4s. 147, 5 June 1905, 693.
[5] HC. Deb. 4s. 147, 6 June 1905, 856; HC. Deb. 4s. 164, 5 November 1906, 117–18.

Office and its men-on-the-spot firmly in control. In June 1912, A. Lyttelton, a former Secretary of State for the Colonies, considered the Crown colony system of government a success mainly because the men-on-the-spot received 'great assistance from the stored wisdom and knowledge of the permanent servants in the Colonial Office'.[1]

It is, however, open to doubt whether the human and other resources of the Colonial Office adequately met the needs of pioneer administration in areas recently brought under British control through protectorate treaties, punitive expeditions and patrols, judicial agreements and the like. The Colonial Office could not competently guide and control the varied activities of its men-on-the-spot without first obtaining adequate knowledge of the problems they encountered in the day-to-day administration of the areas entrusted to their charge.

Certainly the Colonial Office had accumulated wisdom and knowledge based on experience in administering its territories in the Far East, West Indies, and parts of Africa. Yet how much of such information was relevant to the different needs of different localities? There is also the distinction between the accumulation of 'stored wisdom' and its proper use. The accessibility of such knowledge led to the dangerous transplantation of experience gained elsewhere in other territories with a different background. For example, MacGregor's Newspaper Ordinance, 1903, was inspired by similar legislation in Demerara.[2] Egerton's Unlawful Societies Proclamation, 1905, followed the draft of a similar ordinance in the Straits Settlements.[3] His Seditious Offences Ordinance, 1909, amounted to a transplantation, for the most part, of Indian legislation[4] while the Peace Preservation Ordinance, 1912, followed legislation for the Gold Coast and the Irish Coercion Acts.[5]

At best, these attempted short cuts to administration, most of which were severely criticised in Southern Nigeria, helped to expose the Colonial Office's lack of adequate local knowledge. Few of its permanent officials visited the areas they adminis-

---

[1] HC. Deb. 5s. 40, 27 June 1912, 543.
[2] CO. 149/6, Legislative Council Debates, 11 February 4 and 8 June 1903.
[3] CO. 520/26, Egerton to C.O., 6 December 1904, enclosure.
[4] HC. Deb. 5s. 15, 22 March 1910, 929.
[5] CO. 592/11, Legislative Council Debates, 8 February 1912.

tered from afar. The disadvantages of that situation were quite obvious between 1904 and 1911 when the Colonial Office admitted its difficulties in dealing with the controversial issues of tolls and the judicial agreements without having satisfactory maps of the administrative divisions of Lagos Colony and Protectorate.[1] The accumulated knowledge with which Lyttelton credited the Colonial Office was no help here.

Thus limited, the Colonial Office gave its man-on-the-spot much consideration when controversies arose. MacGregor had such public difficulties over the disputed Native Councils and Forestry Ordinances and the tolls question which he undertook without seeking the prior approval of the Colonial Office.[2] Despite its irritation, the Colonial Office eventually supported MacGregor. In the case of the Native Councils Ordinance where MacGregor and the A.P.S. disagreed over the best means of protecting the interests of the chiefs of the Lagos Protectorate, the Colonial Office had 'no hesitation in adopting the opinion of the practical man with local experience as against the opinion of the theorists on such a subject'.[3]

The relationship between the Colonial Office and its man-on-the-spot was best expounded by Lord Onslow in March 1907:

> When I had the honour of taking a share in Colonial administration under Mr Chamberlain, it was the settled policy of the Colonial Office that you ought never, except under very exceptional circumstances, to interfere with the decision and the policy of the man whom you had sent out to administer, and in return we at the Colonial Office only asked for one thing, and that was that we should be kept fully and completely informed of what the man on the spot intended to do and what he advised us to do. So long as we were kept absolutely informed of what was about to be done, the occasions on which the Colonial Office interfered were of the very rarest.[4]

[1] CO. 147/166, C.O. to MacGregor, conf. 21 August 1903; CO. 147/170, Moseley to C.O., 11 June 1904, minute by C.S.; CO. 520/102, Egerton to C.O., 29 April 1911, minute by J.A.

[2] CO. 147/157, C.O. to MacGregor, conf. 27 December 1901; CO. 147/166, MacGregor to C.O., tel. 14 June 1903, minutes by F.G.A.B. and R.L.A.; CO. 147/168, C.O. to MacGregor, conf. 27 November 1903.

[3] CO. 147/164, Fox-Bourne to C.O., 18 March 1902, minute by F.G.A.B.

[4] *J.A.S.*, vol. 6, London 1906–7, pp. 304–5; Speech made by Lord Onslow on 8 March 1907.

Much earlier, in 1899 and 1902, R. L. Antrobus had observed that the Colonial Office considered policies and measures which affected British West Africa on the principle that its function was 'not to administer but to control administration'.[1] Consequently, 'We deliberately leave the initiative in most matters to the local governments, and refrain from interfering with them more than is necessary to secure that the colonies shall be administered on lines which will meet with the approval of Parliament.'[2]

THE MAN-ON-THE-SPOT AND HIS ENVIRONMENT

The seriousness of the responsibility of the Governor or High Commissioner and his deputies becomes quite clear from the rôle assigned to them by the Colonial Office. But how equipped were they to assume that rôle to the satisfaction of the people whose political destiny they controlled? Above all, administration involves men as well as measures. Enlightened foreign rulers would be expected to consider not only the interests of their home government but also those of the people under their charge. That in turn would entail giving the people under their charge an adequate means of expressing their views. But how far were these effective channels open to the people, and did these avenues guarantee reliable controls over authoritarian rule by the men-on-the-spot?

Through the tours of the Governor, High Commissioner and their deputies, the government, theoretically, had ample means of ascertaining the views of the chiefs and people during interviews and discussions with petitioners. In considering the effectiveness of such tours, their frequency over a wide area at a time of difficult means of transportation and communications must be considered as well. Allowance should also be made for the fact that such tours took place while the suspicion and misunderstanding, exacerbated by the newly-established and steadily expanding colonialism, disturbed relations between the new rulers and those they had displaced. Further problems arose from the use of imperfect interpreters. At times, the granting of language bonuses

[1] CO. 444/1, Moor to C.O., 14 June 1899, minute by R.L.A.
[2] CO. 520/16, W. T. Dyer to Lucas, 16 September 1902, minute by R.L.A.

encouraged some of the political staff to learn some of the languages of the people but a lot more relied on interpreters whose command of the English language left much to be desired. The principal men-on-the-spot – Moor, MacGregor, and Egerton – not to mention such deputies as L. Probyn, G. C. Denton, C. H. Moseley, J. J. Thorburn, A. G. Boyle, F. S. James and others, hardly spoke any Nigerian language.

Added to the language difficulty was the poor state of anthropological information necessary for satisfactory administration of an alien people. The practice of indirect administration hardly resolved that problem. In Southern Nigeria, indirect administration dealt mainly with the execution of larger policies already formulated by the British authorities. The making of by-laws by members of the reorganised native councils with their problems of composition and inadequate independent judgment in the presence of British political officers hardly removed the grievances of the people over such matters as punitive expeditions, deportations of chiefs, coercive legislation, tolls, the liquor traffic. forced labour, domestic slavery, the selective ban on secret cults, the prohibition of jujus and witchcraft accusations and the like. The masses had no voice in those vital issues; they were not the policy-makers; they were required to obey the decisions made over their heads.

Even without frequent tours and knowing the languages of the people, the Governor or High Commissioner could rely on the annual, quarterly and other reports from his subordinates to provide the necessary information for making major decisions. But, there also, much depended on the competence of the officers who compiled and wrote such reports and their reliability considering the problems of language, illness and frequent changes in postings.

The work of men-on-the-spot, however, received much approval in June 1912 when Secretary of State Harcourt examined their rôle. In his 'unfeigned admiration' of the 'splendid work of the whole Colonial Service from the top to the bottom', Harcourt observed:

> They spend a great period of the best of their lives on very moderate emoluments in distant and often deadly lands – lost to their friends, removed from public appreciation in the obscurity of the jungle, but, if they err, never spared from

blame. They reap few rewards except the advantage of the native, the credit of the service, and their own good name; but they have at least the testimony of the civilised world to their probity and humanity. The Empire owes more than it will ever pay to her exiled and strenuous sons.[1]

The critical press at Lagos, however, queried both the performance of the men on the spot, and the autocracy associated with the Crown colony system of government.[2]

THE NEWSPAPER ORDINANCE, 1903

In the local press, the educated Africans, denied a place in either the central or the indirect administration, found a convenient means of criticising the government. They formed a problem for the government, however. Either it could suppress them, thus incurring the odium of attacking the British ideal of free speech, or it could allow unrestrained criticism and deal ruthlessly with the resultant public agitation.

Compared with Lagos, the Protectorate of Southern Nigeria did not experience the same problem of criticism in the press. The Calabar-based newspapers had been edited and controlled by the Presbyterian missionaries before they folded in 1904. After seeing the early copies of the *Calabar Observer*, Moor expressed satisfaction that the newspaper was in 'safe hands'.[3] As this newspaper had a relatively short existence, Moor's Newspaper Proclamation, 1903,[4] had the effect of discouraging the establishment of any successors. Hence, a newspaper law was more urgent for Lagos than for the Protectorate of Southern Nigeria.

That MacGregor sponsored such a newspaper law for Lagos at first seemed puzzling. As the man-on-the-spot without the benefit of understanding the Yoruba language or being in touch with the masses, MacGregor did not enjoy seeing criticism by the Lagos press of unpopular government measures. And, despite the mutual respect between MacGregor and the Lagos chiefs, most of his measures were resented. The Native Councils and the Forestry Ordinances and the tolls issue were cases in point.

[1] H.C. Deb. 5s. 40, 27 June 1912, 540.   [2] Omu, *op. cit.*, p. 182.
[3] CO. 520/14, Moor to C.O., 6 June 1902.
[4] CO. 588/1, No. 26 of 1903.

The Mild Autocracy

The Lagos press exploited the situation to MacGregor's embarrassment. MacGregor's answer was the Newspaper Ordinance.

The government sought to justify it as an attempt to check frequent libels. It denied any plans to interfere with the liberty of the press except to provide against any 'reckless statements'.[1] Before proposing this law, MacGregor expressed surprise at the ingenuity of the Lagos press in 'discovering a sinister motive for anything and everything ever done by this government or by a Government Officer'. He therefore urged controls to deal with blasphemous, seditious and other forms of libel.[2]

The opponents of the newspaper law considered it unnecessary,[3] and protested that libel actions had been rare. A petition from Lagos residents to Secretary of State Chamberlain on 20 June 1903 claimed that in the long history of the Lagos press there had been only three cases of newspaper libels.[4] Nor did the Nigerian unofficial members of the Legislative Council – C. A. Sapara-Williams, O. Johnson and C. J. George – see any justification for the proposed law merely to protect young, inexperienced British officers in Lagos from exposure to unrestrained press criticism.[5] Johnson emphasised that press criticism, not gagging, would benefit the public by exposing the activities of such young officers 'with more zeal than discretion'.[6]

In their petition the residents of Lagos also claimed that the public would lose more if, in the attempts to protect government officials, press freedom were lost. Such freedom provided 'the only available means afforded the people of this Colony and the Hinterland for exposing abuses, and for ventilating their opinions and grievances'.[7] Both the petitioners and the Nigerian unofficial members of the Legislative Council considered the proposed law unnecessary because of the well-known loyalty of the Lagos people to the British Crown.[8] MacGregor agreed but emphasised the danger of press indiscretion.[9]

[1] CO. 147/167, MacGregor to C.O., 16 October 1903, enclosure.
[2] CSO. 7/1/4, Legislative Council Debates, 4 June 1903.
[3] *Ibid.* See also debates of 8 June 1903.
[4] CO. 147/168, G. A. Williams to C.O., 22 June 1903, enclosure.
[5] CSO. 7/1/4, Legislative Council Debates, 4 and 8 June 1903.
[6] CSO. 7/1/4, Legislative Council Debates, 8 June 1903.
[7] CO. 147/168, G. A. Williams to C.O., 22 June 1903, enclosure.
[8] *Ibid.* C.S.O. 7/1/4, Legislative Council Debates, 4 June 1903.
[9] CSO. 7/1/4, Legislative Council Debates, 4 June 1903.

The public rejected the government argument that a newspaper law which suited the needs of the people of the British West Indies would be ideal for Lagos with different circumstances.[1] That retort came after Chief Justice W. Nicoll, an official with nine years' previous experience in Demerara, had informed the Lagos Legislative Council that the Demerara newspaper law of 1839 was 'precisely and practically the same as the Press Bill before the Council'.[2]

The original requirement of a £500 bond as a condition for publishing newspapers, as required by the earlier draft of the newspaper bill, met with stiff opposition from the Nigerian unofficial members of the Legislative Council and the proprietors and editors of the Lagos press. In their view, the bond represented an indirect government attempt to destroy the newspaper profession and a denial of the fundamental right of British subjects to freedom of expression.[3] These critics of the Crown colony system of government used the argument of their rights as British subjects, a status they had acquired by virtue of the British annexation of Lagos in 1861. Sapara-Williams stressed:

> I know we are in the minority, and no doubt we are fighting a hopeless battle but this does not alter the fact. And I hold that the principle that Newspapers cannot be published without the proprietor or publisher giving a bond is certainly repugnant to all sense of justice and an outrage upon the established principles of English liberty which we as subjects of His Majesty the King have an undoubted right to.[4]

During the long controversy, the bond issue overshadowed all the other features of the proposed newspaper bill. O. Johnson maintained that the bond demanded would not only hang as 'the sword of Damocles over publishers' but also act as a bait for frequent litigation for libel even on flimsy grounds.[5]

The government declined to follow British practice over the issue of newspaper bonds and press freedom. Acting Chief

[1] CSO. 7/1/4, Legislative Council Debates, 8 June 1903.
[2] CO. 149/6, Legislative Council Debates, 11 February 1903. The practice of allowing the Chief Justice an *ex officio* seat on the Legislative Council in Lagos continued until April 1908.
[3] CO. 147/168, G. A. Williams to C.O., 22 June 1903, enclosure. The bond allowed under the British Guiana press law was £500.
[4] CSO. 7/1/4, Legislative Council Debates, 8 June 1903.
[5] CO. 149/6, Legislative Council Debates, 11 February 1903.

Sir Henry McCallum

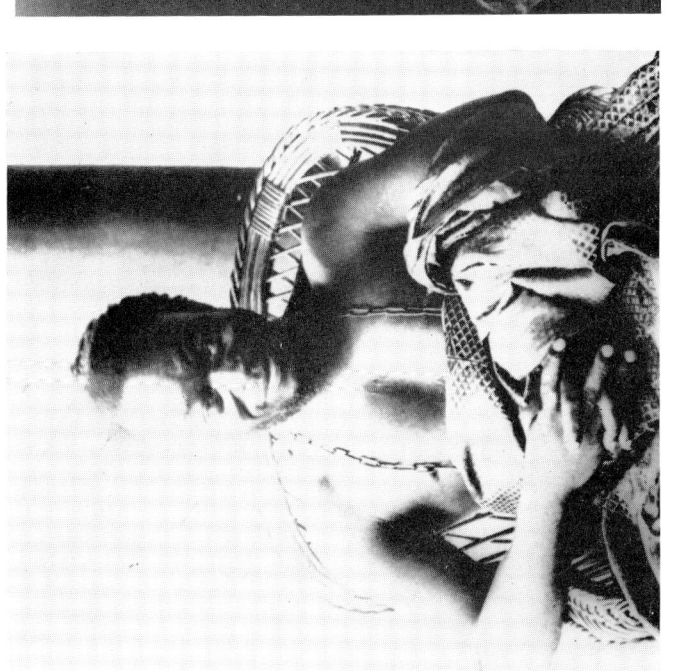
Overami of Benin

H. L. Galway and the Chiefs of Bonny, 1896

The Mild Autocracy

Justice E. A. Speed maintained that because of the huge capital investment made in the newspaper business by English proprietors in the United Kingdom, no similar bond had been required there to protect the public. In the case of the Lagos press, the government sought to employ the bond as a means of imposing 'a sense of responsibility' on newspaper editors and publishers. With reference to the principles of English liberty, Speed stressed the rarity throughout the world of any 'absolutely free press'.[1] The only major concession which the government agreed to make was the reduction of the bond from £500 to £250. In spite of the unofficial members' opposition, the Newspaper Ordinance, (No. 10 of 1903) became law on 5 October 1903.[2]

As this law with the £250 bond made the newspaper business in Lagos more expensive so it checked the previous tendency towards the proliferation of newspapers. No prosecutions under the 1903 ordinance took place until 1930.[3] Press criticism of government policies, however, continued unabated.

THE SEDITIOUS OFFENCES ORDINANCE, 1909

The position later became so serious that Egerton sought to curb press freedom through the Seditious Offences Ordinance enacted on 6 November 1909.[4] Though it applied to the whole of post-1906 Southern Nigeria, this act actually had its roots in discontent in the Western Province between 1906 and 1909. Through it, Egerton sought to control political unrest there and protect the government officers generally from public criticism.

Opposition to the public acquisition of the Hausa Lines and to the proposed water-rate in Lagos were two main reasons for Egerton's urging the Seditious Offences Ordinance.[5] To these should be added his irritation over the pamphlet[6] published in September 1908 by Herbert Macaulay, one of the educated

[1] CSO. 7/1/4, Legislative Council Debates, 8 June 1903.
[2] *Ibid.* C.O. 150/11, Lagos Government Gazette, 10 October 1903.
[3] Omu, *op. cit.*, pp. 339–40.
[4] CO. 588/3, No. 23 of 1909.
[5] CO. 520/67, Egerton to C.O., conf. 27 November 1908; MP. No. 46280.
[6] Its title was: 'Governor Egerton and the Railway'. It was filed in MP. No. 46280. Henceforth this pamphlet will be referred to as *The Macaulay Pamphlet*.

Africans and foremost critics of government policies and practices.

The eviction, between 1907 and 1909, of the African occupants of the piece of land designated the Hausa Lines under the Hausa Lands Ordinance, 1906,[1] caused great resentment. The government said it wanted to provide new accommodation for its staff on that piece of land.[2] The evicted 'unauthorised occupants' of the Hausa Lines were offered 99-year leases at a new site east of the cutting known as the MacGregor Canal. Each lessee could ask for government assistance, not exceeding £12, repayable at the rate of ten shillings a month, to purchase building material. Compassionate grants, up to a maximum of £100 were also available for the affected needy persons willing to build houses on the new 'Hausa settlement'.[3]

There were conflicting reports on the number of persons actually affected by those evictions. W. N. Geary, a former Attorney-General of the Gold Coast but a practising barrister in Lagos at the time of the evictions, put the number of houses pulled down at 1,500–2,000 and claimed that the public petition against the eviction bore 2,000 signatures.[4] The Macaulay pamphlet estimated that some 2,000 persons had been evicted,[5] but J. E. B. Seely (later Lord Mottistone), then Parliamentary Under-Secretary of State for the Colonies, reduced the number to 350.[6]

Public meetings held in Lagos protested against both the 'alienation' and compensation. Sapara Williams considered the compensation offered inadequate.[7]

Seely, however, told the House of Commons in March 1910 that a 'liberal compensation' of £13,347 had been given by the government in Lagos to 92 evicted claimants who owned 59 buildings on the seven-acre site of the Hausa Lines. Though he considered compensation adequate at the rate of over £750 per acre for a piece of land officially described as 'barren, destitute,

---

[1] CO. 588/2, No. 13 of 1906.
[2] Preamble to No. 13 of 1906; HC. Deb. 4s. 164, 6 November 1906, 312 – statement by W. S. Churchill.
[3] CO. 588/2, No. 13 of 1906; preamble, clauses 8, 9, 12(1).
[4] W. N. Geary to the editor, *The Westminster Gazette*, 1 March 1908. Filed in C.O. 520/71, MP. No. 8791.
[5] CO. 520/67, MP. No. 46280, *The Macaulay Pamphlet*, p. 22.
[6] HC. Deb. 4s. 187, 4 May 1908, 1650.
[7] *Anti-Slavery Papers*, MSS. Brit. Emp. S.22. G.212, C. S. Williams to J. H. Harris, 2 May 1910.

and unfenced',[1] those affected saw their eviction not only from the financial viewpoint but also the emotional angle.

Other protests came as a result of the use which the government made of the Hausa Lines after the evictions. In their public statement in December 1907, most of the unofficial members of the Legislative Council viewed 'with grave apprehension proposals to expropriate ground for further official residences' and expressed their conviction that the Public Lands Ordinance, 1876, was 'now being applied to cases which were not contemplated by the framers of that enactment'.[2]

Nevertheless, the government firmly asserted its legal rights under the Public Lands Ordinance (No. 8 of 1876) to acquire land with compensation. In cases of disputed interest or title and compensation, the decision of the Supreme Court was final.[3] The government felt satisfied that under the Hausa Lands Ordinance it had offered and paid compensations in certain cases. The government case was also based on the fact that the Hausa Lines formed part of 'Crown Land' which it had set aside since 1863 for the residential quarters of the Lagos Constabulary (later Hausa Force) 'so long as they remained active members'. However, it discovered that most of the occupants of the Hausa Lines until 1906 were either retired soldiers or 'others having no legal claim or right' to it.[4] Though legal this attitude took no account of the human aspects of the problem.

Even more widespread and intense protest was provoked by the proposal to levy a water rate in Lagos township in 1908. This protest followed the government's attempt to supply the 50,000-odd people in Lagos with a good water scheme rather than relying on well-water and rain-water collected in tanks. In making the proposal for a new water-supply scheme, the government considered the size, importance and site of Lagos near the lagoon,[5] and was supported by its medical advisers who found the existing water supply in Lagos inadequate and dangerous.[6]

[1] HC. Deb. 5s. 15, 23 March 1910, 1035.
[2] *The African Mail*, 10 January 1908, p. 138; *The Lagos Standard*, 11 December 1907. Its signatories were O. Johnson, C. Sapara-Williams, A. Matheson, K. Ajasa and R. Tannock.   [3] No. 8 of 1876, clause 8.
[4] CO. 588/2, No. 13 of 1906, preamble.
[5] CO. 520/77, Thorburn to C.O., conf. 7 January 1909, minute by F.G.A.B.
[6] CO. 520/77, Thorburn, to C.O., conf. 7 January 1909. CO. 520/79, Egerton to C.O., conf. 10 June 1909.

For the new water-scheme, Egerton, with the Colonial Office's approval, sought to avoid saddling the people of the entire Colony and Protectorate of Southern Nigeria with the cost of providing the residents of Lagos with water of better quality and quantity. The government therefore preferred to raise a loan and impose water rates on the house-holders to cover the interest, sinking fund charges and the cost of working the scheme. Estimates in 1908 put the cost of the new water scheme at £130,000.[1]

In asking the people of Lagos to contribute through rates, Egerton was following the same principle he had adopted for the Benin City water project in 1908. The Benin City chiefs and people subscribed £300 to meet the first year's interest and other charges on the loan to the Benin City Native Council guaranteed by the government.[2]

In Lagos, however, the White Cap chiefs actively protested against the water scheme. In petitions and subsequent discussions during the special meeting of the Central Native Council in Lagos, the chiefs explained the grounds of their opposition. They expressed satisfaction with the quantity and quality of the water already available – their favourite excuse for avoiding payment of the rates, which they considered as the thin end of a direct tax wedge. The proposed water rates reminded them of municipal government, which they also opposed. They condemned the support given by the Nigerian unofficial members to the scheme.[3]

They, not the unofficial members, assumed leadership of the masses. The strong resolutions passed against the water scheme during the mass meeting at Lagos on 26 November 1908 underlined the gravity of the situation.[4] Undaunted, the government carried the scheme into effect. But public opposition to it remained a serious issue in Lagos politics till World War I, as the later agitation by the People's Union led by O. Obasa and others from 1907 clearly showed.[5]

[1] CO. 520/77, Thorburn to C.O., conf. 7 January 1909, enclosures and minute by F.G.A.B. C.O. 520/79, C.O. to Egerton, conf. 23 July 1909.
[2] CO. 592/1, Legislative Council Debates, 1 July 1908.
[3] CO. 520/67, Egerton to C.O., conf. 16 November 1908, enclosure – Petition of Chief Aromire and others dated 2 November 1908. C.O. 520/77 Thorburn to C.O., conf. 7 January 1909, enclosure – Central Native Council Debates, 20 July 1908.
[4] CO. 520/67, Egerton to C.O., conf. 29 November 1908, enclosure.
[5] Thomas, I. B.: *Life History of Herbert Macaulay*, Lagos 1947, p. 22.

The Mild Autocracy

Before the agitation over the Hausa Lines evictions and the water scheme died down, Egerton was incensed by the publication and circulation of about 1,000 copies of the Macaulay pamphlet in 1908. Copies of the pamphlet 'in Mr Macaulay's own handwriting' reached Egerton and other government officials.[1] Scurrilous language was used to refer to the Governor and his deputies. Macaulay's allegations against the Railway Department had much justification. He was not alone in criticising the maladministration of that department whose senior officers had been accused of fraud in railway contracts and stores. Macaulay blamed the government for not investigating thoroughly such matters of public concern and punishing the officials found guilty. He upheld the allegation of corruption made by A. Johnston, a former British superintending engineer, against H. Butler-Wright, a former deputy manager of the Railway Department.[2] The Lagos Chamber of Commerce made a similar request for a public inquiry.[3]

Egerton had previously informed the Executive Council in March 1907 of 'the irregular handling of government monies' by Butler-Wright,[4] and Butler-Wright had left Lagos for good. In a subsequent session of the Executive Council in August 1908, the members advised the removal of A. Johnston, another senior railway official. However, they had to admit that the charges against other officials were not proven.[5]

Egerton believed that the Macaulay pamphlet sought to arouse 'feelings of enmity and hatred'[6] between government officials and the public. The Governor felt so concerned over the Macaulay pamphlet that he informed the Acting Chief Justice:

> ... if the publication of such effusions as this is weakly allowed the time of reckoning will surely come – as it has in India. I want advice how to strengthen the government so that such publications can be suppressed and authors punished.[7]

[1] CO. 520/67, Egerton to C.O., conf. 27 November 1908.
[2] *The Macaulay Pamphlet*, pp. 11–22.
[3] CO. 520/68, Egerton to C.O., conf. 7 December 1908, enclosure.
[4] CO. 592/10, Minutes of Executive Council meeting, 25 March 1907.
[5] CO. 592/10, Minutes of Executive Council meeting, 21 August 1908.
[6] CO. 520/67, Egerton to Crewe, conf. 27 November 1908, enclosure, minute dated 27 September 1908.
[7] *Ibid.*, Egerton's minute to Speed, 2 October 1908.

When cooler judgments prevailed, Egerton dropped his contemplated action for libel against Macaulay.[1] However, he requested that the executive should be strengthened by

> a new enactment which, while allowing reasonable freedom of discussion of Government measures, will give the Government power to prevent and repress riotous assemblies and also to punish publications and speeches designed to inflame an excitable and ignorant populace . . .[2]

Egerton wanted an ordinance which should follow closely 'the law of India'.[3] The Colonial Office complied with this request and sent a draft ordinance,[4] which with subsequent additions and alterations became law in 1909.

On several grounds the three Nigerian unofficial members of the Legislative Council strongly opposed the passing of this ordinance. They disliked an ordinance drafted in Britain for application in Southern Nigeria. Not only did they consider the law unnecessary because Yorubas had been historically loyal to the Crown, they also feared that it would be contrary to the principle of a free press. They further objected to the comparison of Southern Nigeria with India whose circumstances were quite different.[5]

The translation of the draft ordinance into Yoruba, in order to enable the chiefs and people in the Western Province to understand its provisions, did not decrease the public opposition to it. Chief Ojora, one of the White Cap chiefs, and others representing the public in the Western Province petitioned Lord Crewe, the Secretary of State for the Colonies, against the draft bill.[6] If anything, the translation into Yoruba of the proposed law increased misinterpretations of its aims. During the discussions in the Central Native Council in November 1909 when the Yoruba text was available, the translators had used *tembelekun* (civil war or conspiracy) in place of 'sedition'. They thereby gave the offence the higher status of treason or insurrection. Chief Eletu,

---

[1] *Ibid.*, enclosures.   [2] *Ibid.*   [3] *Ibid.*

[4] *Ibid.* According to F. G. Butler's minute thereon, India had a press law passed in December 1908. But H. B. Cox, who drafted the draft Seditious Offences Ordinance of Southern Nigeria, based it, he minuted, on the Indian penal code, 1860, as amended up to 1903.

[5] CO. 592/11, Legislative Council Debates, 8 October, 6 November 1909.

[6] CO. 520/91, Egerton to C.O. enclosure.

one of the White Cap chiefs, expressed the resentment of Yorubas at being referred to as *Onitembelekun* (conspirators).¹ Disu Otun, another member of the Central Native Council, stated:

> ... the word *Tembelekun* frightens us. It means civil war. The law is more severe even than the legislation about latrine pans and a water supply. Anyone sitting down quietly at home may easily be caught by this Ordinance without knowing why. We ask that it may be passed in other parts of the Protectorate but not here.²

Outside Southern Nigeria there was more criticism of the law. John Holt considered it coercive and unnecessary:

> These overfed pampered officials are wanting to do as they like without being publicly tackled ... This ordinance is intended to coerce people to say nothing against officialdom ... I am certain there is no necessity for such an ordinance. We have got on very well without all these restrictions on public liberty which have been imported recently and bear the spirit of South Africa and the East where white men are not models of correct conduct towards or treatment of subject peoples ... It is not an easy thing for any man to say anything likely to give offence to despotic officials. Why in addition they should want legal powers to still further terrorise those who would like to speak if they dared to I don't know.³

In the British Parliament C. R. Buxton, M.P. for Ashburton, disliked the provision of the non-limitation of fines and the transplantation, *mutatis mutandis*, of Indian legislation to Southern Nigeria where he considered it 'unsuitable'.⁴ J. Seely, however, told the House of Commons that the Seditious Offences Ordinance of Southern Nigeria merely codified the 'common law of England' which was already applicable to the colony. He maintained that despite the other similarities, the penalty of transportation for life, present in the Indian penal code, had been excluded from the Seditious Offences Ordinance of Southern Nigeria.⁵ Prime Minister Asquith gave a similar reply to the

¹ Central Native Council Debates, 23 November 1909. (University of Ibadan Library).
² *Ibid.*
³ *E.D.M.P.* F/8, Holt to Morel, 15 October 1909.
⁴ HC. Deb. 5s. 15, March 1910, 929.
⁵ HC. Deb. 5s. 15, 22 March 1910, 930.

Commons on 23 March 1910 when questioned by J. King, M.P. for Knutsford.[1]

As enacted on 6 November 1909, the ordinance made penal any offence which by word or deed was meant or likely to incite ill-feeling against the government and its *bona fide* officers. Within defined limits, inciting one section of the public against another amounted to sedition. Conviction meant imprisonment up to a term of two years, an unlimited fine, or both.[2]

Before 1916, there were no prosecutions under the Seditious Offences Ordinance, 1909.[3] The cautious, discreet approach to colonial issues adopted by the chiefs and people of the Western Province had the effect of preventing the offences which came within the meaning of sedition under the 1909 law. The main value of both the 1903 Newspaper Ordinance, and the 1909 Seditious Offences Ordinance was as deterrents.

In the Eastern and Central Provinces of post-1906 Southern Nigeria, violent mass protests against colonialism brought severe reprisals in the form of punitive expeditions, patrols and the three Coercive Acts of 1912, which thereby became the complements of the press and sedition laws.

Exposed to the fire of public criticism, Egerton showed as much apprehension as MacGregor when the latter passed the Newspaper Ordinance, 1903. Both Governors expressed concern less for themselves than for their subordinate officers. In 1903 and 1909, the public in Lagos vehemently opposed these forms of coercive legislation. But the protestations of loyalty and spirited defence of their fundamental right to freedom of expression failed to prevent the enactment of the measures designed to strengthen government control. Despite official anxieties the development of British administrative control over Southern Nigeria proceeded without any patently 'seditious' incidents.

Armed with the press and sedition laws and the 1912 Coercive Acts, the men-on-the-spot in Southern Nigeria had adequate legal powers to deal with serious threats to law and order and public safety. By using these with their broad executive powers – for instance to order and carry out punitive expeditions and patrols – the men-on-the-spot were in a strong position to determine policies and the general course of administrative practice.

[1] HC. Deb. 5s. 15, 23 March 1910, 1047.
[2] CO. 588/3, No. 23 of 1909, clauses 1–5, and 8.
[3] Omu, *op. cit.*, pp. 355 and 361.

The Mild Autocracy

It is true that they had to operate within the further constitutional checks provided by the Executive and Legislative Councils, but no such bodies limited Moor's exercise of power and authority. Although Egerton assumed a similar rôle in the Protectorate of Southern Nigeria between 1904 and 1905, he later became subject to some degree of control from the Executive and Legislative Council, like MacGregor before him in Lagos. To what extent then did these institutions render the exercise of autocracy, particularly by the men-on-the-spot, mild in these sections of the developing Nigerian state?

5 The Executive and Legislative Councils

UNOFFICIAL REPRESENTATION ON THE EXECUTIVE COUNCIL

In theory, the existence of Executive and Legislative Councils limited the autocratic powers of the Governor. In practice, he maintained a firm grip on the formulation of administrative policy. The ordinary people played no part in the Executive Council and relatively little in the Legislative Council. In this chapter, the emphasis will be on the role of both councils as seen by the people. Official expectations will also be put in proper focus.

The exclusion from the Executive Council of Lagos, and later of Southern Nigeria, of unofficial representatives between 1898 and 1914 was not the result of public apathy. On the contrary, the usual functions of the Executive Council in a British Crown colony and the general trend of British colonial policy made their representation there extremely difficult.

The position in Southern Nigeria confirmed M. Wight's argument[1] that generally where a Legislative Council and an Executive Council existed, unofficial members reached the first body much earlier than the second. However, with reference to Southern Nigeria before 1914, his other submission needs substantial qualifications. According to Wight:

> In the majority of colonies, the appointment of unofficial members to the executive council has been dependent on the existence of suitable candidates for the position. This is particularly the case in the colonies of non-European population, where the question did not begin to be agitated by public opinion until after the First World War.

Before World War I, the British government did not adopt the

[1] Wight, M.: *The Development of the Legislative Council, 1606–1945*, London 1946, pp. 130–1.

argument of 'suitable' candidates for rejecting demands for unofficial representation on the Executive Council of Lagos. If by 'suitable' candidates Wight meant Africans willing to co-operate with the government, Lagos Colony and Protectorate had its Kitoyi Ajasas among the educated élite. Yet their pro-government attitude compromised them as popular representatives on the Executive Council.

Two decisive factors could explain the absence of unofficial representatives on the Executive Council at Lagos before 1914. The limited objectives of pre-war advocates of decolonisation had much to do with this. More crucial was the unwillingness of the Colonial Office to share with unofficials the decision-making power.

To appreciate fully the significance of these two factors, the rôle of an Executive Council in a British Crown colony from the middle of the nineteenth century must first be ascertained. Admission into it meant membership of the inner circle of the Crown colony government. Nevertheless it could be an embarrassment to advocates of decolonisation if they were to remain in a permanent minority.

The Executive Council was the policy-making body, particularly in bills for enactment, even though they required the Colonial Office's sanction before becoming law. Its other major function was disciplinary: it could suspend or dismiss government officials and exercise the Governor's power of pardon in cases of capital punishment.[1] Although the council was 'executive' in the sense that it advised the Governor in the exercise of his executive functions, the Governor could dispense with this advice in emergencies, again subject to Colonial Office approval.

There were certain obstacles to the admission of unofficial members. Because of its central position in the Crown colony system of government, the Executive Council's proceedings were confidential. The oath of secrecy imposed upon its members precluded them from disclosing their stand on unpopular government measures. Yet without such disclosures, unofficial members of the Executive Council could lose public support when the government adopted such measures. On the other hand, the public debates in the Legislative Council promised greater convenience and attraction to opponents of colonialism. Therefore, in demanding constitutional reforms during the pre-war

[1] *Ibid.*, pp. 149–50.

period, members of the public in Lagos Colony and Protectorate emphasised representation on the Legislative, not the Executive, Council.

Even the limited demand in 1905 for representation on the Executive Council was rejected, underlining the reluctance of the Colonial Office, before the post-World War II policy of dyarchy or partnership between the British government and dependent peoples in parts of West Africa, to encourage Governors anxious to have unofficial representatives on their Executive Councils so as to promote better public relations.

This reluctance should be related to the two major functions of the Executive Council. The admission of African unofficial members before 1914 would have been an important concession to the principle of responsible government, a principle not then explicitly recognised as applicable to people of Afro-Asian descent. The other problem was the Executive Council's disciplinary rôle under a system of government that was neither representative of nor responsible to Africans. The government did not find it easy to allow unofficials much say in determining issues connected with the services and tenure of its expatriate officials. Under the system of government as practised in Lagos and later Southern Nigeria, British officials dominated the higher cadres of the public service. Matters concerning their discipline – suspension or dismissals – were similarly handled by men of their own race. As M. Wight correctly noted,[1] the disciplinary rôle of the Executive Council was quite serious, particularly under British colonial régimes which, before World War II, lacked independent public service commissions. The British government's unwillingness to separate the disciplinary authority from the powers of the pre-World War II colonial Executive Councils and its initial hesitation to commit itself to the principle of self-determination for dependent peoples seemed more crucial than the question of having 'suitable' candidates as unofficial members of such a colonial Executive Council as that based in Lagos.

The question of unofficial representation did not seriously receive the attention of the men-on-the-spot until the Executive Council was created in March 1886.[2] The Letters Patent and Royal Instructions of 13 January 1886, which provided for the administration of Lagos after its separation from the Gold Coast,

[1] *Ibid.*, pp. 149–50.
[2] CSO. 7/1/3, Executive Council minutes, 3 March 1886.

The Executive and Legislative Councils

encouraged Administrator (later Governor) Alfred Moloney to recommend the appointment of unofficial members to both Executive and Legislative Councils.[1] While suggesting the names of the unofficial members of the Legislative Council, Moloney made no specific recommendations for unofficial members of the Executive Council. The Colonial Office did not regard that as an important omission, nor did it raise the question of suitability of candidates. Assistant Under-Secretary J. Bramston admitted that despite the provision in the Royal Instructions for the appointment of unofficial members of the newly-created Executive Council at Lagos, the Colonial Office found 'no occasion at present for exercising this power, and no intention of doing so'.[2]

Neither Moloney nor Bramston then stated that Lagos did not have 'suitable' candidates. In his confidential dispatch of 19 April 1886, Moloney considered the Colonial Office's approval of his recommendations for un-official membership in the Legislative Council more urgent than action on the Executive Council's unofficial members. His priorities were understandable. From 1872 the Legislative Council of Lagos had had European and African unofficial representatives. There the principle of unofficial representation was recognised and accepted by the Colonial Office. Without this approval, it was not so convenient for Moloney to recommend names of unofficial members of the Executive Council. Bramston's unrefuted comment revealed that the Colonial Office was unwilling to approve, even in principle, the desirability of having unofficial representatives on the Executive Council of Lagos in 1886 and subsequently. That position remained basically unchanged between 1886 and 1914.

Neither MacGregor nor Egerton took the initiative in recommending the appointment of unofficial members of the Executive Council. At that stage, Africans demanded that the Colonial Office make such appointments.

Taking advantage of his visit to the United Kingdom in 1905, Legislative Councillor C. A. Sapara-Williams wrote to the Colonial Office about unofficial representation on the Executive Council of Lagos and followed this with an interview. In view of the government proposals to amalgamate the Lagos Colony and Protectorate with the Protectorate of Southern Nigeria,

[1] CO. 147/55, Moloney to C.O., conf. 19 April 1886.
[2] *Ibid.*, Minute by J.B., dated 3 June 1886.

Sapara-Williams, in his letter of 10 October 1905, made several proposals (including Executive Council and Legislative Council reforms) so as to secure the continuity of policy which he considered desirable. He further considered it desirable that the Africans who contributed the revenues for the administration of a self-supporting territory should be represented on the Executive Council by 'one or more unofficial members'.[1]

Because of the interview between Sapara-Williams and R. L. Antrobus of the Colonial Office, no written reply was recorded. The Colonial Office merely expressed satisfaction with the 'temperately worded and well-written representation from a well known member of the native community of Lagos'.[2] Even so, no Africans reached the Executive Council under the new constitutional arrangements which followed the amalgamation of 1 May 1906.

Leading Africans, including Herbert Macaulay and S. H. Pearse, whose views on the 1906 amalgamation had not been sought, held a public meeting in Lagos on 6 June 1906. The resolutions they passed, which were subsequently forwarded by Egerton to the Colonial Office, included Executive Council and Legislative Council reforms. The petitioners maintained that the time had come ' when members not holding offices in the Colony and Protectorate of Southern Nigeria should be appointed on the Executive Council'.[3] Egerton, however, considered that 'the present condition of West Africa' did not render it 'desirable that any unofficials should be appointed members of the Executive Councils of the British administrations'.[4] The Colonial Office endorsed Egerton's cryptic observation.[5]

Neither Egerton nor the Colonial Office clarified the expression 'present conditions' in British West Africa. They perhaps referred to the efforts then being made to consolidate their administrative control over British West Africa. During the 1880s and 1890s when the British government concentrated on the acquisition of territories, it gladly sought and received informal advice from such educated Africans as the Rev. Samuel Johnson of Lagos. This period of diplomacy, involving the negotiation of

[1] CO. 147/178, Sapara-Williams to Antrobus, 10 October 1905, enclosure.
[2] *Ibid.*, minute by C.S., dated 12 January 1906.
[3] CO. 520/36, Egerton to C.O., 11 August 1906, enclosure.
[4] *Ibid.*   [5] CO. 520/36, C.O. to Egerton, 6 November 1906.

protectorate treaties and agreements, gave way about 1900 to an era of tighter administration.

As the British government's control over its colonies and protectorates in West Africa increased, it understandably felt less and less need of formal or informal advice from educated Africans outside the Legislative Council chambers. During this period, too, educated West Africans were denied higher administrative posts in the public services, thanks mainly to growing racial prejudice which made it inconceivable to encourage Africans in posts which would enable them to discipline such erring expatriate officials as those involved in the railway scandals highlighted in the Macaulay pamphlet.

Nor did the views of the educated élite receive much official attention in the era when the British government in parts of West Africa showed considerable attachment to the principle and practice of indirect administration through recognised chiefs and other officially approved, though occasionally reformed, African institutions. Consequently, the Colonial Office found it difficult to admit educated West Africans into the Executive Councils without encouraging other Africans to hope for similar progress in other branches of their administrations. It was not until September 1942 that, for reasons outside the scope of this book, the British government allowed unofficial representation on the Executive Councils of Nigeria and the Gold Coast.[1]

THE RÔLE OF THE LEGISLATIVE COUNCIL

In ascertaining the usefulness of the Legislative Council to the public in Southern Nigeria, the rôle of the unofficial – particularly the African – members who were in a permanent minority vis-à-vis the official members needs emphasis. In theory, the presence of a few unofficial members in the Legislative Council between 1900 and 1913 suggested that the Crown colony type of government, as in Southern Nigeria, provided for the representation of unofficial opinion. In practice, the limited powers of such councils inclined some sections of the public, as those in Lagos, to regard them as mere window-dressing.

There is force in M. Wight's contention[2] that the Legislative

[1] *The Nigerian Daily Times*, 30 September 1942.
[2] Wight, *op. cit.*, p. 117.

Council's principal function from the middle of the nineteenth century lay in its control of a colony's revenue and expenditure. The financial powers which the Legislative Council could claim were, however, subject to further control by the Secretary of State[1] who was responsible to the British Parliament.

The Legislative Council's other important function, of passing ordinances covering a wide range of subjects, was subject to certain limitations which tended to diminish the effectiveness of unofficial members in controlling legislative proposals. These limitations included the Governor's power to initiate all legislation, his official majority, his double vote where necessary, his veto, his power to reserve such classes of bills as divorce and currency legislation and bills affecting the emoluments of public servants for the Crown's approval, the Crown's power to disallow colonial ordinances, and the overriding powers of Orders in Council and acts of the British Parliament.[2]

It will be seen later that the British government also regarded a Legislative Council with an official majority as a convenient instrument for muffling protests, which would have gained a stronger voice from the absence of a legitimate vent. For political reasons, the government found criticisms of its policies less embarrassing in a Legislative Council with an official majority than in the British Parliament with a formal opposition party. As the development of a formal opposition was discouraged, so co-operation[3] between official and unofficial members was emphasised. This is part of the general safety-valve theme that will later be related to the case of Southern Nigeria.

The limited powers of a Legislative Council with an official majority showed it to be, on balance, a convenient instrument for developing an imperial estate. There is at present no convincing evidence that before 1914 the British government consciously sought to transform the Legislative Council, as in Lagos, into an embryonic Parliament which would provide the unofficial members with valuable experience in self-government. Self-government for people of Afro-Asian descent did not become an explicit goal of general British colonial policy between 1900 and 1914 despite the measure of limited local self-government allowed under the Morley-Minto reforms of 1909 in India. Assessed in general terms, the Indian case before and immediately after the Morley-Minto reforms of 1909 had some relevance to

[1] *Ibid.*, pp. 153-4.   [2] *Ibid.*, pp. 118, 152-3.   [3] *Ibid.*, p. 101.

events in Southern Nigeria. Possibly British officials, already aware of Indian trends, sought to guard against them by limiting the unofficial membership in Legislative Councils, by passing newspaper and seditious offences laws, by seeking to prevent the emergence of a class of 'Bengal Babus' – clerks and agitators – and by cautiously restricting secondary and higher education so as to avoid the mushrooming of such educational institutions as those of India.

Between 1900 and 1913, the Legislative Council of Lagos essentially served the colony. From July 1901, its sphere of jurisdiction legally extended to the Lagos Protectorate. Apart from making possible the discussion and disposal of broad revenue and legislative measures affecting the newly merged territories, the 1906 amalgamation left the Legislative Council's centre of gravity around Lagos. The people of the Central and Eastern Provinces in post-1906 Southern Nigeria therefore had no African representatives in the Legislative Council based in Lagos.

The main functions of a Colonial Legislative Council with an official majority were, according to A. J. Harding of the Colonial Office,[1] the following:

(a) They serve a useful purpose as a safety valve, and give an opportunity for the few persons in a colony, who really have views on public questions, to air those views and to ventilate individual and other grievances.
(b) They do afford the opportunity for unofficial members to give the Government useful advice: how far the unofficials take advantage of this opportunity depends, of course, largely on the calibre of the unofficial members, and therefore depends very largely on the colony.
(c) They afford an opportunity for the Governor to deliver speeches, an occupation dear to some Governors, and to some extent necessary for all.
(d) They may serve as some check on official extravagance.

Harding's safety-valve concept did not unequivocally apply to the Legislative Council based in Lagos between 1900 and 1913. Compared with people in the Protectorate of Southern Nigeria, those of Lagos Colony and Protectorate were relatively peaceful under British control, but the decisive factor was not

[1] CO. 583/100, Clifford to C.O., conf. 26 March 1921, minute by A.J.H., dated 2 June 1921.

the absence of a Legislative Council in one territory and its existence in the other. There were other considerations, among them the type of British personnel entrusted with the administration of subject peoples; the extent to which indigenous institutions were known and utilised; the respect given to the treaties and agreements between the British Crown and the traditional élite; and the degree of understanding and mutual trust existing between the government and the governed. A Legislative Council in which Africans were represented on the basis of nomination had a high potential value as a vent for grievances, but much depended on the type of nominees, the contact between them and the people, the confidence of the people in an assembly dominated by British officials, and how often that body met.

Before 1914, the Legislative Council had an official majority, which did not make it attractive to the African community as a forum for an adequate and sympathetic consideration of its problems. Moreover, the basis of African representation there left much to be desired. Despite the African superiority in numbers, the African and European communities each had two representatives between 1897 and 1900. From 1901 to 1905 there were three African and two European unofficial members. Both communities had equal (3:3) representation between 1906 and 1913.

African confidence in their representatives was further shaken by the fact that the basis of selection was nomination, not election.[1] Obadiah Johnson, one of the African unofficial members of the Legislative Council, drew attention to that defect during a debate in October 1911: 'What I would like to see is that instead of having a nominated Legislative Council, we are allowed an elected one...'[2] On the whole, more persistent Nigerian demands for the principle of elective representation took place, as shown elsewhere,[3] outside the Legislative Council. These demands were partly met much later by the Nigeria (Legislative Council) Order in Council of 1922.

If the basis of unofficial representation caused any satisfaction in Lagos, this was largely among the few European residents engaged in various business enterprises. Until 1913, the Euro-

[1] Tamuno, T. N.: *Nigeria and Elective Representation, 1923–1947*, London 1966, pp. 7–17.
[2] Legislative Council Debates, 26 October 1911.
[3] Tamuno, *op. cit.*, pp. 7–17.

The Executive and Legislative Councils

pean unofficial members of the Legislative Council who represented commercial, banking, and shipping interests understood that the government gave considerable weight to the representation of property as against the claims of Africans who wanted greater representation of men on the basis of population and election. That the government derived nearly 80 per cent of its revenues from indirect taxes – customs dues – was an important factor in the representation of property. The government failed to make allowances for the fact that the tax burden was subsequently passed on by the businessmen to consumers. The equal representation which the government allowed Africans and Europeans in the Legislative Council from 1906 actually conferred more advantages upon the business interests (European and African) in Lagos.

Before 1901, such African professionals as lawyers and medical doctors were not nominated as unofficial members of the Legislative Council. The emphasis previously was on representatives of the mercantile community. Governor MacGregor departed from that tradition in 1901 with the appointment of Dr Obadiah Johnson and a barrister, C. A. Sapara-Williams. In doing so, MacGregor sought[1] to obtain the views of educated Africans who had the confidence of the people at the time when government influence and authority in the Lagos Protectorate increased, particularly with further railway extension from Lagos. Johnson had roots in Oyo, and Sapara-Williams in Ilesha. These two educated gentlemen were joined by a third professional, another barrister, Kitoyi Ajasa, successor to C. J. George, the leading African trader, who died in September 1906 after an unbroken tenure of twenty years.

Through the Nigerian unofficial members some grievances which affected the African community reached the Legislative Council. Among the most important from 1900 were the inadequate compassionate allowances given by the government to the Head of the Dosunmu House, emoluments for the White Cap chiefs of Lagos, the inability of the people to pay rates under a municipal form of government, opposition to the Native Councils, Forestry, Newspapers, and Seditious Offences Ordinances and the colonial chaplaincy and Church question.

[1] CO. 147/154, MacGregor to C.O., conf. 7 February 1901; CO. 147/155, MacGregor to C.O., conf. 26 May 1901; CO. 147/156, MacGregor to CO., conf. 14 August 1901.

The Legislative Council proceedings of this period provided inadequate discussion of the people's grievances over these and other important questions of public interest. The local press in Lagos gave more attention to such issues as the tolls question (1902–3), the judicial agreements of 1904–8, the amalgamation schemes of 1905–6 and 1913–14, the widespread anxiety over British proposals to abolish the liquor traffic in West Africa (1907–9) and dissatisfaction with government proposals affecting the ownership of West African lands (1909–13).

The other channel for expressing public grievances in Lagos lay in protest meetings followed by the drafting of petitions with hundreds of signatures. Inevitably, copies of such petitions sent to the Governor and the members of the Legislative Council reached the Colonial Office for further consideration. In such matters, the Colonial Office often endorsed the recommendations of the Governor, not necessarily those of the Governor in Legislative Council. Occasionally, the contents of such petitions reached sympathetic British parliamentarians who raised them during their own debates. The liquor traffic and the colonial chaplaincy and Church questions were in that category. But where the British Parliament provided a further forum for the discussion of government action which caused public concern in Lagos and later Southern Nigeria, there was rarely much alteration in the policies the government had decided to pursue.

From 1900, at least in theory, the public in Lagos and other parts of Southern Nigeria had alternative channels of expressing their views outside the Legislative Council. Following the Native Councils Ordinance, 1901, the chiefs of the Lagos Protectorate could make their views on local matters known to the British personnel who as advisers sat with them on the reorganised Native Councils. Similar bodies, called native courts, provided nearly the same opportunities for the warrant-chiefs in the Protectorate of Southern Nigeria since 1900. It is true that before and after the 1906 amalgamation the government utilised the principle and practice of indirect administration as an alternative means of obtaining African opinions through the chiefs it recognised. But the imperfections inherent in the system of indirect administration through such reorganised Native Courts and Councils substantially qualified their usefulness as avenues of expressing widespread grievances in several parts of Southern Nigeria.

In Lagos, the Central Native Council, established under the

The Executive and Legislative Councils

Native Councils Ordinance, 1901, enabled MacGregor and Egerton to ascertain the views of the White Cap chiefs and other leaders of the traditional élite on the issues brought to their knowledge by the masses. This will receive more detailed attention in Chapter 6. It is sufficient here to explore the rôle of the Central Native Council as a forum for redressing public grievances. It was the Central Native Council, rather than the Legislative Council, that provided strong opposition to the government's water rate scheme in 1908 and the Seditious Offences Ordinance, 1909. Under Egerton's administration, and prompted by the spirited part it had taken over such controversial matters of public interest, it began to assume the rôle of an active competitor with the Legislative Council.

The members of the Central Native Council began to consider MacGregor's practice of consulting their opinion on certain customary practices as a right to be consulted in all aspects of legislation affecting the public. The clash of interests between the Central Native Council and the Legislative Council was quite clear during the consideration of the Seditious Offences Ordinance, 1909. The members of the Central Native Council, not the unofficial members of the Legislative Council, demanded that the draft bill be translated into Yoruba for closer study and to remove the current, widespread and disturbing rumours that under the proposed law 'two men cannot stand together talking'.[1] Egerton agreed to this request. The debate in the Central Native Council in October 1908 gave Disu Otun an opportunity to express on behalf of the other members their long-felt anxiety:[2]

> Disu Otun: As it is now we have no power as in the olden days. Before, whenever the King and the Chiefs wanted to do anything they always consulted the people, but now things have changed that we cannot know how things are being done until all of a sudden it has been made a law. We beg your Excellency not to pass this law.

> Governor Egerton: This is not the Council for passing laws. We are always glad to call this Council together and to hear what members have to say and to consider their views but it is not the Council that makes the law . . .

[1] Minutes of the Central Native Council meeting, 5 October 1909.
[2] Ibid.

The members of the Central Native Council failed to accept Egerton's clarification of their status when they reassembled about a month later to consider the Yoruba text of the Seditious Offences Ordinance. They again related their discussions to their much-desired status as another legislative chamber. Deputy Governor H. C. Moorhouse represented Egerton at this meeting.[1]

> Sule Giwa: We have read the translated ordinance – we quite understand it: we are sorry and afraid about it. It looks as if the Government thought we were going to conspire in some way against it: we are under the Government, we have no wish whatever to conspire . . . We think the law reflects against our character . . . Therefore we ask that this Ordinance be not passed.
>
> Ali Balogun: Is it a fact that this Council has no power to make or prohibit laws? If so, why are we all here? Apparently there is a higher Council than this who make the laws.
>
> Deputy-Governor Moorhouse: This Council cannot make laws – but its opinion is welcomed with respect to any law that may be under consideration.
>
> Ali Balogun: I shall like this put before the Governor – Kitoyi Ajasa, Sapara Williams and Dr O. Johnson are members of the superior [Legislative] Council – they are supposed to represent Lagos. They are not representative of Lagos: They are not of the Chiefs of Lagos: the Chiefs are here. I should like the Governor informed of this.

H. C. Moorhouse promised to convey the opinions expressed by Ali Balogun on behalf of the Central Native Council to Governor Egerton. Egerton's response was not recorded, but on 23 November 1909 when Moorhouse again met the members of the Central Native Council to continue the debate on the Seditious Offences Ordinance, Chief Ashogbon declared:[2]

> Ali Balogun said the right thing in pointing out that the three Native members of Legislative Council were not representative of Lagos. We had been meaning to say this for a long time, but at each meeting we put it off.

[1] Minutes of the Central Native Council meeting, 18 November 1909.
[2] Minutes of the Central Native Council meeting, 23 November 1909.

Neither Egerton nor Lugard until 1913 altered the constitution and powers of the Central Native Council as authorised by MacGregor when he established it in 1901. The members continued to press for their views to be consulted before the government passed laws in the Legislative Council. The rivalry between the Legislative Council and the Central Native Council continued until 1913. During its last recorded debate on the West African lands question in March 1913, the chiefs informed F. D. Lugard that they desired consultation on 'matters which concerned them, for they could not read and write like the educated party, and had no knowledge of their laws and no voice in them.'[1] As far as the members of the Central Native Council were concerned, Harding's safety-valve theory did not apply. Nor could it be validly extended to the chiefs and people of the Yoruba part of the protectorate, nor to the chiefs and people of the Central and Eastern Provinces even after the 1906 amalgamation. Between 1906 and 1913, the government did not consider giving them an African representative on the Legislative Council. The arguments produced by Moor in 1902 against the establishment of a separate Legislative Council for the people still held good.

Since the three Nigerian unofficial members of the Legislative Council from May 1906 showed no demonstrable interest in debating government measures meant for the Central and Eastern Provinces, the government in that chamber lacked any African advice or criticism in such matters. Since the 1906 amalgamation, these three members regarded themselves as the spokesmen for the people of Western Province (formerly Lagos Colony and Protectorate). For example, they tendered neither useful advice nor criticism in 1912 when the government rushed through the Legislative Council its three Coercive Ordinances.[2] These laws – which sought to legalise the imposition of fines on towns, villages and other communities, provided for the better preservation of the public peace, and enabled certain parts of the protectorate to be declared unsettled districts – affected only the Central and Eastern Provinces of post-1906 Southern Nigeria. Attorney-General Pennington's adverse comments on the people of the Central and Eastern Provinces were left unchallenged by Obadiah

---

[1] Minutes of the Central Native Council meeting, 14 March 1913.
[2] CSO. 592/11, Legislative Council Debates, 1 February 1912; CSO, 592/11, Legislative Council Debates, 8 February 1912; CSO. 592/11. Legislative Council Debates, 31 May 1912.

Johnson, Sapara-Williams and Kitoyi Ajasa. During the first reading of the bill for collective punishment, Pennington observed: '... I can assure Honourable Members that life and property are not blessed with the same certainty in the Central and Eastern Provinces as they are in the Western Province...'[1] In justifying the bill for the better preservation of public peace and safety, Pennington claimed that 'the wildest parts of the Western Provinces are almost as safe as what you may call the most civilised parts of the Central and Eastern Provinces'.[2] On another occasion, Pennington admitted that the draft unsettled districts bill was 'a reversion to a primitive type'.[3] All three draft bills had a quick passage through the Legislative Council without even token opposition from the Nigerian unofficial members.

The views which have developed from the attempt to relate the safety-valve theory to the existence of a Legislative Council with an official majority and other competing avenues for expressing public grievances over government measures will now be summed up. Several people, including the chiefs of Lagos, did not regard the Legislative Council as a legitimate vent. Even when it served as a forum for discussing public grievances, these received inadequate attention.

Harding's second function, to enable the government to receive 'useful advice' from the unofficial members, was made almost impossible to attain by existing official attitudes. This second rôle should be related to the official viewpoint stressed in August 1868 by the Duke of Buckingham, the former Colonial Secretary:

> You will naturally understand that holding his seat by nomination of the Crown, he has been selected for it in the expectation and in the confidence that he will co-operate with the Crown in its general policy, and not oppose the Crown on any important question without strong and substantial reasons...[4]

The emphasis then was on co-operation and loyalty, not on factious opposition.

During a heated debate, it was not always easy to distinguish between 'useful advice' and disloyal criticism. From 1900 to 1913,

[1] CO. 592/11, Legislative Council Debates, 1 February 1912.
[2] CO. 592/11, Legislative Council Debates, 8 February 1912.
[3] CO. 592/11, Legislative Council Debates, 31 May 1912.
[4] Porter, A. T.: 'The social background of decision-makers in Sierra Leone', *Sierra Leone Studies*, New Series, no. 13, June 1960, p. 7. Wight, *op. cit.*, p. 112.

The Executive and Legislative Councils

the unofficial members of the Legislative Council could look back to the career of the Rev. James Johnson who because of repeated criticism of such government measures as the Ijebu expedition of 1892 lost his seat from July 1894 when Governor Carter replaced him with the more pliable African, J. J. Thomas, the 'loyal subject' who 'would not offer any factious opposition' to the government 'when dealing with general legislative business'.[1]

James Johnson's earlier career in the Legislative Council demonstrated the general issue of how much criticism the government could tolerate from unofficial members. Some governors and their deputies were more tolerant of opposition than others. In the tolerant group belonged Acting Governor J. Thorburn, who during a debate in the Legislative Council in November 1910 acknowledged:

> Now Mr Williams has talked of our having pokes at one another ... It is extremely gratifying to me that we had these differences of opinion, because if the honourable unofficial members of this council simply sat here and recorded their assent to everything that was proposed by the administration without any opposition on their part, it would show that the administration was very slack or that the unofficial members were not fit to hold their positions as critics.[2]

Of the Nigerian unofficial members between 1900 and 1913 none criticised government policy as vehemently as James Johnson in the 1890s. On balance, C. J. George and K. Ajasa behaved as loyalists and made few contributions to the debates. By 1906, Sapara-Williams obviously assumed leadership in debate, though Obadiah Johnson was the senior Nigerian member after C. J. George's death. Johnson, too, participated actively in debates, but lacked the lawyer's skill in the presentation of arguments with emphasis on force, coherence, clarity and conviction. K. Ajasa, the third Nigerian unofficial member from September 1906, usually absented himself from the Legislative Council meetings because of private legal engagements. On the few occasions when he was present, he spoke rarely and briefly. Among these Nigerian unofficial members, Sapara-Williams

[1] CSO. 1/7/9, Carter to C.O., conf. 7 March 1894.
[2] *Southern Nigeria Gazette*, 7 December 1910, Legislative Council Debates, 1 November, 1910.

most ably criticised government policies without being considered disloyal and unco-operative. Yet, by October 1910 he was already complaining that Lagos people attacked him because of his friendliness with the government. He therefore chose that opportunity to stress: '... where the Government shows me plainly what their intentions are and I can follow them, no man is more willing to support the government than your humble servant.'[1]

No permanent opposition bloc, comprising the unofficial members, European and African, developed to criticise government measures. No individual unofficial member always stood for, or against, the government. This was partly due to the fact that officials, especially at the committee stage, were willing to consider sympathetically the views of the unofficials only if alterations involved matters of detail rather than policies. Moreover, James Johnson's experience in July 1894 showed that the government detested consistent criticisms from African unofficial members.

The concept of the Legislative Council with an official majority acting as a forum for giving the government useful advice did not quite satisfy British business groups with interests in Nigeria. These groups did not think that unofficials alone in Lagos were competent enough to give the government necessary advice, particularly on revenue and customs and other items of interest to them. The main snag arose from the desire of such business groups to make their views known independently of their representatives in Lagos, who, as has already been shown, were in the Legislative Council. This difficulty Angus Matheson, one of the European unofficial members, highlighted in April 1910 during the second reading of a bill for the limitation of actions and for avoiding suits at law. Matheson then remarked:

> At an interview between the merchants and the Governor [Egerton], His Excellency was good enough to give his word that this ordinance would not be passed until our Principals at home had an opportunity to give their views on the Bill. Under the circumstances, I for one did not think it necessary to express my views to any extent at this meeting of Council.[2]

[1] *Southern Nigeria Gazette*, 23 November 1910, Legislative Council Debates, 24 Oct. 1910.
[2] *Southern Nigeria Gazette*, 15 June 1910, Legislative Council Debates, 30 April 1910.

The Executive and Legislative Councils

The British merchants in the United Kingdom also did not regard the Legislative Council in Lagos as their only means of tendering advice. They preferred making their views known to the Colonial Office through direct correspondence and deputations. The African trade section of the Liverpool Chamber of Commerce used this method with success in July 1912 when it forwarded its criticism of the proposed amendment to Southern Nigeria's merchandise marks legislation.[1]

Quite often, such representations were well received at the Colonial Office. When, for example, the Companies Ordinance of Southern Nigeria became law in March 1912, after the publication of the draft bill in the government *Gazette* in February 1912, the British merchants with interests in West Africa made it clear to Secretary of State Harcourt 'that it sometimes happens that legislation affecting trade in important respects is enacted so quickly that no time is afforded for criticism by the heads of the firms concerned who are normally resident in this country'.[2] Impressed by their petition, Harcourt advised the officials of the Southern Nigeria government 'that, in the absence of special reasons to the contrary, a period of (say) three months might be allowed between first and second reading in the case of important ordinances affecting trading interests, so as to afford due time for criticism by the interests concerned'.[3] The fact that such Colonial Office views were not normally ignored by the government of Southern Nigeria meant that the Legislative Council no longer remained the exclusive source of advice or criticism in matters affecting proposed legislation.

The unofficial members of the Legislative Council also felt that their freedom to criticise or advise the government was circumscribed when the Secretary of State had taken the initiative in recommending desirable legislation. For instance, the criticisms of the unofficial members failed to stop the enactment of the Seditious Offences Ordinance, 1909, with the usual official majority which ultimately had the sanction of the Secretary of State.

Some of the Nigerian unofficial members were similarly handicapped in 1911 when another important but controversial bill, the Foreign Jurisdiction Bill, came before the Legislative

[1] CSO. 1/20/51, C.O. to O.A.G., 16 July 1912.
[2] CSO. 1/20/52, C.O. to O.A.G., 15 August 1912.
[3] *Ibid.*

Council on the instructions of the Secretary of State, as Attorney-General Pennington explained. The aim, he said, was to settle doubts whether the Legislative Council had power to apply the laws of the colony to the protectorate section of the Western Province. O. Johnson had doubts that such an extension was proper in view of the treaties and agreements concluded between the British Crown and the Yoruba chiefs and people. Pennington however, took legal notice of only the 'treaties', not of the 'agreements' and 'undertakings'. Johnson therefore complained:[1] 'The Secretary of State's sanction is now put forward simply to shut our mouths, because whatever the Secretary of State says, we cannot help agreeing to; but the question is, how was the matter put before him before he sanctioned it?' The government did not attempt to answer that query but ruled Johnson's motion to delay the second reading of the bill out of order and continued with its further consideration.

In doing so, the government found it relatively easy because the Nigerian unofficial members disagreed over the necessity of the proposed legislation. Johnson opposed it all through the proceedings; Williams originally opposed it but later yielded to the government. From the beginning, Ajasa warmly welcomed it with the argument:[2]

> The more the Supreme Court Ordinance is extended to the Protectorate the better it will be for the people; it will safeguard their interests and their liberty. That is the way I look at it, and I must say that I have been looking for it a long time.

When eventually the Legislative Council passed it as required by the Secretary of State, only Johnson voted against it.[3] That ordinance of 1911, however, left the question of the limits of British jurisdiction in the Western Province controversial until 1914.

Harding's third function of a Legislative Council as a platform for Governor's speeches raised its own problems. Not all Governors liked speech-making to the same extent, and not every Governor's speech received as much public attention as the debate on the yearly Estimates of Revenue and Expenditure. The proceedings of the Legislative Council could interest the public

[1] CO. 592/11, Legislative Council Debates, 31 January 1911.
[2] *Ibid.*
[3] CO. 592/11, Legislative Council Debates, 2 February 1911.

in other respects: by disclosing the standpoint of the members on the various subjects discussed. The government itself recognised such interest and from December 1904 wanted the local press and the Lagos Chamber of Commerce to have copies of the verbatim reports on the proceedings of the Legislative Council. Sapara-Williams' proposal that such proceedings be published also in the government *Gazette* had the unanimous approval of the other members.[1]

Thereafter, the public had the advantage of following not only the speeches of their Governor and his deputies but also the contributions of the unofficial members. Under the nomination system, however, the people lacked the power to effect the withdrawal of unofficial members who in their opinion inadequately represented their interests. The usefulness of such speeches to the public depended also on the frequency of the Legislative Council meetings and the time allowed unofficial members to study the agenda. During this period, the Legislative Council had irregular sessions, sometimes meeting on six days every year. Unofficial members occasionally complained that the agenda for such meetings reached them too late, and in one case one hour before the meeting began.[2] At such times, the Nigerian unofficial members found it inconvenient to hold private consultations before the proceedings of the Legislative Council began.[3]

The fourth function attributed by Harding to Legislative Councils was their likely usefulness as a check upon official extravagance. The unofficial members in Lagos urged both retrenchment and approval by the Legislative Council before, not after, expenditure. In May 1906, when the Legislative Council debated advances in excess of the financial vote, Egerton and the other members unanimously accepted C. J. George's motion that 'in future all expenditure be approved by this Council before being undertaken'.[4] The government, however, explained that difficult means of transport and communications between Lagos and the outlying districts made it impossible to obtain prior

[1] CSO. 7/1/4, Legislative Council Debates, 12 December 1904.
[2] *Southern Nigeria Gazette*, 18 August 1909. Legislative Council Debates, 30 July 1909.
[3] *Southern Nigeria Gazette*, 27 October 1909, Legislative Council Debates, 6 October 1909.
[4] *Southern Nigerian Gazette*, 27 June 1906, Legislative Council Debates, 31 May 1906.

approval of expenditure in certain cases if unnecessary delays were to be avoided.[1]

A further embarrassment for the unofficial members arose when their approval was sought for expenditure which the Governor had already discussed with the Colonial Office. For example, in May 1906, when they had the opportunity of discussing the list of offices and scale of salaries under Egerton's Amalgamation scheme, C. J. George, O. Johnson and C. Sapara-Williams urged such retrenchment as would not jeopardise efficiency and economic development. Egerton, however, claimed that an expenditure of £160,000 on personal emoluments in a colony with an annual revenue of more than £1 million was not extravagant.[2] When their protests were rejected, Obadiah Johnson pointed out:

> The unofficial members are placed in an awkward position when conclusions arrived at and sanctioned by the Secretary of State are placed before us for adoption. We cannot do anything. Our protests will always be a barren protest... It seems only fair that local matters should be looked into thoroughly.[3]

The question of what the Nigerian unofficial members called 'Command' votes was reopened by Sapara-Williams in January 1911 during the discussion of the supplementary loan of £200,000 to be granted by the government of Southern Nigeria to Northern Nigeria for railway extension in the latter territory.[4] Sapara-Williams regarded the approval sought as a 'Command' because that supplementary loan had already been sanctioned by the Secretary of State. Kitoyi Ajasa wondered whether the Secretary of State's earlier sanction did not compromise the unofficial members' liberty in voting. Egerton, however, reassured them that they were free to vote 'one way or the other on any motion brought before the Council'. Eventually, that supplementary loan received the endorsement of the Legislative Council.

At times, the unofficial members showed an ambiguous attitude towards government expenditure, occasionally urging retrench-

[1] Ibid.
[2] *Southern Nigeria Gazette*, 13 June 1906, Legislative Council Debates, 25 May 1906.   [3] Ibid.
[4] *Southern Nigeria Gazette*, March 1911, Legislative Council Debates, 31 January 1911. An initial loan of £1,230,000 granted by Southern Nigeria for railway construction in Northern Nigeria had already been approved by the Secretary of State for the Colonies.

The Executive and Legislative Councils

ment, but at other times putting forward proposals which entailed increased expenditure. They criticised government extravagance in railway construction. Their criticisms in December 1904, however, failed to prevent the approval of the other members of the Legislative Council to the government's bill to raise a loan of £2 million for railway extension.[1] The Railway Department's extravagance continued and so provided ample material for the Macaulay pamphlet. Nor did criticisms by the Nigerian unofficial members in May 1906 check a further source of extravagance whereby the widows of officers who died before reaching pensionable age received full pensions instead of half, as proposed by Sapara-Williams, George and Johnson.[2]

The colonial chaplaincy and church question provided by far the most glaring aspect of government extravagance which the unofficial members of the Legislative Council condemned more on grounds of principle than for the sums involved. The colonial church question whose history in Lagos dates from 1875[3] was revived by Egerton in 1905 and effected between 1909 and 1910. The stipend of the colonial chaplain who was to serve the European members of the colonial church had a salary scale of £400–20–500 with a duty allowance of £80 a year, both of which the Legislative Council approved. Under the same scheme, the government wanted the public to contribute £1,500 towards the building of the desired colonial church while private donations would provide the rest.

Sapara-Williams, a Wesleyan, objected to this sum of £1,500 being provided for in the Estimates of Expenditure (1910) on three principal grounds. He said that if the 400 Europeans in Lagos desired a church of their own, they should pay for its erection. He cited the precedent in 1906 when, in his opinion, the Legislative Council 'properly' rejected a request for government financial assistance made by Muslims in Lagos for the erection of their central mosque. He maintained that various denominations in Lagos built and supported their own churches privately.[4]

---

[1] *Lagos Government Gazette*, 24 December 1904, Legislative Council Debates, 14 December 1904.
[2] *Southern Nigeria Gazette*, 23 May 1906, Legislative Council Debates, 11 May 1906.
[3] Omu, F. I. A.: *The Nigerian Newspaper Press* (Ph.D. thesis), Ibadan 1965, p. 236.
[4] *Southern Nigeria Gazette*, 18 August 1909, Legislative Council

Opposition to the scheme also came from sources outside the Legislative Council: from the ranks of Christians, Muslims and heathens who were thus called upon to finance a church for the minority of European residents in Lagos. In a strongly worded petition to the Colonial Office in September 1909, the people of Lagos considered the colonial chaplaincy and church scheme one of 'segregation and separation in religious matters' and maintained that the twenty-odd 'constant worshippers' out of the 400 European residents in Lagos could be conveniently accommodated in the available churches there.[1]

John Holt, another consistent critic of government extravagance and exponent of economy, waded into the colonial chaplaincy and church question against the government despite his own contribution to the private donations. He resented the idea of asking Africans to pay for 'a white man's church'. He believed that churches, like shops, should follow the laws of supply and demand but doubted whether the demand for a colonial church for European residents actually existed in Lagos. He expressed strong opposition to the principle of borrowing to build a church on the grounds that it represented evidence of 'economic wickedness' and contravened the strict Biblical teaching: 'Owe no man anything'.[2]

Some Liberal Party members of the British Parliament were equally critical of the colonial chaplaincy and church scheme proposed by Egerton. To them the question of principle was far more important than the sum involved. J. Seely tried to assuage them by citing other precedents in British imperial history to justify the use of public funds for religious purposes. In March 1910, Seely quoted such current examples as the Straits Settlements, Hong Kong, the Federated Malay States, Mauritius, Seychelles, Ceylon, British Guiana, Trinidad and Southern Nigeria.[3] C. Strachey of the Colonial Office considered the creation of the chaplaincy in Lagos 'a mistake'.[4] Egerton, however, expressed no repentance. As a lawyer, he quickly advanced the precedents

---

Debates, 30 July 1909; *Southern Nigeria Gazette*, 4 October 1909, Legislative Council Debates, 6 October 1909.

[1] *Macaulay Papers*, vol. 4/2, Petition dated 20 September 1909.

[2] *E.D.M.P.* F/8, Holt to Morel, 8 October 1909.

[3] CO. 520/98, MP. 7921, Memorandum in Seely's handwriting attached to H. J. Wilson, M.P., to Seely, 20 March 1910.

[4] *Ibid.*, minute by C.S.

Sir William MacGregor

Sir Ralph Moor

Dr Obadiah Johnson

The Rt. Rev. James Johnson

nearer Southern Nigeria – the examples of the Gold Coast where the government contributed £9,000 to support its colonial church in Accra, and the Northern Nigeria government which had spent an unspecified sum to build and maintain its colonial church at Lokoja.¹ He did not, however, succeed in convincing O. Johnson of the C.M.S. nor C. Sapara-Williams, the Wesleyan – the Nigerian unofficial members then present – to withdraw their opposition, but their objections were, in the end, disregarded by the Legislative Council.

On other occasions, the Nigerian unofficial members of the Legislative Council appeared to cast doubts over their sincerity in urging retrenchment and economy. They expressed a desire to increase the allowances granted to Prince Eshugbayi *Eleko* who from 1901 headed the Dosunmu-Oyekan House in Lagos. In 1905, they wanted his allowance increased from £250 a year to £300 but Egerton rejected their proposal.² The government, however, approved their recommendation in March 1903 that the stipends for the White Cap chiefs, amounting to a total expenditure of £300 a year, be increased.³ The Nigerian unofficial members' interest in higher emoluments for civil servants included their plea in March 1904 that the inadequate salaries of clerical and other staff be reconsidered. That proposal Acting Governor Moseley promised to submit to the Secretary of State for the Colonies.⁴ Again no one objected when the Legislative Council approved, in December 1907, the huge sum of £1,000 a year increase in Egerton's emoluments (including duty pay).⁵

The conflicting attitudes of the official and unofficial members to the question of expenditure on personal emoluments was best illustrated in the proceedings of the Legislative Council's select committee appointed to report on the Estimates of Expenditure for 1910. The unofficial members urged salary increases for the British police magistrates, comptroller of customs, assistant superintendents of police and superintendents of police, whereas

[1] *Southern Nigeria Gazette*, 27 October 1909, Legislative Council Debates, 6 October 1909.
[2] *Lagos Government Gazette*, 5 April 1905, Legislative Council Debates, 1 March 1905.
[3] CSO. 7/1/4, Legislative Council Debates, 2 March 1903; 16 March 1904.
[4] *Ibid.*, Debates, 15 and 17 March 1904.
[5] *Southern Nigeria Gazette*, 22 January 1908, Legislative Council Debates, 4 December 1907.

the official members found no justification for this. All the unofficial members, except O. Johnson, wanted the salary of the British Inspector-General of Police increased, but the official members refused. The unofficial members demanded more stipends for the White Cap chiefs of Lagos, but the officials declined. The unofficial members further considered the emoluments of the conservator of forests excessive, but the official members did not agree. Both official and unofficials, however, agreed that the post of inspector of agriculture for British West Africa, then under consideration by the Colonial Office, constituted a 'superfluous and unnecessary luxury'.[1]

What, then, was the value, if any, of unofficial checks upon the expenditure of public funds? The Nigerian members' assessment is best illustrated by the disillusionment expressed by Sapara-Williams in October 1909. Soon after the consideration of the Estimates for 1910 at the committee stage in the Legislative Council, he observed:

> If 'the keen but always absolutely fair criticisms' suggested by the Native Unofficial Members are to be ridden over in such a deplorable and roughshod manner by the Official Members as depicted so very clearly in every line of this Report . . . then I for one must record my extreme regret that I should have been called upon to make such useless sacrifice of my time.[2]

The evidence adduced so far indicates that the unofficial members of the Legislative Council did not uniformly succeed in determining the items and scale of government expenditure. This was partly a result of the inadequate representation of the masses of consumers who ultimately bore the burden of the indirect taxation which provided the government with the bulk of its revenue. It was above all a clear manifestation of the inability of the few unofficial members of the Legislative Council to alter the locus of power and authority under the new régime.

Using Harding's criteria, and relating these to the activities and limitations of the unofficial (mainly Nigerian) members, there is considerable justification for the view that the Legislative Council as then constituted had very limited value even for the

[1] *Southern Nigeria Gazette*, 27 October 1909. Report of the select committee on the Estimates of Expenditure for 1910.
[2] *Ibid.*, Legislative Council Debates, 6 October 1909.

The Executive and Legislative Councils

African community in Lagos, let alone the millions of other Nigerians in the protectorate who were not represented there.

In general, neither the Executive Council nor the Legislative Council altered the nature of the mild autocracy which developed under the Crown colony system of government as it operated in Southern Nigeria. The next chapter will ascertain whether in matters of judicial administration the people of Southern Nigeria had their interests adequately protected at a time when Britain continued to expand and strengthen her authority in parts of the emergent Nigerian state.

6 Law, Justice and Ministerial Duties

BLENDING THE OLD AND THE NEW

The apparatus of law courts in Southern Nigeria was a blend of Western European and African forms and standards of justice. Before 1908, the white man's courts comprised the Supreme, Divisional and District Commissioners' Courts which adopted the British model. Native courts and councils were reorganised on the African model. Links were, however, provided through the intricate procedures for appeals which in certain cases went to the Judicial Committee of the Privy Council in Britain.

The mixing extended to the law itself. In certain cases, the Supreme Courts of the Protectorate of Southern Nigeria and Lagos Colony and Protectorate recognised the common law of England, the doctrines of equity and the statutes of general application as they operated in Southern Nigeria as well as those aspects of Nigerian customary law which were not 'repugnant to natural justice, equity and good conscience' nor incompatible with the existing legislation.[1] At first, the British authorities hardly realised the serious dangers which lay in such attempts to mix two kinds of law.

The mixing process distorted the customary law and seriously threatened its validity in parts of Southern Nigeria. At first the judicial hierarchy failed to take much notice. Later, in their judgment in the famous *Eleko* case, in March 1931, the Lords of the Judicial Committee of the Privy Council expressed an opinion which, *mutatis mutandis*, could also be applied to the period before 1914. Their lordships then observed:

> An interesting question arose at the hearing as to the modification of an original custom to kill into a milder custom to banish. Their Lordships entertain no doubt that the more barbarous

[1] CO. 588/1, The Supreme Court Proclamation, 1900 (No. 6 of 1900). The Supreme Court Ordinance, 1876 (No. 4 of 1876).

customs of earlier days may under the influences of civilisation become milder without losing their essential character of custom. It would, however, appear to be necessary to show that in their milder form they are still recognised in the native community as custom, so as in that form to regulate the relations of the native community *inter se*. In other words, the Court cannot itself transform a barbarous custom into a milder one. If it still stands in its barbarous character it must be rejected as repugnant to 'natural justice, equity and good conscience'. It is the assent of the native community that gives a custom its validity, and therefore, barbarous or mild, it must be shown to be recognised by the native community whose conduct it is supposed to regulate.[1]

This pronouncement had a relevance which transcended the limitations of the *Eleko* case and the customary law concerning deportations and banishment. It could also apply to the modifications in such practices as infanticide, ordeals and the death penalty in witchcraft accusations and offences, reparation in certain cases of homicide, severe penalties for theft, human sacrifices and the like.

At the various stages of the judicial process in Southern Nigeria, the series of law courts exercised their power of modification in several cases which did not necessarily go as appeals to the Privy Council. Thus, they helped to modify the content of customary law without considering the effects of their action among a largely illiterate population.

The mixing process also extended to the personnel of the newly-organised or regulated Native Courts or Councils, where British political officers sat with 'warrant holding' chiefs. Serious human problems eventually resulted.

The dual rôle of native courts and councils as judicial and administrative institutions left the door half-open to instances of cases settled 'politically': for instance the land disputes of the Eastern and Central Provinces of post-1906 Southern Nigeria.

The judicial system revealed further problems which we will now examine, starting with the problems of the Supreme Courts and their Divisional and District Commissioners' Courts and their personnel.

[1] *Macaulay Papers*. Privy Council Appeal No. 42 of 1930, Judgment delivered on 24 March 1931. For some details of the *Eleko* case see Chapter 7.

The Evolution of the Nigerian State

THE STRUCTURE AND RÔLE OF THE BRITISH JUDICIARY

Before 1908, Southern Nigeria had two Supreme Courts and corresponding sets of Divisional and District Commissioners' Courts. By subsequent amendments,[1] the Lagos government adapted its Supreme Court Ordinance, 1876, to meet its needs after 1886 when the colony had administration independent of the Gold Coast. These amendments, which remained in force until 1908, provided for the colony the Supreme Court and Divisional and District Commissioners' Courts.[2] By Orders in Council of 18 March 1899 and 13 March 1901,[3] the railway areas in the Egba and Ibadan territories became districts under the Supreme Court Ordinance, 1876. The jurisdiction of the Supreme Court in Yorubaland expanded under the judicial agreements of the period 1904–8.

Despite protests from Administrator A. Moloney and Chief Justice S. Smith of Lagos, the Colonial Office passed the Order in Council of 24 September 1886 under which the Gold Coast Supreme Court became the Court of Appeal for Lagos. The British government, however, revoked that Order in Council in 1889 and issued a new one on 5 July 1889 under which appeals from the Lagos Supreme Court went to the Privy Council.[4] This in turn was replaced by another Order in Council of 15 February 1909 after the amalgamation of the two Supreme Courts of Lagos and the former Protectorate of Southern Nigeria in 1908. By the 1902 amendment[5] to the Supreme Court Ordinance, 1876, the Supreme Court of Lagos comprised the Chief Justices and other judges of Lagos, of the Gold Coast Supreme Court and of the Supreme Courts of the Protectorates of Northern and

---

[1] Speed, E. A.: *Lagos Revised edition of Ordinances and Orders & rules with appendix*, London 1902, pp. 14–140. Amendments to Ordinance No. 4 of 1876 by Ordinances 3 of 1883, 7 of 1884, 1 of 1888 and 8 of 1895. See also Elias, T. O.: *Groundwork of Nigerian Law*, London 1954, pp. 65–75.

[2] Speed, *op. cit.*, pp. 141–2. By an Order in Council of 31 July 1895, Lagos, Leckie, Badagry, Epe and Ikorodu were constituted into Districts under the Supreme Court Ordinance, 1876.

[3] *Ibid.*, pp. 143–5.

[4] Stallard, G. and Richards, E. H.: *Laws of the Colony of Lagos, 1865–93*, London 1894, pp. 952–5.

[5] CO. 148/3, Ordinance No. 24 of 1902.

Southern Nigeria. The Lagos Chief Justice, or the one acting, presided, the others sitting as puisne judges.[1] By consular instructions issued to MacDonald in 1891, the Supreme Court of Lagos acted as the Court of Appeal for the Oil Rivers Protectorate,[2] which had no 'Chief Judicial Officer' until the appointment of M. R. Menendez in August 1897.[3]

At the beginning of 1900, the judicial staff of the Protectorate of Southern Nigeria comprised Puisne Judge M. R. Menendez and Chief Justice H. G. Kelly. The Legal Department was headed by Attorney-General J. Winkfield, assisted by a police magistrate at Calabar, who in 1903, combined the duties of a judicial officer with those of a District Commissioner.

Under the new judicial system, Moor established three sets of courts – the Supreme Court, District Commissioners' and Native Courts.[4] The new District Commissioners' Courts replaced the old Consular Courts of the Oil Rivers Protectorate. From 1900, when the judicial appeal to the Lagos Supreme Court ended, the former Native Councils of the 1890s became legalised and better organised.

The Supreme Court Proclamation, 1900, established the 'Supreme Court' for Southern Nigeria. The new court comprised the Chief Justice and other judges appointed by the High Commissioner. In 1902,[5] Moor enlarged the constitution of the Supreme Court in cases of appeal. The new Appeal Court, or Full Court, consisted of the Chief Justices and other judges of the Protectorates of Southern Nigeria, Lagos, and Northern Nigeria. The Chief Justice or acting Chief Justice of the Protectorate of Southern Nigeria presided. Thus the territories making up Nigeria, though originally politically distinct, had in appeal cases a judicial unity about twelve years before their formal political amalgamation.

Despite the transformation in the meaning of a protectorate, particularly after 1895, the legal difficulty of an appeal to the Privy Council from the Supreme Court of such a protectorate as

[1] *Ibid.*, clauses 3 and 4.
[2] Elias, *op. cit.*, p. 83.
[3] FO. 2/132, Moor to F.O., 6 August 1897.
[4] CO. 588/1, The Supreme Court, Criminal Procedure, the Commissioners and Native Courts Proclamations, Nos. 6, 7, 8 and 9 respectively of 1900.
[5] CO. 588/1, The Supreme Court Appeal Proclamation, No. 15 of 1902.

Southern Nigeria persisted. Moor spotted that difficulty in 1902[1] and wanted it rectified, but no solution emerged before 1908.[2] The prospect of political amalgamation with the Colony and Protectorate of Lagos and the special position of Egbaland caused the abandonment 'for the present' of R. L. Antrobus' panacea for this and other difficulties. He had earlier hoped to find a solution through the annexation of the Protectorates of Southern Nigeria and Lagos to 'the King's dominions' and their subsequent erection into 'a new colony'.[3]

The 1906 amalgamation notwithstanding, the Supreme Courts at first remained separate. In 1907 Attorney-General E. A. Speed pointed out the inconvenience of having separate Supreme Courts and Supreme Court Ordinances, drawing special attention to the difficulties in transfers and the service conditions of the judicial staff, and the anomaly of having one Chief Justice in the Legislative Council and leaving out the other.[4] In a second memorandum,[5] Speed referred to the difficulties, under the existing dual system, in executing imperial legislation and advocated a single Supreme Court for the colony and protectorate.

The Colonial Office appreciated Speed's points but could not solve the problem of getting rid of one of the two Chief Justices until Chief Justice Nicoll retired for health reasons towards the end of 1907.[6] The other Chief Justice, Kelly, was allowed to retire on 'abolition of office'.[7]

Egerton thus effected the amalgamation of the Supreme Courts on 31 March 1908. A. W. Osborne, the former Attorney-General of the Gold Coast, had the distinction of being the first Chief Justice of the newly-amalgamated Supreme Court. From 1 April 1908, therefore, a single Supreme Court Ordinance[8] applied to the colony and protectorate.

The amalgamation further simplified the previous difficulty

---

[1] CO. 520/16, Moor to C.O., 19 November 1902.
[2] CO. 588/3, Ordinances 3 and 14 of 1908.
[3] *Ibid.*, minutes by R.L.A., dated 17 October 1903 and 15 July 1904.
[4] CO. 520/44, Egerton to C.O., 23 March 1907, enclosure.
[5] CO. 520/45, Egerton to C.O., 4 May 1907, enclosure.
[6] Sir W. Nicoll died on 6 February 1908.
[7] CO. 520/33, MP. No. 42303, minute by F.G.A.B.; CO. 520/54, C.O. to Kelly, 21 September 1907.
[8] CO. 520/95, F. S. James to C.O., 15 August 1910, enclosure; CO. 588/3, Ordinances 3 and 14 of 1908 and 9 of 1909; CO. 588/4, Ordinance No. 4 of 1912.

Law, Justice and Ministerial Duties

in extending to the protectorate certain imperial statutes. By section 2(1) of the Southern Nigeria Protectorate (Imperial Statutes Extension) Order, 1911, the Admiralty Offences (Colonial) Act 1849, sections 7 and 11 of the Evidence Act 1851, the Foreign Tribunals Evidence Act 1856, the Evidence by Commission Act 1859, the British Law Ascertainment Act 1859, and the Evidence by Commission Act 1885, were extended and applied to 'the Protectorate of Southern Nigeria as if it were a British possession'. By section 2(2) of the same order, jurisdiction in these acts was vested in the Supreme Court of Southern Nigeria.[1]

Similarly solved about the same time was the old problem of how to cut the direct links between the judiciary and the legislature through the Chief Justice's *ex officio* membership in the Legislative Council. In June 1905 Egerton had maintained that the 'principle' of allowing the 'Head of the Judiciary' a seat on the Legislative Council was 'inexpedient'.[2] In April 1906, Chief Justices Nicoll and Kelly advised Egerton that 'the Chief Justice should *not* [sic] be a member of the Legislative Council' and that 'his duties should be made purely judicial'.[3] The Colonial Office, however, retained the Chief Justice (Nicoll) in the Legislative Council because of an alleged difficulty in getting 'a sufficient number' of Legislative Councillors.[4] Not until April 1908 did the Chief Justice cease to be an *ex officio* member of the Legislative Council.[5]

Osborne's appointment as the new Chief Justice of the amalgamated Supreme Court illustrated the strained relationship between the judiciary and the executive branches of a colonial government such as post-1906 Southern Nigeria's. Osborne emphasised his claim to the headship of the Judicial Department and urged consultation by the Governor in appointments affecting the judicial staff. He also attempted to make the judiciary independent of the executive, and finally, in 1909, adopted, according to H. B. Cox of the Colonial Office,[6] 'the novel' and 'somewhat unpleasant'

[1] CO. 520/110, Council Office to C.O., 9 March 1911, enclosure – Order dated 4 March 1911.
[2] CO. 147/175, Egerton to C.O., conf. 20 June 1905.
[3] CO. 147/179, Egerton to C.O., 14 April 1906; CO. 520/59, Egerton to C.O., 23 February 1908.
[4] CO. 147/179, C.O. to Egerton, conf. 10 August 1906.
[5] CO. 380/172, Instructions dated 18 April 1908.
[6] CO. 520/83, Egerton to C.O., 20 November 1909, enclosure, and minute by H.B.C.

procedure of presenting a 'humble petition' to the Secretary of State. His main complaint concerned the Governor's transfer of judicial staff to the Legal Department and *vice versa*, sometimes without consulting him.[1] In his second petition of March 1910,[2] Osborne again claimed, though Egerton refused to concede, control over judicial staff appointments. The Colonial Office upheld the Governor's right to appoint judicial officers to permanent or temporary posts, but directed 'that as a matter of propriety, and for the better conduct of business, the Chief Justice should be consulted whenever it is possible to do so'.[3]

Short staffing caused further conflict between the Governor and the Chief Justice. Besides the Chief Justice there was, between 1909 and 1910, a judicial staff comprising four puisne judges, a police magistrate for each of three provinces, an assistant police magistrate for the colony and a complement of registrars and clerks. District Commissioners came within the Judicial Department only as *ex officio* commissioners of the Supreme Court; otherwise, their duties were primarily executive. About the same time, the Legal Department had an Attorney-General, and a Crown Solicitor.[4] The local revenue, well over £1 million between 1906 and 1911 and more than £2 million in 1912, could have adequately covered the salaries of extra staff. But from 1906 Egerton spent more on economic development projects than on the administration of justice.

After 1906, political difficulties in the Eastern and Central Provinces added to the judicial problems. West African-born barristers and their touts harassed Egerton's administration, particularly after the amalgamation of the Supreme Court in 1908. Previously, these lawyers from Sierra Leone, Lagos, and the Gold Coast had the bulk of their private practice in Lagos.[5] In the Eastern and Central Provinces they used as intermediaries the touts who spoke the local languages and dialects. These agents

[1] *Ibid.*, enclosure – petition dated 12 November 1909.
[2] CO. 520/92, Egerton to C.O., 12 April 1910, enclosure.
[3] CO. 520/92, C.O. to O.A.G. (Southern Nigeria), 28 June 1910.
[4] CO. 520/83, Egerton to C.O., 20 November 1909, enclosures and minutes; CO. 520/91, Egerton to C.O., 8 February 1910, enclosures and minutes; CO. 520/92, Egerton to C.O., 12 April 1910, enclosures and minutes.
[5] Adewoye, O.: *The Legal Profession in Southern Nigeria, 1863–1943* (Ph.D. dissertation) Columbia 1968, pp. 89 and 102.

Law, Justice and Ministerial Duties

raked up past cases, increased the costs of cases brought before the British law courts and caused political instability.[1]

Both Egerton and Acting Provincial Commissioner Moorhouse agreed that West African lawyers such as S. Dove of Sierra Leone had fanned to flame the Nzekwe-Okonjor chieftaincy dispute in the Asaba hinterland which played into the hands of the *Ekumeku* Society between 1909 and 1910.[2] Touting by the agents of these lawyers also worsened the unrest in the Awka district in 1910.[3] Most of all they harassed Egerton's administration in disputes over the boundaries of towns and villages. The Supreme Court and its lower courts found such cases exceptionally difficult to handle because of the absence of qualified government and private surveyors whose evidence was vital.[4] With a substantial increase in the number and activities of the West African barristers practising in the Eastern and Central Provinces, the land disputes which previously had been settled 'politically'[5] became the subject of appeals to the British Courts, even though the latter lacked sufficient knowledge of African procedures. Consequently, an interminable series of appeals and frustrations in land disputes ensued. Occasionally, the executive solutions of boundary disputes accompanied punitive expeditions. In 1909 and 1910 when the boundary dispute between the Akunakunas and Abinis created unrest in the north-eastern part of the Eastern Province, Egerton restored order by sending in troops.[6]

To avoid further unrest the government in 1911 limited the jurisdiction of the Supreme Court in land cases to the 'more settled and developed portions of the protectorate in the Eastern and Central Provinces'.[7] The Chief Justice and the Attorney-General considered such reform necessary.[8]

The activities of West African lawyers and their touts raised other problems such as the legality of government actions taken

[1] *Ibid.*, pp. 119–20.
[2] CO. 520/93, Egerton to C.O., conf. 17 May 1910 and enclosure.
[3] CO. 520/93, Egerton to C.O., conf. 21 May 1910 and enclosure.
[4] CO. 520/94, Egerton to C.O., conf. 6 June 1910, enclosures.
[5] CO. 520/92, Egerton to C.O., conf. 5 April 1910, and enclosures.
[6] CO. 520/91, Egerton to C.O., conf. 14 February 1910, enclosures. CO. 520/91, Egerton to C.O., conf. 19 February 1910, enclosures. Until 1910, the Akunakunas and Abinis shared a common Native Court.
[7] CO. 520/103, Egerton to Harcourt 3 May 1911. This order was made under the Supreme Court Ordinance.
[8] CO. 520/92, Egerton to C.O., conf. 5 April 1910, and enclosures.

during punitive expeditions and patrols and the political solutions found to land disputes. On the new situation, Egerton wrote in February 1910:

> Hitherto Government action has never been questioned in the Courts but with native barristers at several stations in [the] Eastern and Central provinces, with agents wandering through the country, it is desirable that government action should be well within the statute law.[1]

The government's difficulties were accentuated by the fact that in the Eastern and Central Provinces the Supreme Court had exercised jurisdiction 'immediately on the heels of the troops'.[2]

These two provinces lacked the jurisdictional obstacles highlighted and sometimes solved by the judicial agreements of 1904–8 in the Yoruba parts of the protectorate. A principal feature of the Egba judicial agreement, in particular, had been the opposition of the E.U.G. to allowing lawyers to appear in the determination of matters involving the powers ceded to the British government and exercisable by the Supreme Court. The Eastern and Central Provinces further lacked control over the integrity of private legal practitioners in the Supreme Court and Divisional Courts – a control indirectly exercised in the Western Province by the Lagos press and enlightened public opinion, the keener competition among Lagos-based lawyers, and the presence there of the senior members of the Bar and Bench.[3]

Because of the jurisdictional difficulties in the Lagos Protectorate, the District Commissioners' Courts and similar tribunals became more important in the Protectorate of Southern Nigeria. Moor gave such courts special attention from 1900 when he was reorganising the judicial system.

In order to deal promptly with cases in areas where a sitting of the Supreme Court would mean undue delays, the High Commissioner had authority from 1901[4] to appoint special courts consisting of the District Commissioner and African chiefs sitting as assessors. These courts had the special duty of trying urgent cases in 'unsettled districts' – those without firm British administrative control.

[1] CO. 520/91, Egerton to C.O., conf. 19 February 1910, enclosure.
[2] *Ibid.*
[3] Adewoye, *op. cit.*, pp. 121–3.
[4] CO. 588-1, The Criminal Amendment Proclamation, No 12 of 1901, clause 62A.

Law, Justice and Ministerial Duties

District Commissioners in the Protectorate of Southern Nigeria and Lagos Colony and Protectorate became *ex officio* commissioners of the pre-1908 Supreme Courts. In the Protectorate of Southern Nigeria, they had authority, from 1 May 1900,[1] to exercise concurrently with the Supreme Court the powers and jurisdiction of a judge of the latter court.[2] Appeals from their decisions went to the Supreme Court and every monthly list sent by a Commissioner to the Chief Justice operated as an appeal in criminal cases. From July 1901,[3] the term 'Commissioner' included Divisional Commissioners, Travelling District Commissioners, Residents, District Commissioners and the Assistant District Commissioners.

AFRICAN TRIBUNALS IN THE PROTECTORATE OF SOUTHERN NIGERIA

Inferior to the Supreme Court and Commissioners' Courts were the native courts reorganised by Moor between 1900 and 1903.[4] Under the new system, the government established two sets of African tribunals – native councils and minor courts. The native council, presided over by the Commissioner in charge of a district, acted as a superior court to the minor court whose president was 'a native authority'. From 1903, the District Commissioner or his assistant had the power to preside over the sessions of any native court though in their absence the African vice-president or the senior member present took charge of the proceedings.

The power to appoint or dismiss members of the native courts lay with the High Commissioner. The government, however, failed to provide any specific legal procedure under the Native Courts Proclamations to guide him in performing these important tasks.

The native courts had power and authority to invite African assessors for consultation on customary law. They were allowed to enforce only African laws and customs 'not opposed to natural

[1] CO. 588/1, The Commissioners Proclamation, No 8 of 1900. This was amended by Proclamations Nos. 13 of 1901 and 6 of 1903.
[2] Elias, *op. cit.*, pp. 92–3.
[3] CO. 588/1, The Commissioners Amendment Proclamation, No. 13 of 1901.
[4] CO. 588/1, Native Courts Proclamations, No. 9 of 1900 and 25 of 1901; No. 17 of 1903; and No. 23 of 1903.

morality and humanity'. Each native council heard and determined appeals from the minor courts located in the same area. When a commissioner presided, a minor court had the same jurisdiction as a native council in the strictly defined categories of civil and criminal matters. Appeals from the native courts reached the Supreme Court through the District Commissioners' Courts.

Counsel, advocates, solicitors, proctors and attorneys were generally barred from participating in the proceedings of the native courts except by the special leave of the commissioner or court. Exceptions were made to allow authorised husbands, wives, guardians, masters and other inmates of a household to appear on behalf of plaintiffs and defendants at their own request.[1]

Every native court was vested with more than judicial powers. Its 'ministerial' powers allowed it to act as a conservator of the peace, execute any order or process of the Supreme Court or of its commissioners, and apprehend, detain and send to the Supreme Court and its commissioners persons accused of any serious offence or crime.[2]

Subject to the High Commissioner's approval, every native council had power to make, amend and revoke rules which embodied customary law for its own district, regulate and promote trade there, and generally provide for the peace, good order and welfare of the people under its jurisdiction.[3] These legislative powers which did not have the same force as 'proclamations' extended only to by-laws.

Funds for the courts came from the fees and fines which they imposed and collected. They were allowed to accept payment in cash or kind. From 1901, brass rods, manillas, tobacco, cloth and other trade goods, but not gin, were accepted from indigent litigants. Out of such funds, the members and clerks and other court functionaries were paid and authorised public works undertaken. Where necessary, the government provided additional financial assistance.[4]

A new Native Court Proclamation[5] passed on 22 March 1906 came into operation on Amalgamation Day (1 May) in the Central and Eastern Provinces. It repealed the former Native Courts Proclamations but retained, basically, their constitution, powers

[1] CO. 588/1, No. 25 of 1901.   [2] *Ibid.*   [3] *Ibid.*
[4] *Southern Nigeria Government Gazette*, 28 February 1900, Circular No. 86 of 1900; CO. 520/18, Moor to C.O., 7 January 1903.
[5] CO. 588/1, No. 7 of 1906, After 1908 it became an ordinance.

and jurisdiction as well as their dichotomy into native councils and minor courts. A new provision,[1] however, kept the judicial control of the native courts closely under the Chief Justice or other judge of the Supreme Court.

The 1906 proclamation consolidated and elaborated the existing provisions affecting appeals from the native courts to the Supreme Court in criminal and civil cases. Within certain defined limits, the criminal cases included in the monthly lists sent by the commissioners in charge of the native courts to the Chief Justice of the Supreme Court acted as 'automatic' appeals.[2]

By far the most remarkable feature of the proclamation was its application to 'native foreigners' – West Africans other than those of the Eastern and Central Provinces – 'as if they were natives of the protectorate'.[3] About 200 such 'native' foreigners consequently petitioned the Secretary of State in May 1906 praying for their exclusion from the provisions of this proclamation.[4]

The petitioners criticised the proclamation on two principal grounds, external and internal. On external grounds, they contended that the African laws and customs which would apply to them were uncertain and unwritten, that the members of the native courts were illiterate, and that there were serious differences of language and belief between them and the 'aboriginal natives'. On internal grounds, they held that litigants generally had no right of choosing the court members who would decide cases affecting them. They further maintained that native court members took no oaths and they feared the development of irregular proceedings. They criticised the want of proportion between fines and imprisonment in default of native court orders and decisions. They also attacked the exclusion of counsel from the native courts and the limitation of the provisions for appeal. In their view, the application to them of the Trade Credit and Native House Rule Proclamations would severely injure their commercial interests and circumscribe their personal freedom.[5]

Although the petitioners presented a strong case, Egerton

[1] *Ibid.*, clause 12.
[2] *Ibid.*, clauses 34 and 35. C.O. 520/47, Thorburn to C.O., 27 June 1907, enclosure; CO. 520/49, Thorburn to C.O., 26 September 1907.
[3] Ordinance 7 of 1906, clause 8.
[4] CO. 520/41, J. W. Maxwell to C.O., 3 December 1906, and enclosure.
[5] *Ibid.*, enclosure.

believed that as native court decisions were 'carefully scrutinised' by the political officers and the judges of the Supreme Court, there would be no injustice to litigants generally. He further maintained that 'when Native Foreigners come to Southern Nigeria they must be prepared to submit themselves to the laws of the country as in India and other parts of the world...'[1] Among Egerton's safeguards against injustice in the native courts were the provisions for automatic and ordinary appeals in the 1906 proclamation. The other lay in the Governor's authority to suspend or dismiss any native court member for abuse of power or inefficiency.[2] Despite the above theoretical guarantees, the Colonial Office ruled that the proclamation should apply only to 'native' foreigners 'of a comparatively uneducated and uncivilised type' and not to those in the 'larger towns' of the protectorate.[3] In those areas, such persons would have the benefit of the District Commissioners' and Divisional Courts of the Supreme Court. These concessions apart, there was no substantial amendment of the proclamation before 1914.

The operational difficulties began much earlier and continued much longer. In January 1903 Moor considered the native courts the bulwark of his administration.[4] Their real value, however, could be assessed only on the basis of how they worked.

The existence of these native courts posed a paradox. To prevent the existence of illegal courts and the reversion to such pre-colonial sanctions as ordeals and references to jujus and other secret cults, more native courts were needed in the areas under British administrative control and in those not firmly controlled. But the larger the number of these courts, the more difficult it became to supervise them effectively.

Moor's administration tried to handle this problem in several ways. A travelling supervisor of native courts was appointed to examine their accounts and other records and report on their working through the Secretariat to the Chief Justice.[5]

The travelling supervisor appointed between 1901 and 1902 at first worked with the clerical staff of the Judicial Department. From 1905, the government transferred the supervision of the

[1] CO. 520/43, Egerton to C.O., 21 February 1907.
[2] Ordinance No. 7 of 1906, clauses 34, 35, 40.
[3] C.O 520/43, C.O. to Egerton, 24 April 1907.
[4] CO. 520/18, Moor to C.O., 7 January 1903.
[5] CO. 520/8, Probyn to C.O., 9 August 1901.

administrative work of the native courts from the Judicial to the Political Department and attached the travelling supervisor to the Secretary's Office. From 1907, the Eastern Province alone had at Calabar and Opobo two African supervisors who travelled round the native courts in the province and checked on the spot the clerical and accounting work of the court staff.[1] Egerton continued Moor's policy and practice.

Through the monthly returns of attendance from the native court clerks, Moor's administration also tried to supervise the working of the native courts. Such returns had to be passed through the District Commissioners to the Judicial Department so that the Chief Justice could easily spot any neglect and take necessary action.[2] In August 1902 Moor sent Puisne Judge Menendez to inspect and report on the courts already established. Where Menendez found lack of effective supervision he reported accordingly, but generally, he considered the native court system 'excellent' and 'without parallel in West Africa'.[3] Menendez certainly underestimated, however, the operational problems encountered in establishing, maintaining and increasing public confidence in the re-organised native courts.

Between 1900 and 1913 some of these courts – particularly those which served Sapele, Obubra Hill, Benin City[4] – covered areas too large for effective supervision. Each court's perimeter was so large that it could have easily encouraged the existence of illegal native courts. The political officers entrusted with the detection of such illegal courts and the supervision of the official courts were too busy with other duties.

Other problems stemmed from the fact that the divisional, district and native court boundaries did not necessarily follow ethnic lines. Consequently, some native courts served people with different languages, customs and habits. In this category belonged the Okrika Native Council on Okrika island which served the mainland Eleme people,[5] the Benin Native Court area

[1] *Southern Nigeria Government Gazette* (*Supplement*), 1 July 1908, Annual report on the Eastern Province, 1907.
[2] CO. 520/18, Moor to CO., 7 January 1903. *Southern Nigeria Government Gazette*, 30 May 1903, Circular No. 145.
[3] CO. 520/18, Moor to C.O., 7 January 1903, enclosure – Report by Menendez.
[4] *Southern Nigeria Government Gazette*, 17 February 3 March, 17 March and 30 March 1905.
[5] Porter, J. C.: *Okrika Intelligence report*, 1933, p. 15.

which included the Ika people of Igbanke (near Agbor) and the court which served not only Auchi and Uzairue people but those of Wefa-Wano, Ekperi and Ukpilla.[1] The Epie-Atissas who attended the Sabagreia Native Court established in 1904 had up to 1933 only one member to represent them in that court. In its official report of 1935 the government noted:

> The Epies were always at a disadvantage because they were not understood in that court and could not understand the language spoken by members of the bench. An Epie man always had to take a friend to court who could understand Ijaw and act as interpreter for him.[2]

A further perennial problem of the native court system arose from the choice of members. Practice in such matters differed from place to place. In certain cases, the chiefs and people were consulted by the British political officers before 'warrants' were issued to the chiefs to become members of the native courts. In others, the arbitrary selection was determined by such considerations as loyalty, personal appeal, and assistance to the British officers.[3] Such unilateral appointments of native court members sometimes led to public protests which the British political officers usually ignored. For example, during District Commissioner A. L. C. Laborde's visit to Iyedi in the Central Province on 27 April 1907, the chiefs and people expressed their disapproval of Chief Ogwa's membership in the native court. Laborde however reported: 'I informed them in reply that Ogwa had been loyal and had helped the D.C. and the D.C. would help him.'[4] This open defiance of public opinion supported a chief who was 'friendly' with the government but displeased the majority who were thereby free to resort to illegal courts. Officers who behaved like Laborde helped to diminish public confidence in the official native courts.

At other times, the political officers who recognised their error in making wrong appointments tried to set things right. When

---

[1] Igbafe, P. A.: *Benin ander British Administration 1897–1938* (Ph.D. thesis) Ibadan 1967. pp. 281–2.

[2] Newns, A. F. F. P.: *Epie-Atissa Group Intelligence Report*, 1935.

[3] Afigbo, A.E.: *The Warrant Chief System in Eastern Nigeria, 1900–1929*, (Ph.D. Thesis) Ibadan 1964, pp. 75–6.

[4] CSO. 4/3/9, Report by Laborde on his visit to Iyedi, dated 9 May 1907.

District Commissioner F. Hives discovered that one Onye-eke, the priest of the *Kamalu* ju-ju, had gone to the extent of applying for and obtaining a warrant to sit as a member of the Oloko Minor Court in Bende district, he investigated Onye-eke's antecedents. Hives thereafter reported in 1909 that the latter's 'warrant would be returned for cancelling'.[1] By 1912 'tremendous competition' had developed for warrants to sit as members of the Ebem (Edem) Native Court. Some of the warrants which the government had earlier given to the members of this Court were withdrawn, partly because of their misconduct, but mainly because most of them 'were not even chiefs'.[2]

The choice of native court members approved by the public had to be related to the wider question of the people's response to the new British administrative control which became firmer every year. As some of the reorganised native courts were not always intra-village but often inter-village assemblies with lots of paper work, the old and illiterate men with traditional authority hesitated to present themselves as court members because of their unwillingness and inability to travel long distances to court centres, difficulties in understanding the many written forms in court processes, distrust of foreign rule, and other causes. Consequently, young and ambitious men found it much easier to seek native court warrants.

Where many people competed for native court warrants, the political officer had to exercise his discretion, rightly or wrongly, without any reliable anthropological data to guide him. In the various districts of the Eastern Province, for instance, the government did not find it easy to choose between the *Okpala, onyeisi, oke-amadi, atamu, ishi-iwu, ozo* title-holder (among the Ibos); the *amanyanabo, waridabo* or House Head (among Ijo groups); the *ntoi, ekpuk* head, *Ekpe* runner, *ntul emang* (among the Qua, Ibibio-Efik and Ekoi clusters); and the host of impostors with legendary titles. In 1930 an official report recalled the exaggerated claims of the persons seeking warrants before 1914. Some of the applicants assumed such non-existent titles as 'King' to impress the political officers. Among the Ngwa Ibos, District Officer J. Jackson stated: 'As no such KING existed, and the village had to send somebody, they usually sent a youngish and intelligent man ... but in many cases slaves were sent and were deposed to

[1] CO. 520/80, Egerton to C.O., conf. 28 August 1909, enclosure.
[2] *Riv. Prof.* 1/32, Annual report on the Bende district, 1912.

be the "KING of ABA" or whatever his village might be.'[1] That such practices were not limited to the Ngwa Ibos was revealed by H. R. Palmer, an officer with considerable administrative experience in Northern Nigeria, after a visit to Southern Nigeria in 1914. Recalling his observations then, Palmer informed the Nigerian Legislative Council in February 1930 during the debates on the Women's Riots of 1929-30: 'I was there in 1913 [sic] and I found in many cases that many unimportant people had been made Chiefs, while the people's real Chiefs were living somewhere out of the way so as not to have any dealings with the Government'.[2]

Occasionally, members of the public put forward their own alternatives to the existing system of native councils based on the arbitrary selection of warrant-holding chiefs. In November 1911, the 'Commons of Bonny' – the young and educated element in that district – petitioned the Commissioner of the Eastern Province asking for 'a purely organised National Assembly or Council in place of the present ill-formed Native Council'.[3] The petitioners proposed a new council comprising the head chief, Prince William Dappa Pepple, other chiefs and about 24 'Commons' (including 12 educated Africans) elected annually. They demanded 'a Native Council entirely under the control of the Prince who with the twenty-four Councillors and Chiefs should decide all matters and keep proper records to be occasionally inspected by the District Commissioner or a Judge of the Supreme Court'. Prince Pepple's sudden death on 31 December 1911 dealt a crushing blow to their grandiose, though unique, scheme with a strong democratic flavour in an era of mild autocracy.

Both Moor and Egerton were plagued by the persistence of illegal, unofficial tribunals, despite the exclusive jurisdiction claimed for the official native courts. Among the strongest threats to the official courts were those of the secret cults and jujus or oracles. Moor had attempted to crush the Aro Long JuJu with a punitive expedition between 1901 and 1902 though its effectiveness, as we have seen, was questioned in 1908 and 1913.

Moor's administration did succeed in eliminating the illegal

[1] Jackson, J.: *Ngwa Clan Intelligence Report with a Supplementary Memorandum by E. J. G. Kelly*, 1930, p. 43.
[2] Legislative Council Debates, 5 February 1930, p. 141. In 1930, Palmer was Lieutenant-Governor of the Northern Provinces. His visit was in 1914, not 1913.   [3] *Riv. prof.* 1/25, Petition dated 17 November 1911.

Law, Justice and Ministerial Duties

arbitration centre provided by the *Eni* or Crocodile JuJu at the Isoko village of Uzere where accusations of serious offences had been dealt with through judgment by ordeal until 1903. Usually, the accused persons had to establish their innocence by swimming from the centre of the crocodile-infested lake to its edge, an ordeal which often ended in death regardless of guilt or innocence. The government persuaded the Uzere chiefs to end the ordeal, which they did by their joint resolution of 9 December 1903.[1] To deal with such matters legally, the government passed the Ordeal, Witchcraft and JuJu Proclamation, 1903.[2] From 1 April 1903, the government used this law to prohibit trials by ordeal as well as punish any accusation of witchcraft and the use of charms or ju-jus.

Despite this proclamation the illegal courts continued to compete with the official ones. Egerton who inherited this problem from 1904 sometimes handled it through punitive expeditions. Between 1904 and 1911 he ordered troops to destroy the *Agballa* oracle at Awka, the Ogoni cults of *Barigogara*, *Ebeka*, *Agbarato* and *Gberete* which had provided ordeal centres for the *Amarikpo* secret cult, the *Iyiobulo* cult at Allabia along the Andoni River, the *Amadioha* oracle at Ozuzu in Etche territory and the *Obonorio* cult in Owerri and Okigwi districts.[3] The above operations excluded those assigned to eliminate the judicial and political threat from the *Ekumeku* between 1904 and 1910.

Another problem arose from the practice of certain members of the official native courts who decided cases at home. In September 1906 four warrant-holding members of the Igbodo Native Court in Agbor sub-district were charged with 'exercising the authority of a Court in Igbodo, imposing fines, levying fees and ... keeping a number of boys whom they used as police'.[4] On conviction, the four men were sentenced to various terms of imprisonment. By impersonating *bona fide* government oflcials, resourceful persons similarly held illegal courts until they were caught and punished. The existing proclamations[5] against the

[1] CO. 520/24, Fosbery to C.O., 15 January 1904, and enclosure.
[2] CO. 588/1, No. 13 of 1903.
[3] CO. 520–26, Egerton to C.O., conf. 11 October 1904, enclosures, *Southern Nigeria Government Gazette* (*Supplement*), 11 September 1912. Annual report on the Eastern Province 1911.
[4] CO. 520/37, Egerton to C.O., conf. 7 October 1906, enclosure.
[5] CO. 588/1, The Uniforms Proclamation, No. 16 of 1903; and No. 11 of 1904 which came into operation on 1 January 1905.

use of discarded government uniforms by 'unauthorised persons' proved ineffective. In his report on the Eastern Province for 1906, Provincial Commissioner H. Bedwell observed:

From various Districts complaints of 'consul men' are reported. This form of living on the native is dying very hard. There appears to be little difficulty in securing some sort of 'so-so' uniform – in one case a water bottle and revolver were secured. This together with a page from a hymn book, or as in another case, a pocket French Dictionary completed the equipment. Such men do a great deal of harm among the native population and are difficult to catch. However, I am glad to say a good portion are eventually brought to justice.[1]

In many districts it was difficult to obtain competent and honest clerks for the native courts. Frequently, the semi-literate clerks exploited the illiteracy of the native court members and the masses of litigants. As long as the salaries of native court clerks remained low and unattractive,[2] few literate Africans applied for such jobs. Mary Slessor, a missionary of the United Presbyterian Church (later United Free Church), solved this problem in a unique manner. As vice-president of the Itu Native Court from May 1905 to November 1909,[3] she performed simultaneously the duties of a court clerk.[4] That solution the illiterate vice-presidents of the other native courts could not adopt.

Even the few native court clerks employed sought to make themselves masters and not merely servants of these courts.[5] Among illiterate members, the clerk with a veneer of Western European education tried to run the courts in the absence, through illness or other cause, of the British officers. The British officers engaged on other duties sometimes encouraged the magisterial rôle assumed by the court clerks. With Acting District Commissioner E. Dawson's approval, J. Halliday, the clerk of the Azumini Native Council in Aba district, constituted himself a watchdog over the members and interfered with their

[1] CO. 592/3, Annual report on the Eastern Province, 1906.
[2] The salaries of the clerks of 4 Native Councils in Ahoada district in 1909 varied between £48 and £166 a year. See *Calprof./2*, Handing-over notes of the Ahoada district dated 20 March 1909.
[3] Brian O'Brien, *She had a magic*, London 1958, pp. 217, 226.
[4] CO. 591/3, *Southern Nigeria Government Gazette*, 24 October 1906.
[5] Cmd. 468, p. 21.

Law, Justice and Ministerial Duties

proceedings.[1] Isaiah Yellow, another African clerk, sent to superintend the erection of a new court house at Okumoku in Degema district in 1907, assumed powers beyond his office and intimidated the chiefs who refused to provide forced labour for road work.[2] Yellow again illegally decided cases with other native court chiefs before his indiscretions there led to a 'rising' in 1907 in which the government houses already erected were destroyed. Government troops subsequently crushed the stiff resistance put up by 2,000 armed men from 23 nearby villages, and Isaiah Yellow was dismissed.

In another district, in 1910, two clerks of the Ebem (Edem) Native Court were successively convicted of 'unscrupulous methods of working the authority of the court for their own aggrandisement'.[3] The Ebem (Edem) Court experienced the tyranny of native court clerks, suffered from the allied problems of its members deciding cases privately and encountered serious rivalry from the illegal courts run by the *Akpam* secret cult in the same area.[4]

Such malpractices by native court staff contributed largely to the loss of confidence in their proceedings. In 1910, the government attributed unrest in Okigwi district to such activities. The people were refusing to obey summonses to attend native court sessions and sometimes assaulted court messengers. Most of the people in this district resorted to the *Obonorio* ju-ju at Ezimoha. To restore law and order the government sent troops and thus repeated the performance of the patrol which had visited the same area between 1905 and 1906. Reports obtained during the 1910 patrol revealed that large sums of money and smaller presents in kind had been given by litigants to the native court staff for their assistance 'in making cases good'.[5]

The effectiveness of the native courts suffered also from the adoption of Western European standards of justice. Traditional sanctions for such offences as theft could no longer be imposed by the new official native courts. Under the old order, theft, for example, had been punished in various communities by heavy

[1] *Calprof./*2, Aba quarterly report, 30 June 1908.
[2] CO. 520/48, Thorburn to C.O., conf. 5 August 1907; CO. 520/49, Thorburn to C.O., conf. 21 October 1907; CO. 520/50, Egerton to CO., conf. 6 December 1907.
[3] *Riv. prof.* 1/13, Annual report, Bende district, 1910.
[4] *Riv. prof.* 1/32, Annual report on the Bende district, 1912.
[5] CO. 592/13, Annual report on the Eastern Province, 1911.

fines, restitution or mutilation. Though 'barbarous' by Western European standards, these pre-colonial forms of punishment effectively checked thieving.[1] Under British rule, the maximum penalty allowed in a native court presided over by a British political officer could not exceed imprisonment for two years. Yet, in 'very many cases',[2] sentences imposing that penalty had been reduced by the Judges of the Supreme Court. Partly because of this and partly because of the stimulation of wants in the rapidly expanding import trade, such areas as Kwale, Aboh and Warri in the Central Province became notorious as 'thief towns', and the people there resorted to such unapproved sanctions as 'eye-cutting'.[3] The government had to send a patrol in 1911 to suppress this practice in the Aboh district.[4]

The Ezzas in the Abakiliki district of the Eastern Province also refused to bring criminal cases before the official native courts because of the ineffective punishment for theft. The government met their resentment by arranging for the British District Commissioner to be present in the native council so that he could impose the maximum penalty in trials involving theft.[5]

Very little authoritative information has so far been obtained on the conduct of the native court members in the Central and Eastern Provinces. Their functions extended beyond strictly judicial matters to those of acting as intermediaries between the public and the British authorities. Political officers used them to transmit such orders as the supply of carriers and the provision of forced labour for the maintenance of public roads and waterways.[6]

In this ministerial rôle, the native court members exercised considerable authority in their respective towns and villages so long as they enjoyed the confidence of the political officers.[7] Hence, several of them became more the envoys of the government than of the people they claimed to represent. The resultant discontent occasionally showed itself in mob violence which led to the burning of native court houses, assault on court messengers, and the disregarding of summonses to appear before these courts.

[1] CO. 520/115, F. S. James to C.O., 19 June 1912, enclosures.
[2] *Ibid.*
[3] *Ibid.* 'Eye-cutting' was a form of mutilating the eye.
[4] CO. 520/103, A. G. Boyle to C.O., conf. 30 May 1911.
[5] *Southern Nigeria Government Gazette* (*Supplement*), 11 September 1912, Annual report on the Eastern Province, 1911.
[6] Jackson, *op. cit.*, p. 43.   [7] *Ibid.*, p. 44.

Law, Justice and Ministerial Duties

In time, the public began to realise that such reactions resulted in bloodier confrontation with government troops during punitive expeditions and patrols.

The dual rôle of the members of the native courts exposed both the public and the functionaries themselves to considerable strains and stresses. To ensure that official orders were obeyed without stiff public opposition which would entail the use of punitive expeditions and patrols, the members of these native courts tried to be good government servants without sacrificing the confidence of their own people. By trying to bridge two stools they – or some of them – fell between them.

Some of the Native Court members who had been former war-leaders did not find it easy to preach and expect their old rank and file to appreciate the blessings of the *Pax Britannica*. Nor could the members who traditionally had been the priests of village cults spread the new doctrine of the evils of witchcraft and ordeals without being ridiculed by their former clients. Again, it was not quite practical to expect a ruler by traditional right, who under the old order initiated policy, to relegate himself unreservedly to the new rôle of an executive of a foreign government whose ways he did not understand. There were of course people who assumed the new rôle loyally through gratitude to the government for giving them a share in the administration. But openly co-operative attitudes among a hostile public merely served to widen the gap of trust between the government and the governed.

Not all the people, however, longed for the return of the 'good old days'. To several chiefs and commoners alike, British rule offered greater freedom of movement, emancipation, employment opportunities, escape from ordeals and the like. Among the native court members and others there were perhaps cases of Sauls turned into Pauls. But whether the new doctrine was political, religious, judicial or a combination of these, the process of conversion sometimes proceeded through upheavals and other forms of restlessness among the members of the old faith.

THE ERA OF NATIVE COUNCILS IN YORUBALAND

The problems raised by the judicial and administrative rôle of the native courts were more disturbing in the areas where

The Evolution of the Nigerian State

British control was firmer and the choice of members more incautious. For the same reasons already given to explain the paucity of punitive expeditions and patrols in the Yoruba part of the Protectorate, the system of native councils there worked with less open friction.

In the reorganisation of native councils in Yorubaland, MacGregor improved upon the work of his predecessor McCallum who between 1897 and 1898 had set up such councils at Ibadan, Abeokuta and Oyo. Except in Abeokuta, the most revolutionary aspect of that reform arose from the British Resident's membership in the Oyo and Ibadan Native Councils which were vested with judicial and administrative functions.[1]

For Lagos Colony, McCallum had also adopted a measure which MacGregor later developed. In 1897 McCallum revived, under a new name, the office of Agent for Native Affairs created in October 1895. As the first Agent for Native Affairs, E. W. Blyden had taken care of the training of African junior civil servants, trade, Muslim education, relations with Ilorin and so on. In 1897 when the Native Advisory Board replaced the office of Agent for Native Affairs, Blyden continued as its secretary until his resignation in 1899.[2] Henry Carr succeeded him.

MacGregor, however, had no enthusiasm for the Native Advisory Board established, he said, to obtain 'carriers for certain expeditions'[3] at the time of the Anglo-French frontier problems along the Western part of Yorubaland. *The Lagos Standard* claimed that the Native Advisory Board which comprised chiefs, educated Africans, Muslims and 'Brazilian repatriates', held consultations and deliberations on African questions.[4] Between 1 November 1897 and 27 April 1899 – a period of 18 months – the Board met only ten times.[5] With the resolution of the Anglo-French border dispute, government interests in the Native Advisory Board lapsed until MacGregor revived it under another name as part of his Native Councils Ordinance, 1901.

[1] Aderibigbe, A. A. B.: *The Expansion of the Lagos Protectorate, 1863–1900* (Ph.D. thesis) London 1959, pp. 329–41; Atanda, J. A., *op. cit.*, pp. 113–14; Agiri, B. A.: *Development of local government in Ogbomosho, 1850–1950* (M.A. Dissertation) Ibadan 1966, p. 102.

[2] Gbadamosi, G. O.: *The growth of Islam among the Yoruba, 1841–1908*, (Ph.D. thesis) Ibadan 1968 (awarded 1969), pp. 275–99.

[3] CO. 147/144, MacGregor to C.O., conf. 20 September 1899.

[4] *The Lagos Standard*, 20 December 1899 and 29 May 1901.

[5] CO. 147/142, Denton to C.O., conf. 9 May 1899.

Law, Justice and Ministerial Duties

For MacGregor, the Native Councils Ordinance represented more than a strictly judicial question. He found it useful as a means of administering the Lagos Protectorate through its chiefs and indigenous institutions. The ordinance was necessary, said MacGregor, because the chiefs had lost power and prestige. Educated Africans and soldiers returning home challenged the chiefs' authority, which was further diminished by the abolition of the slave trade and the stopping or modification of tolls. MacGregor further noticed that 'as the position of the Chiefs was entirely undefined in any way European officers have very frequently caused serious trouble by arbitrarily setting aside the authority of the Chief, by intentionally ignoring him, or even by acting in direct opposition to his wishes, and that without reference to Headquarters'.[1] The chiefs therefore complained to MacGregor who found in the Native Councils Ordinance an adequate means of redress.[2]

The ordinance was severely criticised by the three Nigerian unofficial members of the Legislative Council, the A.P.S. and the Manchester Chamber of Commerce. They contended that it interfered with the internal affairs of the Yoruba states or provinces, contrary to the provisions of the nineteenth century treaties, agreements and pledges. They maintained that through the power of appointment of the members of the native councils, the Governor would upset the pre-colonial institutions of the people. Though willing to trust MacGregor to implement the provisions of this ordinance without any serious detriment to the best interests of the people, they felt reluctant to place similar confidence in his successor.[3]

Despite this opposition, MacGregor secured the passage of the Native Councils Ordinance on 4 November 1901 with its basic principles retained.[4] It provided for the constitution of Native Councils in the Lagos Colony and Protectorate and stipulated that action so taken should be notified in the government *Gazette*. Under this law, the colony had a Central Native Council

[1] CO. 147/157, MacGregor to C.O., conf. 11 November 1901.
[2] CO. 149/6, Legislative Council Debates, 24 September 1901.
[3] CO. 149/6, Legislative Council Debates, 24 September 1901; CO. 147/159, Fox-Bourne to C.O., 27 November 1901; CO. 147/164, Fox-Bourne to C.O., 18 March 1902; CO. 147/162, Manchester Chamber of Commerce to C.O., 11 February 1902.
[4] C.O. 149/6, Legislative Council Debates, 18 October 1901. *Lagos Government Gazette*, 16 November 1901, Ordinance No. 15 of 1901.

whose members were appointed by the Governor, its president. Its meetings would be special and sessional. Its main tasks involved giving the Governor advice on questions affecting 'the good government and the well-being of the native population' which he had submitted to it and making recommendations 'for the benefit of the native population'.[1]

At the same time, the government agreed to recognise the existing Provincial and District Councils. In their absence, the Governor had authority to confer with the chiefs concerning the constitution of such councils 'as far as can be ascertained in accordance with any established custom or usage . . .'. The principal or ruling chief 'recognised' by the government would preside over the Provincial or District Council. British officers in such councils would only 'assist' by 'giving advice or counsel'. The Provincial and District Councils had authority in matters of internal administration. They were responsible for the preservation of peace, the administration of justice and the protection and encouragement of trade and industry.[2]

Town and village councils constituted the last and lowest category of native councils under the 1901 law. Provincial or district councils, and failing these the Governor, had authority to establish town and village Councils to handle 'the business and administrative affairs' of their respective areas.[3]

The ordinance did not specify to whom the chiefs, as members of these councils, were ultimately responsible for the effective performance of the judicial and ministerial duties entrusted to them under this law. P. H. Ezechiel and R. L. Antrobus, however, agreed that the members of the reorganised native councils of Yorubaland owed their responsibility to the British government acting as the new 'paramount power'.[4]

An important difference in the native court system adopted by Moor and MacGregor, and later Egerton, lay in the rôle of the British officers who sat in these councils or courts. Under the Native Council Ordinance of the Lagos Protectorate, these officers sat as advisers, but in the native courts of the Protectorate of Southern Nigeria they assumed the rôle of presidents.

[1] Ordinance No. 15 of 1901, Part 1.
[2] *Ibid.*, Part 2 of the Ordinance.
[3] No. 15 of 1901, Parts 2 and 3.
[4] CO. 147/157, MacGregor to C.O., conf. 11 November 1901, minutes by P.H.E. and marginal comments by R.L.A.

Moor's native court system did not raise as much verbal opposition from the public, the A.P.S. and the European Chambers of Commerce as MacGregor's. In the Protectorate of Southern Nigeria, the public reacted sharply through mob violence after government proclamations. In Lagos, verbal protests, petitions and mass meetings usually preceded enactments. Among a largely illiterate public, few drew attention to the principle of 'treaty rights' in matters of conflict between the people and the government in the Protectorate of Southern Nigeria. In the Lagos Protectorate, these 'treaty rights' became the alpha and omega of non-violent objections to any government measures.

Public opposition in Lagos stemmed from the view that MacGregor's Native Councils Ordinance was a far-reaching innovation. It regulated the existing native councils but did not create them. The idea of regulating native councils in the Lagos hinterland was not new. MacGregor continued McCallum's policy when illness prevented the latter from regulating more native councils than those of Abeokuta, Oyo and Ibadan. MacGregor's Central Native Council developed from McCallum's Native Advisory Board. But, contrary to the precedent of the Native Advisory Board, there were no educated members in the Central Native Council and this constituted a major source of grievance to *The Lagos Standard*.[1]

Considered in contrast to the pre-colonial systems of government, the introduction by both McCallum and MacGregor of British advisers into native councils constituted an important novel element. Indeed, the success or failure of the conciliar system encouraged by McCallum, MacGregor and later Egerton depended very much on the relationship between advisers and advised.

A major defect of the Native Councils Ordinance, 1901, was the absence of a clear definition of the judicial functions of the Provincial and other Councils. In his Amalgamation report of 1920,[2] Lugard seized upon this defect and alleged that the native councils regulated by MacGregor's administration, and maintained by Egerton's, exercised their judicial functions without reference to the colony's Supreme Court. Lugard further stated that the native councils of Yorubaland had authority to inflict

[1] *The Lagos Standard*, 15 January 1902 and 18 February 1903.
[2] Lugard, F. D.: *Amalgamation report et seq.*, 1912–19, Cmd. 468, London 1920, p. 21.

sentences of death without review by the Supreme Court or by its lower courts.

On an earlier occasion, however, Lugard had expressed a different opinion. In June 1913 he had informed the Colonial Office that the Native Councils Ordinance had been enforced throughout the Lagos Protectorate (later Western Province).

> The Native Councils and Courts ... have not been allowed to inflict a death sentence, or to deal with British subjects, and have, in fact, been largely controlled by the local official. The right of executive interference has been equally asserted. Sir W. Egerton deported the Owa of Illesha [sic] for a time for misconduct ... [1]

Lugard was referring to the courts of the Yoruba provinces which had not concluded judicial agreements with the Crown. Lugard's remarks were made after he had studied memoranda submitted by Attorney-General Pennington, Chief Justice Osborne and such high-ranking political officers as F. S. James, who in March 1913 was the Provincial Commissioner in charge of the Western Province of post-1906 Southern Nigeria. In his report of March 1913, F. S. James observed:

> Although the Ileshas assert their independence ... yet we have undoubtedly acquired jurisdiction by usage. From the [Native] Council there is an appeal to the District Commissioner; and the District Commissioner on his travels hears cases and administers justice in the same way as a District Commissioner in the Central and Eastern Provinces ... Ondo is just the same ... Native Councils hear civil cases, except when one party says he would rather go to the District Commissioner ... The District Commissioner, when travelling, apparently does so as a Commissioner of the Supreme Court, and only recently in dealing with a case (civil), as it was beyond his powers, i.e. a matter of £400, he sent a letter down to the Supreme Court at Lagos, who issued a summons and sent it up to the District Commissioner to serve. This was done. This is asserting our jurisdiction with a vengeance.[2]

Besides, MacGregor, Egerton and their deputies occasionally stepped outside the strict provisions of the 1901 ordinance in

[1] *African (West) No. 1005 Confidential*, No. 6, Lugard to C.O., 30 June 1913.   [2] *Ibid.* Enclosure 3 in No. 6, dated 11 March 1913.

dealing with judicial administration. Quite often, without the formality of a supplementary judicial agreement, the Governor's *fiat* settled such matters. For instance, MacGregor fined and reprimanded the Bashorun of Ibadan in 1900 because, with the support of his council, he had tried and executed two burglars without reference to the British Resident there.[1] In 1901, MacGregor advised the Alafin of Oyo that cases of homicide should be tried by the Lagos Chief Justice.[2] Even in Egbaland, where the question of jurisdiction remained seriously in dispute, MacGregor intervened to make it clear to the E.U.G. in 1901 that the Oluwo of Ilawo and the Ogboni chiefs who had executed Akiode for theft could not be above the law and the restraints which British standards of justice demanded in such matters.[3] In September 1901, MacGregor declared it unlawful for the provincial chiefs to order the execution of their subjects without trial and without reference to the Governor for advice.[4] It seemed strange that such a prohibition was not contained in the 1901 Native Councils Ordinance.

In some ways, the judicial agreements with Abeokuta, Ibadan, Oyo, Ife and Ijebu-Ode seemed a last-minute attempt to rectify that omission. By considering the Ijebu-Ode judicial agreement superfluous, the government gave the impression that it preferred the acquisition, through usage, of jurisdiction in judicial matters since there were more native councils than judicial agreements.

Egerton could not necessarily be regarded as a do-nothing Governor in matters connected with the native councils in Yorubaland. His administration passed the Statute Laws Revision Ordinance, 1905, under which it amended the Native Councils Ordinance, 1901, by substituting the words 'the proper exercise of the civil or criminal jurisdiction vested in or usually exercised by the native authority' for the words 'the administration of justice' in the principal ordinance.[5] Thereafter, the convention developed to prevent the infliction of the death penalty by any native council without the Governor's consent.[6]

---

[1] CO. 147/149, MacGregor to C.O., 19 June 1900.
[2] CO. 147/155, MacGregor to C.O., 21 May 1901.
[3] CO. 147/156, MacGregor to C.O., 19 July 1901, enclosures.
[4] CO. 149/6, Legislative Council Debates, 24 September 1901.
[5] Ordinance No. 4 of 1905, clause 13.
[6] CO. 520/84, Egerton to C.O., 16 November 1909, enclosure 3.

In his 1920 report, Lugard declared that during the administrations of MacGregor and Egerton the Native Councils Ordinance, 1901, remained 'practically a dead letter'.[1] C. W. Newbury held a similar view, with reference to Badagry and 'most of the Western Province'.[2] Both these views need qualification.

The copious memoranda submitted by the judicial, legal and political staff to Lugard in 1913 on their own fields of administration under MacGregor and Egerton clearly showed that they did not regard the ordinance, as a dead letter. Indeed, Lugard's main dispatch enclosing these memoranda[3] also revealed his belief then that the ordinance operated throughout the Western Province. It is nevertheless true that in Yorubaland legal uncertainties concerning jurisdiction precluded its uniform application.

In their respective local studies, B. A. Agiri on Ogbomosho, J. A. Atanda on Oyo, S. A. Akintoye on the *Ekiti-parapo*, O. O. Ayantuga on the Ijebu and G. D. Jenkins on Ibadan have confirmed that in its application in these parts of Yorubaland, the Native Councils Ordinance, 1901, led to serious political and other strains.[4] I agree with them.

Despite the perennial problems of legal jurisdiction, MacGregor, Egerton and their deputies tried to implement the ordinance as much as they could. For instance, they exercised the right of intervention in appointing members, as the ordinance allowed, but made sure that they sanctioned the choice of the African authorities. The two educated additional members whom MacGregor approved for Ibadan province in 1903 had been those proposed 'spontaneously', he said, by the Bale and Council of Ibadan.[5] Between February and May 1904, Acting Governor C. Moseley three times intervened to settle disputes among the members of the Ijebu-Ode Native Council as a result of the Awujale's dislike of the presence of Christian and Muslim mem-

---

[1] Cmd. 468, p. 21. Also quoted by Perham, M.: *Native Administration in Nigeria*, p. 74.

[2] Newbury, C. W.: *The Western Slave Coast and its Rulers*, Oxford 1961, p. 193 ff.

[3] *African (West). No. 1005 Confidential*, 15 May 1913–27 January 1914.

[4] Akintoye, *op. cit.*, pp. 336–41. Atanda, *op. cit.*, pp. 126–50. Agiri, *op. cit.*, pp. 117–22. Ayantuga, *op. cit.*, pp. 324–35. Jenkins, G. D.: *Politics in Ibadan* (Ph.D. Dissertation), Evanston 1965, pp. 176–85.

[5] CO. 147/167, MacGregor to Lyttelton, 31 December 1903. These were the Rev. J. Okuseinde and Mr Foster.

bers, who alleged that they had been persecuted because of their 'progressive and enlightened' views. In deference to the Awujale's wishes, Moseley accepted their replacement by sixteen heathen chiefs selected by the Ijebu-Ode indigenous authorities.[1]

In an attempt to settle misunderstandings between the Ilesha Native Council and the Travelling District Commissioner in charge of Ilesha, Egerton in 1905 removed the Owa for 37 days.

The Lagos Standard and the A.P.S. cited the difficulties of the Ilesha Native Council as examples of the dangers which they had earlier foreseen when MacGregor passed his ordinance.[2] The Ilesha Council again demonstrated some of the operational difficulties of MacGregor's conciliar system, particularly over the rôle of the political officer as the 'adviser' to the African authorities within and outside the native councils.

The troubles at Ilesha could be traced to MacGregor's administration. During his visit to Ilesha in April 1901, MacGregor had laid down what Travelling District Commissioner W. G. Ambrose later called the 'Ilesha constitution' – that is, the regulations for the reorganised Ilesha Council.[3] MacGregor then also settled the misunderstandings between Owa Ajimoko (Haastrup) and Travelling District Commissioner W. R. Reeve-Tucker.[4] In September 1903, MacGregor held a further meeting with the 'Ilesha Provincial Council' – the reorganised native council under the 1901 law – to settle the differences between the new Owa Ataiyero and Travelling District Commissioner W. G. Ambrose.[5]

The relationship between Ambrose and Ataiyero and the members of the Ilesha Council steadily deteriorated after MacGregor's departure. Egerton therefore had to heal a running sore at Ilesha. Judged by the records of the dispute between the Ilesha Council and its Travelling District Commissioners between 1901 and 1905, the Native Councils Ordinance there represented more

[1] CO. 147/169, Moseley to C.O., 13 February 1904. CO. 147/170, Moseley to C.O., 14 April 1904. CO. 147/170, Moseley to C.O., 3 May 1904.
[2] *The Lagos Standard*, 10 August 1904. CO. 147/178, Fox-Bourne to C.O., 16 January 1905.
[3] CO. 147/175, Egerton to C.O., conf. 10 June 1905, enclosure. CO. 147/155, MacGregor to C.O., 21 May 1901, enclosure.
[4] CO. 147/155, MacGregor to C.O., 21 May 1901. Owa Ajimoko Haastrup (April 1896 – 21 September 1901). Owa Ataiyero (1902–20).
[5] CO. 147/167, MacGregor to C.O., 31 December 1903.

a failure than a qualified success. The relationship between the Travelling District Commissioners and the Ilesha Council was nearly always difficult. Ambrose, for example, accused the members of the Ilesha Council (including the Owa) of receiving bribes from litigants and of refusing to heed his advice.¹ The Ilesha chiefs said that they received only 'presents', 'customary dues' and 'hush money'.²

During this era of bad feelings between the British Commissioner and the Owa in Council there were two foci of authority in Ilesha – the one at the Owa's palace and the other on Imo Hill. Consequently, the Ilesha Council became powerless and frustrated. The exasperated Owa appealed in vain to his people not to take their complaints to the rival court of the British Commissioner on Imo Hill.³ In these circumstances Oba Odo and the Loro – two Ilesha chiefs and members of the Native Council – incurred a penalty of two years' imprisonment in 1904 for extortion from litigants. They were arrested and detained on government orders but without the consent of the Ilesha Council. Oba Odo died in prison in May 1905 and the government thereafter released the Loro.⁴ Egerton made matters worse for the already discontented Owa Ataiyero by asking him during their meeting of 18 March 1905 'to accompany' the Governor to Benin City to see the relationship between the chiefs there and their District Commissioners.⁵ Ataiyero reluctantly obeyed and so left Ilesha between 19 March and 25 April 1905.

H. (later Lord) Samuel, M.P. for Cleveland in the House of Commons, considered the sight-seeing trip no less than a 'deportation'.⁶ The forced tour of instruction and sightseeing, or temporary deportation, perhaps made Ataiyero a wiser man but it certainly cost the Owa loss of dignity before his people and fellow African authorities. Acting on the advice of the Executive Council, however, Egerton rejected Ambrose's further recommenda-

¹ CO. 147/175, Egerton to C.O., conf. 10 June 1905, enclosure.
² *The Lagos Standard*, 10 August 1904. *The Lagos Weekly Record*, 5 November 1904. CO. 147/171, Egerton to C.O., 29 October 1904, enclosure. CO. 147/173, Fox-Bourne to C.O., 28 December 1904. CO. 147/178, Fox-Bourne to C.O., 13 February 1905.
³ CO. 147/175, Egerton to C.O., conf. 10 June 1905, enclosures.
⁴ CO. 147/171, Egerton to C.O., 29 October 1904, enclosure. C.O. 147/176, Thorburn to C.O., conf. 9 August 1905.
⁵ CO. 147/175, Egerton to C.O., conf. 10 June 1905, enclosure.
⁶ H.C. Deb. 4s. 143, 29 March 1905, 1517/18.

tion in July 1905 to deport the Owa and other members of the Ilesha Native Council permanently.¹

In London, H. R. Fox-Bourne of the A.P.S. had an interview with the Colonial Office and expressed A.P.S. disapproval of the Owa's 'temporary deportation'.² In Lagos, a deputation from the Lagos branch of the A.P.S., led by Sapara-Williams, met Acting Governor Thorburn to discuss the Ilesha situation.³ The protest increased when a petition, drawn up after a mass meeting in Lagos and purporting to represent 4,400 persons, was sent to Secretary of State A. Lyttelton. Among other things, the petitioners, including Herbert Macaulay, complained that MacGregor's policy of peace and conciliation through such institutions as the native council had been reversed by Egerton.⁴ Denying this, Egerton added that his 'wish and intention' was 'to maintain the authority of the native rulers both here [Lagos Protectorate] and in Southern Nigeria provided that authority is properly exercised'.⁵

The Colonial Office similarly maintained that there had been no reversal of MacGregor's assurance to the A.P.S. in 1902 to strengthen and support the African authorities. It pointed out, however, the 'implied necessary condition' in MacGregor's assurance – that the African authorities could only be supported so long as they exercised their authority 'faithfully and honestly in the interests of their communities' which were 'under the protection of Great Britain'. The Colonial Office did not consider a chief like the Loro 'a fit person' to retain in the Ilesha Native Council. It therefore found no justification for amending the Lagos Native Councils Ordinance, 1901, as the A.P.S., urged, 'to relieve it of all uncertainties of interpretation'.⁶

This review of Ilesha events from 1901 to 1905 showed that there the above conciliar system met its severest test. Something went wrong, not with the machinery *per se*, but with the persons required to work it. Neither the Travelling District Commissioners, particularly Ambrose, nor the Owa could be exonerated.

¹ CO. 149/7, Minutes of the Executive Council meeting, 24 July 1905.
² CO. 147/178, Fox-Bourne to C.O., 10 August 1905.
³ *The Lagos Standard*, 23 August 1905.
⁴ CO. 147/175, Egerton to C.O., conf. 16 July 1905, enclosure.
⁵ CO. 147/175, Egerton to C.O., conf. 16 July 1905.
⁶ CO. 147/178, Fox-Bourne to C.O., 16 January 1905. C·O 147/178, C.O. to the Aborigines Protection Society, 7 February 1905.

The experiment of having a British officer to advise the members of an unco-operative native council was a total failure in Ilesha. Although financial matters helped to widen the gulf between the British Commissioners and the Owa in Council, the ultimate cause of the rift came from the poor human relationship between the adviser and those he sought to advise. Each side suspected the other's good intentions and an atmosphere of distrust was hardly helpful to giving and taking advice. In 1906, when Egerton replaced Ambrose with F. C. Palmer, an atmosphere of better understanding resulted. The Owa at once reported to the Governor satisfaction with Palmer's services.[1]

That the Ibadan Council at first worked with less open friction than Ilesha's largely resulted from the good human relationship between Resident C. H. Elgee and the Bale and Council. As MacGregor's disciple, whom he had served as Private Secretary and Secretary to the Executive Council, Elgee understood both the spirit and the letter of the 1901 ordinance and of its sponsor's general policy towards the African authorities in Yorubaland. Elgee therefore adopted a 'pro-native' policy in Ibadan.[2] The Bale and Chiefs of Ibadan reciprocated Elgee's respect and allowed him to exercise great influence among them inside and outside the native council. Elgee's support for the chiefs became so great that he often paid little attention to the complaints of the masses.[3]

Egerton, however, did not, and could not, get too involved in the details of Ibadan politics. He preferred to see there the smooth running of the conciliar system. In doing so, he tried to check certain malpractices. For some time, the Ibadan chiefs were apathetic to the advisory court – the native council by another name – and preferred to settle cases privately. To represent them in the advisory court they sent 'messengers'. Dissatisfied with their procedure, Elgee attempted a further reform of the advisory court by bringing in two Ibadan-born 'Justices of the Peace' to sit with him in that tribunal in the absence of the chiefs. Egerton, however, sternly opposed that move. In his memorandum to Elgee in June 1905, Egerton remarked that the native council

> at any rate in Ibadan . . . has been allowed to degenerate from what it originally was and what it was intended by Sir William

[1] *The Lagos Weekly Record*, 18 August 1906.
[2] CO. 147/169, MacGregor to C.O., 2 January 1964, minute by P.H.E.
[3] Akinyele, I. B.: *The Outlines of Ibadan History*, Lagos 1946, pp. 77 and 79.

MacGregor to be, namely, a Legislative and Deliberative Assembly of the Chiefs and a Judicial Tribunal for the administration of Justice *by the chiefs* [sic] advised by the British Resident.[1]

The Colonial Office supported Egerton in asking Elgee to do all he could to rouse the chiefs' interest in the advisory court's proceedings, though it disapproved of private hearings and trials by the chiefs.[2]

Egerton's administration took nearly three years to reorganise the Ibadan Native Council. In 1908 it eventually reconstituted the Ibadan Native Court to function as the judicial branch of the native council. The new court had full jurisdiction except in matters concerning which the Supreme Court had assumed power under the 1904 judicial agreement.

The new Ibadan Native Court comprised the British Resident, the Assistant District Commissioner and the chiefs appointed by the Bale in Council subject to the Governor's approval. The Resident, or in his absence the Assistant District Commissioner, was its president. In their absence, the senior local chief present presided. The sittings of the Ibadan Native Court were public. Barristers and solicitors could not practise there. Appeals lay, as a last resort, to the Governor.[3]

A few years later, the judicial arrangements of 1908 were so radically transformed that the Ibadan chiefs became mere ciphers in the judicial administration of their territory. The British representative there, W. A. Ross, who succeeded Elgee in 1912, openly and gladly assumed direct control over the judicial affairs of the people of Ibadan and Oyo. Lugard's arrival in Nigeria in late 1912, as Egerton's successor, further strengthened Ross' hand in dealing with Ibadan affairs. Ross' assessment of the repository of power and authority in Ibadan affairs can be ascertained from his comments on a letter from the Alafin of Oyo to the Resident in December 1912 concerning the organisation and control of the law courts there. In his undated 'Note' Ross remarked:

[1] CO. 147/175, Egerton to C.O., conf. 13 July 1905, and enclosure.
[2] CO. 147/175, C.O. to O.A.G. (Lagos), conf. 5 October 1905.
[3] *Southern Nigeria Government Gazette* (*Supplement*), 28 October 1908, Native Court Rules and Regulations passed by the Ibadan Council on 3 July 1908 and approved by Egerton on 12 July 1908.

> The right of His Excellency the Governor to interfere in any case has never been questioned by the Alafin and his Chiefs ... with regard to Ibadan ... I reminded the Chiefs ... that I must record in writing what has been a recognised fact, namely, that the Resident, as representing the Governor, has the power at any time to remove any case from the Native Courts, and that his decision shall be binding.[1]

Under Ross' inspiration, the Ibadan Council in January 1913 passed a resolution which betrayed both the spirit and the letter of the Native Councils Ordinance, 1901. Ross' version of that resolution read:

> The [Ibadan] Council agreed that the Resident, as representing the Government, had the right to deal with any case that he thought fit to deal with, regardless of the Chiefs or their decision; and that his sentence should be binding on all parties.[2]

In those significant words Ross sounded the death-knell of MacGregor's ordinance but the bells tolled even more loudly during the 1912–13 phase of Lugard's administration. Both Ross' undated 'Note' and the resolution of January 1913 may have given Lugard the impression that generally the ordinance had been a failure or largely inoperative under the administrations of his immediate predecessors in Southern Nigeria.

A further act of omission by Egerton encouraged the idea that the 1901 Native Councils Ordinance ceased to operate the moment MacGregor left Lagos. As required under the 1901 law, MacGregor zealously gazetted[3] the native councils as soon as these were constituted in various parts of the protectorate. After the 1906 amalgamation, Egerton, however, concentrated on larger issues, particularly economic development, and failed to continue MacGregor's practice.

Those who argued that the Native Councils Ordinance, 1901,

---

[1] *African (West) No. 1005, Confidential*, p. 125.
[2] *Ibid.* Enclosure 7 in No. 6, Extract from Minutes of Ibadan Council, dated 20 January, 1913.
[3] *Lagos Government Gazette*, 15 February, 8 March, 12 April 1902; 10 May, 9 August, 23 August, 11 October, 1902; 21 February, 24 October, 21 November, 1903; 9 January 1904 (instrument not given); 30 January, 13 February, 12 March, 21 May 1904; 28 January, 4 February, 22 March, 16 August, 1905; 14 March 1903 (instrument not given).

became a dead letter did not reckon with the activities of the Central Native Council based in Lagos. They failed to realise that on 14 March 1913 Lugard himself presided over the last recorded meeting of the Central Native Council whose sessions thrilled its members under MacGregor's administration. But as the activities of the Central Native Council were more political than judicial, its rôle will be more conveniently discussed in the next chapter.

7 Direct and Indirect Administration

THE CENTRAL ADMINISTRATION

Between 1900 and 1914 in Southern Nigeria there emerged three approaches to administration – the soldier's (Moor's and Lugard's) of meeting fire with fire, the physician's (MacGregor's) of giving the war-weary Yorubas time to heal their wounds, and the lawyer's (Egerton's) of following precedent.

Moor learnt the details of colonial administration exclusively in West Africa with the additional benefit of his Royal Irish Constabulary experience. His was the soldier's approach. Laconic in expression, intolerant of opposition, he believed in action, in the prompt execution of his orders. Not hampered by Executive and Legislative Councils, not exposed to the full glare of a critical press, saved from the watchful eyes of a vocal educated élite, not unduly disturbed by the linguistic plurality of the people under his control, nor by arguments based on protectorate treaty rights claimed by the people, Moor cut through bureaucratic bottlenecks with the precision of a disciplined officer. Moor, Lugard and others of their kind showed that soldiers were not necessarily devoid of administrative talent.

As long as Moor controlled the affairs of Southern Nigeria he demonstrated independence in judgment and action subject only to the Secretary of State. Even so, John Holt, an outside but careful observer of men and measures in Southern Nigeria, implied that the influence of A. L. Jones on Moor continued until his retirement on grounds of ill-health in October 1903, and was instrumental in Moor's appointment, after his retirement, as head of the African section of the London Chamber of Commerce and as London Agent of the British Cotton Growing Association (B.C.G.A.), besides other business directorships.[1]

Between 1900 and 1903, however, Moor was more successful

[1] E.D.M.P. F/8, Holt to Morel, conf. 14 January 1909.

in handling military and political matters than those connected with economic development. His principal contribution to the history of the evolution of the Nigerian state lay in his giving the Protectorate of Southern Nigeria firm political and judicial institutions which remained practically unchanged until 1913. He concentrated on the many political and judicial questions awaiting settlement between 1900 and 1903, attending to matters of economic development as circumstances allowed. Trade and such development needed peace which Moor sought to provide through punitive expeditions, patrols and the system of native courts.

Moor adopted no consistent views on the African 'systems' of government. Sometimes he saw himself as an innovator;[1] at other times, when he considered the institutions of the former city-states of the Niger Delta, Moor maintained 'that their native systems of government should be strenuously upheld and enforced with such improvements as may from time to time be found for the general welfare of the people and the country'.[2] Moor consulted the coastal chiefs whenever he found it expedient; otherwise he made his own decisions. The cynical Holt hardly believed that Moor genuinely took the chiefs into his confidence before issuing and carrying out his proclamations. In May 1902 Holt queried: 'What Chiefs? Where? ... It would be well to ask for the names of these chiefs when they were consulted and if minutes of the meeting could be furnished.'[3]

It was MacGregor's administration in Lagos Protectorate, not Moor's in the Protectorate of Southern Nigeria, that provided the classical example of indirect administration.

Guided by his Far Eastern experience in Fiji and New Guinea, MacGregor willingly sought the African viewpoint during his administration from 1899 to 1904. In time, MacGregor achieved a 'pro-native' posture without being anti-European in the Yoruba-speaking parts of the evolving Nigerian state.

Chamberlain's choice of the patient and cautious MacGregor as Governor to replace McCallum was amply justified by MacGregor's record in Lagos. His principal contribution lay in building firm political and judicial institutions. MacGregor weathered many a political storm; he always kept cool and emerged

[1] CO. 520/15, Moor to C.O., 8 August 1902.
[2] CO. 520/12, Moor to C.O., 7 July 1901.
[3] *E.D.M.P.* F/8, Holt to Morel, 10 May 1902.

triumphant. His great asset was that he was prepared to wait to achieve his ends. He would introduce a draft bill, face severe opposition to it, weather the storm, delay action on it while negotiations continued and ultimately enact it with its main provisions unchanged.

In his practice of indirect administration, MacGregor showed courtesy to the Yoruba traditional élite without losing the dignity of his position as Governor. Whereas Moor had been generally allergic to African kingship, MacGregor found much pleasure in respecting and maintaining this institution in Yorubaland. Whereas Moor kept a measured distance between the Obongs of Calabar and others, MacGregor treated the Alake of Abeokuta and others as friends. The Yoruba chiefs similarly held Mac-Gregor in high esteem. To the Akarigbo of Shagamu, MacGregor proved himself the 'Natives' friend'.[1] Alake Gbadebo I also commended MacGregor for his 'pro-native' policy.[2]

The Colonial Office, however, did not approve of MacGregor's friendliness with the Yoruba chiefs, nor of his general administrative policy and practice in Yorubaland. Shortly before MacGregor left Lagos permanently to assume the governorship of Newfoundland, Permanent Under-Secretary M. F. Ommanney observed that the Governor had 'not been altogether a success'.[3] Judged on other grounds, however, MacGregor was an eminent success. His administration synchronised with the declaration of a formal, though ill-defined, protectorate over the Lagos hinterland in July 1901. Over this protectorate he sought to extend and consolidate British administrative control and ensure peace, preferring persuasion and personal influence to Maxim guns and other fire-arms. Except in the Itori and Kemta cases, he eschewed even the show of force.

MacGregor's governorship by peaceful methods contrasted sharply with other contemporary administrations in British West Africa. In Sierra Leone, Ashanti, Southern and Northern Nigeria, coercion became the principal means adopted by the Governors and High Commissioners to strengthen British authority.

MacGregor, on the other hand, preferred to obtain the co-operation of the chiefs and people of Yorubaland. Above all,

[1] CO. 147/161, MacGregor to C.O., 23 May 1902, enclosure.
[2] CO. 147/166, MacGregor to C.O., conf. 9 June 1903, enclosure.
[3] CO. 147/167, MacGregor to C.O., tel. 19 December 1903, minute by M.F.O.

MacGregor convincingly proved himself the right man in the right place at the right time. His charm and transparent honesty impressed such outside observers as John Holt. After interviews with MacGregor, Holt wrote in December 1902:

> The more I see of him the more I like him. He has a lot of humour in him. His knowledge is great, his experience of men and matters most varied and wide. His grip of many subjects is thorough. His energy and industry are wonderful. His aims are practical, his ideas sound, his humanity most praiseworthy, his native policy all we can desire. His crowning virtue is that of being a man of peace, patient and tactful and with an earnest wish to be just to his fellow creatures. He is honest beyond doubt.[1]

Despite the controversies over such measures as the Native Councils, Forestry and Newspaper Ordinances and the tolls question, John Holt continued to hold favourable views on the Governor and his administration. When it became known in July 1904 that MacGregor was leaving Lagos to govern Newfoundland, Holt informed Morel:

> MacGregor is not going back again to Lagos and I am really sorry for it. He has done excellent service for his country there. Above all he has been a man of peace. He has been most patient and tactful, and sympathetic in his dealings with the natives. He has tried to carry out our ideas of maintaining whatever is good in their institutions and to lead them in the work of administration. He is an honest man and upholds the character of our country for good faith and honour in dealing with natives. His native policy on the whole should meet with our warm approval. It is based on regard for native rights. He would make use of them in the government of their people . . . I feel his going will be a distinct loss to us. All his work will be undone and possibly great mischief may result if he be followed by a man who has no love for the natives. He has wrought very hard and very ably. He has loved his work too. His previous knowledge and experience fitted him for the post he held . . . I should not be suprised to see Egerton placed over a united Lagos and Southern Nigeria. If that is to be they had better also include Northern Nigeria and make one administration of the three provinces.[2]

[1] *E.D.M.P.* F/8, Holt to Morel, 13 December 1902.
[2] *E.D.M.P.* F/8, Holt to Morel, 11 July 1904.

MacGregor's successor, W. Egerton, assumed the administration of the Protectorate of Southern Nigeria on 2 April 1904; from 26 September 1904 he administered in addition the Lagos Colony and Protectorate. His appointment was a major step towards the amalgamation of both territories.[1] Before 1904 Egerton had had no West African experience. His previous career, lasting twenty-three years, had been spent in the Malay peninsula. He none the less later adjusted himself adequately to West African conditions and tackled with some success the problems of his new administration.

During their first meeting in Britain, Egerton impressed Holt as 'a pacific man' who promised 'well'. Holt used that opportunity to give Egerton 'some broad and candid hints on administration'. Thereafter, Holt found in Egerton's honesty the only praiseworthy aspect of the entire administration which he often criticised for its extravagance.[2]

The triumvirate of Moor, MacGregor and Egerton provided interesting differences in methods of administering a developing colonial state. Moor's administration was memorable for its method of 'pacification' through coercion, MacGregor's as a study of indirect administration, and Egerton's for economic development.

Egerton, however, failed to stamp his administration with as much personality as his two immediate predecessors. It is not surprising. He performed a task which the Colonial Office had previously entrusted to two men. Initially, his difficulties were formidable. The combined territories were large, the means of internal transportation and communications poor, and his staff not as numerous as would be expected for efficient administration.

Largely because of his concentration on economic development, Egerton failed to give his subordinate staff the much needed central direction by means of political memoranda similar to Lugard's in Northern Nigeria. This major defect in Egerton's administration was reported to Lugard in 1913 by F. S. James, whose administrative experience since 1896 had been obtained in the Central and Eastern Provinces (the former Protectorate of Southern Nigeria) and who was now Provincial Commissioner in charge of the Western Province. He reported:

[1] CO. 520/27, MP. No. 21004, minute by R.L.A. on 8 June 1904.
[2] *E.D.M.P.* F/8, Holt to Morel, 5 March 1904. *E.D.M.P.* F/8, Holt to Morel, 10 September 1908.

Direct and Indirect Administration

Since your departure I have been engaged principally in travelling and seeing for myself how things are. I must confess to a feeling of disappointment throughout, as the more one goes into matters the more evident is the want of any useful administration in the past. There is, of course, no question that this Province has been allowed to run itself from the early days. Before the amalgamation the various officers, on arrival out, were apparently ordered off to their respective districts, the great desire being that nothing more should be heard of them in Lagos ... After amalgamation there was certainly created a Provincial Commissioner for the Western Province ... After a few months his job was merged into the Secretariat ... It will thus be seen that, outside the Governor's visits, no inspection was ever carried out, and no control was, as a matter of fact, exercised over the various Political Officers, who were all acting, apparently, on lines laid down by themselves, with an occasional interruption – the result of a petition to the Governor.[1]

The problem of how to control the activities of the smaller men-on-the-spot was not limited to the Western Province nor to Egerton's administration. From 1896, F. S. James lived under the system which allowed the Commissioners in charge of the various districts much control over the day-to-day administration of their areas.

Egerton did not hide his indebtedness to his 'loyal', 'zealous', 'hardworking' and 'intelligent' civil servants. He told his audience at the Liverpool banquet of the West African Trade Association in October 1905 that the 'great progress' made in Southern Nigeria represented the work of 'the most excellent officers' he had there. Egerton then admitted that 'the bigger a country becomes the less a Governor can look into details for himself'.[2] Between October 1905 and February 1912, when he left Southern Nigeria to become the Governor of British Guiana, Egerton stuck to that idea of decentralised control over administrative details in the vastly expanded parts of the colonial state.

The political staff of the civil service occupied a unique position. Even among them, the District Commissioners and other

---

[1] *African (West). No. 1005 Confidential.* Enclosure 3 in No. 6, report dated 2 May 1913.
[2] *The West African Mail*, 13 October 1905, p. 682.

staff of equivalent status assumed a major rôle. As the government servant most directly in touch with the public, the District Commissioner wielded an influence for good or evil. Considering the varied nature of his functions – political, judicial, police, treasury, survey, postal, medical, sanitary and others[1] – it would have been unrealistic to appoint to this office only men with legal qualifications.

MacGregor disapproved of District Commissioners with only legal experience. He preferred persons with tropical experience and others acquainted with African institutions and British country life. Their duties, he thought, should be 'far more executive and administrative than legal'.[2] The Colonial Office, however, made it clear to MacGregor that the District Commissioner's judicial duties were as important as his executive ones,[3] and pointed out serious difficulties in obtaining the type of District Commissioners MacGregor desired.[4]

Though he himself was a lawyer, Egerton stated in May 1905 that he did not consider legal qualifications essential for District Commissioners.[5] Another official recommended that[6]

> ... a District Commissioner should be thoroughly sound in body and limb, with a clean bill of health in the past, and an excellent constitution to carry him safely through the future. He must be hard as nails and have 'nerves' of steel. He must be prepared to take kindly to 'roughing it', and be always ready to make the best of things and to take a cheery view of whatever may occur.

To these qualities should be added sound common sense and sane judgement, particularly in dealing with emergencies in remote areas without adequate guidance from the central secretariat. In his station, the District Commissioner was 'the administration' the people knew, not the distant and seldom seen high-ranking personnel at headquarters. In M. Perham's phrase, the District Commissioner was 'the uncrowned king' of his district.[7]

---

[1] Partridge, C.: *Cross River Natives*, London 1905, pp. 12–31. Morel, E. D.: *Nigeria: its peoples and its problems*, London 1911, pp. 65–6.

[2] CO. 147/145, MacGregor to C.O., conf. 19 October 1899.

[3] CO. 147/155, C.O. to MacGregor, conf. 3 June 1901.

[4] CO. 147/145, MacGregor to Chamberlain, conf. 19 October 1899, minute.   [5] CO. 147/175, Egerton to C.O., 28 May 1905.

[6] Partridge, *op. cit.*, p. 25.

[7] Perham, M.: *The Colonial reckoning*, London 1961, p. 125.

The important rôle of the District Commissioners and other members of the political staff impressed and disturbed John Holt, the consistent critic of government autocracy and high-handedness whatever the skin pigmentation of the perpetrators. Writing to Morel in July 1906, Holt stated:

> A lot of the young fellows sent into our West African colonies for the purpose of administration are wholly unfit for the job. They have neither age nor experience to qualify them, whilst they have unlimited ideas of their own self-importance and contempt for the natives, out of whose labours they are living. They have only one idea of ruling, and that is by force. It is high time that with all the multiplicity of laws we have for regulating traders and natives in these countries there should be some laws to govern the governors as well as those governed, and some check put to the arrogance and intemperate use of power which these young people possess, and use to the destruction of life and property of others ... [1]

EDUCATED AFRICANS AND THE CIVIL SERVICE

In January 1906, Holt proposed colonial policy guide-lines for Lord Elgin, the Secretary of State. He recommended the reduction in the number of British civil servants in West Africa, thereby saving nearly half the money spent on giving them accommodation, and demanded that West Africans be 'employed as much as possible in the administration'.[2] It is not clear whether these and other proposals made by Holt in his correspondence with Morel eventually reached the Colonial Office. Certainly the problems were already well known to them. In Lagos, Calabar, Accra, Freetown and other parts of West Africa, lived thousands of educated Africans. If allowed, these persons, some of them products of Christian missionary education from the nineteenth century, could have readily served in the higher branches of the British West African public services. But quite often, they received little or no encouragement from the government.

In May 1883, *The Lagos Times* advocated the employment of 'negro officials in West Africa'.[3] In September 1911, *The Lagos*

[1] *E.D.M.P.* F/8, Holt to Morel, 13 July 1906.
[2] *E.D.M.P.* F/8, Holt to Morel, 21 January 1906.
[3] *The Lagos Times*, 23 May 1883.

Standard urged that West Africans who, in its opinion, had better qualifications than expatriates to understand the languages and institutions of the people should be given District Commissionerships.[1]

There was a noticeable change in attitude to employing West Africans in their own public services. The earlier, nineteenth-century, policy of associating educated West Africans closely with the British administrations gave way to one which emphasised British personnel during the first four decades of the twentieth century.[2]

For example, in the Gold Coast, G. E. Ferguson had distinguished himself as a political agent during the 1880s and 1890s. Similarly, other West Africans there had served as District Commissioners.[3] In Sierra Leone, J. C. E. Parkes, as Secretary for Native Affairs, W. Hughes, as Assistant District Commissioner, and E. Faulkner, as Assistant Colonial Secretary and District Commissioner, worked efficiently in the central administration from the 1880s.[4] In Lagos Colony, the nineteenth century promised opportunities for capable West Africans who sought careers in the civil service. Of these, the most successful included C. Forsythe, the Postmaster and Treasurer who left the public service in 1874; C. D. Turton, the Acting Crown Prosecutor, District Commissioner, Acting Colonial Secretary, Auditor, Coroner, Inspector of Prisons, Stipendiary Magistrate and Puisne Judge of the Supreme Court on various occasions until the 1880s; I. H. Willoughby, A. C. Willoughby and A. Pratt who served as Superintendents of Police; and J. A. Otonba-Payne, the Registrar of the Supreme Court from 1877 to 1899.[5] In the Niger Coast Protectorate and later Protectorate of Southern Nigeria, the government at first

[1] *The Lagos Standard*, 13 September 1911.
[2] Kimble, D.: *A Political History of Ghana*, Oxford 1963, pp. 61–109. Symonds, R.: *The British and their Successors*, London 1966, p. 119. Kopytoff, J. H.: *A Preface to Modern Nigeria*, Madison 1965, p. 214.
[3] Sampson, M. J.: 'George Ekem Ferguson of Anomabu', *TGCTHS.*, vol. 2, 1956, pp. 30–45.
[4] Fyfe, C.: *A History of Sierra Leone*, London 1962, pp. 479, 492, 538, 545, 615.
[5] Kopytoff, *op. cit.*, pp. 205–12. Adewoye, O.: *The Legal Profession in Southern Nigeria 1863–1943* (Ph.D. Dissertation) New York 1968, pp. 40–5. CO. 147/1, Freeman to C.O., 10 June 1862. CO. 147/24, Hennessy to C.O., 4 November 1872, enclosure. *The Lagos Observer*, 19 June, 17 July, 11 September 1884. CSO. 1/1/12, Moloney to C.O., 3 November 1888.

encouraged only loyal political agents. That trend continued after 1900. Between 1903 and 1904, the Protectorate of Southern Nigeria's Political and Administrative Department included J. Coco Bassey, the Native Political Agent at Itu since 17 April 1899; R. Henshaw, Agent for Native Affairs at Calabar since 11 June 1904; and A. Ja Ja, Native Political Agent at Aba since 1 April 1898.[1] Other West Africans on the staff were not even people of this territory. These included J. H. Mills, the Assistant Secretary, and J. E. A. Jones, the travelling supervisor of native courts.[2]

From the turn of the century, however, the numbers of West Africans in key administrative posts in Lagos Colony began to dwindle. The highest political administrative appointment given to a West African in Lagos thereafter was that occupied by Henry Carr, the Assistant Colonial Secretary for Native Affairs, 1900-1, and third Assistant Colonial Secretary, 1903-6, before he reverted to the Education Department where he later acted as Director of Education. Henry Carr's career in the Central Secretariat illustrated MacGregor's difficulties in his attempts to encourage an educated African of considerable talent and promise. From September 1899 MacGregor felt the lack of an African in the Secretariat, who could concentrate on African questions and provide continuity in policy during the temporary absence of the British officials.[3] Henry Carr's loyalty and high reputation in Lagos encouraged MacGregor to recommend him for the post of Assistant Colonial Secretary for Native Affairs. Carr also had an excellent record as the Inspector of Schools since 1892. In 1897 he had succeeded E. W. Blyden as the Secretary to the Native Advisory Board. In 1901 when MacGregor founded the Lagos Institute[4] to educate public opinion on questions affecting the administration of the colony and protectorate, Carr was easily chosen as its first Vice-President.

In combining the duties of Acting Inspector of Schools with his secretariat work, Carr showed less enthusiasm for the latter.[5]

[1] CO. 473/4, Southern Nigeria Blue Book, 1903. CO. 473/5, Southern Nigeria Blue Book, 1904.
[2] CO. 473/4, Southern Nigeria Blue Book, 1903.
[3] CO. 147/144. MacGregor to C.O., conf. 20 September 1899. CO. 147/145, MacGregor to C.O., 9 November 1899.
[4] MacGregor became the first president. In 1901, the Institute had about 100 members.
[5] CO. 149/7, Minutes of the Executive Council meeting, 18 March 1901.

This involved constant travelling between headquarters and the various towns of Yorubaland for discussions with the chiefs and people there, so that through him new District Commissioners and other officers could obtain information on local politics.[1] But Carr, who often complained of gout and rheumatism, dreaded exposure to rain and dampness through such travelling.[2] Clearly Carr used this fear merely as an excuse, since his job as Inspector of Schools equally entailed travelling. Basically, Carr preferred his inspectorate work to that of Assistant Colonial Secretary, partly because of his special training, but mainly through fear that after MacGregor's departure the Secretariat assignment would not be equally emphasised.[3] Accordingly Carrr reverted to his earlier post as Inspector of Schools between 1901 and 1902, while an African first class clerk filled his place in the Secretariat.[4]

Through MacGregor's further persuasion, Carr returned to the Secretariat in 1903 as the third Assistant Colonial Secretary to deal with the increased clerical work and provide the missing link in the continuity of work there.[5] Carr once more wanted to return to his 'true vocation' in the inspectorate,[6] and was allowed to do so after the 1906 amalgamation.

The Carr episode marked MacGregor's failure to bring a trusted African close to the central administration. Disappointed by Carr's reluctance to serve in such a capacity, MacGregor did not try others.

The Carr experiment assumed further significance, coming as it did after the plea made by the Rev. James Johnson, in an interview with Antrobus at the Colonial Office in July 1899, for the enlistment of African co-operation in working the machinery of government, and the removal of any barrier of 'race or colour' in government appointments from Africans with 'intellectual capacity, a good character and general fitness'.[7]

The reply which Johnson received during or after that inter-

[1] CO. 147/144, MacGregor to C.O., conf. 20 September 1899.
[2] CO. 147/153, MacGregor to C.O., 13 September 1900. CO. 147/165, MacGregor to C.O., conf. 28 April 1903.
[3] CO. 147/170, Moseley to C.O., conf. 23 May 1904, enclosure.
[4] CO. 147/154, MacGregor to C.O., 22 March 1901, minute by P.H.E.
[5] CO. 147/165, MacGregor to C.O., conf. 4 February 1903.
[6] CO. 147/170, Moseley to C.O., conf. 23 May 1904, enclosure.
[7] CO. 147/147, J. Johnson to Chamberlain, 27 December 1899. Johnson became an Assistant Bishop in the diocese of Western Equatorial Africa in February 1900.

view is not recorded. A letter from James Johnson in December 1899 stated the representations made orally during the interview in July. The unchallenged comments on that letter made by a member of the Colonial Office's staff disclosed the official attitude then to the question of giving Africans high administrative posts. F. G. A. Butler of the Colonial Office then noted:

> When a first class native does appear, such as Mr Ferguson of the Gold Coast, and Dr Blyden and Mr Carr of Lagos, he gets reasonable recognition, but our experience of natives in high positions has not been one of undiluted satisfaction. It would be impossible to explain this to Mr Johnson, but I don't think his appeal on this score need cause us much searching of heart.[1]

Carr complained of a 'colour bar' during his interview with J. Seely in Britain in 1909. He resented the appointment, over his head, of E. G. Rowden as the Director of Education. In fairness to Rowden, he had been transferred from a similar post in the Gold Coast. Although Seely told Carr, 'that, broadly speaking, this Office was opposed to the imposition of a colour bar . . .', confidentially, he recorded: 'I am aware the colour bar does exist to some extent in West Africa . . . It may be that the prejudice is increasing as Mr Carr fears'.[2] C. Strachey of the Colonial Office recalled that there had been differences with the British officials in the Education Department in consequence of appointing Carr the Senior Inspector of Schools in May 1906 and of allowing him thereafter to act as Director of Education. The government, he said, could only support Carr that far. As a matter of general policy, Strachey emphasised: 'it is necessary to recognise that the administration of the West African Colonies is British, and that as long as this is the case, no native African can *expect* [sic] to be appointed to any but subordinate posts'.[3] Strachey believed that, academic qualifications apart, Africans hardly demonstrated as much capability as Englishmen in exercising authority. He also observed that Englishmen, especially artisans, objected to working under Africans. He therefore feared that the number of such Englishmen willing to serve in West Africa, already 'small', would be reduced to 'nil' if informed that they could receive orders from West Africans.[4]

---

[1] *Ibid.*, minute by F.G.A.B.
[2] CO. 520/87, MP. No. 40542, minute by J.S. dated 2 December 1909.
[3] *Ibid.*, minute by C.S. dated 10 December 1909.   [4] *Ibid.*

These considerations influenced the Colonial Office's attitude to a petition received in 1909 from four West African Medical Officers serving in Southern Nigeria. C. J. Lumpkin, O. Sapara, W. A. Cole and C. C. Adeniyi-Jones complained of their exclusion from the West African Medical Service since its establishment in 1902. To their disappointment they discovered that the Colonial Office's Committee appointed in 1908 to enquire into the recruitment, duties, organisation and emoluments of the West African Medical Staff still decided to exclude them in favour of their British counterparts. Through such exclusion they suffered loss of status and salary. At first, they had believed that 'colour bar' had been the only factor for their exclusion but after reading the report of the 1908 Committee, they realised that their professional qualifications, obtained in the United Kingdom, had not been fully recognised.[1]

Neither Egerton nor the Colonial Office met the objections of the petitioners. Egerton refused to plead for their inclusion in the West African Medical Staff and urged a subordinate status similar to that of India for West African medical doctors.[2] That colour constituted the main yardstick for their disqualification was clear in the comments made by A. Fiddian and C. Strachey of the Colonial Office. A. Fiddian maintained:

> It is possible that the [1908] Committee were biased. I confess that, for myself, I should not call in a native medical man if anyone else were available, and that the idea of a West African native attending on white women is one which I cannot bring myself to consider in a judicial spirit.[3]

C. Strachey put the deciding factor more frankly:

> The memorialists make a good debating point over the opinion of the Committee that men with rather second-rate 'professional capabilities' are good enough for purely native hospitals etc. The fact is, that their capabilities have nothing to do with the question. No matter how magnificent these might be, we should never get officers to fill our West African staff if they were informed that when they fell sick, they would be treated by black doctors.[4]

[1] CO. 520/83, Egerton to C.O., 6 December 1909, enclosure.
[2] *Ibid.*, minute by A.F., dated 10 February 1910.
[3] *Ibid.*   [4] *Ibid.*, minute by C.S., 28 February 1910.

Colour bar and racial prejudice continued to discourage the employment of more West Africans in the public service of Southern Nigeria. In 1911, G. D. Agbebi, a qualified engineer, trained in Britain, applied for service in the Public Works Department at Lagos. C. V. Bellamy, the Director of Public Works, repeatedly objected to employing Agbebi not on the basis of his professional standing but because of the probable effect of his employment on the subordinate British staff. Instead he recommended that Agbebi seek employment in private business as a contractor to the government or as an employee of the E.U.G., the Ibadan provincial government and the Lagos Municipal Board of Health.[1]

After a further interview with A. J. Harding of the Colonial Office, Bellamy stressed:

> I would here confirm the opinions expressed on Tuesday last that the appointment of Natives as Assistant Engineers in the P.W.D. would be unsuitable until in the process of time and with the progress of Technical Education we are able to employ Natives as Foremen of Works, but so long as we are obliged to employ only Europeans in this capacity it will be impossible to give any Native the position of authority as a Professional Assistant over Europeans, such as that of an Assistant Engineer under the present system.[2]

Agbebi had his chance at last in August 1912 but resigned in less than two years when he found his position and work in the Public Works Department intolerable.[3]

The cumulative effect of such discriminatory practices was an exceedingly high dependence on British personnel, even for the executive functions of government. Thus, the political and administrative staff for the Lagos Colony and Protectorate in 1900 comprised ten District Commissioners (attached also to the Supreme Court), a Resident at Ibadan, and three Travelling Commissioners.[4] All these officers were British. The same year, in the Protectorate of Southern Nigeria, the political staff consisted

---

[1] CO. 520/106, Egerton to C.O., conf. 12 October 1911, enclosure and attachment to MP. No. 35957.
[2] *Ibid.* C. V. Bellamy to Harding, 24 May 1912, attached to MP. No. 35957.
[3] Adewoye, *op. cit.*, pp. 65–6.
[4] CO. 151/38, Lagos Blue Book, 1900.

of four Divisional Commissioners, three Travelling Commissioners, ten District Commissioners, 25 Assistant District Commissioners and one Resident at Benin City[1] – also all British.

In 1912, the political and administrative department of Southern Nigeria comprised two Provincial Commissioners, two Assistant Provincial Commissioners and Provincial Secretaries, seven Senior District Commissioners, ten District Commissioners (first grade), 31 District Commissioners (second grade) and 79 Assistant District Commissioners.[2] Not one of these was African. Only a few of them held university degrees; several were either seconded from the British armed services or retired soldiers.

Correspondingly, the majority of Africans recruited into the government service occupied the lower rungs of the civil service ladder; they were clerks, interpreters, store-keepers, the rank and file of the military and police forces, native court clerks, messengers and so on.

This British dominance of the higher grades of the civil service in Southern Nigeria can be explained by certain basic and interrelated factors.

The link between malaria and the mosquito discovered by R. Ross in 1897–98 provided the major clue to the means of eradicating the malaria pestilence which had previously made West Africa the white man's graveyard. The wider implications of this discovery became known to the Colonial Office through P. Manson, its medical adviser.[3]

The subsequent interest shown in tropical hygiene and public sanitation by Moor, MacGregor and Egerton greatly improved the chances of European survival in Southern Nigeria. As a medical man, MacGregor particularly appreciated the importance of Ross's discovery and championed public sanitation programmes during his administration in Lagos.[4]

Generally in British West Africa, the progress made in public health satisfied Secretary of State Harcourt who informed Parliament in June 1912 that in the previous nine years, the death rate

[1] CO. 473/1, Southern Nigeria Blue Book, 1900.
[2] C.O 473/14, Southern Nigeria Blue Book, 1912.
[3] Dumett, R. E.: 'The campaign against malaria and the expansion of scientific, medical and sanitary services in British West Africa, 1898–1910'. *African Historical Studies*, vol. 1, no. 2, 1968, pp. 153, 161–2.
[4] *Ibid.*, pp. 181–4.

of expatriate officials there had dropped from 21 to 13 per 1,000 and the invaliding rate from 56 to 25 per 1,000.[1] Now long tenures in Nigeria were possible, such as the twenty years' service of F. S. James[2] and the career of W. A. Ross who stayed in the administration service of Nigeria for about a quarter of a century.[3]

In making appointments to the Colonial Service, the patronage system begun by Secretary of State Chamberlain and continued by his successors[4] also had much to do with the preponderance of British personnel in the public services of West Africa before 1914. The long-term effects of that system again depended on the chances of survival in West Africa of those already appointed.

Discrimination on grounds of colour was amply demonstrated by the Henry Carr episode in the Education Department, the plight of Doctors Lumpkin, Sapara, Cole and Adeniyi-Jones, and the G. D. Agbebi case in 1911.

Strachey's emphasis on the government's desire to make its control British in word and deed gave aspirants of non-British descent very little chance for high civil service jobs in West Africa. Consequently, the civil service share of the spoils of empire-building went to reward deserving British citizens.

The Colonial Office's confidence was not always well-placed. Such outside observers as John Holt believed that some chosen officials lacked both age and experience. More crucially, such officers lacked adequate knowledge of the people and the institutions under their control.

THE RELEVANCE OF ANTHROPOLOGICAL DATA TO ADMINISTRATION

Hindsight indicates that a foreign power seeking to govern along indigenous lines needs a thorough, trustworthy knowledge of their institutions and general way of life.

As early as 1889 H. H. Johnston urged

> a thorough and scientific examination on the natural history and ethnology of these lands, so that we can be better guideed

[1] HC. Deb. 5s. 40. 27 June 1912, 528.
[2] *Who was who, 1929–40*, London, 1947.
[3] Atanda, J. A.: *The New Oyo Empire* (Ph.D. thesis) Ibadan 1967, p. 131.
[4] Kimble, *op. cit.*, pp. 61–109.

in our administration of them, both by increasing our knowledge of their natural resources, and by becoming more acquainted with the character of the races whom we are to rule.[1]

Few administrations in British West Africa took this seriously.

For a while, through bonus schemes for language study, the government expected individual political officers to acquire useful anthropological data by their own efforts. In Southern Nigeria such officials as W. A. Ross, G. S. Podevin, P. A. Talbot, C. Partridge, S. W. Sprotson and F. Hives undertook private anthropological studies in the Western, Central and Eastern Provinces. But as they were saddled with many official duties it would have been unrealistic to consider their investigations thorough and their findings authoritative.

In Southern Nigeria, the government made a significant departure from such amateur efforts in 1909 when it appointed for the first time a professional anthropologist. It is not clear whether the initiative for his appointment came from the Colonial Office or from Egerton. The government, however, restricted the activities of the first appointee, N. Thomas, to the Central Province of post-1906 Southern Nigeria.[2]

The Committee of the Royal Anthropological Institute, whose meetings A. Fiddian and C. Strachey attended as representatives of the Colonial Office, discussed the value of desirability of continuing Thomas' work. In 1910, the Committee expressed the

> emphatic opinion that in the interests of the efficient administration of these territories it is most desirable that enquiries of the kind carried out by Mr Thomas should be undertaken on a larger scale and for a more extended period. We are convinced that as the country is opened up and property increases in value there will continually be greater need for accurate knowledge of the people and their usages if mistakes which may entail serious consequences are to be avoided. That has been the experience of India and the principle involved seems equally applicable to Africa.[3]

[1] Johnston, H. H.: 'British West Africa and the trade of the interior'. Paper read on 15 January 1889. *P.R.C.I.*, vol. 20, 1888–89, p. 110.

[2] CO. 520/81, Egerton to C.O., 18 September 1909.

[3] CO. 520/99, Royal Anthropological Institute to C.O., 21 June 1910. The members of this committee were H. H. Risley, C. H. Read, R. R. Marett, A. C. Haddon, W. H. R. Rivers and S. H. Ray. See: CO. 520/99, Royal Anthropological Institute to C.O., 27 April 1910.

In Southern Nigeria, the views of the government on the value of Thomas' work differed. In 1909, Egerton expressed satisfaction that it would benefit the administration and facilitate the acquisition of a 'correct knowledge' of African institutions by the government.[1] Acting Governor F. S. James, however, complained that Thomas failed to take 'the trouble to keep in touch with the Political Officers in charge of the districts in which he has carried out his work . . .' Even so, James recognised that 'the real question at issue' lay in 'the ultimate value of anthropology in connection with the administration of native races rather than the qualities of the individual selected to carry out that work'.[2]

The available evidence does not indicate that Thomas' anthropological surveys between 1909 and 1913 had much influence on administration. In fact, as F. S. James contended in June 1912, 'an anthropologist is not always of service from an administrative point of view'.[3] About a year later, Lugard terminated Thomas' services on the ground 'that researches into native law and custom were best conducted by Political Officers'.[4]

In the light of subsequent experience in Nigeria and other parts of West Africa, there can be no doubt that between 1909 and 1913 the British authorities lost a valuable opportunity of making, and gaining from, detailed investigations into the institutions of the people whom they hardly understood and who scarcely understood them. The sad moment of realisation came during the Women's Riots in parts of South-Eastern Nigeria between 1929 and 1930. In the same context, the government failed to heed another warning after Thomas' dismissal. In 1926, W. G. A. Ormsby-Gore (later Lord Harlech) rightly emphasised, after a tour of British West Africa, the 'axiom that any system of administration or any plans for the progressive development of any African people must be based on a thorough knowledge of their history and their very varied characteristics'.[5] When, eventually, the government faced the bloody consequences of the Women's Riots, the acts of omission in the past were quite

[1] CO. 520/81, Egerton to C.O., 18 September 1909.
[2] CO. 520/115, James to C.O., 19 June 1912.
[3] *Ibid.*
[4] Cmd. 3784, 1931, p. 6. CSO. 1/19/59, Lugard to C.O., 11 September 1913.
[5] Cmd. 2744, London 1926, p. 12.

obvious. The comment made in 1931 by Lord Passfield, Secretary of State for the Colonies, on some aspects of these riots came too late. He drew attention to the danger of introducing direct taxation 'among a population of whom comparatively little was known'.[1]

It was more to the want of such information than to the absence of chiefs with central authority, or to so-called barbarism, that the frequent punitive expeditions and patrols in parts of Southern Nigeria between 1900 and 1913 should be traced. The disturbances of 1929-30 were more than mere tax riots, representing delayed reactions to the public grievances which had accumulated in the preceding decades.

So far in this work, an attempt has been made to portray the major problems of establishing a colonial state and maintaining the central administration dominated by British officials. Under the system of indirect administration as practised in Southern Nigeria until 1914, the governing or ruling class was made up of British officials, whereas Africans, particularly the chiefs, exercised no more than executive powers. It is now time to explore other aspects of that administrative trend.

THE RÔLE OF THE ELEKO AND WHITE CAP CHIEFS OF LAGOS

Since the British annexation of Lagos Colony in 1861, administrators there inherited the long-standing problem of what to do with ex-King Dosunmu and his descendants and the White Cap chiefs who traditionally owned the lands there. The problem was threefold. First, the government had to determine whether or not Dosunmu's descendants and the White Cap chiefs could enjoy any emoluments even on compassionate grounds. Second, the government had to decide what rôle, if any, it would assign the traditional élite of Lagos. Third, and closely connected with the first two, the government had to indicate whether or not the principle of indirect administration could apply to the British colony vis à vis the protectorate. These problems became quite serious and complex under the administrations which respected African chiefs and their institutions in the territories adjacent to Lagos colony. The British authorities did not find it easy to

[1] Cmd. 3784, London 1931, pp. 5-6.

explain their different attitudes to such institutions on the basis of the technical distinctions between colonies and protectorates.

Other complications arose from the fact that when the British government annexed Lagos in 1861 it allowed Dosunmu a pension of £1,000 a year for his lifetime only. Under the 1861 arrangements, his descendants could not benefit from similar pensions.[1] Moreover, as king, Dosunmu had a special status which the government recognised before the annexation. From August 1861, Dosunmu and his descendants lost the high office of King of Lagos. As Administrator Moloney explained to the Legislative Council in February 1888: 'In the Queen's Colony no assumption by anyone of a regal position could be tolerated'.[2] That dictum continued to influence the government's attitude to Dosunmu's successors after his death in February 1885. Following protracted discussions, Prince Oyekan, Dosunmu's successor, began with a compassionate allowance of £200 a year which subsequently reached £400 before his death in 1900.[3] The choice of Oyekan's successor and the determination of the compassionate allowance to be granted him involved the British government in serious controversies.

MacGregor rejected the notion of a 'contract' which bound the government to support the head of the Dosunmu-Oyekan House. The government, he said, accepted only a 'moral obligation' to do so. He therefore allowed the new head of the Dosunmu-Oyekan house in 1901 a compassionate allowance of £200 a year.[4] Before doing so, MacGregor undertook to settle a hotly disputed succession to the headship of the Dosunmu-Oyekan House in 1901. There were claimants – Oduntan, Ajose and Prince Eshugbayi Eleko – who posed difficult problems since Oyekan left no adult son as heir-apparent.

MacGregor thereby assumed the rôle which in such matters had been traditionally performed by the priesthood of the *Ifa* oracle and a select committee of the senior White Cap chiefs and warlords of Lagos.[5] Oduntan, Dosunmu's son, who at first won

[1] CO. 147/154, MacGregor to C.O., 23 February 1901, minute by R.L.A.
[2] CSO. 7/1/2, Legislative Council Debates, 17 February 1888.
[3] CSO. 7/1/2, Legislative Council Debates, 17 February 1888; 14 February 1888; 27 May 1888; 25 January 1894. CO. 147/154, MacGregor to C.O., 23 February 1901.
[4] CO. 147/154, MacGregor to C.O., 23 February 1901.
[5] Thomas, I. B.: *The House of Docemo: full proceedings of an inquiry into*

the approval of the family, was later disqualified on the grounds of his Islamic religion, since tradition frowned upon a Muslim Oba of Lagos. The female members of the Dosunmu-Oyekan family rejected Ajose's candidature because of his descent through the maternal line whereas patrilineal descent usually prevailed in choosing the Oba of Lagos. The White Cap chiefs who previously supported Ajose, the son of Dosunmu's sister, later switched to MacGregor's choice – Prince Eshugbayi Eleko, Dosunmu's son and Oyekan's brother, who fifteen years before this crisis had renounced his Muslim faith for heathenism. Eshugbayi's excellent character impressed MacGregor most.[1]

MacGregor made it clear to the Eleko and the White Cap chiefs that the new head had no official status with the government and that his headship had 'no political importance'.[2] The Colonial Office approved MacGregor's action.[3]

Subsequent events showed that in several ways the Eleko's shadow hung darkly over Lagos politics until the 1930s. The issue of his compassionate allowance and that of his White Cap chiefs interested the Nigerian unofficial members of the Legislative Council. In March 1905, they demanded that the Eleko's allowance be increased to £300 a year but the government refused.[4] They persisted in making similar demands for the Eleko and the White Cap chiefs during the committee stage of the Estimates for 1910. When the government again blocked their efforts, C. Sapara-Williams declared indignantly:

> I beg to express my dissent from the conclusion arrived at by the Official Members in regard to the proposal of the Unofficial Members for the grant of subsidies to the White Cap chiefs . . . It argues a lack of knowledge . . . of the rights and position of the White Cap chiefs, because instead of expecting them to 'render any useful service in the work of controlling', it is the Government that is laid under moral obligation to make adequate provision not only to maintain them but sustain their

---

the method of selection of a Head to the House of Docemo before H. L. Ward-Price, Commissioner, Lagos, 1933, pp. 114 and 120–3.

[1] CO. 147/154, MacGregor to C.O., 23 February 1901. *Macaulay Papers*, File 4/11.

[2] *Ibid.*

[3] CO. 147/154, C.O. to MacGregor, 12 April 1901.

[4] *Lagos Government Gazette*, 5 April 1905, Legislative Council Debates, 1 March 1905.

dignity. The Government is collecting the customs revenue in the exercise of its rights under the Treaty of Cession, but then owing to the ignorance of the times, no demand was made for any reciprocal provision to serve as a compensating advantage for the loss, either of their prescriptive rights to farm the revenue or of the portion thereof to which they were entitled or which it was customary for the King to apportion to them.[1]

In May 1912 the A.S.-A.P.S. revived the question of increased stipends for the Eleko and the White Cap chiefs.[2] The government then agreed to increase the Eleko's allowance to £300 a year and the total sums paid to the White Cap chiefs from £200 a year to £460.[3]

More controversial was the issue of their status in the affairs of Lagos. In 1901, MacGregor had included in his 'Charter' to Prince Eshugbayi the provisions that the Eleko had no 'political' status in Lagos and no official standing in his relations with the government. But, despite the views of the government, the Lagos masses strongly believed that the Eleko and the White Cap chiefs had a political part to play. In their claims for consultation by the government before bills became law in the Legislative Council, the White Cap chiefs reminded the British authorities of their political ambitions.

The government soon saw from the leading rôle assumed by the White Cap chiefs in such issues as the water-rate scheme in Lagos that they had considerable influence among the masses. At an unguarded moment in that controversy, Egerton qualified MacGregor's earlier dictum that the Eleko and his White Cap chiefs had no political significance in Lagos. During the meeting of the Central Native Council in November 1908, Egerton informed the Eleko and the other chiefs present:

> It has been represented to me that the Eleko's bell was sent round the town and a proclamation was made that the people should come together and make a demonstration against taxes. I understand that the people were being stirred up in order that there should be a riot. Now the reason that the British

---

[1] *Southern Nigeria Gazette*, 27 October 1909, Legislative Council Debates, 6 October 1909.
[2] C.O. 554/10, T. Buxton to C.O., 1 May 1912.
[3] *Ibid.*, minute by C.S. dated 9 May 1912.

> Government recognises Eleko and the White Cap Chiefs is because it wishes to rule the people through them. Instead of stirring up the people to do unlawful acts, the Government expects the Chiefs to instruct the people to observe law and order... Chief Aromire has said to me that the Chiefs of Lagos have not been given an important position in the Town. How could I give an important position to persons who behave in the way you have done...[1]

In this statement, Egerton admitted that an element of indirect administration through the Eleko and White Cap chiefs was possible but no more. Although in the same statement Egerton rejected the political significance of the Eleko, the issue continued to disturb Lagos politics in the celebrated Eleko case.

Briefly, the Eleko case involved the government's withdrawal in December 1920 of recognition from Prince Eshugbayi and the simultaneous cancellation of his compassionate allowance of £300 a year for refusing to fulfil a political assignment. The government had earlier asked the Eleko to send round his bellmen to repudiate allegations made against it by H. Macaulay who accompanied the White Cap chief Oluwa (Amodu Tijani) to Britain during the hearing of the appeal in the famous Apapa Land Case. When Prince Eshugbayi persistently refused, the government deported him in August 1925 to Oyo against the protests of the majority of the princes of the Dosunmu-Oyekan family, who said that his deposition and deportation contravened customary law.

During the Eleko case, the government frequently cited MacGregor's 'Charter' to Eshugbayi in 1901. For their part, the Eleko's supporters, particularly H. Macaulay, referred to African law and custom as if the 1861 annexation and its serious constitutional aspects were null and void. It then became clear that the major issues postponed since 1901, if not much earlier, needed urgent juridical and political resolution during the 1920s and 1930s. The Privy Council heard aspects of the appeal made by Prince Eshugbayi for a writ of *habeas corpus* which was earlier rejected by the Supreme Court and Full Court of Nigeria. Twice, on 19 June 1928 and 24 March 1931, the Judicial Committee of the Privy Council ordered aspects of this case to be reopened by the law courts in Nigeria.

In the end, the Eleko case was resolved through the political

---

[1] Minutes of the Central Native Council Meeting, 4 November 1908.

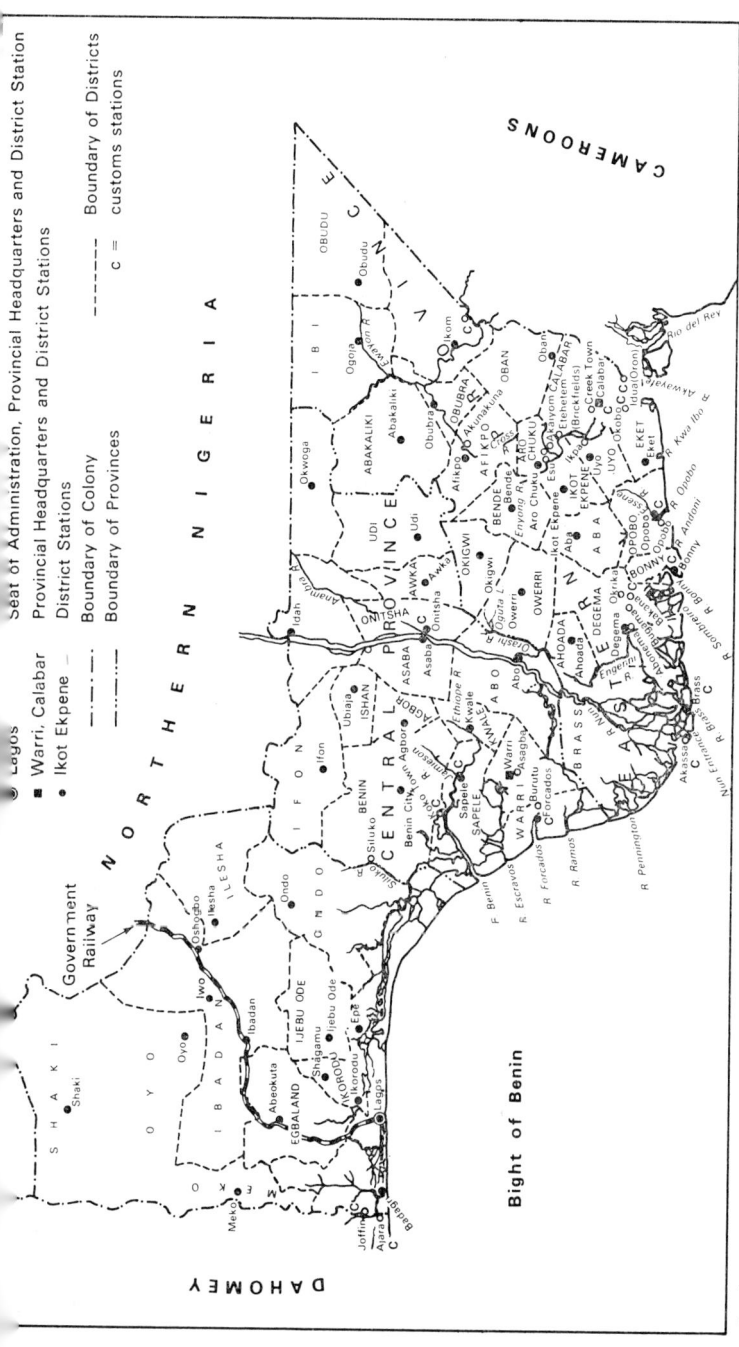

Outline map of Southern Nigeria, 1909

intervention of Governor D. Cameron in 1931 when he cancelled the government's deportation orders of 6 and 8 August 1925 against Eshugbayi. Consequently, Cameron allowed Eshugbayi to return from exile in July 1931 with considerable public support.[1] Until his death on 24 October 1932, Eshugbayi demonstrated clearly to a succession of Governors, including MacGregor and Egerton, that despite the 1861 annexation, the institution of chieftaincy in Lagos could not be easily cast aside in favour of more direct administration.

The third aspect of the issues raised by the demands of the Eleko and the White Cap chiefs – their use under the system of indirect administration – partly resolved itself by the creation in 1901 of the Central Native Council. In it sat Prince Eshugbayi, other White Cap chiefs and Muslim leaders. Denied substantial political power, the Eleko and the White Cap chiefs nevertheless found in the Central Native Council their recognised forum for expressing their views.

The place of the Central Native Council in the administration of the colony should not be exaggerated. Even under its architect, the Central Native Council was no more than a deliberative and advisory council on local issues. It concerned itself primarily with advising the Governor on African law and custom covering such varied subjects as tolls, land tenure, possession of children in the event of the separation of their parents, the use of ceremonial umbrellas by the traditional élite and the right to wear crowns. In return, the Governor informed the members about any matters of public interest. Under MacGregor, the Central Native Council became a quasi-anthropological sub-department of his administration.

In 1903, the Central Native Council had its golden year with a record of eight sessions, the largest number in its career after its inaugural meeting on 20 December 1901. Since February 1902, the Eleko sat as its vice-president during the sessions which conveniently took place at night.[2] Apart from its twenty-odd members, the Governor, on special occasions, invited officials

[1] Information obtained from the *Macaulay Papers* in the Africana section of the University of Ibadan Library. Till August 1970, these private papers were not completely classified.

[2] For the proceedings of the Central Native Council under MacGregor's administration, see *Lagos Government Gazette*, 14 December 1901; 28 December 1901; 24 May 1902; 17 January, 31 January, 7 February, 28 February, 11 April, 13 June, 1 August, 24 December 1903; 5 March 1904.

and such other distinguished visitors as the Oni of Ife who attended its session in February 1903.

Out of respect for MacGregor, the Oni of Ife disregarded the tradition which forbade such a journey in order to attend a special meeting at Lagos of the Central Native Council. As the highest traditional authority[1] on the right of Yoruba chiefs to wear crowns, the Oni, on MacGregor's invitation, had gone to Lagos to advise the Central Native Council in the dispute between the Akarigbo of Shagamu and the Elepe of Epe. In his attempt to expound the pre-colonial practice, the Oni of Ife put himself in an embarrassing position because a face-to-face meeting with such a crowned head as the Akarigbo would have contravened African law and custom. MacGregor solved that problem by a sitting arrangement which allowed the Oni of Ife to back the other members of the Central Native Council while giving his verdict on the dispute between the Akarigbo and the Elepe.

MacGregor had invited the Oni for two principal reasons. First, the Central Native Council itself lacked the authority to decide the issue of crowns outside the colony. Second, Mac-Gregor considered the issue quite important as it affected 'the dignity, authority and position of an Oba'.[2] The Oni confirmed the Akarigbo's right to wear a crown and rejected the Elepe's claim to a crown in the same territory. MacGregor and the Central Native Council felt satisfied with that authoritative pronouncement.

No such meetings of the Central Native Council took place after MacGregor's era. Egerton failed to call meetings as regularly as MacGregor and there were complaints from the members in September 1904, March 1906 and September 1907.[3] In March 1906, Egerton informed them that because of the pressure of administrative work he preferred meetings every three months instead of monthly.[4] In terms of recorded sittings, its worst period was 1911–12 when it seemed inactive. The practice of calling special sessions of the Central Native Council to deal with particular issues, however, continued unchanged at least till 1910.

[1] By tradition, Ife was regarded as the cradle of the Yorubas in Nigeria; the Oni was its traditional ruler.
[2] *Lagos Government Gazette*, 28 February 1903.
[3] Minutes of the Central Native Council meetings, 3 September 1904, 7 March 1906, 12 September, 1907.
[4] Minutes of the Central Native Council meeting, 7 March 1906.

Between December 1903 and its last recorded session in March 1913, the Central Native Council interested itself in various matters which, though important to the chiefs and masses, received inadequate attention in the Legislative Council. These included intra-mural burials, fishing stakes in the lagoon, the disposal of night soil, the water-rate, the Seditious Offences Ordinance, the building rules proposed by the Lagos Municipal Board of Health, the public acquisition of land without compensation and various chieftaincy disputes.[1]

Though the members of the Central Native Council were pleased to discuss such issues, they regretted their inferior status to the members of the Legislative Council.[2] The Central Native Council did not die as a result of poor attendance, lack of zeal or inadequate debate. On the contrary, its meetings were full and its debates lively. Its end in 1913 could partly be explained by the decreasing government interest in its critical approach to legislation, partly by increasing official disapproval of the exaggerated estimate which the members had of their importance and rôle in the administration of the colony.

GOVERNMENT ATTITUDE TOWARDS THE CHIEFS OF THE PROTECTORATE

In several ways, MacGregor, Egerton and their deputies sought to protect the authority and dignity of the traditional élite, but they were inconsistent. Frequently, the government made only token gestures in maintaining the dignity of such important Yoruba chiefs as the Oni of Ife. Though MacGregor appreciated the Oni's political significance, he could do no more than recommend to the Legislative Council in February 1903 the approval of a yearly stipend of £100 for him.[3] Occasionally, MacGregor and his immediate successor tried to catch the shadow of Yoruba

[1] Minutes of the Central Native Council meetings, 8 December 1903, 3 September 1904, 1 February 1905, 4 July 1905, 7 March 1906, 23 July 1906, 12 September 1907, 20 July 1908, 4 November 1908, 24 September 1909, 5 October 1909, 18 November 1909, 23 November 1909, 25 May 1910, 14 March 1913.
[2] *Ibid.*, 5 October 1909, 18 November 1909, 23 November 1909, 14 March 1913.
[3] *Lagos Government Gazette*, 7 March 1903, Legislative Council Debates, 26 February 1903.

chieftaincy but left its substance unprotected during the expansion of British authority and influence in that part of the protectorate. Thus, through fines and warnings, MacGregor in 1903 and Acting Governor Moseley in 1904 tried to discourage the pro-government Muslim leader, Kuku, from using the type of ceremonial umbrella reserved to the Awujale of Ijebu-Ode.[1]

Government attitude towards the Owa and Council of Ilesha demonstrated most the inconsistencies of British policies and practices. MacGregor noticed in May 1901 that the British Commissioner at Ilesha had, without the Governor's approval, fined the Owa and his daughter for administrative irregularities.[2] MacGregor's disapproval hardly lessened the public ridicule caused by the officer's initial ill judgment, nor did temporary deportation of the Owa in 1905 show much change of attitude.

The long-awaited change came in 1908 when the government intervened to support the authority of the Owa and Council and suppress the defiance on the part of the chiefs of the tributary Ipetu. Supported by troops, Acting Provincial Commissioner H. C. Moorhouse visited Ipetu, destroyed houses and dug up yams in the farms for the escort in the attempt to arrest Apetu, the leader of the Ipetu dissidents. When the party successfully accomplished its task, Moorhouse informed the people of Ipetu about the government's intention to support the Owa and Council whose orders they had attempted to defy. With the approval of the Colonial Office, the government deported Apetu to an undisclosed destination.[3]

The same inconsistency was apparent in the government's attitude towards the Akarigbo of Ijebu-Remo in 1911. On the orders of District Commissioner H. F. Duncombe, the Akarigbo of Ijebu-Remo was arrested on charges of larceny and obtaining money under false pretences, and was refused release on bail. When this news reached Lagos, Acting Provincial Commissioner Moorhouse rushed to Shagamu, where, after a thorough investigation, the police withdrew the charges against the Akarigbo, whom they later released. Egerton and Moorhouse blamed Duncombe for 'arresting so important a chief on charges which it

[1] CO. 147/169, Moseley to C.O., 13 February 1904.
[2] CO. 147/155, MacGregor to C.O., 21 May 1901.
[3] CO. 520/64, Egerton to C.O., 31 August 1908, enclosure and minutes by J.S. and Lord Crewe.

The Evolution of the Nigerian State

should be apparent to him were based on ill-feeling and malice'. By so doing, Moorhouse continued, Duncombe had obstructed the general policy of indirect administration through such chiefs as the Akarigbo.[1] This belated admonition hardly removed the adverse effects of Duncombe's attempt to ensure that in their fairness the standards of British justice had no respect for African kings.

The Pinnock case in Oyo between 1909 and 1910 arose from the disagreements between the Alafin of Oyo and the Rev. S. G. Pinnock who, though a British subject, had 'property and interests' which were American.[2] Pinnock had gone to West Africa as the representative of the 'Gospel News Mission' but later attached himself to the American Baptist Mission. He combined his Christian missionary work with his commercial rôle as the Oyo branch agent of the Lagos Stores Limited. Since 1895, Pinnock had incurred the displeasure of Oyo's indigenous authorities because of his criticism of the Alafin's administration and his activities as informer to the government before the bombardment of the Alafin's palace.[3]

Pinnock later extended his criticisms to the friendly relationship between District Commissioner W. A. Ross and the Alafin. Pinnock further assumed the rôle of the protector of the rights of Christian converts in Oyo, who challenged the authority of the Alafin and the District Commissioner. Ross investigated cases of cruelty against such malcontents in the Oyo Native Court reported by Pinnock, but found no justification for Pinnock's allegations.[4] Vexed by Pinnock's accusations and intransigence, the Alafin approached the government to protect him under the terms of the 1893 treaty. Before the government took any positive action, the Alafin found Pinnock's continued opposition intolerable and early in 1909 ordered his expulsion from Oyo. After considerable difficulties, Pinnock voluntarily left Oyo on 7 June 1909.

The government sympathised with the difficulties of the Alafin and the District Commissioner but lacked the legal authority to deport a British subject from the protectorate. Furthermore, under the 1893 treaty the government had under-

[1] CO. 520/106, Egerton to C.O., 5 October 1911, enclosure.
[2] CO. 520/86, F.O. to C.O., 20 July 1909, enclosure.
[3] Atanda, *op. cit.*, p. 141. Ayandele, *op. cit.*, p. 167.
[4] CO. 520/79, Egerton to C.O., conf. 19 June 1909, enclosure.

Direct and Indirect Administration

taken to protect the Alafin so long as its provisions were faithfully observed. These same provisions however included the British government's protection of such European Christian missionaries and commercial firms as those represented by Pinnock at Oyo. Moreover, after 1893 British policy had been to administer indirectly through such chiefs as the Alafin, whose authority Pinnock had consistently defied.

Hence, there were at least two inter-related crises over the Pinnock-Alafin controversy. The conflict in protectorate obligations raised for the government a serious constitutional dilemma. Second, it threatened the policy and practice of indirect administration in a sensitive part of Yorubaland. The stalemate became more embarrassing for the government because, under the existing laws and conventions, the offences of Europeans in such areas as Oyo were not justiciable in their Native Councils. The Oyo judicial agreement of 1904 merely confirmed the operative agreement with Ibadan; hence Oyo as such had none for itself. Nor did the Alafin have any legal right to deport Pinnock without the government's approval in 1909. To deal with cases similar to Pinnock's the government passed the Deportation of Prisoners (Amendment) Ordinance, 1910, which enabled them to support the authority of the chiefs and to rid them of 'turbulent persons'.[1]

The activities of African Christian converts in Ekiti in 1911 reopened the issue of protectorate obligations and demonstrated the clash of interests between indirect administration and vestry authority. Egerton and the District Commissioner in Ekiti noticed the threat to the authority of the chiefs from the defiant attitude of the African Christian converts who were defended by Bishop I. Oluwole, one of the Assistant Bishops in the C.M.S. diocese of Western Equatorial Africa.[2] Egerton believed that in terms of loyalty to African chiefs Muslims and heathens had a better record than Christian converts.[3]

Oluwole rejected the government charges of disloyalty and disrespect brought against the Christian converts in Ekiti.[4] He upheld the conduct of these converts in refusing to pay the customary respects during such traditional, but heathen, festivals

---

[1] CO. 592/11, Legislative Council Debates, 15 February 1910.
[2] *E.D.M.P.* F/8, Egerton to Morel, 1 October 1911, enclosure.
[3] *E.D.M.P.* F/8, Egerton to Morel, 26 November 1911.
[4] *E.D.M.P.* F/8, Egerton to Morel, 1 October 1911, enclosure.

as the *Egungun* displays dedicated to the worship of Yoruba ancestral gods. The historical Christian duty in such cases, Oluwole emphasised, was to 'refuse to offer incense to the gods even at the bidding of a pro-consul'.[1] He further defended his converts in their rejection of polygamy contrary to the wishes of the chiefs. He maintained that despite their refusal to supply communal labour on Sundays when required by the chiefs, they were willing to work extra hours during week-days. He admitted that converts looked to the pastors and catechists, and not to their chiefs, for guidance but approved that trend of vestry rule. Far from seeing in the conduct of the converts an important cause of the loss of the chiefs' dignity and authority, Oluwole held responsible the British practice of arresting and publicly ridiculing the very chiefs for 'trivial causes'.

Oluwole highlighted the two opposing concepts of protection advanced by the chiefs and Christian converts under British administration. The chiefs, he said, wanted the British government 'to protect their land from Christianity'. But on behalf of the Christian converts, Oluwole called upon the government 'to protect them from injustice and oppression'. Despite Egerton's irritation at the conduct of the Christian converts, he advised the British Commissioner in the Ekiti area 'to be more sympathetic towards the Christians'.

Oluwole rightly argued that far more harm came to the chiefs from the excesses of the British administrators themselves. Developments in Ibadan in 1912 confirmed this.

W. A. Ross, the Resident for Oyo and Ibadan, showed no shame at writing to Morel in October 1912:

> I have killed the Bale of Ibadan; the poor old man was very feeble and it's a good thing he's dead. The new Bale is my slave and absolutely loyal to the Alafin ... he publicly – at the native ceremony – declared he would go to Oyo directly he is called and would at all times faithfully obey the Alafin's orders and put his mark to the paper. All is well here and the people are beginning to eat out of my hand and I believe don't dislike me. I didn't think I have spoken to a man yet about taking his hat off but they are all gradually doing it and all the chiefs prostrate including the Bale when they come up here, it's a good sign.[1]

[1] *E.D.M.P.* F/9, W. A. Ross to Morel, 6 October 1912.

OYO-IBADAN RELATIONS

Ross's triumphal entry into the district commissionership of Oyo in May 1906 and his subsequent activities there inclined B. A. Agiri and J. A. Atanda to re-examine the basis of British administrative policy towards the Alafin since 1893. In their view, MacGregor, Egerton and Ross were parties to a conscious policy of encouraging the Alafin to reassert his control over Ibadan and its chiefs.[1] For the period 1900–13, the evidence does not completely support the view that the Colonial Office actively encouraged such a policy. It is nevertheless true that from 1906, for the reasons already advanced, Egerton failed to control the details of administration in various parts of Southern Nigeria.

MacGregor's association with such a policy has been mistakenly attributed to a speech he made in February 1903 to the Legislative Council. He then said:

> Personally I have always had good reason to be satisfied with the demeanour of that great chief, the acknowledged political Head of the Yoruba nation. He has always been ready and willing, indeed most anxious, to adopt as far as lay in his power whatever advice has been given to him for improving the condition of his country and people. Several of the members of this Council have been witnesses of a great weakening of the political power and authority of the Alafin. No doubt there must have existed at the time serious reasons for adopting such a policy. I humbly think it was carried too far. Ever since I made the acquaintance of this chief I have consistently endeavoured to strengthen his rule, because I entertain a high opinion of his wisdom, and of his loyalty to the King and to his own country and people. In this policy it is certainly the case that considerable progress has been made. The authority and influence of the Alafin is clearly stronger and better established than I found it. Were it practicable to do so, it would be very desirable that the authority and influence of the Alafin should be extended beyond its present limits, over districts formerly ruled by him and his predecessors. But it is a fact that, if the

[1] Agiri, B. A.: *Development of Local Government in Ogbomoso* (M.A. Dissertation) Ibadan 1966, pp. 101–4. Atanda, *op. cit.*, pp. 123–6, 146–150.

prestige and authority of a chief are once seriously weakened, it takes time and care to repair the damage.[1]

Clearly MacGregor here was first emphasising the need for *strengthening* the authority of the Alafin within the existing boundaries of Oyo, then discussing the prospects of *extending* the Alafin's control to territories formerly under his jurisdiction. These remarks, however, were framed in conditional terms.

As a means of strengthening chiefs' authority MacGregor relied on stipends. In the same speech of February 1903 MacGregor simultaneously promised £100 a year stipends to the Alafin of Oyo and Oni of Ife respectively.[2] The government increased the Alafin's stipend by £100 in December 1903 as compensation for the abolition of tolls.[3] Until the end of his administration MacGregor seemed more eager to strengthen the authority of the Alake of Abeokuta than that of the Alafin of Oyo. The 1903 speech did not alter this preference. In 1904 MacGregor actively tried to modify the interpretation of his February 1903 speech during the process of requiring the Alafin of Oyo to confirm the Ibadan judicial agreement of 1904 following the procedural precedent of the 1893 treaty. The clash of views of Acting Governor Moseley and MacGregor then came to the knowledge of the Colonial Office, which advised action along the new line of approach recommended by the Governor.[4]

In June 1904, Moseley had emphasised that Oyo province was more important than Ibadan and recommended the restoration of Oyo 'to its former position of primacy in Yorubaland, to the great and immediate prosperity of the cotton industry'.[5] Then in Britain, MacGregor disagreed that 'Oyo is or will be as important as Ibadan'.[6] In a further discussion with C. Strachey, MacGregor affirmed that the 'overlordship' of the Alafin over Ibadan had become so shadowy that it was an error to emphasise it.

---

[1] *Lagos Government Gazette*, 7 March 1903, MacGregor's address to the Legislative Council on 26 February 1903.   [2] *Ibid.*

[3] CO. 147/167, MacGregor to C.O. tel. 7 December 1903.

[4] CO. 147/170, Moseley to C.O., conf. 11 June 1904. CO. 147/170, Moseley to C.O., conf. 27 June 1904, minute by P.H.E. CO. 147/170, Moseley to C.O., 29 June 1904, minute by C.S. CO. 147/171, C.O. to O.A.G., conf. 24 August 1904. CO. 147/171, Moseley to C.O., conf. 23 September 1904. CO. 147/171, C.O. to Egerton, conf. 18 November 1904.   [5] CO. 147/170, Moseley to C.O., conf. 27 June 1904.

[6] *Ibid.*, minute by P.H.E., dated 16 August 1904.

Direct and Indirect Administration

The fact that MacGregor did not consult the Alafin during the crucial stages of the tolls agitation in which Ibadan and Abeokuta led the fight against European merchants further illustrated the limitations of Oyo's primacy then.[1] On the basis of MacGregor's 1904 plea, the Colonial Office decided to warn Moseley against any attempts to make the Alafin's overlordship more realistic than sentiment and tradition allowed.[2] It therefore reminded Moseley not 'to do anything further to recognise any actual control by Oyo over Ibadan'.[3]

Dissatisfied with the Colonial Office's warning, Moseley in September 1904 reminded it of MacGregor's pro-Alafin speech of February 1903 and reiterated instances of the Alafin's influence over the selection of Bashoruns of Ibadan, the precedent set in the treaty of 3 February 1893 and its repetition in Ibadan's judicial agreement of 1904.[4] The Colonial Office, however, impressed upon Moseley in November 1904 that even under the 1893 treaty Ibadan remained 'practically independent of Oyo' and recognised only its 'nominal or formal overlordship'. It admitted that the government had previously required the Alafin's authority to confirm Ibadan's judicial agreement. It nevertheless asked Egerton not 'to coerce the latter [Ibadan] into admitting the Alafin of Oyo to any practical control over their political or administrative affairs.'[5] The Colonial Office noted the conditional aspects of MacGregor's 1903 speech and affirmed that it did not apply to Ibadan nor to any of its tributary towns.[6]

This confidential dispatch of November 1904 contained the specific guide-lines which the Colonial Office desired in Ibadan-Oyo relations. The over-zealous activities of such provincial proconsuls as W. A. Ross overstepped the limits of these guide-lines, and not checking them in time, Egerton and his successors left a sad administrative legacy in Oyo-Ibadan relations which was not reversed until the 1930s.[7]

[1] CO. 147/170, Moseley to C.O., 29 June 1904, minute by C.S., 5 August 1904.
[2] Ibid.
[3] CO. 147/171, C.O. to O.A.G., conf. 24 August 1904.
[4] CO. 147/171, Moseley to C.O., conf. 23 September 1904.
[5] CO. 147/171, C.O. to Egerton, conf. 18 November 1904.
[6] Ibid.
[7] Awe, B. A.: *The Rise of Ibadan as a Yoruba Power in the Nineteenth Century* (D.Phil. Thesis) Oxford 1964, p. 333.

The Evolution of the Nigerian State

TRIBUTARY RELATIONSHIPS

Again out of respect to the wishes of the big chiefs, the government before 1914 generally declined to alter well-known tributary relationships. Ibadan, however, did not pay tribute to the Alafin but retained control over the 80-odd dependent towns and villages despite the wishes of such towns as Ede, Ogbomosho and Iwo to break away, which were not fulfilled until the 1930s.[1]

Until 1913 the government continued the tributary relationship between some Ekiti towns and Ilesha despite the attempts of several Ekiti rulers to declare themselves independent of the Owa of Ilesha. Chief Fabumi of Oke-Messi-Ipoli, for instance, attempted to assert his independence of the Owa in December 1903, but MacGregor steadfastly refused to recognise him as an 'independent' crowned Oba.[2] By rejecting the Ekiti attempts to break away from a tributary or other political relationship with the Owa and other chiefs of Ilesha, neither MacGregor nor Egerton realised that the new conditions established by their administrations had removed some of the pre-colonial factors which had led to the inauguration of the late nineteenth century fighting organisation – the *Ekitiparapo* – which had co-ordinated the military activities of the Ekiti and Ijesha troops against their arch-enemies in Ibadan and Ilorin.

The end of the Yoruba wars in 1893, the appointment of the British Resident in Ibadan in 1894, the Royal Niger Company's conquest of Ilorin in 1897 and the Niger Coast Protectorate's punitive expeditions against Benin in 1897 freed the Ekiti from the formidable enemies who had previously surrounded them on all sides. The expansion and consolidation thereafter of British administrative control in Southern Nigeria and the prospects of exploiting the commercial resources of their territories and the educational opportunities provided by Christian missionaries in their midst encouraged the Ekiti to lose interest in closer relations with the chiefs and people of Ilesha, a wish granted them only in 1913.[3]

The government showed less eagerness in respecting the tributary rights claimed by some Benin chiefs in such districts as

[1] *Ibid.*, p. 334.
[2] CO. 147/167, MacGregor to C.O., 31 December 1903.
[3] Akintoye, *op. cit.*, pp. 338–52.

Ishan and Agbor. Here again the phenomenon of the government's double standards in handling administrative problems affecting the Yoruba parts of the protectorate appeared. The government acted quickly to check excesses and high-handedness of the Benin chiefs towards Ishan and Agbor. Hence, Egerton in 1906 cancelled their tributary rights in the Ishan and Agbor districts. But in the remaining areas, he allowed tributes to be collected on behalf of the Benin chiefs by the District Commissioners.[1]

POLICY TOWARDS UNPOPULAR CHIEFS

During the 1906 Benin City 'scare' over public expectation of Overami's return following Nana's arrival from exile, the government received serious complaints from the majority of Benin chiefs against two of their fellow members – Obaseki and Obayagbon. Through their loyalty to the government, both these chiefs had assumed a rôle out of proportion to their status under pre-colonial conditions. The other chiefs' irritation stemmed from Obaseki's phenomenal rise to prominence and authority despite his original status as a 'junior' chief in pre-1897 Benin.[2]

Neither Egerton nor Moorhouse, whom the former had sent to Benin with troops to handle the serious public discontent which had accumulated since the 1897 punitive expedition, agreed to demote Obaseki in order to appease the other chiefs and people. Instead, in an interview with the leading Benin chiefs, Moorhouse explained to them how Obaseki had earned his high status because of his industry and loyalty to the government. Moorhouse further stated: 'it was not the custom of the Government to drag such a man down to the level of others who having had similar chances had failed to take advantage of them'.[3] Egerton endorsed that viewpoint.[4]

In Ibadan, the problem of unpopular chiefs took a different form. In 1902, the chiefs there complained of the unpopularity of Kongi, a former war-lord who had been 'extremely disloyal' to the Bashorun of Ibadan. The chiefs accused Kongi of being

[1] CO. 520/37, Egerton to C.O., conf. 31 October 1906.
[2] *Ibid.*
[3] *Ibid.*, enclosure.
[4] *Ibid.*, main dispatch.

privy to the death of the Bashorun and of attempting to set up a rival court contrary to tradition.¹ Through pressure from the British officer at Ibadan, the chiefs at first allowed Kongi, who had been stripped of his warlord title and dismissed from the Ibadan Council, to remain a private citizen in the town. When his continued presence raised more threats to internal security, the chiefs changed their minds and asked the government to deport Kongi to their tributary Iwo town, about 30 miles distant from Ibadan.² Kongi's deportation raised legal problems for the government which had no such authority under the Order in Council of July 1901, though the Ibadan Council had power to do so under the Native Councils Ordinance, 1901. The problem arose from the Ibadan chiefs asking Acting Governor Moseley to depose and deport Kongi for them. The Colonial Office, however, treated the matter as 'a voluntary arrangement' between the Acting Governor and the Ibadan chiefs without serious protests from Kongi himself.³

In 1907 Resident Elgee reported to Egerton that Bale Dada of Ibadan disagreed with his council, chiefs and people who consequently lost confidence in him. They had accused him of abusing his office through his collusion with thieves, attempting to influence Native Council decisions and refusing to consult his chiefs in matters affecting the general administration of the town.⁴

Dada, the centre of the controversy, had been elected Bale in December 1904 upon the recommendation of the Resident after consultation with the Alafin of Oyo. Having approved Dada's appointment⁵ Egerton found it embarrassing to recommend his deposition without further inquiries into the allegations against him. For this purpose, Egerton appointed Acting Chief Justice J. Winkfield and Acting Provincial Commissioner A. G. B. Harcourt to investigate the complaints. To satisfy the strong anti-Dada faction in the town, they recommended his removal from office and the choice of a successor under their own law and custom.⁶ Egerton accepted their recommendations and informed Dada accordingly on 14 December 1907 with the promise of a grant of £200 a year pension.⁷ Dada probably resolved the matter for the government and the public by dying mysteriously

¹ CO. 147/162, Moseley to C.O., 8 September 1902.
² *Ibid.*   ³ *Ibid.*, minute by H.B.C.
⁴ C.O 520/50, Egerton to C.O., conf. 16 December 1907, enclosures.
⁵ *Ibid.*   ⁶ *Ibid.*   ⁷ *Ibid.*

a day or two later. Ibadan's discredited ruler at last knew the path of respectable conduct when his people felt compelled to send him – as they would have done literally in pre-colonial times – the traditional parrot's eggs, the customary invitation to commit suicide.

The following year, however, W. A. Ross imposed another unpopular Bale upon the people of Ibadan. With the approval of the Alafin he chose the puppet Irefin. Balogun Situ, the popular contestant, thus lost the race whose ground-rules were no longer determined by the chiefs and people of Ibadan.[1] Ross was fulfilling the promise he had made to Morel in April 1912 when he reported: 'I'm delighted with the Alafin of Oyo. I hope to exert his influence on these people.'[2]

In retrospect, the position in several parts of Southern Nigeria showed clearly who were the rulers and who the executives. By 1913, the government could hardly disguise the fact that contrary to its wishes, its smaller men-on-the-spot had inaugurated or consolidated their own era of the administrative pantomime with chiefs. Such smaller men-on-the-spot as W. A. Ross expressed satisfaction with indirect administration when practised through puppet chiefs.

The position analysed so far has shown a high degree of government interference in the political aspects of the people's internal affairs in the southern parts of the developing Nigerian State. Similar trends occurred in the government's attempts to demarcate and adjust internal boundaries and in the plans to amalgamate its administrations in Nigeria.

[1] Agiri, *op. cit.*, p. 107. Atanda, *op. cit.*, pp. 146–9.
[2] *E.D.M.P.* F/9, W. A. Ross to Morel, 23 April, 1912.

8 Internal Boundaries and Amalgamation

THE INTERNAL BOUNDARY QUESTIONS

Ethnic plurality, pre-colonial historical associations and British administrative trends partly explain the course of the serious internal boundary questions of the late nineteenth and early twentieth centuries. In pre-colonial times such problems were decided by Africans either through wars or peaceful negotiations. But in the colonial era, the *Pax Britannica* frowned upon any African wars, whatever the motive. Moreover, the major decision-makers in boundary disputes were now no longer Africans.

The degree of ethnic heterogeneity in Southern Nigeria can be ascertained from the census figures for 1911.[1] The Ibos (3 millions) and the Yorubas (2 millions) then formed the major ethnic groups out of $7\frac{3}{4}$ million inhabitants in Southern Nigeria. The table on the next page indicates, in numerical order, the remaining ethnic distribution.

A detailed examination of this table indicates that its compilers did not adopt an exact classification. Nor did they take sufficient account of the similarities in languages and dialects. But what impressed the government most in 1911 was the picture of cultural diversity. In its view,

> A perusal of the tables showing all the tribes of 2,000 and over, and the languages in each province, indicates a very marked difference between the general conditions in the Western (Lagos) Province, where for all practical purposes only one language (Yoruba) is spoken, and the Eastern, where there are an extraordinary number of different peoples and tongues. According to the returns received from the District Commissioners in that province, there are no fewer than 82 tribes and 57 languages. Even in the Central Province, 23 tribes and

[1] C.O 592/9, Report on the Southern Nigeria Census, 1911.

Internal Boundaries and Amalgamation

Ibibios	210,000	Ngbos	50,000
Sobos (Urhobos)	209,000	Jekris (Itsekiris)	35,000
Ezzas	180,000	Nsokpongs	33,000
Ezzis	140,000	Ekpaffias	33,000
Anangs	119,000	Okobos	32,000
Ishans	114,000	Ogbayons (Ogbeyans)	31,000
Munchis (Tiv)[1]	97,000	Bokis	31,000
Kwales	97,000	Ikwes	30,000
Ijaws (Ijo)	93,000	Igarras	29,000
Kwas (Qua)	90,000	Abuas	26,000
Ogonis	78,000	Yalas	26,000
Binis	75,000	Etchis (Etches)	25,000
Ikas	74,000	Orons	25,000
Efiks	62,000	Ekois	24,000
Okpotos (Akpotos)	60,000	Akons (Akunakunas?)	22,000
Ekets	60,000	Yakoras (Yakos)	22,000
Igabos	56,000	Abos (Abohs)	21,000
Ikonors (Ikonos)	50,000	New Calabars (Kala-	
Kukurukus (Afenmai)	50,000	bari)	20,000

18 tongues appear on the district census schedules. Doubtless several of the tribes and languages in both provinces are offshoots or dialects, but even allowing for this, it would appear that there was a remarkable diversity, and the difficulties of administering tracts of country where so many different languages are spoken, as in the Eastern Province, must be very much greater than is experienced in this respect in the Western.[2]

The administrative inconveniences of cultural pluralism were evident in the unsatisfactory district, divisional and provincial boundaries and in those which separated one protectorate from another under colonial rule. These difficulties were more complicated under the British administrative arrangements which, in certain areas, paid little regard to the basis of pre-colonial political relationships. These relationships had been largely determined by commercial factors and prescriptive rights, particularly those relating to tribute systems and military conquests. Originally part of the old Oyo Empire, Ilorin was lost by the Yorubas in Southern Nigeria early in the nineteenth century to their kinsmen under the leadership of the Fulani jihadists. To the Yorubas in Southern

---

[1] This was perhaps a misleading reference to the 'Udam' or 'people of Ogoja' who had affinities with the Tiv of Northern Nigeria. See *West Africa*, 1 August 1970, p. 869.   [2] *Ibid.*

Nigeria, Ilorin and their related enclaves in Kabba constituted the major 'lost territories'[1] which they repeatedly sought to regain.

The *Ekitiparapo*, another major product of the Yoruba wars, later became associated with a serious internal boundary problem. Although in 1886[2] the British government had recognised the independence of the *Ekitiparapo*, it subsequently made serious administrative errors which split the Ekiti kingdoms and put them under different governments, much to the people's displeasure. Nor were the people adequately consulted when British-made boundaries divided the Owo people, as well as the Afenmai (formerly Kukuruku), between the Protectorate of Northern and Southern Nigeria, causing considerable misunderstanding in these areas.[3]

The western boundaries of the Benin kingdom which claimed Edo enclaves and tributary villages among the Ekiti, Owo and Akure similarly caused administrative difficulties during the 1890s. These disputes were not settled in favour of the Yoruba-speaking areas there until 1897[4] when the British punitive expedition against Oba Overami assisted the 'independence' struggles of the Yorubas along the western boundary of the pre-colonial Benin kingdom. The British-inspired boundary arrangements which affected the Igala people around Idah and its neighbourhood, the Idoma along the Benue river, and the Brass-Akassa people of the Lower Niger also led to considerable administrative problems.

At the end of the Berlin West Africa Conference of 1884–85, when the British government obtained new territories and still hoped to assume minimum responsibilities for their administration, it had allowed three agencies, not one, to protect its interests in the Niger districts or territories. Consequently, it had arbitrarily drawn lines of demarcation between the territories administered by the Lagos Colony and Protectorate, the Oil Rivers (Niger Coast) Protectorate and the Royal Niger Company. These soon caused trouble. For example, Akassa in the Lower Niger Delta came within the jurisdiction of the Royal Niger

---

[1] CO. 520/80, Egerton to C.O., conf. 4 July 1909, enclosure.
[2] Akintoye, S. A.: *The Ekiti-parapo and the Kiriji War* (Ph.D. thesis) Ibadan 1966, p. 337.
[3] CO. 520/67, Egerton to C.O., conf. 2 November 1908.
[4] Akintoye, *op. cit.*, pp. 343–4.

Internal Boundaries and Amalgamation

Company, whereas the Oil Rivers (Niger Coast) Protectorate controlled such areas as Nembe and Brass which were politically, ethnically and commercially related to the Akassa Ijos. The restrictive trade practices adopted by the Royal Niger Company at Akassa and its other trading depots precipitated the Akassa Raid of 1895 by the aggrieved Nembe-Brass chiefs and people. The result was a punitive expedition against the Akassa raiders by the Niger Coast Protectorate administration, which had assumed no responsibility for the monopolistic policies of the Royal Niger Company and the arbitrary boundary demarcation.

The controversial eastern boundary of Lagos and Protectorate near the Benin River also caused trouble. The Niger Coast Protectorate and the Lagos administrations were embarrassed in 1894 when Nana fled to Lagos territory to avoid arrest. They finally resolved their misunderstandings when Nana was compelled to surrender himself 'unconditionally' to face the charges against him.[1]

Moor, who had been actively involved in the government handling of the Nana and Akassa Raid episodes, became an early advocate of amalgamation as the answer to the issues raised by separate boundaries and jurisdictional conflicts. In November 1896, he advocated 'one main administration for the entire Niger Territories, with one or two sub-administrations . . .'[2] Three separate administrations, he said, were expensive and not favourable to commercial development, and he urged one fiscal system and the removal of fiscal boundaries. Revenues, he proposed, should be pooled and allocated for expenditure according to local requirements. Moor reiterated these views in June 1897.[3]

The Imperial Treasury memorandum of December 1896 similarly pointed out the disadvantages of dividing 'jurisdiction' over the Niger territories between the Niger Coast Protectorate, the Royal Niger Company and Lagos Colony. In a reference to the rival customs duties and conflicting responsibilities for 'good order' among the indigenous inhabitants, the Treasury remarked:[4]

> The company looks to dividends only. The protectorate is bound by the Brussels Act to look after the welfare of the

[1] FO. 2-64, MacDonald to F.O., 12 November 1894.
[2] FO. 2/102, Moor to F.O., 24 November 1896.
[3] FO. 2/122, Moor to F.O., 26 June 1897.
[4] FO. 2/102, Treasury Memorandum of 14 December 1896 filed with Moor to F.O., 24 November 1896.

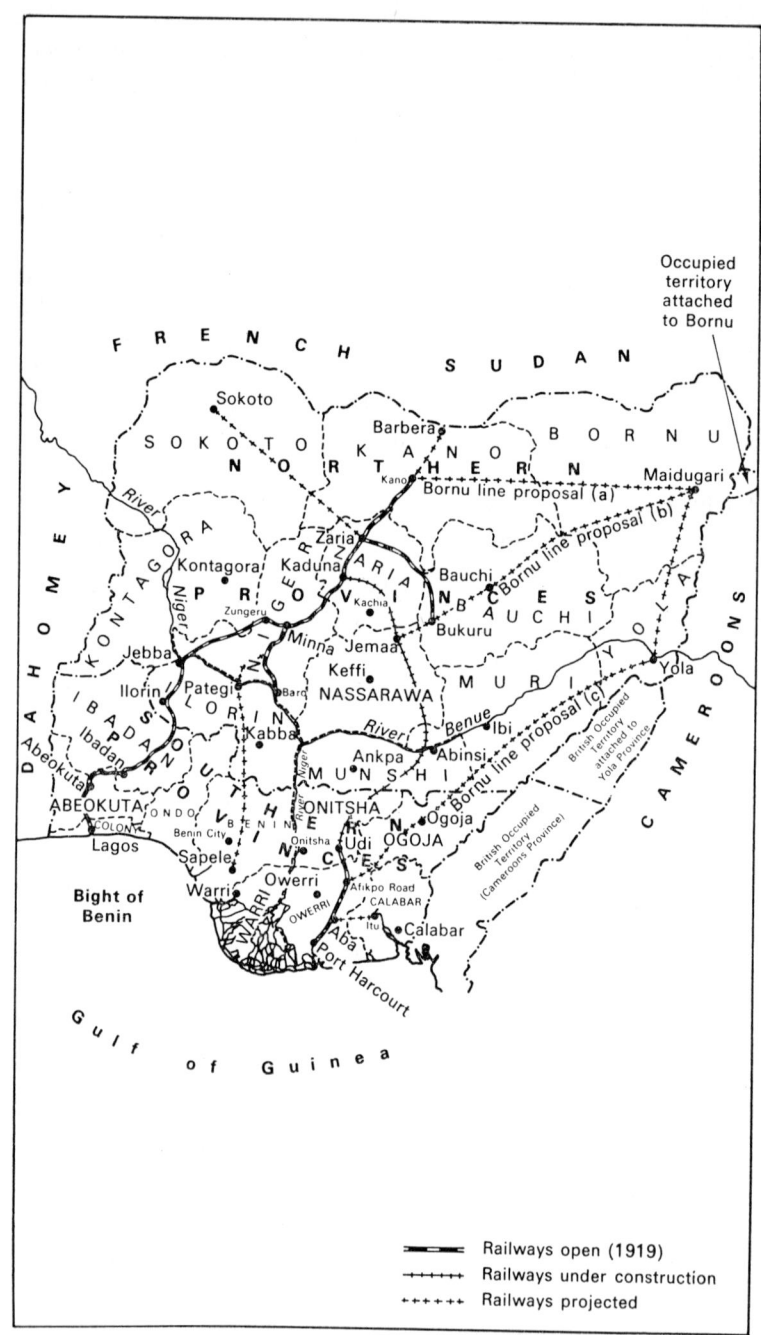

Railways completed and projected in Nigeria, 1920

Internal Boundaries and Amalgamation

natives. The company ousts the Brass-men from the Niger trade, and the latter, to save themselves from starvation, make a raid into the company's province . . . The protectorate has then to pay [£20,000] damages because the Brass-men are within the protectorate jurisdiction.

During the late 1890s when company administration of subject peoples became discredited and the Royal Niger Company consequently lost its charter, its successor-administrations inherited some of the old boundary problems. Even in 1900 the British government still adopted tripartite administration of its territories in Nigeria subject to a few boundary changes.

From January 1900, the Protectorate of Southern Nigeria took over from the Royal Niger Company its stations south of Lokoja. Thereafter, Moor's administration assumed responsibility for Idah, Akassa, Onitsha, Asaba and Aboh. In Northern Nigeria, also in 1900, Lugard inherited the areas hitherto claimed or administered by the Royal Niger Company: Ilorin, Kabba, and the cluster of ethnic groups north of Idah but within the Niger-Benue valley.

In dealing with the various internal boundary disputes which affected their three administrations, the government spokesmen propounded three major principles which often conflicted. MacGregor and Egerton maintained the principle of ethnicity. Moor consistently and Egerton occasionally advocated administrative convenience. Lugard, however, stressed the principle of established local jurisdiction. Even though the Colonial Office encouraged its men-on-the-spot to resolve such differences through further discussions among themselves, it often lent its weight to the theory of established local jurisdiction.

The controversy over the Idah section of the boundary between the Protectorates of Northern and Southern Nigeria illustrated these differences. In October 1902 Lugard objected to the loss of about 500 square miles of territory north of Idah to the Protectorate of Southern Nigeria according to the new boundary delimitation proposed by Moor.[1] Since the Attah of Idah had had hereditary and pre-colonial tributary claims to the people who lived about 16 miles north of Idah in the disputed territory, but for over ten years had not collected regular tribute

[1] CO. 520/18, L. Probyn to C.O., 23 February 1903, enclosure, Lugard to Moor, 11 October 1902.

227

from them, Lugard found no evidence of established local jurisdiction to validate the transfer to the Attah of more villages on the basis of tributary relationships. Lugard later maintained that the Attahs of Idah had exercised no more than 'religious or ceremonial influence' over the people in the area under discussion.[1]

Moor insisted that the chiefs and people of Idah had property and commercial interests in the disputed territory, but informed Lugard in November 1902 that he had based his demands not on the hereditary and tributary lands of the Attahs of Idah but on 'general convenience and facility of administration'.[2] Moor explained:

> I am not at all desirous to add to the territories of Southern Nigeria, but must be guided by the requirements and general convenience of the natives and what appears to me to be the most efficient method of administration. I submit for your consideration that it is unreasonable to have an officer stationed at Idah carrying on administration over natives who in two or three hours journey would be outside his jurisdiction and the majority of whose property and interest are under another Administration.[3]

In January 1903, Lugard skilfully reduced to absurdity Moor's argument about protectorate officials administering the affairs of people who in two or three hours' journey disappeared from the limits of their jurisdiction. He stressed that such a situation 'must apply wherever the frontier is placed . . .'[4]

During their meeting at the Colonial Office on 13 October 1903, Moor and Lugard, however, reached a compromise solution. Under this arrangement, the Protectorate of Southern Nigeria gained certain lands fifteen miles north-east of Idah.[5]

Lugard's emphasis on the principle of established local jurisdiction met its severest test over the controversial boundary between Lagos Colony and Protectorate and the Protectorate of Northern Nigeria. The Ekiti claim to Otun in particular and the general Yoruba claim to Ilorin provided the two most important boundary disputes in the West. Until 1900, Otun had been the

---

[1] *Ibid.*, enclosure – Lugard to Moor, 15 January 1903.
[2] *Ibid.*, enclosure: Moor to Lugard, 19 November 1902.
[3] *Ibid.*
[4] *Ibid.*, enclosure: Lugard to Moor, 14 January 1903.
[5] *Ibid.*, minute by R.L.A., dated 13 October 1903.

leader of the *Ekitiparapo* or confederation. The 16 Ekiti kingdoms constantly acknowledged Otun's prescriptive right to leadership.[1] Otun had formed part of the Lagos Protectorate until 30 April 1900 when, during a boundary delimitation exercise between MacGregor and Lugard, the former wrongly signed it away to Northern Nigeria.[2] MacGregor admitted his error, saying that he had not known that Otun headed the Ekiti kingdoms, and wanted it rectified.[3]

Travelling Commissioner W. G. Ambrose, who supervised the North-Eastern District – including the Ekiti part of the Lagos Protectorate – informed the Secretariat at Lagos that without the presence of Otun, any Native Council embracing the Ekiti people would be regarded by them as no more than 'a dummy Council'.[4] The Ore of Otun petitioned the Lagos government to restore his territory to his kinsmen.[5] He was arrested and detained at Ilorin.[6] Lugard said that Otun had been a tributary state to Ilorin and that lately the Ore had refused to pay 'his customary tribute' to his 'suzerain chief'. The Ore was also suspected of being a member of the Yoruba *Ogboni* secret society.[7]

The controversy over the Otun and Ilorin boundaries enabled Lugard to enunciate his basic principles for the demarcation of boundaries. Writing in March 1904, Lugard stated:[8]

> It is a matter of little Imperial importance whether a section of a particular district is administered by one British authority or another; but it is a matter of much local importance, whether existing customs are arbitrarily interfered with. It is a wholly novel theory that all 'racial relations' should necessarily be under the same rule. The province of Illorin [sic] contains, for instance, a section of the Yorubas conquered by the Fulani and comprising now the Emirate of Illorin, which itself was again an appanage of Gando ... Lines of demarcation in Africa must proceed on decisions of local jurisdiction not on 'racial relations' ... The existing boundaries are tolerably good in

[1] CO. 147/169, Moseley to C.O., 29 February 1904.
[2] CO. 147/162, Moseley to C.O., 24 October 1902.
[3] CI. 147/167, MacGregor to C.O., 31 December 1903. CO. 147/169, MacGregor to C.O., 1 January 1904.
[4] CO. 147/162, Moseley to C.O., 24 October 1902, enclosure: Ambrose's letter dated 18 June 1902.
[5] CO. 147/162. Moseley to C.O., 24 October 1902.
[6] CO. 147/169, Moseley to C.O., 29 February 1904.
[7] CSO. 1/27/4, Lugard to C.O., conf. 28 March 1904.   [8] *Ibid.*

this respect, and have now received the sanction of time and usage . . . I venture to protest against any fresh disturbance of this frontier, the more so . . . I presume that, in the not very distant future, the two Administrations will be merged.

Neither the 1906 amalgamation nor that of 1914, as such, restored Otun or Ilorin to the Yorubas. Otun's restoration to the Ekiti came only in 1936.[1]

Egerton reopened this perennial boundary question as the extension of the Lagos Railway approached and eventually passed Ilorin,[2] reminding the Yorubas of their historical and ethnic claims to Ilorin. On 7 June 1906, the Legislative Council unanimously adopted the resolution moved by C. Sapara-Williams and seconded by O. Johnson:

> That this Council is of opinion that . . . the Secretary of State for the Colonies be asked to sanction that the Railway now being carried on to Oshogbo be continued at once into the Territory of Northern Nigeria, in order to connect the trade of the two places and to facilitate the development of the countries around. And also that the present boundary between the Colony and Protectorate of Southern Nigeria and the Protectorate of Northern Nigeria be re-adjusted by bringing the Southern portion of Northern Nigeria into Southern Nigeria, so that the entire tribes of Yoruba-speaking people should be under one and the same administration.[3]

In July 1909, C. Sapara-Williams, O. Johnson, and K. Ajasa forwarded their own petition to Egerton embodying this resolution and demanding that the Lagos government's control of its railway, which then had reached Jebba, should extend to the 'banks of the Niger' and so include all the Yoruba-speaking people resident there. They considered the existing boundaries 'purely artificial' and 'a source of untold inconveniences and much dissatisfaction, separating as they do farmsteads from homesteads, sub-chiefs and people from their overlords; dividing farms and estates into two portions under different Governments'.[4]

Egerton, the advocate of 'racial boundaries', supported both

---

[1] Akintoye, *op. cit.*, p. 338.
[2] CO. 520/67, Egerton to C.O., conf. 2 November 1908. CO. 520/80, Egerton to C.O., conf. 4 July 1909.
[3] CO. 520/80, Egerton to C.O., conf. 4 July 1909, enclosure.
[4] *Ibid.*, enclosure, petition dated 3 July 1909.

Internal Boundaries and Amalgamation

the 1906 resolution and the 1909 petition. Since 1908, he had strongly advocated the alteration of the Ilorin boundary as well as the reunification under his administration of all the Ekiti towns and Owo and Afenmai territories, part of which were then included in the Protectorate of Northern Nigeria.[1] When he discussed these questions with Governor P. Girouard of Northern Nigeria, he was warned 'that it would be better, as far as possible, to let these boundary disputes sleep pending the amalgamation of the two territories'.[2]

Over the Ilorin boundary question, as in similar cases, the Colonial Office adopted the general principle based on considerations of established local jurisdiction and not kinship. It left villages and towns which had been subject to the pre-colonial rule of the Fulani emirs in Northern Nigeria in that protectorate.[3] Shortly after the 1906 amalgamation, S. Olivier of the Colonial Office further opposed burdening Egerton with the additional work of administering more territories while he faced the great responsibilities of the combined territories in the south.[4] Egerton, however, seemed eager to assume more responsibilities and so learnt with misgiving the desire of the government of the Protectorate of Northern Nigeria to assume complete control over all the 'pagan' settlements divided between the two administrations in post-1906 Nigeria. He would have preferred to administer all the Tiv and Okpoto (Akpoto) areas himself.[5] In advocating such far-reaching boundary alterations, particularly in Tivland, Egerton combined the two principles of ethnicity and administrative convenience. He maintained that, as far as possible, such 'pagan' ethnic communities as the Akpoto and Tiv should be administered by the officials of Southern Nigeria who, in his view, had a longer tradition of handling such people than the authorities of Northern Nigeria. The latter, he said, had specialised in the control of Muslims.[6]

---

[1] CO. 520/67, Egerton to C.O. conf. 2 November 1908. CO. 520/80, Egerton to C.O., conf. 4 July 1909.

[2] CO. 520/61, Egerton to C.O., conf. 18 May 1908.

[3] CO. 520/61, Egerton to C.O., conf. 15 May 1908, minute by C.S.

[4] CO. 520/37, Egerton to C.O., conf. 14 September 1906, minute by S.O. (Later Lord Olivier).

[5] CO. 520/67, Egerton to C.O., conf. 2 November 1908. The term 'Munshi' was used in this document. This was perhaps a reference to the 'Udam' in Ogoja, who were related to the Tiv. See *West Africa*, 1 August 1970, p. 869.   [6] *Ibid*.

Egerton buttressed his recommendations with financial arguments. By assuming control over the Tiv, Okpoto (Akpoto), Ilorin, Otun, and the entire Owo and Afenmai settlements, he would relieve Northern Nigeria of needless financial expenditure. As Northern Nigeria then heavily relied on imperial grants-in-aid and Southern Nigeria was self-sufficient, Egerton thought this a fair deal. He also believed that transferring these territories to Southern Nigeria would offer Northern Nigeria the 'best way' of preparing itself for the larger amalgamation with the rest of the country. Egerton wanted major boundary alterations, such as those he had recommended, settled before the larger amalgamation. Minor disputes, he said, could be undertaken afterwards.[1]

Egerton related the boundary problem with the Tiv and other 'pagan' groups to the need for concerted action with Northern Nigeria in military operations against these people from 1908.[2] By then Egerton had realised the failure of unilateral moves against the tough-minded Tiv close to the northern limits of Southern Nigeria. Without informing the Colonial Office, Trenchard, with Egerton's knowledge, had entered Tiv territory in November 1907. But in the attempts to construct a new road through parts of Tivland in 1909, Egerton's government clashed with the Tiv.[3] Tiv unrest continued. In June 1912 Lugard promised to re-examine the questions of bringing the Tiv under firm British control.[4]

Opinion in the Colonial Office was divided. F. G. A. Butler observed that as the Colonial Office was not then in a hurry to develop Tivland, the financial factor raised earlier by Egerton had no urgency. For political reasons, Butler felt convinced that the slower methods of Northern Nigeria in establishing control over the Tiv would be preferred.[5] R. L. Antrobus, on the other hand, accepted Egerton's view that Southern Nigeria had greater experience and success in 'pagan' administration than Northern

[1] *Ibid.*
[2] *Ibid.* C.O. 520/83, Egerton to C.O., conf. 26 November 1909. CO. 520/91, Egerton to C.O., tel. 10 January 1910. CO. 520/91, Egerton to C.O., conf. 11 February 1910. CO. 510/93, Egerton to C.O., conf. 25 April 1910. CO. 520/103, Egerton to C.O., conf. 17 May 1911.
[3] Boyle: *Trenchard*, London 1962, pp. 88–90.
[4] CO. 520/115, James to C.O., conf. 26 May 1912, minute by F.D.L., dated 22 June 1912.
[5] CO. 520/67, Egerton to C.O., conf. 2 November 1908, minute by F.G.A.B., dated 24 November 1908.

Nigeria. He therefore regretted the presence of several 'pagan' groups north and south of the eastern boundary between both protectorates. Antrobus recalled that 'when we were drawing the line in 1899, our intention was to draw it as far as possible so as to assign pagans to Southern, and Mohammedans to Northern Nigeria'.[1] Even so, Antrobus found it 'unnecessary to consider at present the question of altering the boundary'.[2] Lord Crewe, the Secretary of State, emphasised that without the agreement of the Northern Nigeria authorities, those of Southern Nigeria should not undertake any action, even of a peaceful kind, against the Tiv.[3] No such co-operation took place before Lugard's era from late 1912.

Generally, the government dodged the issue of the boundary questions which arose before 1914. Although some high-ranking officials occasionally recommended that such questions await the implementation of the amalgamation schemes, none of these provided any worthwhile solution.

GRADUAL AMALGAMATION

The various amalgamation schemes undertaken by the government up to January 1914 dealt with the problem of inconvenient internal boundary questions only marginally. Basically, these amalgamation schemes responded gradually to more urgent economic and fiscal necessities. Economic factors were therefore paramount.

To a large extent, the views expressed by Moor in November 1896 and June 1897 in favour of amalgamation and the pooling of revenues were vindicated in the Niger Committee's report of 1898. Comprising Lord Selborne (Chairman), G. Goldie (representing the Royal Niger Company), C. Hill (the Foreign Office), R. Moor (the Niger Coast Protectorate), R. L. Antrobus (the Colonial Office) and H. McCallum (Lagos), this committee had considered, among other things, the question of amalgamating the 'Niger Territories' and unanimously recommended amalgamation as the goal of future British policy in Nigeria. The members

[1] *Ibid*. Minute by R.L.A., dated 25 November 1908.
[2] *Ibid*.
[3] *Ibid*. Minute by C., dated 27 November 1908.

The Evolution of the Nigerian State

agreed that 'the object to be aimed at' should be 'the eventual establishment of a Governor General' over the amalgamated territories.¹

In view of practical difficulties, the committee advised against immediate amalgamation. Indeed two major obstacles made it impossible: the climatic and health hazards on one hand and the inadequate transportation and communications on the other. To solve this last problem the committee recommended the construction of railways.

Meanwhile, the committee proposed the establishment of two groups or provinces – the 'Soudan' and the 'Maritime'. The ninth parallel constituted the line of demarcation between the two provinces. Broadly, the 'Soudan' (interior) Provinces included the bulk of the Muslim population in Nigeria whereas the 'Maritime' (coastal) covered 'pagan' territory except the Muslims in Yorubaland. The committee favoured a common military force for the two provinces though its units would be interchangeable in emergencies. It further welcomed the amalgamation of the colonial military forces of British West Africa. Concerning fiscal arrangements, the committee recommended a 'Customs Union' for the two provinces based on the existing Lagos tariff. It also advised that revenue should be pooled and divided 'according to the budget requirements of the provinces'.

On Chamberlain's instructions, Moor and McCallum in August 1898 re-examined the Niger Committee's recommendations about constituting the Niger Coast Protectorate and Lagos into a Maritime Province. Given adequate staff and allowing for improved means of transport and communications, Moor considered such a province administratively feasible.² McCallum, however, disagreed. The existing difficulties in transportation and communications, McCallum observed, made it desirable to continue the bi-partite administrative arrangements for Lagos and the Niger Coast Protectorate until the situation improved.³ McCallum's arguments impressed Antrobus.⁴ By November 1898 Chamberlain himself had come round to the view that 'for

[1] CO. 446/3, MP. No. 17887, Report of the Niger Committee dated 4 August 1898. By the 'Niger Territories' the committee meant Lagos, the Niger Coast Protectorate and the territory administered by the Royal Niger Company.

[2] CO. 446/3, Moor to C.O., 18 August 1898.

[3] CO. 446/3, McCallum to C.O., 14 August 1898, enclosure.

[4] CO. 446/3, Moor to C.O., 18 August 1898, minute by R.L.A.

the present' there should continue to be three administrations in the Niger territories.¹ Chamberlain communicated his decision to the Treasury in June 1899.² He approved amalgamation in principle and hoped that 'in the course of a few years' it would be possible to place the Niger territories under 'one administration'. But until the means of transportation and communication improved and better arrangements for public health and sanitation had been made for 'the seat of government', he felt unable to recommend the appointment of a 'Governor-General'.

On the establishment of the Customs Union recommended by the Niger Committee, Chamberlain advised, and the Treasury approved, the assimilation of the customs tariffs of all the three territories.³ But, as the government found it difficult to determine precisely the amount of customs duties derived from goods consumed in Northern Nigeria, Chamberlain proposed a basis for revenue allocation, and the Treasury agreed 'that customs receipts should be allotted to the three divisions in such proportions as the Secretary of State may from time to time direct, having regard to the requirements both of the divisions on the coast and of the inland division'.⁴

It is clear that from 1898, the British government had provided a general outline for the amalgamation of the Niger territories. Thereafter, only detailed amalgamation schemes were required, provided the practical difficulties could be solved. These problems were tackled by Moor, MacGregor and Egerton in Southern Nigeria and their colleagues in the north.

In response to Chamberlain's 'verbal instructions', Moor in 1901 drew up a scheme for amalgamating the Protectorate of Southern Nigeria with Lagos.⁵ By failing to consult MacGregor, Moor himself experienced diffidence in recommending the scheme strongly for Chamberlain's favourable consideration.⁶

MacGregor favoured large political units and thought union between Lagos and Northern Nigeria most urgent. The Lagos

[1] CO. 446/3, MP No. 25517, minute by R.L.A., 13 November 1898.
[2] *African (West)*, No. 591, September 1899. C.O. to Treasury, 6 June 1899.
[3] *Ibid*. Treasury to C.O., 20 July 1899.
[4] *Ibid*. Consequently, Southern Nigeria, particularly after the 1906 amalgamation, paid Northern Nigeria a yearly sum of £70,000. A much smaller sum was reluctantly paid by Southern Nigeria before May 1906.
[5] CO. 520/7, Moor to C.O., 14 January 1901.
[6] *Ibid*.

235

Railway which MacGregor wanted extended towards Lake Chad seemed to him the best means of accomplishing the union.¹ For personal reasons, MacGregor considered Lagos Colony and Protectorate too small to give his administrative ability sufficient scope. He therefore informed Antrobus in 1899 and 1900 that he wished to administer Northern Nigeria, a suggestion which the latter thought had influenced his desire for political union.² MacGregor and Lord Selborne thought alike in condemning 'small colonies' as uneconomical and having a tendency to narrow the 'political horizon' of able administrators.³

MacGregor was not alone in his desire for a Lagos-Northern Nigeria merger. John Holt, who consistently admired MacGregor, at first thought of amalgamation in instalments beginning with a Lagos-Northern Nigeria union headed by his favourite Governor. In December 1902, Holt had wrongly assumed that Lugard would leave Northern Nigeria even before undertaking the punitive expeditions against Kano and Sokoto. He therefore informed Morel:

> By all means let us get Sir W. MacGregor appointed Governor there and if you like throw Lagos and Northern Nigeria into one – Southern [Nigeria] will follow. We must get rid of these military Governors.⁴

Even in January 1906, Holt advocated amalgamation on the basis of three 'provinces' administered by 'sub-governors' under the direction of MacGregor as the 'first Governor-General'.⁵

Holt also hoped that by amalgamation the whole of Nigeria would have uniform laws and regulations, particularly in such matters as licences for rubber collection. He further expected amalgamation to help prevent evasions of the seasonal stoppage of illegal rubber exports.⁶

The Colonial Office from 1898 had no doubts about the other economic and fiscal merits of amalgamation. It did not ignore, however, the political and personnel angles, and, taking these into

¹ CO. 147/154, MacGregor to C.O., 23 March 1901, enclosure.
² CO. 446/3, Moor to C.O., 18 August 1898, minute by R.L.A., 8 October 1900.
³ *Ibid.*, minute by S. dated 12 October 1898.
⁴ *E.D.M.P.* F/8, Holt to Morel, 16 December 1902.
⁵ *E.D.M.P.* F/8, Holt to Morel, 21 January 1906.
⁶ *E.D.M.P.* F/8, Holt to Morel, 25 June 1901. *E.D.M.P.* F/8, Holt to Morel, 23 August 1906.

Internal Boundaries and Amalgamation

consideration, decided to move gradually towards amalgamation. The Colonial Office had reasons for its caution. It then considered further amalgamation schemes inauspicious until the major problems, which from 1900 to 1903 had confronted the administrations in Nigeria, had been solved. For example, in the Protectorate of Southern Nigeria, the Aro problem remained serious between 1900 and 1902. In the Protectorate of Northern Nigeria, Kano and Sokoto caused anxiety to Chamberlain[1] until their submission in early 1903. Pending the decline of the political unrest in Northern Nigeria, the Colonial Office did not encourage MacGregor's desire for union with Lagos. Nor did it seek to amalgamate Lagos with the Protectorate of Southern Nigeria as long as MacGregor desired to remain Governor of Lagos, for it did not wish to demote MacGregor to the rank of a 'Lieutenant-Governor'[2] in the event of amalgamation.

While the Colonial Office delayed action, the Protectorate of Southern Nigeria continued to experience considerable jurisdictional difficulties, including the enforcement of its Native House Rule Proclamation, 1901.[3] People seeking to avoid its provisions frequently fled to Lagos Colony and Protectorate, as, in March 1903, Acting High Commissioner L. Probyn unsuccessfully complained.[4] He later appreciated that the Lagos government could hardly endorse warrants for the arrest of such fugitives, as its Travelling District Commissioners near its eastern boundary with the Protectorate of Southern Nigeria lacked the status of judicial officers.[5] Such difficulties were occasionally complicated by the fact that through mistakes about the boundary, the Benin River Native Council, as in 1903, served summonses on offenders within the jurisdiction of Lagos Colony and Protectorate.[6] These difficulties were less acute from 1904 when Egerton began to manage the affairs of Lagos and the Protectorate of Southern Nigeria.

Egerton saw Moor's amalgamation scheme in 1901 before drafting a more elaborate one[7] of his own which was ready in

[1] CO. 446/2, Moor to C.O., 18 August 1898, minute by J.C., dated 24 July 1900.
[2] *Ibid.*, minutes by R.L.A. and M.F.O.
[3] For the details of this law see Chapter 11.
[4] CSO. 8/2/7, L. Probyn to MacGregor, 11 March 1903.
[5] CSO. 8/2/7, L. Probyn to MacGregor, 11 June 1903.
[6] CSO. 8/2/7, Moor to MacGregor, 9 January 1903.
[7] CO. 592/2, S.P. No. 5 of 1906: Paper laid on the table of the Legislative

January 1905, and which he was able to discuss with the Colonial Office during his leave later in the year. Following these discussions, the Colonial Office modified Egerton's earlier proposal to keep separate revenues for Lagos and the Protectorate of Southern Nigeria. The combined territories therefore had a single treasury. This suited Antrobus' long-cherished idea of making 'fiscal union' the 'principal object' of amalgamation.[1] Antrobus had attached very great importance to this in view of the loans to be raised for such projects as the extension of the Lagos Railway. After studying Egerton's draft scheme, Antrobus very strenuously insisted on this fiscal union because of the difficulty that loans raised on the security of the revenue of a protectorate would not be admitted by the Imperial Treasury as a 'trustee investment'.[2]

The Colonial Office further modified Egerton's proposal to keep legislation in the combined territories separate. Instead it advised that the existing laws in both territories should remain in force subject to their future re-examination so as to apply suitable ones to the whole territory.[3] In other respects, the Colonial Office closely followed Egerton's recommendations. Lagos became the headquarters of the amalgamated territories which comprised the colony and a wider protectorate. Lagos continued thereafter as the capital of the developing Nigerian state.

In 1906 the government carved three provinces – Western, Central and Eastern – out of the combined territories. The Western Province comprised the former Lagos Colony and Protectorate with its headquarters at Lagos. The Central Province embraced the western and central divisions of the former Protectorate of Southern Nigeria with the capital at Warri. The Eastern Province included the former Calabar, Eastern and Cross River divisions with headquarters at Calabar. Geographical considerations, accessibility to provincial headquarters, and the need for giving provincial heads adequate salaries compelled Egerton to recommend no more than three provinces.[4]

Council on 11 May 1906. Henceforth, this document will be briefly cited as *The Amalgamation Correspondence*, 1906.

[1] C.O. 520/27, MP. No. 21004, minute by R.L.A., 8 June 1904.
[2] C.O. 520/29, Egerton to C.O., conf. 29 January 1905, minute by R.L.A.
[3] *The Amalgamation Correspondence*, 1906, C.O. to O.A.G., 12 January 1906. [4] *Ibid.* Egerton to C.O., 29 January 1905.

As head of the central administration, the Governor was assisted by a Lieutenant-Governor who was also the Colonial Secretary. A Provincial Commissioner administered each province 'in all departments' without reference to Lagos except in 'important matters'. Such a delegation of powers mainly resulted from the difficult means of transport and communications between Lagos and the provincial headquarters. Egerton further justified it because the system had 'been well proved in the Federated Malay States...'[1]

Egerton also provided for provincial secretariats in addition to the Central Secretariat. The approved political and administrative staff comprised the Provincial Commissioners, Assistant Provincial and District Commissioners.

By amalgamating the Customs and Treasury Departments, Egerton created the new office of Financial Commissioner on the model of the Federated Malay States. Egerton also provided for the posts of provincial treasurer and local auditors.[2]

As the government gained more experience in handling the affairs of the amalgamated territories, it made further adjustments. For example, Egerton modified the 1906 arrangements for provincial commissionerships when experience dictated the need for further reform. Towards the end of 1908, he merged the commissionership of the Western Province with the Central Secretariat. The location of the headquarters of that province at Lagos, he explained, made a separate Provincial Commissioner there unnecessary.[3]

Egerton also found that the merging of the Customs and Treasury Departments did not work satisfactorily and urged their separation in 1908.[4] Although Egerton allowed the retention of the title and emoluments of the Financial Commissioner, he separated the Treasury and Customs Departments in January 1909 and appointed a Comptroller of Customs in the same year.[5]

Railway developments in Northern and Southern Nigeria after 1906 accelerated the pace towards the larger amalgamation

[1] *Ibid.*

[2] Southern Nigeria's accounts were again audited by the Comptroller and Auditor-General, Exchequer and Audit Department, London. See CO. 592/3, Annual report, Southern Nigeria, 1906.

[3] CO. 520/63, Egerton to C.O., conf. 11 July 1908. CO. 520/66, Egerton to C.O., 6 October 1908, minute by J.A.

[4] CO. 520/64, Egerton to C.O., conf. 14 August 1908.

[5] CO. 520/67, Egerton to C.O., conf. 20 November 1908.

The Evolution of the Nigerian State

effected in January 1914. With that amalgamation in view, the imperial Treasury in 1907 recommended that the richer southern administration provide credit 'for railway purposes of the Northern territory which it will eventually absorb'.[1] That proposal involved a loan of £1,230,000 for the construction of the Baro-Kano Railway in Northern Nigeria. Lord Elgin, then Secretary of State for the Colonies, agreed that

> as the amalgamation of Northern and Southern Nigeria has been decided upon in principle, and will probably be carried out within the next few years, it would be justifiable to utilise the credit of Southern Nigeria in order to ensure the construction of the railway, which, on amalgamation, will become the property of the Colony of 'Nigeria' as a whole.[2]

W. S. Churchill announced this decision to the House of Commons on 5 August 1907.[3]

The question of control over the extended Lagos Railway, 200 miles of which lay in Northern Nigeria, made it necessary for the government to co-ordinate its freight rates and eliminate undue rivalries.[4] As a solution to these problems, the government on 3 October 1912, combined the Railway Departments of Northern and Southern Nigeria whose new head took charge of the 'Nigerian Railway'.[5]

In terms of financial considerations, the larger amalgamation of 1914 represented an act of faith on the part of the Colonial Office, in view of the initial staggering estimated deficits ranging from £200,000 to £350,000 a year.[6] Despite the original pessimism over these financial predictions, G. V. Fiddes assumed 'that if we lump together the prosperous Southern [sic] and the struggling Northern Protectorate, the results will be to diminish the burden on the Treasury'.[7]

[1] Cd. 4523, Lond., 1909, No. 21: Treasury to C.O., 1 August 1907.
[2] *Ibid.*, No. 22: C.O. to Treasury, 1 August 1907. This loan was subsequently increased by about £200,000.
[3] *Ibid.* No. 27. HC. Deb. 4s. 179, 5 August 1907, 1535.
[4] CO. 520/103, Egerton to C.O., 26 May 1911. CO. 520/110, Egerton to C.O., 15 November 1911. CO. 520/110, MP. No. 24249, minutes of the Railway Committee meeting, 20 July 1911.
[5] CO. 657/1, Nigerian Railway administrative report, 1912.
[6] CO. 520/110, MP. No. 38852, Strachey's memorandum dated 20 November 1911 and minutes of 11 December 1911.
[7] *Ibid.*, minute by G.V.F., 13 December 1911.

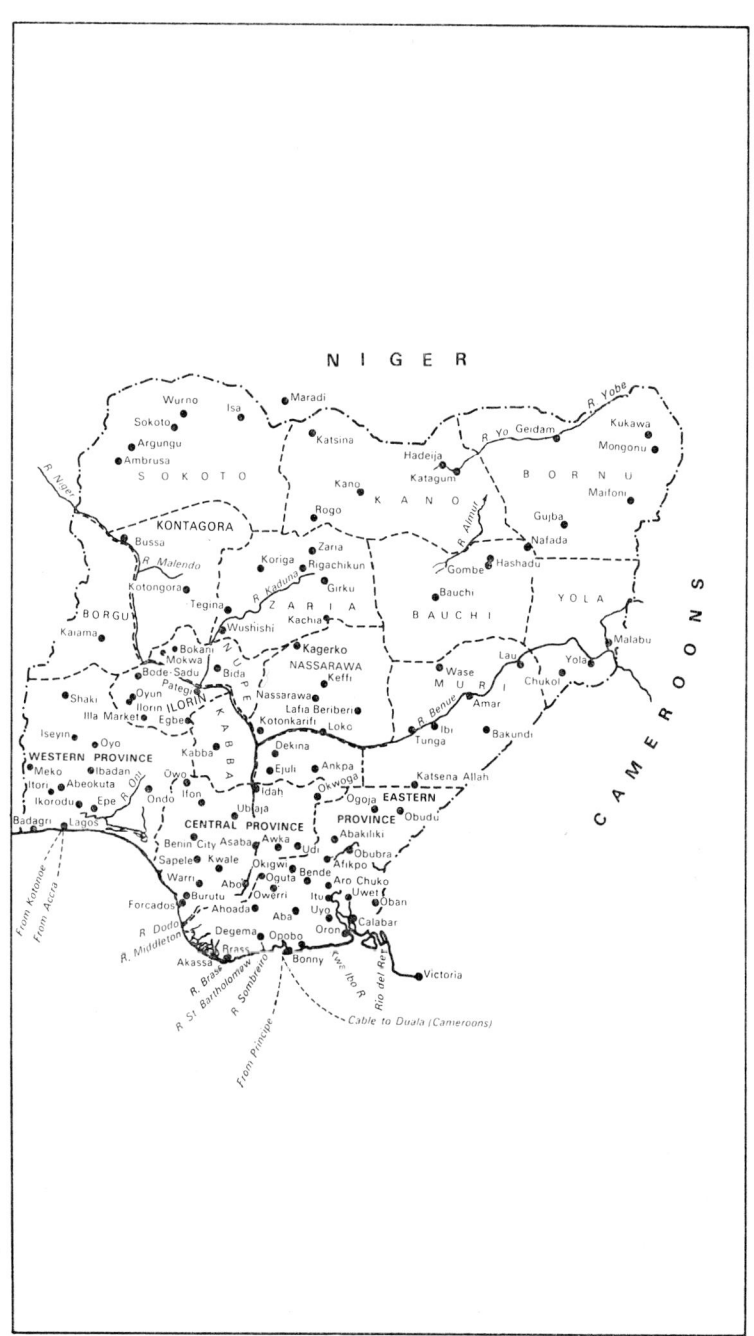

Nigeria, January 1911

The Evolution of the Nigerian State

The 1906 amalgamation, a major step in the scheme of merging the hitherto separate administrations in Nigeria, should be regarded as a means rather than an end. Its prime motive was economic, not political. Amalgamation in 1906, as in 1914, became a convenient method of helping a less economically fortunate partner – Lagos in 1906 and Northern Nigeria in 1914.

In 1906, the Lagos press showed little enthusiasm for the amalgamation accomplished with fanfare in May. Their considerable misgiving partly stemmed from the public awareness of the neglect of Lagos interests during the earlier administrative combinations of which Lagos had formed a part between 1866 and 1886.[1] Secondly, the press seriously criticised the salaries and allowances sanctioned under the amalgamation scheme,[2] and so did a special public meeting called at Lagos on 6 June 1906.[3] There was some justification for this anxiety. Between 1900 and 1901, the expenditure on personal emoluments for Lagos and the Protectorate of Southern Nigeria reached £208,290 4s. 8d. and £335,617 in 1905.[4] It rose from £382,337 in 1906 to £630,031 in 1912.[5] These increases followed naturally from the expanded departmental establishments needed to supervise the new areas brought under control. Egerton, however, defended such expenditure on the grounds of paying 'a good price' to obtain 'good service'.[6]

The Colonial Office decided in favour of the further amalgamation from 1912, when it invited Lugard to prepare a plan for the next stage. In 1911, Secretary of State Harcourt would have 'let the project drop for the present' if he had failed to obtain Lugard's services, 'as its success must depend on the quality of the man whom I could obtain to carry it out'.[7] In June 1912, Harcourt made this decisive factor clear to the House of Commons:

[1] *The Lagos Standard*, 9 May 1906.
[2] *The Lagos Standard*, 13 June 1906. *The African Mail*, 31 January 1908.
[3] CO. 520/36, Egerton to C.O., 11 August 1906, enclosure.
[4] Cd. 2564, London 1905.
[5] *Colonial reports, annual*, Southern Nigeria, 1906. CO. 592/16, Financial report, Southern Nigeria, 1912.
[6] CO. 591/3, Southern Nigeria Government Gazette, 6 June 1906: Legislative Council Debates, 18 May 1906.
[7] *Lugard Papers*, MSS. Brit. Emp. s.73. Harcourt to Lugard, 12 September 1911.

Internal Boundaries and Amalgamation

> Though I have been convinced ever since I came to the Colonial Office that this amalgamation was desirable, I frankly admit that I should not have thought the moment opportune unless I had happened to know and been able to command the services of the one man marked out for this great work, Sir Frederick Lugard...[1]

Despite Egerton's interest in the same post, Harcourt eliminated him outright. After eight years in Southern Nigeria, Egerton by 1912 was a tired man. However, Egerton and his predecessors in Southern Nigeria had in various ways made the 1914 amalgamation possible. Together, they had tackled the two major obstacles noticed by the Niger Committee in 1898. Between 1900 and 1913 Southern Nigeria had improved means of transport and communications. Moreover, Lagos, the administrative and commercial capital, had benefited from the public health and sanitation projects centred on it since the turn of the century.

Similar developments had also taken place in Northern Nigeria during the pre-1914 amalgamation period. Lugard himself recognised that the delay in carrying out the 1914 phase of the amalgamation had further enabled Northern Nigeria to develop at its own rate. In November 1912, Lugard therefore informed the Legislative Council of Southern Nigeria:

> In the opinion of Sir Ralph Moor, and of your former Governor, Sir W. MacGregor, and of myself, the country was ripe for Amalgamation some years ago. But there is no doubt that, if Amalgamation had been carried out at that date, it would have involved a very great strain on the finances of Lagos and Southern Nigeria. Sir W. Egerton in his last Message to Council said that 'Lagos was much disappointed at the delay which had taken place' in effecting this change, – but the interval between 1904 and 1912 has transformed Northern Nigeria from a country with practically no Revenue at all to one which has a very substantial and constantly increasing Revenue ... It has moreover a new and considerable mineral industry and great potentialities in the matter of cotton and other agricultural products. Instead, therefore, of being amalgamated with a wholly undeveloped Hinterland, you will be associated with a country upon which ... the British taxpayer has spent £3,760,830 in Grants in Aid, and which is, therefore ...
>
> [1] HC. Deb. 5s. 40, 27 June 1912, 512.

unburdened by public debt except for the comparatively small sum of £1,630,000 spent on 460 miles of railway which is likely to prove highly remunerative.[1]

Lugard rejected the view that the larger amalgamation inflicted the financial burdens of Northern Nigeria on the south. Convinced of the merits of economic inter-dependence, Lugard stressed that whereas in 1912 Northern Nigeria had incurred a loan responsibility of only £1,630,000, Southern Nigeria then had a public debt of about £7 million whose burden fell equally on all Nigerians.[2]

Lugard, Egerton, MacGregor and Moor all ably played their parts as the principal executives of the policy to amalgamate the Niger territories, a policy whose broad outlines had been laid down since 1898. The onus or honour of amalgamation cannot be attached to any single Governor or High Commissioner. The British government, whose servants they were, did not then consider amalgamation a moral issue. It was basically a major political means of solving a serious economic problem. Its main weakness however, lay in the British government's failure to consult the wishes of the people in matters of such great political and economic significance between 1898 and 1914. This was a reflection of how the people's right to consultations had been steadily lost under the mild autocracy which then typified Southern Nigeria's administration and development.

If, in consequence, the 1898–1914 amalgamation arrangements ever made Nigeria an 'artificial' British creation, so were the various *administrative* districts, divisions and provinces which developed arbitrarily.[3] The administrative parts were not more

---

[1] CSO. 1/19/54, Legard to C.O., 26 November 1912, enclosure: Governor's Message to the Legislative Council, 19 November 1912.   [2] *Ibid.*

[3] The question of administrative units in Southern Nigeria raised the least difficulties within the Yoruba-speaking part of Southern Nigeria except in relation to Ilorin, Otun and Owo. There, the territorial limits of the post-1906 Western Province agreed with those of the Lagos Colony and Protectorate. But the position became more complex in the culturally diverse Protectorate of Southern Nigeria which between 1900 and 1905 had four main administrative 'divisions' – Eastern, Central Western and Cross River. Between 1906 and 1912, these had been transformed into two 'provinces' – Eastern and Central. It should be further recalled that between 1886 and 1899, Idah, Onitsha, Asaba, Aboh and Akassa had been administered by the Royal Niger Company, and from 1900 by the Protectorate of Southern Nigeria.

Internal Boundaries and Amalgamation

natural and sacrosanct than the whole. Ethnic plurality and the various internal boundary questions underlined that historical fact. Administratively, the 1898–1914 amalgamation arrangements constituted important landmarks in Southern Nigeria's political developments. Important in themselves, these arrangements, however, proceeded simultaneously with equally significant economic and social measures designed to promote Southern Nigeria's general development.

9 Development and Structural Changes in the Economy

THE INTERDEPENDENCE OF ADMINISTRATION AND DEVELOPMENT

The close links between administration and development cannot be over-emphasised. New territories brought under control increased the cost of administration. They also contributed to the area under export-import economy, and that in turn helped to increase revenues. Far from being an end in itself, administration thus became a means of promoting internal and external trade. The economy of Southern Nigeria expanded. Before long, the government was emphasising the production of cash crops for exports, particularly in areas where relatively little capital investment was needed to ensure the desired marketable surplus.

Until 1914 the development of the economy of Southern Nigeria gained from a combination of factors. The territory had natural resources and suitable climate for profitable agricultural production. Government policies directly and indirectly helped economic development. In the absence of sufficiently attractive alternative wage-earning opportunities, subsistence and cash-crop farmers became firmly tied to the land.

For a variety of reasons the government avoided any long-term plans. Piecemeal progress, rather than planned economy, was the more convenient approach. The government became too preoccupied with routine administrative matters, punitive expeditions and patrols to spare much time for economic development planning. It lacked the detailed statistics required for making tolerable projections of development goals and implementation time-schedules. In this respect, the census figures, including those of 1911, remained estimates. The government also lacked enough skilled staff to devote to development schemes. Besides, the expected revenues for further development projects depended very much on the vagaries of climate and fluctuations in market

Development and Structural Changes in the Economy

prices. Consequently, estimates of expenditure on development or other projects from potential revenues were too hypothetical and unstable for the requirements of any planned development scheme. The bulk of the funds for Southern Nigeria's administration came from revenue. The major exception was in loans for large-scale public works whose service costs depended on the revenue figures.

IMPERIAL ECONOMIC OBJECTIVES AND ADMINISTRATIVE MEANS

Since 1807, British statesmen, philanthropists and businessmen had consistently emphasised the development of legitimate commerce. Control through coercion, diplomacy, usage and political amalgamation were all means to that end.

At the Colonial Office, Chamberlain's interest in developing imperial 'undeveloped estates' continued to influence his successors. During the House of Commons debate in April 1904 on increased cotton cultivation in Africa, A. Lyttelton declared: '... our business is cautiously and prudently to develop the great estate of which we are the stewards.'[1] In July 1906, the Duke of Marlborough, the former Parliamentary Under-Secretary of State for the Colonies, hoped to 'see in the next ten years a considerable development of the products from the sub-tropical soil in our Colonies in West Africa' and wished that such 'products may find their way into the English market'. One way of doing so, he suggested, lay in using the 'cotton fields in West Africa' to feed the Lancashire mills.[2] In March 1907, Parliamentary Under-Secretary of State W. S. Churchill expressed similar interest in developing 'those vast and yet only partially developed estates... in West and East Africa'. In those territories and particularly in Sierra Leone and post-1906 Southern Nigeria, Churchill stressed development in cotton cultivation and in railway construction.[3]

[1] HC. Deb. 4s. 133, 27 April 1905, 1391.
[2] Presidential address given on 5 July 1906 by Marlborough, the Under-Secretary of State, July 1903 – December 1905. See *J.A.S.*, vol. 6, 1906–7 London, p. 6.
[3] *Ibid.*, pp. 292–3 and 305. Address on 'The development of Africa' on 8 March 1907 by Churchill, Parliamentary Under-Secretary of State for the Colonies, 1905–8.

In Southern Nigeria, Moor, MacGregor and Egerton undertook the task of accomplishing these economic objectives. Of the three, Egerton was by far the most successful. Economic development was the key word of Egerton's administration, and it was for this that the Nigerian unofficial members of the Legislative Council and sections of the public most remembered him.[1]

Egerton's zeal and pertinacity in carrying out economic development measures – some envisaged or begun by Moor and MacGregor – were remarkable. These measures covered a wide range. They involved partly the expansion of the basis and volume of Southern Nigeria's export-import economy and partly the improvement of transport and communications.

Egerton had left the Straits Settlements and the Federated Malay States well aware of the importance of commerce in the development of overseas territories. Roads and railways, as experience in the Malay peninsula had taught him, were essential to this.[2] An overland journey which Egerton and a small party made on push-bicycles from Lagos to Calabar, between 8 March and 19 April 1905, over a 500-mile route confirmed his belief in Southern Nigeria's need for better road development.[3]

Later the same year Egerton declared: 'It is particularly pleasant to know, as my experience has taught me, that the more you develop British trade in a country the better it is for that country . . . The greater the trade, the greater the revenue, and the greater the revenue, if it is well spent, the better the lot of the people we govern.'[4]

Throughout his service in Southern Nigeria, Egerton advocated the administrative and economic advantages of good roads and railways[5] with particular emphasis on mechanical transport,[6] thus reflecting the priority which the British government continued to give to this issue in the development of its territories

[1] CO. 592/11, Legislative Council Debates, 2 November 1911. *The Lagos Weekly Record.* 4 June 1910.   [2] *West Africa*, 31 May 1919, pp. 397–8.

[3] *Colonial reports, Annual,* Southern Nigeria, 1905. *West African Pamphlets,* vol. 3, 9346, No. 71. 'Sir Walter Egerton's pioneer adventure: cycling across Nigeria in 1905' by A. A. Cowan, September 1933.

[4] *The West African Mail,* 13 October 1905, pp. 682–3. Speech during a banquet given by the West African Trade Association in Liverpool on 5 October 1905.

[5] CO. 150/12, Lagos Government Gazette, 8 March 1905, Legislative Council Debates, 28 February 1905.

[6] CO. 157/174, Egerton to C.O., 27 January 1905. CO. 520/60, Egerton to C.O., 3 April 1908.

Development and Structural Changes in the Economy

overseas. In the circular dispatch of August 1907, Lord Elgin, then Secretary of State for the Colonies, announced the formation of the Mechanical Transport Committee to advise on such transport other than railways in British territories overseas.[1] Egerton's administration sent information to this committee but how far its advice was sought and utilised is not clear.

Egerton's special interest in road development encouraged him to establish, at the end of 1904, a separate Roads Department headed by the Supervisor of Roads.[2] Six years later, the government amalgamated the Public Works and Roads Departments.[3]

Administrative arrangements for the development of agriculture were less satisfactory. From 1904 to 1910, the Conservator of Forests – a post created by Moor in January 1903 – also supervised agriculture. That Southern Nigeria's agricultural interests did not suffer unduly during these years partly resulted from the forestry officers' hard work and partly from that of the farmers. The double duties of the forestry staff, however, made forestry administration perfunctory until 1910.

The Colonial Office-inspired arrangement concerning agricultural development in West Africa hardly improved matters. In August 1905, the Colonial Office notified Southern Nigeria that it had selected G. C. Dudgeon as Superintendent of Agriculture for all the British West African territories.[4] Dudgeon's primary duties included reports on the steps taken to extend cotton cultivation in British West Africa and investigations into the possibilities of developing its agricultural resources. Dudgeon was under the supervision of the Director of the Imperial Institute in the United Kingdom.[5] Egerton did not approve, considering British West Africa too large and communications too poor for one man to guide its agricultural development effectively.[6] In the three years after Dudgeon's appointment in 1905, Egerton had only met him once.[7]

---

[1] Cd. 4589, London 1909.
[2] *Colonial reports, annual*, Southern Nigeria, 1904.
[3] CO. 520/94, Thorburn to C.O., 23 June 1910.
[4] CO. 592/2, Paper laid on the table of the Legislative Council of Southern Nigeria on 31 May 1906 (No. 14 of 1906).   [5] *Ibid*.
[6] CO. 520/51, Egerton to C.O., conf. 8 June 1908. Egerton's figures for areas under Dudgeon's superintendence were: Gambia, 3,619 square miles; Sierra Leone, 30,000; Gold Coast, 80,000; Southern Nigeria, 77,260; and Northern Nigeria, 256,400. Total: 447,279 square miles.
[7] C.O. 520/62, Egerton to C.O., conf. 7 July 1908.

Despite Egerton's criticisms, F. G. Butler of the Colonial Office stressed in March 1907 that the Secretary of State needed such an officer as Dudgeon to advise, report on and co-ordinate the work done and experience gained in Southern Nigeria with those of the other British West African territories.[1] However, Egerton's administration became disinterested in Dudgeon's work after its own Director of Agriculture was appointed in 1910. It had taken three years for Egerton's request for his own Director of Agriculture to be granted, because of the difficulty of getting a suitably qualified person. Eventually, W. H. Johnson, the former Director of Agriculture of the Gold Coast Colony and Portuguese Mozambique, was appointed on 3 June 1910.[2]

The administrative direction of commercial development fared best. At the end of 1904, Egerton created the post of the Commercial Intelligence Officer, mainly because he needed accurate trade statistics, particularly information on new sources of trade. Egerton chose an officer with wide local knowledge of the commercial possibilities in the colony and protectorate: C. A. Birtwistle, the former General Manager of the Lagos Stores Limited.[3]

EGERTON'S ADVANTAGES

In carrying out his various measures for economic development, Egerton possessed certain advantages over Moor and MacGregor. First, the 1906 amalgamation gave him unity of direction concerning the pace and content of Southern Nigeria's economic progress. It also made possible a sizable combined revenue, which not only bore part of the cost of large-scale public works and the salaries and other emoluments of the expanded establishments, but also served as security for loans. Partly from loans and partly from revenue, Egerton's administration carried out public works begun or delayed before the 1906 amalgamation.

Two cases illustrate such economic trends. Between 1901 and 1903, the Colonial Office did not authorise railway extension in

[1] CO. 520/43, Egerton to C.O., 26 January 1907, minute by F.G.A.B.
[2] CO. 520/43, Egerton to C.O., 26 January 1907. CO. 520/100, W. H. Johnson to C.O., 22 February 1910, enclosure. CO. 520/96, Egerton to C.O., 27 December 1910.
[3] *Colonial reports, annual*, Southern Nigeria, 1904.

Lagos despite MacGregor's requests for imperial assistance in guaranteeing a loan. Railway extension began when the new loan of £2 million raised in the United Kingdom money market was issued to Southern Nigeria in March 1905,[1] in anticipation of the 1906 amalgamation. It is true that the favourable position of the United Kingdom market helped in raising the loan but the poor Lagos Colony and Protectorate alone could not have obtained it without an imperial guarantee. Making adequate use of the financial advantages of the amalgamated territories, Southern Nigeria raised further loans for development projects in 1908 and 1911 and thus brought its total loan responsibility on 31 December 1912 to £8,267,665.[2]

Similarly, the harbour improvements which the Lagos government had needed for a long time were financially not feasible until the 1906 amalgamation. Part of the loans obtained since 1905 went as expenditure on the Lagos Wharf scheme and harbour works. On 31 December 1912 the government spent a total sum of £377,994 on these projects.[3]

Financial considerations caused the delay in undertaking such heavy expenditure. Since 1892 Messrs Coode, Son, and Matthews, the firm of marine engineers, had submitted proposals to the Colonial Office for improving the Lagos harbour. The firm submitted further reports in October 1893 and June 1898 under a scheme which, excluding dredging, was estimated to cost £797, 000. By 1906, the figure, including dredging, had risen to £897,000.[4]

Till 1906, Lagos revenue alone was insufficient to undertake costly harbour works as well as railway construction. This was obvious to MacGregor in 1901, when he estimated £1 million to provide Lagos with an 'excellent' harbour, but could not recommend such an expenditure. The £40,000 a year interest on a £1 million loan at 4 per cent, MacGregor reckoned, would exceed expenditure on maintaining 'branch boats' between Lagos and Forcados. MacGregor therefore considered railway extension more urgent and financially more desirable.[5]

With the 1906 amalgamation, the financial position improved.

[1] CO. 147/177, Crown Agents to C.O., 3 March 1905, enclosure.
[2] CO. 592/16, Annual financial report, Southern Nigeria, 1912.
[3] *Ibid.*
[4] Cd. 4523, London 1909, enclosures in No. 3 and No. 48.
[5] CO. 147/154, MacGregor to C.O., 23 March 1901, enclosure.

The Evolution of the Nigerian State

Hence, in September 1906, Lord Elgin authorised an initial expenditure of £253,000 on harbour works,[1] and the first stone for constructing the eastern mole was tipped on 8 June 1908[2] – a decade after Messrs Coode, Son, and Matthews had definitely recommended it.

Egerton had the further advantage over Moor and MacGregor of time. Their firmly established political and judicial institutions gave him time to concentrate on economic development. Also, his eight-year term of office in Southern Nigeria was long enough for him to consolidate it.

Generally, Moor, MacGregor and Egerton all relied, for economic development, on the combination of favourable climate, considerable forest and agricultural produce and ample labour supplies.

STRUCTURAL CHANGES IN THE ECONOMY

So far as major structural changes in the economy of Southern Nigeria were concerned, most of the developments already noticed during the late nineteenth century continued until 1914. It is again convenient to examine these trends closely under production, trade, exchange, distribution network, transportation and the balance sheet.

(i) *Sylvan and agricultural produce*
Since the late nineteenth century, the earliest attempts of the government to influence economic production aimed at forest conservation and the diversification of export crops. Moor, Mac-Gregor and Egerton actively promoted such measures.

In the Protectorate of Southern Nigeria, Moor departed early from MacDonald's emphasis on botanical stations in favour of forestry laws. Botanic stations had been established at Lagos (1887), in the Royal Niger Company's territories (1889), the Gold Coast (1890), the Niger Coast Protectorate (1893), the Gambia (1894) and Sierra Leone (1895). Their purposes included experimental work, agricultural teaching, the collection and distribution of information and such miscellaneous functions as the collection of non-economic plants or 'ornamental' work. In some cases, they had deviated from their original objectives.

[1] Cd. 4523, London 1909, No. 6.   [2] *Ibid.*, No. 48.

Development and Structural Changes in the Economy

Thus, there had been too much 'ornamental' work in Lagos and the Niger Coast Protectorate, vegetable-growing in Lagos and the Gold Coast, and cattle-raising in Sierra Leone.[1] Moor converted the botanic station established at Old Calabar in 1893 into 'ornamental gardens'. In his view, the prerequisite of the protectorate lay in a forestry department which would concentrate on forest conservation. Despite disappointment at the fate of botanic stations in British West Africa, W. T. Dyer, the Director of Kew Gardens, regarded Moor's new emphasis as 'perfectly sound'. He warned, however, that its ultimate success depended on the degree of permanence which Moor could secure for the emphasis on forest conservation.[2]

Moor had been preoccupied with forest conservation since the Benin City territories had come under British control in 1897. Disturbed by the destruction of forests in Lagos and the Gold Coast, Moor in October 1900 approached the Colonial Office for uniform forestry legislation in his territory, Lagos Colony and Protectorate and the Protectorate of Northern Nigeria.[3] The Colonial Office advised Moor to discuss his proposals with MacGregor but leave out Northern Nigeria 'at present'.[4] That advice Moor carried out before enacting his Forestry Proclamation,[5] which came into force on 11 December 1901. The proclamation primarily aimed at the conservation of timber, rubber and other 'forest produce'. It empowered the High Commissioner to constitute forest reserves and to prohibit, by order, the cutting, collecting, sale, purchase and export of any forest produce except by concessionaires and licencees and during specified periods in the year. The chiefs in whose territories rubber was collected were allowed royalties subject to the undertaking to spend part of that sum on establishing and maintaining rubber nurseries as directed by the forestry officers who from January 1903 came under the control of H. N. Thompson, the newly-appointed Conservator of Forests.[6]

[1] CO. 520/16, Dyer to Lucas, 16 September 1902, minute by E.R.D. (arnley).
[2] CO. 520/16, Dyer to Lucas, 16 September 1902.
[3] CO. 520/2, Gallway to C.O., 3 August 1900, minute by R. Moor (then on leave), dated 9 October 1900.
[4] Ibid., minute by P.H.E.
[5] CO. 588/1, No. 28 of 1901.
[6] Before Thompson's appointment, P. Hitchens, a Eurasian, had since 1899 acted as the forestry officer for the Benin City territories.

That the Protectorate of Lagos, if not the less forested colony, required a forest conservation law was already obvious to MacGregor even before his discussions with Moor. The reports of his District Commissioners in the Lagos Protectorate had constantly drawn attention to the menace of the destruction of forests. For example, counting over a specific area in the Mamo forest confirmed the incidence of destruction.[1]

If MacGregor had had his way, the Legislative Council would have more easily passed a forestry law for the colony in the first place. He would then have sought to secure its adoption for the jurisdictionally more difficult Yoruba provinces in the protectorate which had forests.[2] However, his freedom of action at the time was severely limited by the Colonial Office's request[3] to collate the methods of forest control with those already adopted in the Protectorate of Southern Nigeria and to make the Lagos forestry law acceptable to the Yoruba provinces in the protectorate. Consequently, the forestry bill which MacGregor submitted to the Legislative Council on 2 September 1901 represented the draft following his conference with Moor.[4]

Both MacGregor's Forestry Bill, 1901 and Moor's Forestry Proclamation, 1901, sought to conserve timber, rubber and other forest produce by prohibiting such dealings generally without a licence or concession. They differed in details, however.

In the Protectorate of Southern Nigeria, where the Forestry Proclamation met with no recorded opposition from the chiefs and people, the issue of licences and concessions was entrusted to the British authorities who also decided cases arising from forestry matters. There also the government shared with the chiefs the revenue from rubber royalties. Fees for concessions and licences went into its treasury. Not so in Lagos. There the Forestry Bill met with so much opposition from the Nigerian unofficial members that it was severely amended at the committee stage. Thereafter, legal proceedings in forestry matters were to be taken, no longer before British officers only as in the draft, but to the African authorities or before them and the British officers in charge of the

[1] CO. 149/5, Lagos annual reports, 1899–1905: the Ikorodu district (1899), Badagry district (1900–1), Report by C. Punch, the Superintendent of Forests on the Lagos Forests, 1900–March 1901. CO. 149/6, Legislative Council Debates, 2 September 1901.
[2] CO. 147/160, MacGregor to C.O., conf. 10 February 1902.
[3] CO. 147/157, C.O. to MacGregor, conf. 27 December 1901.
[4] CO. 147/157, MacGregor to C.O., conf. 2 October 1901.

Development and Structural Changes in the Economy

various districts.¹ To placate producers and traders, the government exempted the oil palm and kola nut trees from the 'forest produce' to be regulated. Licences were to be issued 'in the name of' the African authorities. Half the receipts from licences and royalties were to be paid to the chiefs 'for their own use' and the other half into the provincial or district 'prison fund'² and not into the government treasury as in the Protectorate of Southern Nigeria.³

In view of mounting opposition, the Colonial Office by the end of 1901 dropped its former insistence on uniformity of forestry legislation in the Protectorates of Southern Nigeria and Lagos.⁴ MacGregor thereby had greater freedom to amend further the method of applying the provisions of the forestry bill.

According to the earlier drafts, only the Governor in Legislative Council could apply the provisions of the proposed law to places where it was required. As amended, and subsequently provided for in the Forestry Ordinance of 24 May 1902,⁵ the Governor in Legislative Council had power to make orders and rules for the regulation of forests only after receiving the consent, signified by resolution, of the native councils of the provinces and districts concerned. Such orders and rules were again subject to disallowance by the British Crown. A further amendment of the earlier provisions, which the Colonial Office requested in April 1902 and MacGregor carried out in October 1902, enabled the Governor in Legislative Council to prohibit by order, and without a resolution from the native councils concerned, the export of all kinds of rubber 'wheresoever collected' during a specified period.⁶ That amendment aimed at preventing rubber collected in the Protectorate of Southern Nigeria during the prohibited

¹ CO. 147/157, MacGregor to C.O., conf. 2 October 1901. *Lagos Government Gazette*, 24 May 1902, Forestry Ordinance, No. 14 of 1902. For comparison see *Lagos Government Gazette*, 7 September 1901, draft forestry bill, clause 9.
² Each province or district had its treasury called the prison fund, with which prisons were maintained and public works executed.
³ CO. 147/157, MacGregor to C.O., conf. 2 October 1901.
⁴ CO. 147/157, C.O. to MacGregor, conf. 27 December 1901. CO. 147/160, C.O. to MacGregor, conf. 14 April 1902.
⁵ CO. 147/162, C.O. to London Chamber of Commerce, 30 July 1902. For Ordinance No. 14 of 1902, see *Lagos Government Gazette*, 24 May 1901.
⁶ CO. 147/160, C.O. to MacGregor, conf. 14 April 1902. CO. 148/3, The Forests Ordinance, dated 20 October 1902.

period (1 March to 31 May of every year) from entry into Lagos for export.

Contrary to earlier public fears, the Lagos Forestry Ordinance of May 1902 and its subsequent amendments left intact the proprietary rights of African landowners as sanctioned by customary law.[1]

Both the Forestry Proclamation of 1901 of the Protectorate of Southern Nigeria and the Forestry Ordinance of 1902 of the Lagos Colony and Protectorate provoked much criticism and opposition, especially in Lagos. To the Lagos press and public MacGregor's proposed forestry law was oppressive.[2] Following the 'monster' mass meeting at Lagos on 14 September 1901, during which Sapara-Williams explained to the people the main provisions of the draft bill, over 700 people signed the protest sent to MacGregor and the members of the Legislative Council. The petitioners feared government interference with land tenure in the protectorate through the forestry bill. They also objected to giving British officers jurisdiction in forestry matters.[3]

Later, the A.P.S. wrote to the Colonial Office, drawing attention to the sanctity of the nineteenth century treaties, agreements and pledges.[4] The A.P.S. expressed similar disapproval of Moor's forestry law in the Protectorate of Southern Nigeria. It claimed that it encroached upon 'native lands' and considered it more dangerous than the forestry law proposed for Lagos.[5]

Chamberlain maintained that the Forestry Proclamation, 1901, would not interfere with the use of the land and its products by the people. It merely sought, he said, to check the exploitation of forest produce by African and European adventurers who, in view of immediate gains, failed to consider the permanent interests of the indigenous owners of the land.[6]

John Holt was again prominent in attacking both laws. Always an advocate of free exploitation of the natural resources of Southern Nigeria, Holt had an ideal like that of the American frontiersman before 1890. In his firm belief in free private

[1] The Forestry Ordinance, No. 14 of 1902, clause 14.
[2] *The Lagos Standard*, 18 and 25 September 1901.
[3] CO. 147/160, MacGregor to C.O., conf. 10 February 1902, enclosure – petition dated 14 September 1901.
[4] CO. 147/159, Fox-Bourne to C.O., 2 November 1901. CO. 147/159, Fox-Bourne to C.O., 31 December 1901.
[5] CO. 520/17, Fox-Bourne to C.O., 18 April 1902.
[6] CO. 520/17, C.O. to Fox-Bourne, 2 May 1902.

enterprise, Holt failed to appreciate the risks of reckless exploitation and the heavy costs of forest regeneration.

Holt considered the Forestry Department of the Protectorate of Southern Nigeria an 'incubus' which created nothing. The concession laws, he said, were abused by African and European monopolists who failed to work them fully. Government forest reserves, he argued, took more land from the Africans and provided jobs for 'more of these official pests and blood-suckers'.[1] Holt urged unrestricted forest exploitation, not ordinances and proclamations which would have the effect of 'shutting up that forest for all time'.[2] He considered the forestry laws of Southern Nigeria and the rest of British West Africa 'idiotic' and admitted: '... if I had my way out there I would take out of those forests anything of economic and commercial value.'[3] In Holt's view, the Imperial Institute which since November 1903 had undertaken mineral surveys in Southern Nigeria,[4] was of greater value than Kew Gardens whose directors emphasised botanical gardens and forest conservation, which he considered luxurious and mischievous.[5] Holt complained that forestry laws like those of Southern Nigeria hindered the investment of new private capital in economic development.[6] He, however, felt relieved that the oil palm escaped regulation under the forestry laws 'or they might have killed the trade, which after all is our backbone'.[7]

Far from being impressed by Chamberlain's arguments based on the long-term needs of the people, Holt denied that traders were short-sighted in forestry and other matters. He strongly rejected the view that in such matters Chamberlain behaved as an innocent 'lamb' among the pack of mercantile wolves.[8]

In April 1902, Chamberlain had employed his argument of the future forestry needs of the people to counter the protests from

[1] E.D.M.P. F/8, Holt to Morel, 30 September 1909.
[2] E.D.M.P. F/8, Holt to Morel, 23 April, 1902.
[3] E.D.M.P. F/8, Holt to Morel, 24 September 1906.
[4] CO. 520/22, W. R. Dunstan to C.O. 14 September 1903. During the 1908–9 programme, the survey discovered the existence of coal of excellent quality in the Udi area – sources later used as fuel for the railway.
[5] E.D.M.P. F/8, Holt to Morel, 6 May, 1901. E.D.M.P. F/8, Holt to Morel, 24 September 1906. E.D.M.P. F/8, Holt to Morel, 4 October 1902.
[6] E.D.M.P. F/8, Holt to Morel, 27 November 1901.
[7] E.D.M.P. F/8, Holt to Morel, 14 October 1901.
[8] E.D.M.P. F/8, Holt to Morel, 10 May 1902.

the Liverpool and Manchester Chambers of Commerce to Moor's Forestry Proclamation.[1] The Liverpool Chamber of Commerce had earlier opposed the wide scope of Moor's law and complained that it conferred 'too absolute powers' in forestry measures on the High Commissioner without considering the likely loss of revenue by lessening the volume of trade in wood.[2] The Manchester Chamber of Commerce made a similar remonstrance.[3]

Egerton reluctantly continued the forestry regulations passed by his predecessors, though between May 1905 and April 1907 he almost revoked the restrictions on forest produce. At first, Egerton had considered the difficulty of effective supervision by the overworked forestry staff. In forest regeneration, he also favoured a departure from the protection of mahogany to an emphasis on the cultivation of indigenous and exotic species of rubber.

The abolition of the existing forestry regulations would have been, as Egerton admitted, 'a very serious reversal' of his predecessors' policies.[4] H. N. Thompson, the Conservator of Forests, also helped to check a hasty change of policy.[5] Hence, the continuity of policy which W. T. Dyer, the Director of Kew Gardens, had considered essential to the success of forestry legislation in Southern Nigeria was secured.

Egerton encouraged forest conservation by establishing and maintaining 'forest reserves' and 'communal rubber plantations' owned by the people. In the Idah district, for example, 'communal officials' supervised these 'plantations' in co-operation with the District Commissioner and the staff of the Forestry Department.[6]

In its attempts to regenerate forests by 'artificial' means, Egerton's administration encouraged rubber planting. On Egerton's instructions, N. C. McLeod, the Deputy Conservator of

[1] CO. 520/16, C.O. to Liverpool Chamber of Commerce, 12 April 1902.
[2] CO. 520/16, Liverpool Chamber of Commerce to Co., 27 March 1902 and enclosure.
[3] CO. 520/16, Manchester Chamber of Commerce to C.O., 1 May 1902.
[4] CO. 147/175, Egerton to C.O., 31 May 1905. CO. 520/45, Egerton to C.O, 14 April 1907.
[5] CO. 520/45, Egerton to C.O., 13 May 1907.
[6] *J.A.S.*, vol. 10, 1910–11, London p. 132. CO. 657/1, Annual report on forest administration, Southern Nigeria, 1912.

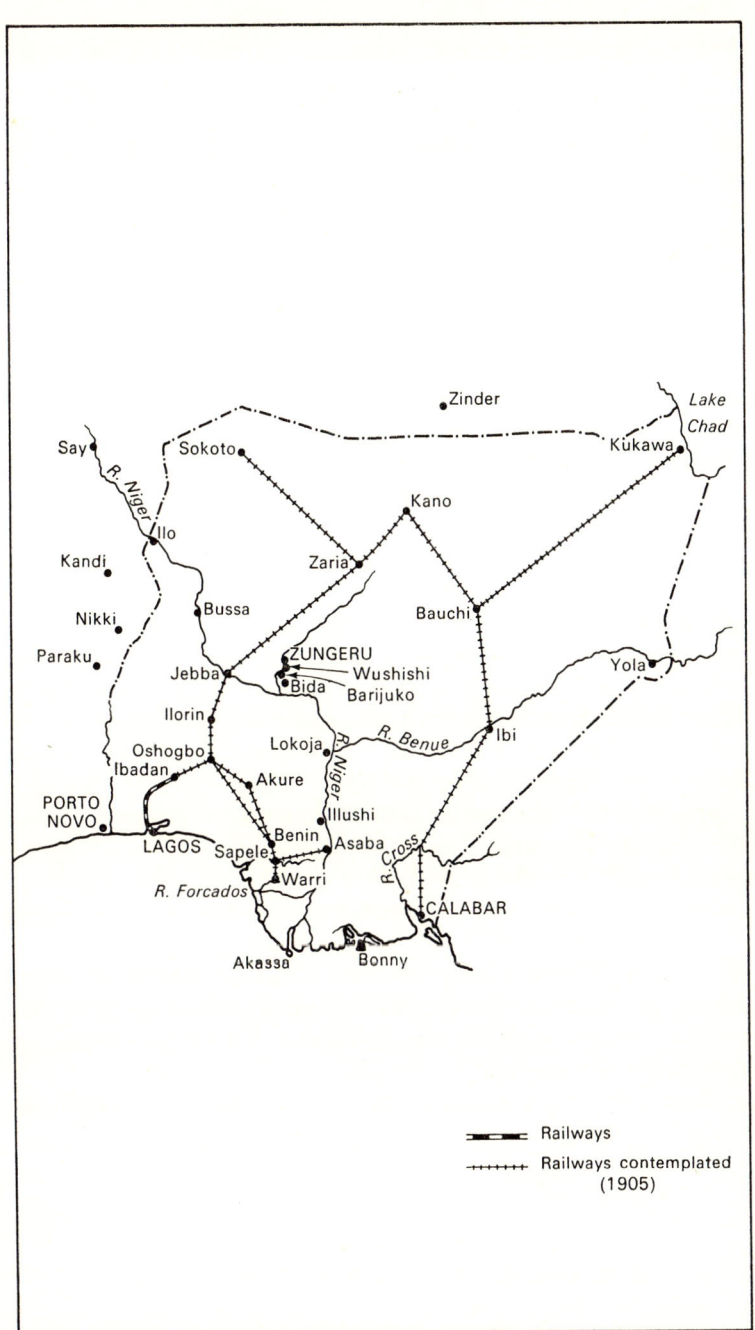

Railway plans for Nigeria, 1905

Forests, visited the Straits Settlements and the Federated Malay States, in September 1907, to study and report on rubber plantations there. His report that Southern Nigeria's climatal conditions suited the cultivation of *para* rubber (*Hevea brasiliensis*)[1] encouraged Egerton's administration to continue the practice begun in 1905 of importing large quantities of *para* seeds from the Malay peninsula for planters in Southern Nigeria.[2] The indigenous variety of rubber (*Funtumia elastica*) grew widely and wildly in the rain forest belt of the colony and protectorate, the same habitat for hardwood and the oil palms. To encourage the cultivation of the indigenous and exotic varieties for export, the government in 1905 granted large rubber concessions along the Benin River to Messrs Miller Brothers and Company Limited and *para* rubber concessions to the African Association at Warri.[3]

At least three-quarters of Southern Nigeria's total exports came from palm produce – oil and kernels.[4] To protect these vital interests, Egerton undertook measures between 1904 and 1905 to ensure the quality of palm produce exports. From 1904, the government introduced in Lagos the system of palm kernel inspection to prevent the export of soaked kernels or kernels mixed with shell, dust and other stuff. For this service, rendered in Lagos by the Customs officials, the merchants paid 6*d* per ton of palm kernels exported. A similar service began in 1905 for the rest of Southern Nigeria, supervised by the District Commissioners.[5]

Afraid of too much reliance on palm produce, Egerton sought to diversify the basis of the economy by developing 'other branches of agriculture'.[6] Birtwistle, the Commercial Intelligence Officer, supported this procedure so as to prevent excessive dependence upon 'one product, which may possibly some day fail us'.[7] The government therefore encouraged the cultivation for export of groundnuts in the Central Province, cocoa in the three provinces, maize in the Western Province, and cotton in certain districts of the three provinces.[8]

Imperially, the cultivation of cotton for export in Southern

[1] CO. 592/4, Paper laid on the table of the Legislative Council, 19 May 1908 (S.P. No. 32 of 1908).   [2] *Ibid.*
[3] CO. 592/3, Trade report on Southern Nigeria, 1906.
[4] CO. 592/3, Trade report on Southern Nigeria, 1907.
[5] CO. 592/3, Trade report on Southern Nigeria, 1906.
[6] CO. 520/64, Egerton to C.O., 23 August 1908.
[7] *Ibid.*, enclosure.
[8] CO. 592/3, Trade report on Southern Nigeria, 1906.

Nigeria evoked the greatest excitement. High hopes were entertained because of the earlier record of cotton cultivation in Yorubaland. Cotton ginned manually had been exported from Lagos to the United States during and after the civil war. In 1869 alone, cotton exports from Lagos to the United States had a total value of about £77,000. The absence of powered ginneries and the dislocation caused by world price fluctuations later helped to diminish interest in cotton exports from Yorubaland.[1]

Between 1902 and 1903, the British Cotton Growing Association (B.C.G.A.) tried to revive this interest in the cultivation of cotton. Both Moor and MacGregor responded favourably in their own attempts to diversify the basis of the export trade in their respective territories. The cotton experiments begun towards the end of 1902 in the plains of Urhoboland and at N'Kissi in co-operation with the B.C.G.A. produced disappointing results, however. The low price offered ($1\frac{1}{2}d$ per lb. of seed cotton) could not compete with that received for palm produce and other crops.[2] Since 1902, MacGregor had discussed the prospects of cotton cultivation in Lagos with representatives of the Liverpool, Oldham and Manchester Chambers of Commerce.[3] He supported the B.C.G.A., which early in 1903 sent two cotton experts to Lagos at the government's expense. These experts held various meetings with the Yoruba chiefs and people and superintended the cultivation with varieties of American and indigenous cotton of about 3,800 acres of land in the Abeokuta, Ibadan, Ekiti, Oyo, Ogbomosho and Meko districts.[4]

To stimulate further interest, the Lagos government urged the guarantee of a steady local price for cotton ($1d$ a lb. of seed cotton), transport facilities, the supply of good seed and ginning machinery. MacGregor agreed to exempt from freight charges the B.C.G.A.'s cotton carried on the railway for an experimental period of two years, provided Messrs Elder, Dempster and Company did likewise on their West Africa shipping lines.[5]

[1] CO. 592/3, Trade report on Southern Nigeria, 1907.
[2] *Colonial reports, annual*, Southern Nigeria, 1902.
[3] CO. 147/164, MacGregor to C.O., 31 July 1902.
[4] CO. 147/169, Moseley to C.O., 30 January 1905, enclosure. The cotton experts arrived in Lagos in April 1903. See CO. 147/165, MacGregor to C.O., 16 April 1903.
[5] CO. 147/164, MacGregor to C.O., 31 July 1902. CO. 147/157, MacGregor to C.O., 28 December 1903. CO. 147/165, MacGregor to C.O., 12 December 1902.

This shipping company co-operated as required until 1904.[1] The Colonial Office approved MacGregor's proposal. Lord Onslow, the Parliamentary Under-Secretary at the time, expressed much enthusiasm because 'an Imperial Zollverein' would encounter 'the greatest difficulties in connection with cotton and tobacco'.[2] Despite all the government's support, however, cotton did not constitute a major export crop during MacGregor's administration.

Egerton inherited the B.C.G.A. albatross, which he found particularly difficult to cast aside following the prominence given, during the King's Speech and House of Commons resolution of 1904, to the task of expanding the areas under cotton cultivation within the British Empire.[3]

From 1904, the B.C.G.A., formed in 1902 to extend cotton cultivation within the British Empire, looked upon British West Africa with great optimism. It sought to avoid too much dependence on American-produced cotton and the price fluctuations and speculation which resulted from the climatal effects on the same crop.[4] As a remedy, W. S. Churchill in March 1907 proposed:

> ... we should vary the sources of supply ... we should not be dependent upon one particular country, but draw our supply from many lands and many climates, so that a bad year in one part of the world might be compensated by a good one elsewhere ... It is for that reason that we welcome most particularly cotton-growing in Lagos, Sierra Leone and Southern Nigeria ...[5]

By 1904, the B.C.G.A. had passed from the predominantly 'experimental' stage of its work in such centres as the Protectorate of Southern Nigeria and Lagos Colony and Protectorate to

[1] CO. 147/159, Moseley to C.O., 19 January 1904, enclosure.

[2] CO. 147/164, MacGregor to C.O., 12 December 1902, minute by Lord Onslow.

[3] HL. Deb. 4s. 129, 2 February 1904, 4. HC. Deb. 4s. 133, 27 April 1904, 1404.

[4] Birtwistle, C. A.: 'Cotton growing and Nigeria', paper read on 18 December 1907, *P.R.C.I.*, vol. 39, 1907–8, London pp. 80–104. Bruce, C.: 'The Crown colonies and places', paper read on 14 March 1905, *P.R.C.I.*, vol. 36, 1905, pp. 221–2. Bruce, C.: *The Broad Stone of Empire*, vol. 1, London 1910, pp. 17–20.

[5] W. S. Churchill, 'The development of Africa', paper read 8 March 1907, *J.A.S.*, vol. 6, 1906–7, London, p. 293.

the 'commercial'.¹ In 1904, J. A. Hutton, the Vice-President of the B.C.G.A., expected at least 10 million bales of cotton from British West Africa alone. The cotton variety produced in Southern Nigeria, he said, represented 'just the cotton we want in Lancashire'.²

With Egerton's encouragement, the B.C.G.A. in March 1905 acquired for 30 years, subject to further extension, the lease of 5,000 acres of land with a nominal annual compensation of $3d$ per acre from the chiefs and people of Ibadan for cotton cultivation. The site, later called Moor's Plantation, had been previously used by the people of Ibadan for the cultivation of farm crops.³ Before obtaining this lease, the B.C.G.A. had approached the E.U.G. for the acquisition of land for cotton cultivation, but the chiefs and people there refused on the grounds that they had 'no public land to spare'.⁴ Among the largely illiterate people of Ibadan, the B.C.G.A. intrusion was not first opposed by the traditional élite who negotiated the 1905 lease.

The opposition came too late to stop the B.C.G.A. operations at Moor's Plantation. Later, the chiefs complained of inadequate land for food cultivation after the loss of the 5,000 acres. To them starvation represented a more urgent problem than the prospect of raising improved American cotton staples. They also considered the alienation, through coercion, of Moor's Plantation a contravention of the pledges given by the government before they signed the 1893 agreement. O. Johnson, who raised these objections during the debates of the Legislative Council, failed to gain any adequate redress from the government.⁵

John Holt disliked the B.C.G.A. monopoly of cotton ginning in Southern Nigeria. By fixing cotton prices, he argued, the B.C.G.A. prevented the Southern Nigerian cultivators from access to the 'free market' in Europe for their cotton.⁶ He also disliked the principle of government subsidies for the monopolist B.C.G.A. He much preferred allowing the people of West Africa generally to grow only economically beneficial crops, not those dictated to them for political and other reasons. In his view, the

¹ HC. Deb. 4s. 133, 27 April 1904, 1395.
² *West Africa*, 13 February 1904, p. 156. Hutton's address to the Manchester Statistical Society on 10 February 1904.
³ *E.D.M.P.* F/9, O. Johnson to Morel, 22 April 1905 and enclosures.
⁴ *Ibid.*
⁵ *Ibid.*
⁶ *E.D.M.P.* F/8, Holt to Morel, 28 January 1910.

B.C.G.A. had become involved in such politically-loaded issues as imperial tariff reform.[1]

Egerton at first gave the B.C.G.A. his support, and it was given special privileges between 1904 and 1907. From 1 April 1904, the government contributed £5,000 annually to the B.C.G.A. under certain conditions.[2] The B.C.G.A. agreed to provide cotton experts to continue its experimental work to the satisfaction of the government. It further undertook to spend no less than £10,000 annually or £30,000 gross in four years on the Protectorate of Southern Nigeria, Lagos Colony and Protectorate and Sierra Leone. It also agreed to buy cotton grown in Southern Nigeria at the fixed price of 1d a lb. of seed cotton at all the buying stations. In the event of a fall in prices, amounting to a loss of £25,000, the Secretary of State agreed to review the buying price in Southern Nigeria. The Colonial Office, however, in November 1906 relieved the B.C.G.A. of its obligation to pay 1d a lb. of seed cotton.[3]

Three years later the government discontinued the free freight of the B.C.G.A.'s cotton, and, after March 1910, the undertaking to pay the B.C.G.A. £5,000 annually. In April of that year the B.C.G.A.'s experimental work came under the government's newly established Agricultural Department. The government estimated that between 1904 and 1910 it had spent at least £40,000 to aid the B.C.G.A. for 'cotton development' but admitted that the benefit to Southern Nigeria was 'not clear'.[4]

Between 1904 and 1908, the British government approved the buying and ginning monopoly by the private B.C.G.A. because of its desire to keep in reliable hands the selection and distribution of cotton seed. In 1904, the Colonial Office did not consider Southern Nigeria, then without a competent Department of Agriculture, capable of selecting seed of good quality. Moreover, it then believed that the B.C.G.A. could encourage cotton cultivation without too much regard for profit.[5]

The B.C.G.A.'s work in Southern Nigeria between 1904 and

[1] *E.D.M.P.* F/8, Holt to Morel, 15 January 1910.
[2] CO. 592/4, Paper laid on the table of the Legislative Council on 18 September 1908 (No. 56 of 1908).
[3] *Ibid.*
[4] CSO. 1/19/51, Boyle to C.O., 12 September 1912, enclosure.
[5] CO. 520/67 Egerton to C.O., conf. 21 November 1908, minute by R.L.A. CO. 520/73, K. A. Hutton to C.O., 10 January 1908, minute by F.G.A.B.

1912 represented a partial success. It failed to get many indigenous producers interested in cotton cultivation. Only in the Ishan district of the Central Province did the B.C.G.A. and the government obtain encouraging results. There, a staple 'far superior to any other West African cotton' was obtained.[1] Otherwise, as the Director of Agriculture reported for 1910, the farmers considered cotton secondary to their food crops.[2] Even so, N. C. McLeod, the Acting Conservator of Forests, had in November 1908 considered the B.C.G.A.'s experimental work 'very satisfactory'.[3] The statistics of cotton exports, though much below the exaggerated expectations of 1904, remained fairly high. The quality of cotton exported by the B.C.G.A. increased from 2,000 bales of 400 lbs each in 1904 to 12,000 in 1909. Cotton lint exported from Southern Nigeria for 1910, 1911 and 1912 amounted to 2,478,000 lbs, 2,238,000 lbs and 4,373,000 lbs respectively.[4] Compared with the nineteenth-century export figures for cotton from Yorubaland, the period 1902–13 showed a significant revival of cotton as an export crop. Nevertheless, such progress in cotton, maize, cocoa, groundnuts, *para* rubber cultivation and mahogany regeneration for exports failed to alter the primacy of palm produce.

(ii) *Trade*
The export-import trade of Southern Nigeria expanded remarkably during the administrations of Moor, MacGregor and Egerton. In 1907, Egerton expressed much satisfaction with the significant trend he observed in the competition between trade routes. For much of the nineteenth century, the products of Northern Nigeria had gone northwards across the Sahara to the ports of North Africa through which it also obtained several of its imports. But with railway extension from Lagos to Ilorin and beyond, Southern Nigeria increasingly exported through Lagos the hides and skins produced in Kano and other cities in Northern Nigeria. Northern caravan traders also brought to Southern Nigeria large quantities of potash and livestock.[5]

[1] CO. 520/67, Egerton to C.O., 17 November 1908.
[2] CO. 592/9, Annual report on the Agricultural Department, 1910.
[3] CO. 520/67, Egerton to C.O., conf. 21 November 1908, enclosure.
[4] CO. 520/110, J. A. Hutton to C.O., 3 April 1911. *Colonial reports, annual*, Southern Nigeria, 1912.
[5] CO. 592/3, Trade report on Southern Nigeria.

The government valued its expanding export-import trade because of the revenue derived mainly from customs duties. In 1912 alone customs duties yielded £1,569,290 – 70.2 per cent of the total revenue. Of these, the duty on spirits provided 64.6 per cent of the total customs revenue for 1912. The government placed spirits, tobacco, and a few other selected items on the list for specific duties. In general, *ad valorem* duties – 10 per cent during this period – suited the needs of the government for a majority of its imports. In the latter group came cotton goods, which in 1912 contributed three-quarters of the total receipts from *ad valorem* duties.[1]

As a result of the judicious expenditure on large-scale public works and firm administration in the expanding area under British control, the trade figures[2] for Southern Nigeria steadily increased between 1900 and 1912 when clear statistics were available. The United Kingdom and Germany then remained the principal overseas competitors for Southern Nigeria's trade.

In 1900, the total export-import trade of the Protectorate of Southern Nigeria came to £2,249,188 5s 7d. Of this, the United Kingdom contributed £1,600,805 2s 6d as against Germany's £473,296 5s 6d. The total Lagos trade in 1900 amounted to £1,715,581 8s 9d out of which the United Kingdom provided £984,120 10s 8d and Germany £554,539 14s 6d. In 1912, Southern Nigeria's total trade had risen to £12,520,307 7s 5d in which the United Kingdom share leapt to £7,249,050 12s 4d and Germany's to £3,321,518 2s 4d.

Statistics for the period 1904–11, which witnessed phenomenal economic development in Southern Nigeria, revealed more clearly the relative contributions made to its commercial progress by the United Kingdom and German markets. Of the total average import trade in Southern Nigeria during the period 1904–6, the United Kingdom supplied 75.97 per cent as against Germany's 12.04 per cent. The corresponding contributions to the export trade were 56.85 per cent and 39.25 per cent. The United Kingdom's contributions to Southern Nigeria's total

---

[1] CO. 592/16, Financial report on Southern Nigeria, 1912.
[2] CO. 473/1, Blue Book, Southern Nigeria, 1900. CO. 151/38, Blue Book, Lagos, 1900. CO. 473/14, Blue Book, Southern Nigeria, 1912. CO. 592/3, Trade report on Southern Nigeria, 1906. CO. 592/15, Trade statistical abstract, Southern Nigeria, 1911: Paper laid on the table of the Legislative Council on 31 May, 1912 (No. 20 of 1912).

trade in 1911 represented 53.3 per cent as compared with 55 per cent in 1910. The German contribution amounted to 30.1 per cent and 28.3 per cent respectively. These figures indicated that despite the strong German competition, the United Kingdom derived substantial benefits from the commercial development of Southern Nigeria. These same statistics further revealed the extent to which Southern Nigeria's export-import economy had been sucked into the vortex of international commerce.

(iii) *Exchange*

International currency, mainly British, gradually displaced barter and such other means of exchange as manillas, brass and copper rods and wires which previously had served as legal tender in Southern Nigeria and other parts of British West Africa. Manillas at first met the currency needs of the people in the 'interior villages' of Southern Nigeria, but, like cowries, they had the demerits of bulk and weight of transport, loss of time in counting, inequality in exchange in various towns and villages, and occasional withdrawal from circulation of large stocks which then ceased to earn interest.[1] Since the nineteenth century, these manillas had dominated the palm oil trade of such centres as Bonny and Opobo where on 31 December 1912 the European merchants alone held 8 million stocks valued at £57,000. Commercial Intelligence Officer Birtwistle reckoned that about one million people in the Opobo, Bonny and Eket districts then possessed 20 million manillas.[2]

The government handled problems connected with the manilla currency gradually. Through his proclamation in 1902, Moor prohibited further imports of manillas into the Protectorate of Southern Nigeria. The government followed this limitation with fixing the rates of exchange which in 1902 allowed 16 manillas for 1s and 12 manillas for 1s from January 1906. The government, however, demonetised manillas as well as brass rods in 1911.[3] Though economically sound, the demonitisation of manillas seemed harsh on the grounds that the government until 1913 allowed no compensation for the large stocks held by Europeans and Africans. In June 1913 the government opposed any compensation, hoping that the railway projects which it envisaged for Port-Harcourt and the eastern part of Southern Nigeria would

[1] CSO. 1/19/58, Lugard to C.O., 23 June 1913, and enclosure.
[2] *Ibid.*   [3] *Ibid.*

provide enough labour for payment in West African silver. It further hoped that silver currency would drive manillas out of circulation even without compensation.[1]

In 1911, the government, not Africans and European businessmen, took the initiative for replacing the sterling silver already circulating in Southern Nigeria and other parts of West Africa with the special West African silver currency. The government wished to rectify the Colonial Office's grievances which arose out of the £2 million profits made by the Imperial Treasury from the sterling silver used in West Africa between 1900 and 1910.[2] In 1906, the British Crown allowed Southern and Northern Nigeria to use special subsidiary nickel coinage of the denominations of one penny and one-tenth of a penny. Though marking an improvement on barter, both the sterling silver and the subsidiary nickel coinage in use in Southern Nigeria had certain disadvantages. Shortages of coins arose partly from the African practice in melting down the silver coins for ornaments and from the absence of banking facilities in the hinterland of Southern Nigeria.[3] Other difficulties were the results of the inadequate renewal of worn silver and the absence of redemption in gold at par following any foreign drain.[4]

Egerton's advocacy of 'a sound currency' to meet all the 'reasonable requirements of trade' reflected the needs of Southern Nigeria's expanding population and economy. He not only wanted silver coins redeemable in gold in Britain but also demanded from 1904 that Southern Nigeria's currency be placed 'on a decimal basis', which impressed him as simpler. He therefore objected to the continued circulation of the threepenny pieces of sterling silver in British West Africa.[5] The British government failed to adopt Egerton's early advocacy of decimal currency for Southern Nigeria until 1914. Instead, it sanctioned special silver coins of the value of 2s, 1s, 6d and 3d for British West Africa. These new coins, exactly the same size, value and weight of the sterling silver, circulated side by side with the latter. Although the new silver coins did not circulate in the

[1] CSO. 1/19/58, Lugard to C.O., 23 June 1913.
[2] Newlyn, W. T. and Rowan, D. C.: *Money and Banking in British Colonial Africa*, Oxford 1954, pp. 35–6.
[3] Loynes, J. B.: *The West African Currency Board 1912–1962*, London 1962 p. 6.
[4] CSO. 1/22/8, C.O. to Egerton, conf. 9 January 1912, enclosures.
[5] CSO. 1/21/10, Egerton to C.O., conf. 8 February 1912.

Development and Structural Changes in the Economy

United Kingdom, the government allowed their exchange 'at par' with British coins through the Bank of British West Africa,[1] which since 1911 had ceased to monopolise the supply of the old silver coins. Writing in 1962, J. B. Loynes observed that the new silver coins introduced in 1912 were well received by Africans.[2] Under the steady advance of colonialism African opposition to currency had less chance of success. Since the 1880s they had gradually lost the right to choose their own means of exchange. They were not consulted about the demonitisation of cowries, brass rods and manillas and the introduction of sterling silver, the special subsidiary nickel coinage and the special silver coins for British West Africa. Their autonomy in such matters as currency and exchange had by 1912 been completely lost.

(iv) *Distribution problems*
With the development of British administrative control over Southern Nigeria and the progress of economic development, the people had to make a series of adjustments to gradual or rapid changes in their political and economic life. Success or failure depended very much on individual ability. A. G. Hopkins noted[3] that the collapse of middlemen in Yorubaland was less disastrous than in the Niger Delta where the links in the chain of demand and supply had been less flexible. In the Yoruba part of the protectorate, particularly at Abeokuta and Ibadan, Hopkins also noticed the steady increase in the branches of European mercantile establishments since 1898, and especially during the period of intense economic prosperity, 1906–14.[4]

In the other parts of Southern Nigeria, the earlier reluctance of British firms to establish branches inland changed during the period 1905–7.[5] Thereafter, they competed more seriously with the African traders who had previously dominated that field.

---

[1] CSO. 1/20/57, C.O. to Lugard, 29 April 1913. CSO. 1/20/58, C.O. to Lugard, 10 June 1913, enclosure. CSO. 1/19/54, Lugard to C.O., 26 November 1911. No currency notes were issued in Nigeria until June 1916 and that because of war-time scarcity of coins. See Loynes: *op. cit.*, p. 16.
[2] Loynes, *op. cit.*, p. 19.
[3] Hopkins, A. G.: *An Economic History of Lagos, 1880–1914* (Ph.D. thesis) London 1964, pp. 452–3.
[4] *Ibid.*, pp. 393–437.
[5] CO. 520/44, Egerton to C.O., 18 March 1907.

The main sources of friction between the people and the government did not stem from the commercial rivalries between Africans and Europeans, except in the controversy over tolls in Yorubaland. As tolls affected the channels of internal trade, they became involved with the questions of autonomy, prescriptive rights, and the guarantees made under the nineteenth century treaties, agreements and pledges. The tolls, or local imposts, on goods passing through the Yoruba provinces affected both the caravan trade with Northern Nigeria and the internal trade within Lagos Colony and Protectorate. These tolls fell on Europeans and Africans alike, but whereas they were opposed by the European traders in the colony and protectorate, with the backing of the Manchester and Liverpool Chambers of Commerce, the Yoruba chiefs and people insisted on their continuation. MacGregor therefore encountered a difficult problem, which he weathered with his usual tact and patience.

The choice between free and restricted trade did not become simple. Much as MacGregor saw the advantages of trade unfettered by tolls, he nevertheless did not want an open clash with the chiefs and people. Moreover, as a firm believer in indirect administration, he did not wish to abolish tolls which would have deprived the native councils of the much-needed funds for essential public works. The alternative of a government subsidy, the people, for political and sentimental reasons, at first refused to accept. Hence, in some parts of Yorubaland, MacGregor adopted the compromise of regulated tolls.

In June 1900 MacGregor had already made known his 'fixed policy' about tolls. That policy involved the disallowance of new tolls and increases in the existing ones and the commutation of such well-established tolls as those of Ibadan and Abeokuta by some other form of payment when and where possible.[1] He discovered that the unregulated tolls in cowries and produce had been arbitrarily imposed and collected by the chiefs' messengers at the toll-gates. In the absence of printed tariffs, the traders were at the mercy of the toll-collectors. The proceeds of such unregulated internal trade taxes went to the chiefs who frequently used them as pocket money. For example, the Ibadan budget for the period 1902–3 showed 'nil' under revenue from tolls.[2] Until

[1] CO. 147/149, MacGregor to C.O., conf. 17 June 1900.
[2] CO. 147/166, MacGregor to C.O., 5 May 1903, enclosure and minute by C.S.

July 1903 Ibadan province had no regulated tolls. The difference with Abeokuta was remarkable. There, MacGregor had in July 1900 regulated tolls by ordering a printed tariff. Under the new arrangement, tolls on goods in transit to and from Lagos were exempted. From the regulated tolls, Abeokuta derived a revenue of about £12,000 for the year ending 31 December 1902.[1] MacGregor's attempt in April 1903 to regulate Ibadan's tolls on Abeokuta's pattern precipitated the tolls crisis.[2] The European merchants with branches at Abeokuta raised no objection to paying the regulated Egba tolls, but in Ibadan, the European merchants claimed exemption.[3]

The tolls agitation developed into a four-dimensional problem which involved the Yoruba provinces led by Ibadan and Abeokuta, the European merchants in Lagos and abroad, MacGregor and the Colonial Office. MacGregor inclined to support Ibadan and Abeokuta. The Colonial Office, whose sympathies lay with the European merchants, insisted on the abolition of tolls and favoured a government subsidy to the people concerned.[4]

As in many a controversial issue, John Holt intervened not necessarily on humanitarian grounds but for economic self-interest. In Nigeria, as well as the Gold Coast, Holt insisted, tolls must go.[5] European merchants in British West Africa, he stressed, were not the 'interlopers' that Africans thought.[6] The tolls agitation enabled Holt to admit that he did not conceive of 'native political and fiscal independence'.[7] He instead stood solidly for the principle of one flag, one customs house in the Protectorate of Southern Nigeria, Lagos Colony and Protectorate and Protectorate of Northern Nigeria.[8] He found practical difficulties in having separate 'customs frontiers' for each territory or province

[1] CO. 147/166, MacGregor to C.O., conf. 7 July 1903, enclosure, appendix 8.
[2] *Lagos Government Gazette*, 28 July 1900. *Lagos Government Gazette*, 25 April 1903.
[3] CO. 147/166, MacGregor to C.O., tel. 30 June 1903, minutes by C.S. and R.L.A. The European merchants affected included John Holt and Co., G. L. Gaiser, Lagos Stores, Patterson and Zochonis at Abeokuta and Ibadan; and Witt & Busch at Ibadan. See CO.1 47/166, MacGregor to C.O., conf. 7 July, 1903.
[4] CO. 147/166, C.O. to MacGregor, tel. 9 June 1903.
[5] *E.D.M.P.* F/8, Holt to Morel, 22 January 1906.
[6] *E.D.M.P.* F/8, Holt to Morel, 16 July 1903.
[7] *E.D.M.P.* F/8, Holt to Morel, 4 July 1903.
[8] *E.D.M.P.* F/8, Holt to A. L. Jones, 28 July 1903.

as the merchants would then have had to deal with a multiplicity of customs-house examinations and the complexity of drawbacks for re-exports besides the inevitable waste of time.[1]

At the height of the tolls controversy, a deputation from the Liverpool and Manchester Chambers of Commerce met Chamberlain at the Colonial Office on 18 June 1903 to raise its political and commercial objections. It alleged that tolls collected by Africans would be subject to abuses and evasions by their kinsmen, whereas Europeans only would be asked to pay. It feared a multiplication of customs-houses and consequent additional expenditure on passing entries. The chiefs and people of Yorubaland, it maintained, were 'unfit' to spend the revenue from tolls which would increase as more and more of the territory was developed by the railway. The deputation further expressed 'most serious apprehension' that the authority given 'for [the] first time' to Africans 'to tax Europeans' would make the former 'arrogant' and lead to the 'abuse of their present qualified independence . . .' Once such a 'right' were conceded, it could never be withdrawn 'without a conflict'.[2]

The deputation proposed the abolition of tolls and the grant of government subsidies to the chiefs and people of Yorubaland. For that purpose, it added, the European merchants would willingly pay 'additional customs duties on spirits and even cotton goods'.[3] Chamberlain agreed with the deputation's submissions. He therefore asked MacGregor by telegram to 'consider whether with your great influence with native chiefs you could not obtain arrangement on these lines'.[4]

The Lagos Chamber of Commerce raised a further protest based on treaty obligations. They maintained that by interfering with trade, the Egba tolls contravened the stipulations of the 1893 treaty.[5]

Ibadan and Abeokuta, for their part, emphasised that their 1893 agreement and treaty justified their levy of tolls. The Bale and other chiefs of Ibadan considered a government subsidy to replace tolls a threat to their control of internal affairs. The E.U.G. regarded such a subsidy as a loss of their 'independence'.

[1] *E.D.M.P.* F/8, Holt to Morel, 10 June 1903.
[2] CO. 147/166, C.O. to MacGregor, tel. 18 June 1903.   [3] *Ibid.*   [4] *Ibid.*
[5] CO. 147/166, MacGregor to C.O., conf. 7 July 1903, enclosure appendix 5. CO. 147/168, Liverpool Chamber of Commerce to C.O., 29 June 1903, enclosure.

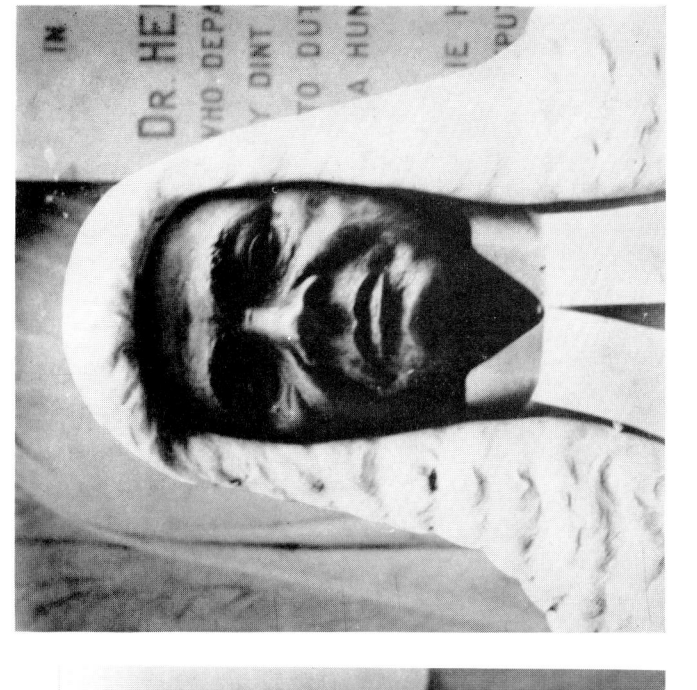

Henry Carr

C. A. Sapara-Williams

Sir Walter Egerton

Herbert Macaulay

After a series of mass meetings whose resolutions were transmitted through MacGregor to the Colonial Office, members of the public in Ibadan and Abeokuta declared themselves willing to pay tolls. In both provinces, the people drew attention to the antiquity of the tolls which had been paid 'from time immemorial'.[1]

The Egbas claimed that the imposition of tolls on European traders in their territory had precedents. Such traders, they said, had paid tolls in Abeokuta since the 1850s 'without hesitation'.[2] James Johnson, the African Christian missionary then with nearly 26 years' experience of evangelism in the Lagos Protectorate, agreed that the collection of tolls represented part of Yoruba tradition and history. He opposed, however, the payment of government subsidies to the African authorities who could spend part of such assistance on heathen religious festivals.[3]

For financial reasons, MacGregor was at first unwilling to replace tolls with subsidies whose funds would have been derived from increasing the customs duties on such imports as cotton goods and spirits, which constituted the principal sources of customs revenue. Further increases of customs duties, he feared, would drive Lagos trade to the neighbouring French colony of Dahomey, besides encouraging smuggling along that frontier.[4] He felt satisfied that the regulated tolls did not interfere with trade, and would provide the provincial administrations with more and more revenue as the number of European traders increased in the areas along the railway.[5]

MacGregor feared that abolishing tolls would diminish Yoruba interest in the imperially desired goal of expanding the area under cotton cultivation, jeopardise his plans to undertake and complete the judicial agreement with Abeokuta as well as raise

[1] CO. 147/166, MacGregor to C.O., conf. 7 July 1903, and appendixes 1, 4, 8, 9, 10(a), (b), and 15. CO. 147/166, MacGregor to C.O., tel. 12 June 1903. CO. 147/166, MacGregor to C.O., conf. 13 July 1903, enclosures.

[2] CO. 147/166, MacGregor to C.O., conf. 7 July 1903. The examples which the E.U.G. gave included G. B. Scalla (Italian), Herr Bergmeyer (German), and the six English firms of W. McKoskry, Southam Wike and Co., Banner Brothers and Co., J. Hughes, W. Fell and the West African Co.

[3] CO. 147/166, MacGregor to C.O., conf. 25 July 1903, enclosure.

[4] CO. 147/166, MacGregor to C.O., conf. 7 July 1903.

[5] CO. 149/6, Legislative Council Debates, 4 June 1903. CO. 147/165, MacGregor to C.O., conf. 22 March 1903.

obstacles to the concessions he expected from the Bale and chiefs of Ibadan over certain lands along the railway to be leased to the government.[1] He further expressed alarm at the prospect of arousing the open hostility of Yoruba secret cults which could use the tolls agitation to foment serious political trouble. He very much misconstrued the objectives of the Ekitiparapo political-cum-military organisation as a secret society which, if given the chance in Ilesha, could embarrass his administration politically over the issue of tolls.[2]

As always, MacGregor hoped for better results from amicable negotiations and diplomacy. He was not mistaken. Through his persuasion, the Ibadan and Abeokuta chiefs and people, who led the tolls agitation, agreed to publish annual estimates of revenue and expenditure and reports by trained auditors. Ibadan also consented to submit its estimates for the Secretary of State's approval. Both Ibadan and Abeokuta further agreed that they would not increase the existing regulated tolls without the Secretary of State's sanction.[3] These concessions provided a check against the abuses complained of by the Chambers of Commerce deputation of June 1903. A further concession made all railway-borne goods to and from Ibadan and Abeokuta tolls-free. The Ibadan and Abeokuta chiefs and people again decided to allow draw-backs 'in full' on all goods re-exported from their provinces.[4]

The results of MacGregor's negotiated settlement over tolls satisfied the Colonial Office. P. H. Ezechiel deemed Abeokuta's concessions 'most important' as they amounted to a 'renunciation' of 'a portion of the theoretical independence' which it had hitherto claimed and enjoyed.[5] Antrobus felt satisfied that the same concessions enabled the government 'to interfere' in the collection of tolls and the expenditure of the proceeds in Ibadan and Abeokuta.[6]

The fear that the sanction of the Ibadan and Abeokuta tolls

[1] CO. 147/166, MacGregor to C.O., tel. 12 June 1903. CO. 147/167, MacGregor to C.O., 30 November 1903.
[2] CO. 147/167, MacGregor to C.O., conf. 31 October 1903.
[3] CO. 147/166, MacGregor to C.O., tel. 30 June 1903.
[4] CO. 147/166, MacGregor to C.O., conf. 7 July 1903, appendices 1 and 16.
[5] CO. 147/166, MacGregor to C.O., tel. 30 June 1903, minute by P.H.E.
[6] *Ibid.*, minute by R.L.A.

would make the abolition of similar tolls in other parts of Yorubaland difficult hardly materialised. MacGregor distinguished between the tolls allowed in such important provincial centres as Ibadan and Abeokuta and those collected at places with little or no resident European population. He seemed less eager to retain tolls in such places. Hence, through further negotiations, he abolished the Ilesha tolls in September 1903 and did the same in Oyo in the same year.[1] MacGregor also saw to it that no tolls were levied by the towns along the route proposed for the extension of the railway. He therefore arranged that goods on which tolls had been paid once in Ibadan territory should be free for Iwo, Ede, Oshogbo, Ikirun and Ogbomosho, the principal towns to be affected by the railway extension.[2] By February 1904, P. H. Ezechiel noted that MacGregor deserved 'much credit' for all he had done concerning tolls.[3]

On the basis of MacGregor's representations, the Colonial Office sanctioned the regulated tolls in Ibadan and Abeokuta by telegram on 28 July 1903.[4] Alake Gbadebo of Abeokuta celebrated that decision by distributing large quantities of cotton seed, hitherto held up, to the Egba farmers. Egerton, however, in 1907 commuted the Ibadan tolls to an annual subsidy of £2,500.

(v) *Transportation*
In their attempts to promote Southern Nigeria's economic development and the free flow of goods and services, Moor, MacGregor and Egerton tackled the related problem of transportation.

The magnitude of the transport problem in the Protectorate of Southern Nigeria was partly demonstrated by its physical features which in the Niger Delta presented a vast complex of creeks and rivers. Sudd blocked the passages of some of these waterways; others were inaccessible during the dry season (November–February) except to craft of shallow draught. Unable to keep open over 3,000 miles of inland waterways from

[1] CO. 147/167, MacGregor to C.O., conf. 31 October 1903, enclosure. CO. 147/167, MacGregor to C.O., tel. 7 December 1903. CO. 147/167, CO. to MacGregor, conf. 24 December 1903. CO. 147/167, MacGregor to C.O., conf. 30 December 1903, enclosure.
[2] CO. 147/166, MacGregor to C.O., conf. 7 July 1903.
[3] CO. 147/167, MacGregor to C.O., conf. 30 December 1903, minute by P.H.E.
[4] CO. 147/166, C.O. to MacGregor, conf. 21 August 1903.

revenue alone, the government of Southern Nigeria encouraged the chiefs and people to provide compulsory labour to clear neighbouring waterways under the provisions of the Roads and Creeks Proclamation, 1903.[1]

Moor also invited the European trading agents in the protectorate to invest in the development of transport. At the end of the Aro expedition, he met the European agents trading at Old Calabar and promised them government aid if they could provide transport to tap the resources of the interior, even at the risk of competition with the African middlemen traders whose financial resources proved inadequate for a thorough and rapid development of trade in the protectorate. Content with trade at their coastal 'factories', the agents were not attracted by schemes involving vast expenditure. Disappointed, Moor remarked that in such matters trade waited for the flag to take the initiative, which seemed to him the 'reverse of the order of things which is supposed in the past to have been one of the guiding principles of genuine British commerce'.[2]

Moor showed an early interest in the development of railways with branch lines to supplement the existing water transport during the dry season.[3] But his proposal in 1897 that Forcados, with its deeper and more navigable entrance than Lagos, be made the outlet for a railway into the hinterland west of the Niger was turned down by the Foreign and Colonial Offices on the grounds that the construction of the Lagos Railway had already begun.[4]

Convinced, however, that Southern Nigeria's development required more than one railway, Moor in 1901 proposed another railway east of the Niger which would ultimately be connected with Old Calabar.[5] No decision by the Colonial Office was recorded in the next two years. Undaunted, Moor in February 1903 recommended the construction of a light electric railway, 25–30 miles long, to tap the resources of the territory within the loop of the Cross river, hoping that in future years the line would be extended to connect Old Calabar with the Benue river. The

[1] CO. 588/1, No. 15 of 1903.
[2] CO. 520/15, Moor to C.O., 10 September 1902. CO. 520/15, Moor to C.O., 26 August 1902. CO. 520/15, Moor to C.O., 14 October 1902.
[3] CO. 520/7, Moor to C.O., 17 January 1901.
[4] FO. 2/122, Moor to F.O., 26 June 1897. CO. 147/124, F.O. to C.O., 11 August 1897, minute by W.H.M. HL. Deb. 4s. 156, 10 May 1906, 1440: statement by Lord Elgin.
[5] CO. 520/7, Moor to C.O., 17 January 1901.

Development and Structural Changes in the Economy

Colonial Office sanctioned only the survey of the proposed route.[1] The main obstacles to Moor's railway proposals between 1897 and 1903 came from the inadequate funds for the construction and extension of the Lagos Railway.

The construction of the Lagos Railway sanctioned by Chamberlain in March 1896 proceeded by stages, reaching Otta (20 miles) in September 1897, Abeokuta (60 miles) in 1899 and Ibadan (125 miles) in December 1900.[2] At the formal opening of the Lagos–Ibadan section on 4 March 1901, MacGregor stressed the importance of railway extension beyond Ibadan. He hoped that such an extension would help the political union of Lagos and Northern Nigeria, meet the strategic needs of the colony and protectorate in view of parallel railway developments in French Conakry and Dahomey, as well as help the commercial development of Lagos and Northern Nigeria. He therefore called upon all Yorubas to 'push on the railway stage by stage, and never rest satisfied till your iron horse drinks of the waters of Tchad'.[3]

In May 1901 MacGregor explored alternative routes for extension. He chose the eastern, though longer, route for reasons of population and the agricultural and forest produce prospects. The eastern route traversed such populous towns as Ibadan (200,000), Iwo (50,000), Ede (30,000), Oshogbo (50,000), Ikirun (35,000) and the not too distant Ilesha (5,000) as opposed to Ogbomosho (65,000) and Oyo (40,000) along the western route. He, of course, made an allowance for a 15–20 per cent over-estimation. Even so, the eastern route had the added attraction of fertile land, timber and oil palms.[4] When eventually authorised, the extension of the railway in 1905 followed the eastern route which MacGregor proposed four years earlier.

A combination of factors contributed to this delay. The Colonial Office did not consider the financial position of the colony favourable for further loan expenditure until experience in working the Lagos–Ibadan section had been gained. Over £1 million out of the total sum of £1,210,729 spent on the Lagos Railway until 31 March 1903 had come as Treasury loans and

---

[1] CO. 520/18, Moor to C.O., 9 February 1903. CO. 520/21, Crown Agents to C.O., 17 December 1903, minute by C.S. CO. 520/23, Moor to C.O., 29 September 1903.
[2] Cd. 2325, London 1904, p. 6.
[3] CO. 147/154, MacGregor to C.O., 23 March 1901, enclosure.
[4] CO. 147/155, MacGregor to C.O., 21 May 1901.

advances by the Crown Agents.¹ Because of the South African war, Lagos Colony and Protectorate found it extremely difficult to obtain loans on reasonable terms, in the British open market, without an imperial guarantee. Again, Secretary of State Chamberlain declined to ask Parliament either for a further loan from the imperial exchequer or for an imperial guarantee for a loan. Since he did not consider the proposed extension urgent, Chamberlain further desired to experiment with construction by 'contract' in view of the criticisms made of the costly 'departmental' system under which the Lagos–Ibadan section of the railway had been built.²

After 1901, Chamberlain's reluctance to act seemed out of tune with his celebrated House of Commons speech of 22 August 1895 concerning the development of the 'undeveloped states' by railways and by parliamentary financial assistance.³ In a letter to Lady Lugard in November 1902, Chamberlain affirmed that British public opinion, disappointed by 'the slow progress and the enormous cost of the Uganda Railway', opposed 'too rapid progress'. Chamberlain advised that until commercial prospects became more convincing, investments in large undertakings seemed speculative.⁴ In March 1905, Chamberlain privately advised F. D. Lugard that the time was not suitable to ask Parliament for large sums of money for railway developments.⁵ High taxation in Britain, he stated, accounted for this situation.⁶

By the time of Egerton's administration, a more favourable climate for railway extension was beginning to develop. The extension of the Lagos Railway, the Colonial Office believed in

¹ CO. 147/173, MacGregor to C.O., 19 August 1904, enclosure.
Imperial Treasury loan	£792,500
Surplus funds of the colony	£129,705
Advances obtained by the Crown Agents	£288,524
Total	£1,210,729

² CO. 147/169, MacGregor to C.O., 10 January 1904, minute by P.H.E. CO. 147/169, C.O. to Treasury, 15 March 1904. CO. 147/168, Manchester Chamber of Commerce to C.O., 26 June 1903, minute by J.C. CO. 147/165, MacGregor to C.O., conf. 4 March 1903, minute by J.C. For the details of the two systems of railway construction, see Cd. 2325, London, 1904, pp. 8–10.

³ HC. Deb. 4s. 36, 22 August 1895, 640–2.

⁴ *Lugard Papers*. M.S.S. Brit. Emp. S. 62, Chamberlain to Lady Lugard 20 November 1902.

⁵ *Ibid.*, Chamberlain to F. D. Lugard, 22 March 1905.

⁶ *Ibid.*, Chamberlain to F. D. Lugard, 30 May 1905.

Development and Structural Changes in the Economy

March 1904, would help to develop Northern Nigeria and make it independent of imperial grants-in-aid.[1] Egerton and Birtwistle also wanted to encourage the European merchants with depots at Lagos to open branches in Northern Nigeria whose cotton, groundnuts, shea-nuts and livestock would be carried southwards by the Lagos Railway.[2] Moreover, the development of the Dahomey Railway, which had reached Tchaourou, aroused British fears that the French sought to divert to it Lagos-bound trade.[3]

In November 1904 the Colonial Office sanctioned the construction of the Ibadan–Oshogbo section.[4] Construction began early in 1905 and the railway reached Jebba (on the Niger) in January 1909[5] The 467-mile-long Iddo–Minna section cost the government a total sum of £4,089,605 on 31 December 1912.[6]

Year	Miles open (mean mileage)	Gross earnings £	Working expenses £	Net earnings £	Proportion of working expenses to gross receipts %	Profit on capital applied
1903	124	51,259	45,863	5,396	89.4	NOT AVAILABLE
1904/5	124	60,336	53,394	6,942	88.5	
1905	124	72,649	56,776	15,873	78.2	
1906	131	84,663	60,295	24,368	71.2	
1907	178	139,747	74,435	65,312	53.3	
1908	214	146,382	103,425	42,957	70.7	
1909	272	203,558	131,820	71,738	64.7	2.88
1910	307	253,604	157,868	95,736	62.2	3.29
1911	307	307,092	176,961	130,131	57.6	4.38
1912	467	394,919	236,280	158,639	59.8	3.69

[1] CO. 147/169, C.O. to Treasury, 15 March 1904.
[2] Cd. 4523, 1909, No. 14 and its enclosures; and enclosure in No. 18.
[3] CO. 147/169, MacGregor to C.O., 10 January 1904, minute by C.S. CO. 147/169, C.O. to Treasury, 15 March 1904.
[4] Cd. 4523, 1909, No. 56.
[5] *Ibid.*
[6] CO. 592/16, Annual financial report, Southern Nigeria, 1912. This figure excluded the sum of £161,512 spent on the Lagos tramway and the Carter-Denton bridges.

Several factors should be considered in assessing the profitability or otherwise of the Lagos Railway. The table on p. 279[1] gives a concise financial picture between 1903 and 1912.

Generally, the proportion of working expenses to gross receipts decreased as the length of the railway increased. There were, however, exceptions at the 214th mile and in the last 160 miles of the whole line. As the government foresaw in 1907,[2] the 160-mile-long section between Jebba and Minna failed to show direct profits. Though that section was not populous, it formed a necessary link with the more populous agricultural districts between Zaria and Kano. A similar necessary link lay between the 200th and 307th miles.

General Manager F. B. Glasier distinguished between the profitable sections, the 'commercial line', and others of less commercial value, the 'political line'. By Glasier's division, from Iddo to Ikirun, the 200th mile, the railway came under the commercial section as distinct from the political line – the 107-mile-long Ikirun–Jebba section.[3] Roughly, Ikirun represented the limit of the oil palm zone up to which the railway commercially justified itself. For instance, the receipts from the Ikirun–Jebba section averaged £160 a week in November 1909 as against £2,800 a week from the 200-mile-long commercial section.[4]

In assessing the profitability of the railway, allowance should be made for the low freight rates charged to carry stone quarried at Abeokuta for the Lagos harbour works. Stone including laterite was carried at special rates to improve the lines of the railway opened to traffic.[5]

Above all, the Lagos Railway served the purpose conceived by MacGregor and Egerton – not as a profit-making concern but as a means of benefiting the territory's general development directly and indirectly. That function the Lagos Railway carried out mainly because of parallel development of 'feeder' roads in the Western Province and other roads in the Central and Eastern Provinces.

Neither Moor nor MacGregor gave any serious attention to

[1] CO. 657/1, Nigerian Railway administrative report, 1912, table 9.
[2] Cd. 4523, 1909, enclosure in No. 14 – Egerton to C.O., 10 May 1907.
[3] CO. 520/91, Egerton to C.O., 31 January 1910, enclosure.
[4] *Ibid.*
[5] CO. 592/13, Lagos Railway administrative report, 1911.

Development and Structural Changes in the Economy

road development. Egerton, however, made good his predecessors' shortcomings. In 1902 the Protectorate of Southern Nigeria and Lagos Colony and Protectorate together spent only £1,669 for road construction and £2,683 in 1903.[1] By 1907, roads and bridges accounted for £65,744 for the combined territories.[2]

With road development, Egerton also encouraged motor transport. Nigeria's first motor service began with vans on the Ibadan–Oyo road in 1906.[3] These developments helped to stimulate economic and social progress besides assisting administration generally.[4]

Railway extension, road development and motor transport went on apace with harbour works and the clearance of waterways. The further the Lagos Railway was extended into Northern Nigeria, the greater the need became to make its outlet a safe harbour for ocean steamers. The practice of transferring goods by 'branch boats' to the deeper and safer port of Forcados, more than a hundred miles east of Lagos, caused delays besides increasing the costs of imports and exports. In damp weather, goods were destroyed.[5] To minimise these risks, the government considered expenditure on improving the Lagos harbour justified. This scheme comprised the construction of stone moles or breakwaters on each side of the harbour entrance, the deepening of the channel and portions of the harbour by dredging, the extension and strengthening of the existing customs wharf at Lagos and the erection of quays for ocean steamers near Wilmot Point.[6] The plan included the construction of a branch railway to Apapa wharf to relieve the Iddo wharf of harbour stone traffic. That branch route – 37 miles long and opened in November 1911 – also dealt with traffic for the Lagos water works.[7]

As in railway extension, the Colonial Office's sanction of expenditure on harbour improvements depended on the results obtained from the sections of these works approved from time to time.[8] Being the first to be sanctioned, the eastern mole reached

[1] CO. 520/49, Thorburn to C.O., 28 September 1907, enclosure.
[2] CO. 520/67, Egerton to C.O., 20 November 1908, enclosure.
[3] Cd. 4523, 1909, enclosure in No. 18. Cd. 4589, 1909, enclosure 2 in No. 12.
[4] CO. 520/115, James to C.O., 28 May 1912.
[5] Cd. 4523, 1909, enclosure in No. 18, Nos. 48–49, and 51.
[6] CO. 659/1, Lagos Customs and Trade Journal, 2 June 1911.
[7] CO. 592/13, Lagos Railway administrative report, 1911.
[8] Cd. 4523, 1909, No. 49.

the length of 6,479 feet on 14 December 1912. On the same date, only 888 feet of the western mole, which had been lately sanctioned, had been built. As a result of these harbour projects, the Lagos bar draught on 29 November 1912 permitted steamers drawing twelve feet to enter it.[1]

Outside the colony, Egerton continued the policy of clearing waterways. Between 1903 and 1904 expenditure under this head for Lagos and the Protectorate of Southern Nigeria amounted to only £500. Egerton increased it six-fold during the period 1904–5 and ten-fold in 1908.[2]

(vi) *The balance sheet*

All these important development projects cost a lot of money – sums mainly derived from revenue which in turn relied on customs duties. To that extent, such businessmen as John Holt felt greatly concerned over the high cost of economic development. Holt did not share MacGregor's enthusiasm in having the Lagos Railway extended to Lake Chad except, as he said, to carry cattle and fish.[3] Holt felt that the British government's enthusiasm for such railways had been exploited by the British shipping firms which charged such exorbitant rates as 45*s* per ton for carrying railway stocks from the United Kingdom to Lagos. Any freight charges in excess of the 'ordinary market rates' he considered 'a robbery of the colonies who pay them'. He therefore called upon the British government to break up such monopolies.[4] Despite these views, the government did not seek to end the shipping privileges enjoyed by the British firm of Messrs Elder, Dempster and Company Limited in West Africa. Holt further demanded that government development projects in British West Africa must be self-supporting and 'show a profit or be abandoned to private enterprise'.[5] Yet, the latter alternative could not avoid the trend towards private monopolies which in railway and other economic development projects Holt strongly detested.

By far Holt's most consistent criticism of such economic development programmes as Chamberlain and others advocated was of the inadequate consideration given to budget-

[1] CO. 659/1, Lagos Customs and Trade Journal, 17 December 1912.
[2] CO. 520/64, Egerton to C.O., 21 August 1908. The actual figures were 1904–5: £3,143; 1908: £5,000.
[3] *E.D.M.P.* F/8, Holt to Morel, 6 May 1901.
[4] *E.D.M.P.* F/8, Holt to Morel, 7 November 1906.
[5] *E.D.M.P.* F/8, Holt to Morel, 21 January 1906.

Development and Structural Changes in the Economy

balancing. Holt detested the idea of deficit-spending, fearing that 'reckless expenditure' would result in the creation of 'another West Indies in West Africa'.[1] Holt therefore felt alarmed at the economic trends which he had observed during the Colonial Secretaryship of Joseph Chamberlain (1895–1903). In November 1902, Holt painfully informed Morel:

> Until J.C. came with his 'development of our estates' ideas, it was the pride of our W[est] A[frican] colonies to work their administrative machinery on modest lines with a small tariff, and have a balance to their credit, but now under the present regime they are being run on extravagant lines, such as the Prodigal son would have employed and the end must mean either bankruptcy or a load of debt which will absorb the labour of half the population to pay the interest thereon. It serves to parade an artificial appearance of progress, but it is imprudent and will earn the malediction of future generations who will have to bear the burden.[2]

Holt consistently[3] questioned the morality of deficit-spending which would confer immediate economic and social benefits on the present generation leaving heavy debts to its successors. He did not, however, recognise that in such matters the moral standards required of individuals do not necessarily extend to states. With a buoyant economy, and revenues sufficient to repay the debt charges – provided they were mainly domestic loans – deficit-spending was not necessarily as monstrous as Holt had believed.

Holt put the blame on Egerton and 'his overpaid, underworked, extravagant and luxurious officials'.[4] E. A. Speed, a former official in Southern Nigeria, who was later transferred to Northern Nigeria, confirmed some of these charges in July 1911. After a brief visit to Lagos, Speed informed Morel:

> What strikes me about the lavish expenditure of money there is that no sort of provision seems to be made for a lean time, and no sort of attempt to substitute another form of revenue for the 'gin-money' which, or at all events the continued expansion of which, is surely doomed.[5]

[1] *E.D.M.P.* F/8, Holt to Morel, 16 April 1902.
[2] *E.D.M.P.* F/8, Holt to Morel, 23 November 1902.
[3] *E.D.M.P.* F/8, Holt to Morel, 22 January 1906.
[4] CO. 520/67, Egerton to C.O., 29 November 1908.
[5] *E.D.M.P.* F/9, E. A. Speed to Morel, 19 July 1911.

Despite these criticisms, Egerton did not have as much freedom as he desired in spending money on 'productive' public works. To him the old adage 'money makes money' commended itself. He considered expenditure on large-scale public works 'beneficial and directly or indirectly revenue-producing'.[1]

Some of the Colonial Office staff, however, failed to share Egerton's enthusiasm. F. G. A. Butler observed in 1908:

> The comfortable principle that the more you spend the more you will have cannot be applied blindly. It is all to the good that Sir W. Egerton should have such an abounding faith in the future of Southern Nigeria. The responsibility is on him to put forward positive proposals for the development of the country. He discharges his responsibility admirably. The responsibility is on the S[ecretary] of S[tate] to judge proposals calmly and dispassionately, and with a long look ahead. If any mistake is to be made in the Colonial Office, it should be that of excess of caution, rather than the opposite. The Gov[erno]r ought to understand and appreciate our essential function of cautious criticism, just as we appreciate his of enthusiastic development.[2]

Eleven years later, Egerton admitted that he had appreciated the rôle of the Colonial Office 'in checking the rash wishes of Governors to cram into the short term of their administration what the Colonial Office thought would be better spread over 20 or 30 years...'[3] But during his administration in Southern Nigeria, Egerton's enthusiasm for expenditure on special public works knew no bounds. Between 1906 and 1912, his administration spent a total sum of £1,905,548 from revenue on such projects:[4]

Railway capital works	£212,725
Works and building extraordinary	£887,346
Roads and bridges	£297,009
Telegraphs	£ 91,603
Marine	£416,865
Total	£1,905,548

[1] CO. 520/67, Egerton to C.O., 20 November 1908.
[2] *Ibid.*, minute by F.G.A.B., dated 12 December 1908.
[3] *West Africa*, 31 May 1919, p. 398.
[4] CO. 592/16, Annual financial report, Southern Nigeria, 1912.

Development and Structural Changes in the Economy

The government then also spent £3,358,369 from loan funds. This excluded, however, the £1,410,000 advanced by Egerton's administration to Northern Nigeria for the construction of the Baro-Kano Railway and the dredging of the Niger south of Baro. In Southern Nigeria, the loan funds paid for railway construction, the harbour and water works at Lagos, the Apapa wharf and the Carter-Denton bridges.[1]

The remarkable economic progress made by Southern Nigeria between 1906 and 1912 can be summarily assessed by examining the figures triennially:[2]

		1906 £	1909 £	1912 £	Increase 1906–12 £
1.	Revenue	1,088,717	1,361,891	2,235,412	1,146,695
2.	Expenditure	1,056,290	1,648,680	2,110,498	1,054,208
3.	Assets over liabilities, excluding loans	475,497	375,761	1,132,540	657,044
4.	Total expenditure from loans	1,677,756	4,263,042	6,183,782	4,506,026
5.	Total liability on loans	2,000,000	5,142,461	8,267,665	6,267,665
6.	Loan sinking (redemption) fund	–	30,885	115,268	115,268
7.	Imports (excluding specie).	2,847,316	4,529,604	5,951,883	3,104,567
8.	Exports (excluding specie).	2,950,392	4,114,237	5,773,488	2,823,096
9.	Total trade (excluding specie).	5,797,708	8,643,841	11,725,371	5,927,663
10.	Customs duties	885,858	987,571	1,569,290	683,432

Expenditure on public works remained so high that in 1911 alone the ratio of expenditure represented 87.7 per cent of the total revenue as against 94.4 per cent in 1912.[3] Despite its large-scale spending, Egerton's administration was a success. It is true that Egerton raised Southern Nigeria's loan responsibility to £8,267,665 in 1912 – about eight times the 1903 amount. But the redemption charges and the revenue figures then amply indicated Southern Nigeria's capacity to redeem its loans. Under Egerton's encouragement and intelligent spending on 'extra-

[1] *Ibid.*   [2] *Ibid.*   [3] *Ibid.*

ordinary' and 'special works', Southern Nigeria in 1906 became the first British West African territory to earn a revenue exceeding £1 million. Between 1907 and 1912 that revenue doubled.[1]

Another example of the financial stability of Egerton's administration lay in the balance of assets over liabilities (excluding loans) which increased from £475,497 in 1906 to £1,132,540 in 1912. That record showed a considerable improvement on the combined balance of assets over liabilities of £361,720 0s 10d for Lagos and the Protectorate of Southern Nigeria on 31 March 1904.[2]

Generally, the economic record of the administrations of Moor, MacGregor and Egerton indicated that they did not neglect the question of development even though they had worked within the narrow limits of the funds at their disposal. In carrying out their various economic measures they and the Colonial Office made the big decisions. Some of these major decisions, as in the liquor trade, had social as well as economic impacts. The main social effects of the increasing British administrative control over Southern Nigeria were just as important as the economic consequences.

[1] *Ibid.*
[2] *Colonial reports, annual,* Southern Nigeria, 1904, *Colonial reports, annual,* Lagos, 1904.

10 Social Obligations and Performance

FORMAL SOCIAL OBLIGATIONS

If administration did not constitute an end in itself neither did economic development. Taken in a wider sense, economic development measures have their social aspect, the link being provided by the human beings whose interests are affected. The common goal of human development clearly illustrates the interdependence of measures for economic and social welfare. Among other things, the good health and education of the masses provide valuable economic assets, particularly in the fields of labour and markets for goods and services. Let us therefore examine the major social obligations which the British government constitutionally undertook in its relations with the people of Southern Nigeria until 1914.

These social obligations had been made abundantly clear since 1886. The Letters Patent and Royal Instructions of 13 January 1886 and the additional Royal Instructions of 31 October 1898 remained in force till February 1899 when MacGregor inherited them on becoming Governor of Lagos.[1] Egerton, too, undertook the same social obligations under the Royal Instructions to the Governor of Southern Nigeria in February 1906.[2]

In these instructions the British government spelt out the principal functions of the Governor towards the people in his territory.

> The Governor is, to the utmost of his power, to promote religion and education among the native inhabitants of the Colony, and he is especially to take care to protect them in their persons and in the free enjoyment of their possessions, and by all lawful means to prevent and restrain all violence and

---
[1] CO. 380/152, C.O. to MacGregor, 23 March 1899.
[2] CSO. 5/8/4, Instructions dated 28 February 1906, clause 36.

injustice which may in any manner be practised or attempted against them.[1]

The Governor therefore had wide powers to intervene in various aspects of the social life of the people. Gradually the people lost their powers of control. However, as social welfare did not at first attract much government interest, there was comparatively little direct interference there until 1914.

As in economic development, the government then lacked adequate human and financial resources and the time to undertake wide-ranging social welfare measures. Its efforts were therefore limited to the major towns and the immediate vicinity of its out-stations. Consequently, millions of villagers lacked adequate protection from policemen on beat-duty. Often their only experiences with the police and troops were during punitive expeditions and patrols. In such areas, the secret cults, oracles and other pre-colonial law enforcement agencies not spotted for destruction by the government continued to operate discreetly underground.

In several communities, railways, motorable roads, harbour facilities, electric lights and good water supplies did not come within the reach of the masses. They went on using bush-paths, dug-outs, public wells, drinking water from running streams, bush fires, the fuel-power of palm-oil and kernel fibres and the seasonal bonuses of moonlight and rainfall.

These villagers did not measure progress in material terms. They resigned themselves to such facilities as long as these met their limited needs, even preferring them to paying direct taxes for major development projects which benefited them only peripherally or not at all. They expressed anxieties, however, over the economic measures which had serious social implications, such as the liquor controversy, government public health and sanitation measures, Western European education, and land policy. These involved the power to tax and spend, the good health of the farmers, consumers and labourers, interference with vital aspects of their pre-colonial religious institutions and threats to the main source of the territory's agricultural and sylvan produce, which in turn supported the expanding import trade.

[1] CSO. 5/8/2. Instructions dated 13 January 1886, clause 31. C.S.O. 5/8/4. Instructions dated 28 February 1886, clause 36.

THE LIQUOR CONTROVERSY

In Southern Nigeria and other parts of West Africa, the liquor question antedated the era of British colonialism.[1] Gin, rum, brandy, whisky and other brands and blends of liquor had featured prominently in West African commerce long before the abolition of the slave trade in 1807. By 1909, the German and Dutch ports of Hamburg and Rotterdam provided 90 per cent of Southern Nigeria's liquor imports.[2]

Similarly, the international aspects of the liquor question did not give Britain as much freedom in dealing with it as she desired in Southern Nigeria and other West African territories under her control. As a leading signatory to the various international conventions which dealt with this traffic in Africa, Britain had to co-operate with other nations. She had to operate within the limits of the General Act of Brussels (2 July 1890), the Convention respecting the Liquor Traffic in Africa (8 June 1899) and the Convention respecting Liquors in Africa (3 November 1906).[3] Under these conventions, Lagos and the Protectorate of Southern Nigeria did not come within the prohibited zones for the liquor trade. But the predominantly Muslim Protectorate of Northern Nigeria did.

Considering the age and antecedents of the liquor trade in West Africa, it was significant that in 1909 the agitation for its control or abolition became so intense that the government authorised and carried out a special inquiry. It is important to find out why the inquiry was held when and where it was. The major issues preceding the inquiry and the significance of the entire liquor controversy in Southern Nigeria must also be examined.

Certain factors inside and outside Southern Nigeria influenced the timing of the 1909 inquiry, which proved more comprehensive than the limited quality tests of liquor samples undertaken, as in 1897,[4] in response to public agitation.

---

[1] HC. Deb. 5s. 28, 20 July 1911, 1347.
[2] CO. 520/87, The Southern Nigeria Liquor Trade Committee Report dated 17 September 1909, p. 5. (Also printed as Cd. 4906, October 1909.)
[3] HC. Deb. 4s. 192, 20 July 1908, 1458.
[4] CO. 520/86, M.P. No. 3864, minute by C.S. dated 2 February 1909.

The British advocates of stricter control of abolition of the liquor trade in West Africa apparently expected a more favourable response from the Liberal Party governments led by H. Campbell-Bannerman (1906–8) and H. H. Asquith (1908–16). The spate of parliamentary questions and petitions from the N.R.–L.T.U.C. on the liquor issue showed a marked increase during the Liberal Party's ascendancy in British politics.

The leaders of temperance societies in the United Kingdom expected the government to impose on West Africans the same liquor restrictions as those enforced among black South Africans shortly before the Liberal Party assumed office in 1906. The Most Rev. R. T. Davidson, Archbishop of Canterbury (1903–28), in June 1905 strongly favoured action along South African lines.[1] In July 1908, the N.R.–L.T.U.C. reminded the Liberal Party government that restrictions imposed in South Africa had been 'justified by results'.[2]

In its renewed agitation against the liquor traffic in West Africa, the N.R.-L.T.U.C. had timed its tactics so as to exploit the recent 'unanimity' of opinion in the House of Commons over the banning of the opium trade elsewhere in the British Empire. It therefore reminded the Colonial Office in July 1908 of the absurdity in prohibiting the opium traffic without also banning the 'more harmful' liquor trade in West Africa.[3]

Another major development affected the timing of the 1909 inquiry. Egerton's enthusiasm for railway extension seriously threatened the effectiveness of the prohibition in Northern Nigeria as the iron horse sped from Lagos towards Ilorin, Jebba, Minna and Kano. The Archbishop of Canterbury informed Parliament soon after the end of the Brussels Convention of November 1906:

> Most of all, my Lords, the matter is, to my mind, important because of the very prosaic but vital fact that the railway is weekly or monthly advancing and bringing with it fresh difficulties which we have hitherto not been called upon to face. . . . When I spoke before [June 1905], the railway was still . . . a long way off the frontier. It is now close to the frontier . . . In a short time the railway will be carrying goods right into the region of the prohibited area.[4]

[1] HL. Deb. 4s. 147, 6 June 1905, 835–6.
[2] CO. 520/73, NR-LTUC to C.O., 6 July 1908.   [3] *Ibid.*
[4] HL. Deb. 4s. 170, 27 February 1907, 6–9.

Archbishop Davidson feared that such rapid railway extension towards the prohibited zone threatened with liquor the lives of about 10 million people in Northern Nigeria. In the House of Commons, J. Kennaway (Devonshire) complained of rail-borne liquor being smuggled into Northern Nigeria.[1]

The critical stage came on 1 March 1908 when the Lagos Railway reached Ikirun, about 12 miles from the boundary with Northern Nigeria. Simultaneously, Egerton forbade rail-borne liquor beyond Ikirun.[2] But despite this 'a certain amount of gin' filtered from Southern to Northern Nigeria.[3]

The critics of the liquor traffic seized the opportunity provided by the extension of the Lagos Railway to demand stricter restrictions. The N.R.-L.T.U.C. therefore proposed, and the Colonial Office agreed, that Southern Nigeria provide the test-case for a thorough investigation into the liquor trade in West Africa. Southern Nigeria impressed them as presenting the 'facts' of the liquor traffic among an indigenous population on a considerable scale yet in an area not too large for precise investigation.[4]

The critics of the liquor trade aroused the fervour and emotionalism typical of temperance and prohibition movements. Before 1909, the problem was five-dimensional. The government spokesmen stressed revenue, the humanitarian evangelicals emphasised morality and welfare, such humanitarian traders as John Holt harped on the power to tax and spend, the European liquor traders tailored their arguments to suit business profits, and the Africans found it more convenient to pay an indirect tax than a direct levy.

Although Moor, MacGregor and Egerton, as well as their predecessors, all faced the liquor problem, none found an easy alternative source of revenue. They felt less alarm over the volume of the trade and the supposed harmful nature of the imported liquor than over the loss of the revenue derived. In the last three years before the 1909 inquiry, the revenue from the customs duties on spirits proved considerable:[5]

[1] HC. Deb. 4s. 191, 29 June 1908, 351.
[2] CO. 520/64, Egerton to C.O., conf. 8 August 1908. CO. 520/64, Egerton to C.O., 6 August 1908, enclosure.
[3] *The liquor traffic report*, 1909, p. 8.
[4] CO. 520/73, N.R.-L.T.U.C. to C.O., 6 July 1908. CO. 520/73, N.R.-L.T.U.C. to C.O., 28 July 1908. CO. 520/73, C.O. to N.R.-L.T.U.C., 30 September 1908. [5] *The liquor traffic report*, 1909, p. 6.

	Total revenue £	Duty from spirits £
1906	1,088,717	600,784
1907	1,459,554	806,942
1908	1,388,243	691,186

Much of this revenue had come from the specific duties imposed on imported spirits. From the 1890s to 1909 these duties had been steadily increased from 6d per 'proof' gallon to 5s per gallon of 50 degrees Tralles, with surcharges and rebates above and below that strength subject to a minimum of 4s a gallon.[1] Consequently, the specific duties on gin and rum, for example, were as high as 200 per cent and 300 per cent respectively, of their 'declared values'.[2] These high duties, the government hoped, would discourage imports as well as raise revenue,[3] and indeed the policy had had a steadying effect on the volume of the liquor trade. In spite of generally expanding trade and increasing population, the volume[4] of spirits consumed in Southern Nigeria between 1902 and 1910 did not rise astronomically:

	Average imports of 'proof spirit' Gallons
1902–4	8,900,000
1905–7	8,700,000
1908–10	8,600,000

So Moor, MacGregor and Egerton declined to interfere. For example, when, in December 1901, T. Welsh, a Liverpool trader based at Old Calabar who refused to participate in the liquor traffic, approached Moor to alter radically the structure of customs duties, including the specific duties on spirits, Moor considered the proposals not practical,[5] saying they would disturb the existing channels of trade to the advantage of smuggling

[1] Ibid.
[2] Ibid. 'Declared value': the f.o.b. at the port of export (value minus freight, duty, insurance and landing charges).
[3] CO. 520/62, Egerton to C.O., conf. 6 July 1908.
[4] HC. Deb. 5s. 28, 20 July 1911, 1346.
[5] CO. 520/10, Moor to C.O., 4 December 1901.

between Nigeria and its neighbouring French and German colonies.[1]

MacGregor also declined to increase the specific duties on spirits without simultaneous reciprocation in French Dahomey.[2] He found it more rewarding to wage war against such diseases as malaria, diarrhoea, dysentery and small-pox than to involve the government in 'the liquor "will-o-the-wisp".'[3]

Egerton emphasised the problem of smuggling over Southern Nigeria's boundaries with French Dahomey in the West and the German Cameroons in the East if the specific duties on spirits in his territory exceeded by far those in the neighbouring territories. Egerton admitted that he already found it difficult to police a territory as large and populous as Southern Nigeria with his limited complement of troops and law enforcement agencies. He reiterated, however, his willingness to maintain the restrictions imposed on rail-borne spirits carried beyond Ikirun for purchase, under special licence, by the expatriate staff in Northern Nigeria. He similarly agreed to continue the prohibition line north of the junction of the River Niger with its Anambra tributary for water-borne liquor and similar restrictions along the Cross River and the inland zones between these and the boundary with Northern Nigeria. The other check through the system of licences for wholesale and retail traders in liquor he also continued to enforce.

Egerton nevertheless opposed any general prohibition or excessive duties. Either, he said, would be very difficult to enforce and would encourage 'shebeening' – the selling of excisable liquor without licences – and excessive tapping of the oil palm for fermented palm wine.[4]

The Colonial Office stuck to the revenue aspect. In August 1908, C. Strachey regretted the fact that the prohibitionists failed to see 'the beauty of the system by which the consumers of spirits are made to contribute more than anyone else to the cost of governing the country'.[5] Even so, R. L. Antrobus, the consistent

[1] Ibid.
[2] CO. 147/157, MacGregor to C.O., 21 September 1901.
[3] CO. 147/157, MacGregor to C.O., conf. 7 November 1901, enclosure.
[4] CO. 520/56, Egerton to C.O., 29 September 1907. C.O. 520/62, Egerton to C.O., conf. 6 July 1908. C.O. 520/92, Egerton to C.O., conf. 21 March 1910.
[5] CO. 520/62, Egerton to C.O., conf. 6 July 1908, minute by C.S., dated 5 August 1908.

advocate of direct taxation, considered it 'wrong' to be so heavily dependent on revenue from such indirect taxes as the customs duties on spirits.[1] In such matters British policy differed from France's in her West African territories. The French obtained only 12 per cent of their revenues from duties on spirits as against 50 per cent in British West Africa. At the same time, the French derived 43 per cent of their revenue through direct taxation whereas Britain relied on about 5 per cent.[2] Egerton, however, disliked direct taxation partly because it was burdensome but mainly because it was expensive to collect.[3]

Egerton admitted that the government had received gin as payment for native court fees and fines.[4] Inquiries showed that the four minor courts of Ogbeyan, Sabagreia, Amassoma, and Ekowe in Brass district had received gin as payment of fines, a practice promptly stopped in June 1908.[5] Gin-currency, particularly in 'Peters' gin, had featured prominently in Brass trade since the 1850s.[6] From 1901, Moor had, however, prohibited its use. Egerton therefore claimed that the payments in the four minor courts in Brass district did not represent a regular or widespread practice.[7]

Concerning the further allegation that the spirits traffic had displaced other imports, figures during the administrations of Moor, MacGregor and Egerton failed to justify the concern of Parliament and the humanitarian critics. During the five-year period 1903–7, the total value of Southern Nigeria's imports, exclusive of specie, was as shown in the table on p. 295.[8]

The relatively high value of imports of spirits and other imports for 1907 merely reflected the fact that 1907 generally represented a 'bumper year' for Southern Nigeria's import-export trade.[9]

[1] CO. 520/56, Egerton to C.O., 29 September 1907, R.L.A.'s marginal comments on minute by F.G.A.B. dated 10 December 1907.
[2] *Ibid.*, minute by F.G.A.B.
[3] CO. 520/103, Egerton to C.O., conf. 30 May 1911.
[4] CO. 520/64, Egerton to C.O., conf. 8 August 1908. CO. 520/72, MP. 41979, Bishop Tugwell's letter to *The Times*, 14 November 1908.
[5] CO. 520/66, Egerton to C.O., conf. 26 September 1908.
[6] CO. 520/66, Egerton to C.O., 28 September 1908. Till July 1908, the Cross River people also used gin currency. See, CO. 520/66, Egerton to C.O., conf. 6 July 1908.
[7] CO. 520/66, Egerton to C.O., conf. 26 September 1908.
[8] HC. Deb. 4s. 198, 9 December 1908.
[9] *The Liquor traffic report*, 1909, p. 3.

Social Obligations and Performance

	1903 £	1904 £	1905 £	1906 £	1907 £
Government	236,120	211,855	390,566	390,567	298,615
Commercial:					
(i) Spirits	220,871	277,300	262,256	301,738	385,505
(ii) Other	1,671,151	1,933,558	2,020,584	2,236,013	3,165,219
Total	2,128,142	2,422,713	2,592,406	2,847,318	3,839,339

On the moral issue, Egerton, as did MacGregor before him, claimed that cases of drunkenness were rare in Southern Nigeria.[1] Nor did Egerton believe that prohibition could or would promote morality among the masses.[2]

The protests of such evangelical humanitarians as Bishops H. Tugwell, J. Johnson and I. Oluwole from Southern Nigeria, all members of the C.M.S. in the diocese of Western Equatorial Africa, and the N.R.-L.T.U.C. in Britain, constantly emphasised moral arguments against the liquor traffic. In their responses to MacGregor's paper on 'Lagos' read before the Lagos Institute in 1901, Tugwell and Oluwole poured scorn on the Governor's lack of interest in imposing stricter controls on the liquor traffic. To Oluwole, the liquor traffic constituted the 'vexed subject' not the 'liquor phantom' or 'airy nothing' that MacGregor considered it.[3] Tugwell, a fervent advocate of direct taxation, condemned the principle of deriving revenues from the liquor trade:

> We import Spirits for the purposes of Revenue. How is the Railway being built? By Gin. How was the Carter-Denton Bridge built? By Gin. How is the Town lighted? By Gin. And now if it be asked How is the Town to be drained, or how are we to secure a good supply and good pure water? The answer is, with Gin! Such a situation is absolutely dishonest.

Bishop James Johnson, who since 1887 had addressed Members of Parliament privately on the liquor question, considered the spirits, particularly the gin and rum, sold in West Africa

---

[1] CO. 520/62, Egerton to C.O., conf. 6 July 1908. CO. 147/157, MacGregor to C.O., conf. 7 November 1901, enclosure.
[2] CO. 520/62, Egerton to C.O., conf. 6 July 1908.
[3] CO. 147/157, MacGregor to C.O., conf. 7 November 1901, enclosure: paper read on 16 October 1901.

'very cheap, low and vile in character' and debilitating to the farmers who produced valuable export crops. The liquor traffic, he said, further impoverished Southern Nigeria and caused physical degeneracy and premature death.[1] He cited the examples of Uganda, South Africa and Northern Nigeria where Britain protected Africans from the liquor traffic. He did not see why West Africa, which had for centuries been exposed to the evil effects of the slave trade, should again be afflicted with such a 'destructive traffic' as the liquor trade. He continued:

> We are tempted to ask why this difference of treatment when there is no evidence to show that West Africa is more capable of resisting the evil effects of this Traffic than the other African Territories?[2]

Neither J. Seely, to whom he forwarded his petition, nor the staff of the Colonial Office found an answer to Johnson's question. The government, however, agreed that until July 1908, at any rate, it continued to prohibit the sale of spirits to Africans in the Northern Territories of the Gold Coast, Northern Nigeria, British Somaliland, the British East Africa Protectorate, Uganda, Nyasaland and Rhodesia.[3]

In January 1909 James Johnson reminded the Colonial Office of resolutions passed by the West African clergy and laity against the liquor traffic. The Lagos Conference of bishops and laity in West Africa in 1906 had condemned the liquor trade as 'immoral in principle and ruinous to the people'.[4] The 1908 Abeokuta Synod of the Episcopal Native Church in the diocese of Western Equatorial Africa had also passed a similar resolution.[5]

Not content with protests in West Africa, the humanitarian evangelicals lobbied British Members of Parliament and followed these with a deputation to the Colonial Office on July 1908. Bishops Tugwell, Oluwole and Johnson were active in these moves.[6] In the United Kingdom, Tugwell and the N.R.-L.T.U.C. took the lead in the propaganda war against the liquor traffic in Southern Nigeria and the rest of British West Africa. In

[1] CO. 520/89, J. Johnson to Seely, 14 January 1909.
[2] *Ibid.*
[3] HC. Deb. 4s. 192, 20 July 1908, 1457.
[4] CO. 520/89, Johnson to Seely, 14 January 1909.
[5] *Ibid.*
[6] CO. 520/87, N.R.-L.T.U.C. to C.O., 7 April 1909, enclosure.

his address to the Pan-Anglican Congress in June 1908, Tugwell emphasised that the liquor traffic was commercially unsound, socially destructive, morally indefensible and a scandal to the British administration. He charged that the government improperly derived more revenue from spirits than from cotton goods and other 'useful articles' of 'legitimate trade'. He maintained that as a trustee power, Britain had the responsibility of protecting Africans from the alleged evils of the liquor traffic.[1]

The 'facts' of the liquor trade which Tugwell and other evangelical humanitarians with a knowledge of West African conditions supplied, the N.R.-L.T.U.C. magnified in its petitions and deputations. In July 1908,[2] the N.R.-L.T.U.C. informed the Colonial Office that the 'great Missionary and Temperance Societies' of the United Kingdom had unanimously asked for the prohibition of the liquor traffic in Southern Nigeria and other parts of West Africa as an act of 'practical statesmanship'. It again stressed the 'demoralising' aspects of the trade and advocated direct taxation in the event of prohibition. It felt satisfied that Southern Nigeria's difficult coast-line and a 'small' preventive service along the borders with Dahomey and the Cameroons would substantially check the incidence of smuggling. Revenue from direct taxation, it further observed, would meet the needs of the preventive service and administration generally. The N.R.-L.T.U.C. relentlessly maintained its pressure on the Colonial Office over the liquor controversy. In April 1909, it drew the attention of the Colonial Office to the British government's trustee rôle in West Africa and charged that the liquor traffic constituted 'the most serious obstacle' to Christian missionary and philanthropic work there.[3]

In Liverpool, John Holt's brand of humanitarianism evoked a different response. The liquor trade, in which Holt had no direct interests, gave him the opportunity of commenting freely on government policy and the conduct of the Christian missionaries. During the early stages of the controversy, Holt adopted a sane, moderate and constructive line. In 1896, for example, he had advised that the liquor trade be made a government monopoly. Under such a scheme, selected firms would then act as the licensed distributing agents of the government, who would thus

---

[1] CO. 520/72, MP. No. 26972A, address on 18 June 1908.
[2] CO. 520/73, N.R.-L.T.U.C. to C.O. 6 July 1908.
[3] CO. 520/87, N.R.-L.T.U.C. to C.O., 7 April 1909, enclosure.

have a better chance of controlling the liquor trade and watching its effects on the people.¹

When the government failed to adopt his suggestions and proceeded with the policy of increasing the specific duties on liquor for revenue and other purposes, Holt became more belligerent. He admitted the soundness of Egerton's policy in increasing taxes on spirits and other 'objectionable' imports in lieu of revenue from such necessities of life as salt, rice, and other food items, even though the revenue would benefit both the public and the government officials.² However, as a general principle, Holt emphasised:

> No man or men or govt. has any right to tax anybody unless there is a necessary public object upon which to spend the money. The first thing is the necessary public object for which money is needed, and then the least objectionable way of raising the money from the public. These servants of the state do not consider the interests of the public whose interests they ought to be the jealous guardians . . . They first think of how much they can squeeze out of the public by taxation in order that they may spend it in their own way and largely for their own enjoyment.³

Over the liquor question, Holt quickly advanced beyond the constitutional arguments based on the power to tax and spend. The activities of the humanitarian evangelicals in Southern Nigeria and the United Kingdom left him cold. In September 1908 Holt revealed to Morel:

> All that Tugwell talks about infantile mortality, the birthrate, the physical degeneration of the race through drink, I regard as the offspring of a disordered mind. . . . You will find that when you have made full inquiry . . . that the whiteman – man for man – is in Africa a much greater drinker and drunkard that [sic] the blackman who is the object of the special solicitude of the Tugwellites, and other hare-brained cranks, who are plundering the native whilst pretending to save him.⁴

¹ CO. 520/72, Liverpool Chamber of Commerce to C.O., 5 September 1908, enclosure.
² *E.D.M.P.* F/8, Holt to Morel, 10 September 1908.
³ *Ibid.*
⁴ *Ibid.*

Concerning the propaganda tactics of the humanitarians of the Tugwell school, Holt in January 1910 observed:

> The worst drinkers on the West Coast are the Europeans first, and then the civilised natives but the Dukes and Bishops ignore them. Why? Because they are comparatively few and the theme would not impress an ordinary meeting here ... Do you suppose they are going to let the liquor traffic drop? Not they! They would have nothing to get their listeners here to fret about and worry over and part with their coppers for, if they did.[1]

The other Liverpool traders with more direct interests in the liquor traffic in West Africa similarly endeavoured to demonstrate that they also had a vibrant humanitarian conscience. In September 1908, the members of the African trade section of the Liverpool Chamber of Commerce impressed upon J. Seely that merchants did not intend to kill their customers as that would destroy their commerce. They maintained that the limits of the prohibited zones for the liquor traffic under the international conventions were too ill-defined to be useful, and that foreign powers could not effectively prohibit the illicit distillation of spirits and fermented liquors in their territories. They also feared that smuggling and costly preventive services would result from the unwillingness of the governments of the neighbouring territories to reciprocate higher duties imposed on spirits in British West Africa.[2]

African consumers – the target of different kinds of humanitarianism – considered the liquor controversy practically and on the basis of self-interest. They found it more convenient to pay this form of indirect tax than a direct levy.[3] As it fell heaviest on the consumers of spirits, those who could not afford the costlier varieties of brandy, whisky, gin and rum had ready access to the cheaper locally-fermented brews. Such locally-produced drinks included 'tombo' or 'emu' (palm wine), 'peto' (fermented spirit from corn or millet), 'sekete' (guinea corn liquor), 'oti-oka' (maize-wine liquid) and 'agadagidi' (plantain-wine liquor).[4]

[1] *E.D.M.P.* F/8, Holt to Morel, 9 January 1910.
[2] CO. 520/72, Liverpool Chamber of Commerce to C.O., 5 September 1908, enclosure.
[3] *The liquor traffic report*, 1909, p. 11.
[4] Cd. 4907, Evidence before the Liquor Traffic Committee, Southern Nigeria, 1909, Appendix A, pp. 423 and 425.

Whereas the well-to-do educated Africans had regular access to whisky, brandy and other spirits, the masses waited for such festive occasions as marriages and funeral rites to indulge their appetite for European liquor.[1] Those who could ill afford spirits for entertainment continued to use kola-nuts. Contrary to the allegations of Bishops Tugwell and Johnson, the gin traffic did not displace the kola-nut trade in Southern Nigeria.[2]

To ascertain the disputed 'facts' of the liquor traffic in Southern Nigeria, the British government early in 1909 appointed a four-man committee headed by Mackenzie Chalmers, a distinguished former British civil servant in India. As an independent observer, Chalmers was the more acceptable since he had had neither official nor private business connections with British West Africa. This professionally qualified lawyer was also held in much respect by the Permanent Under-Secretary of State, Home Department, between 1903 and 1908.[3] The other members of the committee were chosen for their long-standing experience of conditions in West Africa. They included A. A. Cowan of the liquor-trading Liverpool firm of Alexander Miller, Brothers and Company; C. H. Elgee, the pro-African Resident of Ibadan; and T. Welsh of the Liverpool firm of Thomas Welsh and Company which had no dealings in the spirits trade.[4] After an exhaustive inquiry, the members of the committee unanimously agreed:

> There is absolutely no evidence of race deterioration due to drink. In Southern Nigeria mortality is high and disease is rife, but drink is only an insignificant factor in producing these results. There is hardly any alcoholic disease amongst the native population, and with the exception of one or two isolated cases we found no connection between drink and crime. On the occasions of feasts and festivals the natives often drink more than is good for them, both of trade spirits and native liquors. Individuals injured themselves both morally and physically by indulgence in drink, but the people generally are a sober people, who are able to drink in moderation with-

[1] *Ibid.*, p. 17.
[2] *Ibid.*, p. 20.
[3] CO. 520/73, N.R.-L.T.U.C. to Crewe, 21 October, 1908, minute by J.S.
[4] HC. Deb. 5s. 1, 24 February 1909, 713/17. HC. Deb. 5s. 1, 3 March 1909, 1402-3.

Social Obligations and Performance

out falling into excess . . . The expert evidence taken in England shows that there is nothing to complain of as regards the quality of the spirits imported into Nigeria.[1]

The committee's verdict, however, did not immediately end the evangelical criticism of 'the Drink Traffic' in West Africa. In its resolutions passed at the Leeds meeting of February 1911, the Central Board of Missions of the Church of England regarded the liquor trade as 'a serious hindrance to the advance of Christianity'. It also called upon the British government not only to ensure that in Southern Nigeria the liquor traffic came 'under effective supervision and control' but also to guarantee 'adequate protection' for Northern Nigeria.[2]

Generally, the Chalmers report satisfied the Colonial Office. The 'indifference' of Christian missionaries, other than those of the C.M.S., to the proceedings of the Chalmers committee caught the special attention of the Colonial Office. It noted that only one European Wesleyan missionary gave evidence while the Roman Catholic missionaries had to be 'coerced' to give evidence.[3] Permanent Under-Secretary F. J. S. Hopwood felt so satisfied with the Chalmers report that he expected it to 'serve as good defensive matter in debate and otherwise for some years to come'.[4] J. Seely, however, found the same report embarrassing by making it more difficult for the government to justify prohibition in Northern Nigeria and other British protectorates in Africa if Africans in Southern Nigeria exercised sufficient self-control.[5] Less embarrassed, Lord Crewe regarded the existence of Islam in Northern Nigeria, at any rate, as a sufficiently 'good reason' for maintaining prohibition in that protectorate.[6] In June 1912 Harcourt assured Parliament that the government would protect the prohibited zone in Northern Nigeria and increase the specific duties on spirits imported into West Africa whether or not international co-operation through the Brussels Liquor conference of 1911–12 succeeded.[7]

[1] *The liquor traffic report*, 1909, p. 23.
[2] CO. 520/111, The Archbishop of Canterbury to C.O., 11 March 1911, enclosure.
[3] CO. 520/87, M.P. No. 31229, minute by C.S., dated 2 October 1909.
[4] *Ibid.*, minute dated 5 October 1909.
[5] *Ibid.*
[6] *Ibid.*, minute dated 11 October 1909.
[7] HC. Deb. 5s. 40. 27 June 1912, 535–6.

The Chalmers report did not make Egerton's administration feel complacent. Instead, through further ordinances in 1910 and 1912, it improved the legal machinery for dealing with illicit distillation of spirits.[1] In 1912, it accompanied these measures with increasing the specific duty on spirits at 50 degrees Tralles from 5s to 5s 6d per imperial gallon.[2]

For Southern Nigeria, the entire liquor controversy which led to the 1909 inquiry had several significant aspects. It demonstrated that the relationship between the Cross and the flag did not represent a solid partnership. Over this basic issue of revenue versus morality, the government failed to back the vociferous critics among the Anglican clergy. In this controversy, the clash of interests between the administrative and evangelical viewpoints proved remarkably sharp. On this occasion, as in the Pinnock case and the Oluwole-led protests of the Ekiti Christian converts, the government failed to protect the Cross as much as the clergy desired.

The entire liquor crisis indicated that the government did not consider it practical politics to end the 'drink traffic' in Southern Nigeria during this period. The main obstacle lay in the public opposition to direct taxation. By the favourable nature of its major conclusions, the Chalmers report indirectly helped to postpone the immediate consideration of direct taxation in Southern Nigeria.

The 1905–9 phase of the liquor controversy in West Africa focused particular attention on Southern Nigeria, mainly because of railway extension towards the prohibited zone in Northern Nigeria. To that extent, the pre-inquiry stage of the agitation gave Southern Nigeria's administration adverse world publicity. The Chalmers report set right that picture, again with much publicity though, in some quarters, its findings were contested. The conclusion in the Chalmers report that generally the people of Southern Nigeria were sober failed to impress some officials in Northern Nigeria. One of these, G. J. F. Tomlinson, observed in August 1911 that compared with Sokoto, Onitsha remained 'a pandemonium of alcoholic debauchery'.[3]

---

[1] CO. 588/3, The Distilleries Ordinance, 1910 (No. 13 of 1910) dated 2 August 1910. CO. 588/4, the Distillation of Spirits Prohibition Ordinance (No. 2), 1912 (No. 30 of 1912) dated 27 September 1912.

[2] CO. 520/113, Egerton to C.O., tel. 12 February 1912.

[3] *E.D.M.P.* F/9, G. J. F. Tomlinson to Morel, 7 August 1911.

The controversy ended the irregular use of gin currency for the payment of native court fees and fines in the Brass district. However, the detection of this malpractice in 1908 indicated the strong attachment of some of the people of Southern Nigeria to the pre-colonial gin currency, in spite of its increasing competition with sterling silver and British subsidiary copper coinage.

The liquor agitation drew public attention to the presence of cheaper substitutes brewed or fermented locally. The two related problems of illicit distillation and shebeening continued to raise serious problems for the police and other law enforcement agencies.

Moreover, the Anglican clergy and the N.R.-L.T.U.C. gave considerable emphasis to the theme of trusteeship during the entire agitation against the liquor traffic in West Africa. Directly and indirectly, these repeated references to trusteeship served to remind the government of its general social obligations to the people under its charge in such territories as Southern and Northern Nigeria.

PUBLIC HEALTH AND SANITATION

Although the controversy over the liquor traffic revealed the importance which its critics attached to the good health of the ordinary people of Southern Nigeria, the government did not systematically show much interest in public health and sanitation except in relation to its officials. Government expenditure on such matters of public health fell much below the sums devoted to the railway, harbour, roads, bridges, and the like. Part of John Holt's criticism of the government attitude to the liquor traffic resulted from his strong views on the power to tax and spend. On his list of priorities for government expenditure, as indicated in January 1906, public health and education had precedence over the railway, roads and so on.[1] Moor, MacGregor and Egerton thought differently.

Of the three, MacGregor showed the greatest enthusiasm for public health and sanitation measures, without achieving correspondingly satisfactory results outside Lagos and its neighbourhood. He as well as Egerton concentrated on the improvement of

[1] *E.D.M.P.* F/8, Holt to Morel, 21 January 1906. Holt regarded education as the first major item of expenditure and public health next in importance.

public health facilities at Lagos and a few government stations elsewhere. As the political and commercial capital of the colony, and later of Southern Nigeria, Lagos understandably received first consideration in such matters from MacGregor and Egerton. Both used the General Board of Health established under the Public Health Ordinance, 1899[1] to improve the sanitary district of Lagos and its neighbouring areas to which the government subsequently extended the law. Even the anti-malaria campaign undertaken, through MacGregor's encouragement, by the Ladies' League founded in January 1901, concentrated its efforts around Lagos.[2] There, the members of the Ladies League distributed to poor patients medicines from the stocks in the government dispensary at Ereko. The League also actively interested itself in the fight against infant mortality. With the end of the MacGregor era, the Ladies' League declined as an active, but private, adjunct to the Medical Department. MacGregor's interest in the reclamation of swamps again centred on Lagos. The clearance of the Kokomaiko swamp[3] and the construction of the MacGregor canal were noticeable aspects of his attempts to get rid of the miasma which surrounded Lagos city and constituted serious public health hazards there.

The first government-sponsored improved water scheme, undertaken in 1908, sought to benefit the people of Lagos and the officials resident there. By comparison with Lagos, the Benin water scheme, about the same time, represented a much smaller project. During the same period, other towns in Southern Nigeria lacked similar facilities. The emphasis on Lagos needs increased after the establishment in December 1908 of the Municipal Board of Health. Thereafter, the newly-established Board carried out in Lagos township and Ebute Metta the sanitary work which previously the Public Works Department had undertaken with the advice of the Medical Department.[4]

Although the scourge of smallpox threatened the lives of

[1] *Lagos Government Gazette*, 16 September 1899, Ordinance dated 13 September 1899.

[2] CO. 147/154, MacGregor to C.O., 23 February 1901. The officers of the Ladies' League included: President, Mrs. C. A. Sapara-Williams; Vice-President, Mrs. I. Oluwole; Secretary, Mrs. O. Johnson. Its inaugural meeting took place on 25 January 1901.

[3] CO. 147/157, MacGregor to C.O., conf. 7 November 1901, enclosure.

[4] CO. 592/5, Annual report on the Medical Department, 1908.

Political and military staff in Southern Nigeria, 1910

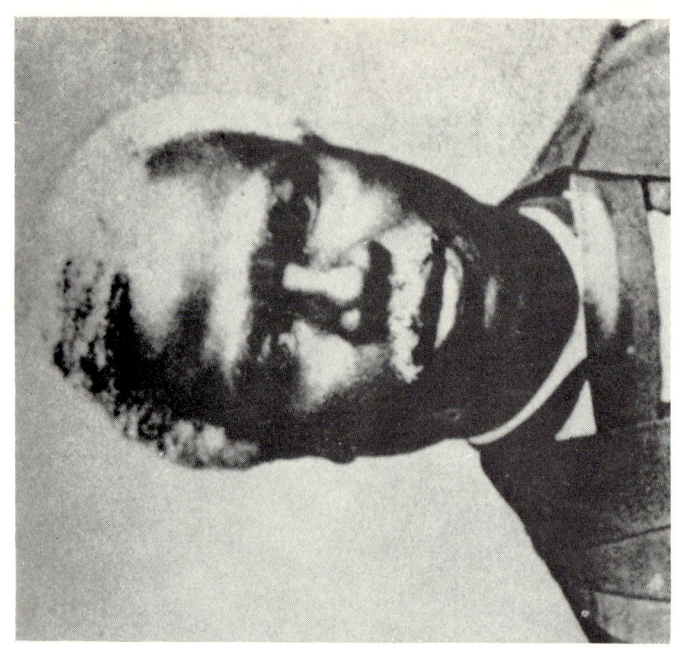

The Rt. Rev. Isaac Oluwole

John Holt

Social Obligations and Performance

millions of people in Southern Nigeria, the government emphasised its eradication in Lagos and its adjoining districts. In its attempts to control the activities of the *Sopono* (smallpox) cult among the Yoruba, the government in 1909 banned the invocation of any smallpox juju in Lagos township, Iddo island, Ebute Metta, Apapa and its neighbourhood.[1] In other parts of Southern Nigeria, the Medical Department, which in March 1910 had a sanitary branch, approached the problem of smallpox through vaccination. But relatively few people benefited from the activities of the Hinterland Vaccination Staff already in existence in 1906.[2] The inadequacy of the public health and sanitation measures adopted by the government outside Lagos and its neighbourhood could be seen from the statistics for 1908 when only 83,315 successful cases out of 114,524 persons vaccinated against smallpox in the Western, Eastern and Central Provinces were reported. In the same year, the Medical Department treated only 73,786 persons[3] out of a population of over 7 million.

Generally, the Christian missionaries assisted considerably in providing medical and public health facilities even where the government felt unable to take the initiative. Through the combined efforts of the government and the Christian missionaries, Southern Nigeria in 1912, had a few hospitals, lunatic asylums, leper asylums and settlements and a pauper house situated in key areas. The Western Province had a hospital in each of the districts of Lagos, Badagry, Epe and Ibadan. In the Eastern Province, Calabar district had two hospitals as against one each for the districts of Opobo, Bonny, Brass and Degema. The Central Province topped the hospitals list with nine, six of which were located in the Onitsha district, and one each in the districts of Warri, Sapele and Forcados. Only Lagos District had a Lunatic Asylum and the Pauper House which in 1912 had 21 patients supported by the government. Ibusa had two Leper Asylums and a Leper Settlement some of which were maintained by the

---

[1] CO. 520/82, Egerton to C.O., 9 October 1909, enclosure. To its worshippers, smallpox was known as 'Oba Ilu Aiye' (the King of the world). According to Dr. O. Sapara: 'It is the only disease that is greeted with royal honours. A person, however poor, when suffering from that disease, is greeted with salutation and prostration usually accorded the Alafin of Oyo in his palace'.
[2] CO. 592/3, Annual report on the Medical Department, 1906.
[3] CO. 592/5, Annual report on the Medical Department, 1908.

'friends' of the inmates and others by the government. Yaba and Onitsha each had a Leper Asylum.[1]

In the field of public health and education, the government made relatively little impact on the people during this period. By far the greater beneficiaries were the government officials and the few Africans near their stations.

PUBLIC EDUCATION

Similarly undistinguished was the government's record in public education. There also the Christian missionaries became the pioneers. Neither the government nor the missionaries had adequate funds for mass education. More important, public distrust of the government extended to the Christian missionaries whose general work threatened the social solidarity of the various communities whose own religious and cultural values suffered as a result. With its emphasis on individualism, literacy in English, and lessons on foreign cultural values, the secular and religious content of Western European education did not at first impress the men and women of the old order who held back most of their children from cultural contamination in the newly-established schools.

Without the time and skilled man-power to break down these cultural barriers, the government and the Christian missionaries had a particularly difficult task to establish public education. For a while, the government contented itself with making token gestures in the areas under its control. Elsewhere, government schools had to wait until administrative control was established. A good example of the close relationship between firm administrative control and the establishment of government schools can be seen from the time-table of the first set of such schools established in the Eastern Province. There, the government in April 1900 opened its first school at Bonny along the coast. The other schools at Opobo, Owerri, Akassa, Azumini, Aro-Chuku, Oban, Uwet, Eket, Obubra and Nkarhia were opened, in that order, between July 1905 and January 1907.[2]

[1] CO. 473/14, Blue Book, Southern Nigeria, 1912. The record did not make the distinction between a Leper Asylum and a Leper Settlement clear.

[2] CO. 592/3, Annual report on the Eastern Province, 1906. This report was dated 27 April 1907.

Social Obligations and Performance

From 1900 to 1913, the government had only one secondary school, King's School (later College), established on 20 September 1909.¹ Beginning with 11 students in 1909, King's College had 59 on its roll in 1912.² The lead established by the Christian missionaries in public education they maintained in the larger number of secondary and primary schools under their control. In 1912 alone Southern Nigeria had five assisted and four unassisted secondary schools run by Christian missionaries.³ The number of schools established by the government and Christian missionaries had attendance rolls which indicated the degree of support they received from the 7 million-odd people of Southern Nigeria. In 1912, the few government and assisted schools served:⁴

Assisted Secondary Schools	Unassisted Secondary Schools
Hope Waddell Institute	C.M.S. Grammar School, Abeokuta
St. Gregory's Grammar School	Wesleyan (Boys) High School, Lagos
C.M.S. Grammar School, Lagos	Wesleyan (Girls) High School, Lagos
C.M.S. Girls' Seminary	New High Class School, Lagos
St. Mary's Convent, Lagos	

Province	Government	Assisted
Western	12	38
Central	26	22
Eastern	21	30
Total	59	90

The 90 assisted denominational schools inspected by the staff of the Education Department in 1912 had a total of 15,426 pupils distributed thus:⁵

¹ CO. 592/7, Annual report on the Education Department, 1909. In 1910, it became King's College.
² *Ibid.* C.O. 592/16, Annual report on the Education Department, 1912.
³ CO. 592/16, Annual report on the Education Department, 1912.
⁴ *Ibid.*   ⁵ *Ibid.*

Denomination	No. of Shcools	Pupils enrolled
Anglican	27	4,690
R.C.M.	35	7,041
United Free Church	19	2,495
Wesleyan	6	872
United Native African	2	257
Qua Ibo	1	71
Total	90	15,426

In 1912, the 59 government schools had only 5,682 enrolled:[1]

Province	Boys	Girls	Total
Western	914	13	927
Central	2,647	108	2,755
Eastern	1,947	53	2,000
Total	5,508	174	5,682

The government assisted educational development through grants-in-aid to selected schools inspected regularly by the staff of the Education Department. In 1912, the government spent only £10,475 10s 3d[2] under this item out of a total expenditure then of £2,110,498.

The few Koranic Schools in the Western Province did not receive any government grants-in-aid, for instance, in 1910. The estimated 3,000 pupils who then attended the Koranic Schools received purely religious instructions[3] which did not sufficiently attract the government's attention.

Under the Educational Code and additional instructions from the Director of Education, the government controlled curriculum development. During Egerton's administration with its emphasis on economic development, the government actively encouraged a measure of technical and industrial instruction in some of its own schools and those established by the Christian missionaries. In the Eastern, Central and Western Provinces, special emphasis was given to carpentry, coopering, agriculture, typewriting, tele-

[1] Ibid.
[2] Ibid.
[3] CO. 592/9, Annual report on the Education Department, 1910.

Social Obligations and Performance

graphy, printing, tailoring, smithery, art-needlework, laundry, cookery, baking and poultry keeping. In agriculture, the B.C.G.A. supplied cotton seed for use in the school gardens. In addition, the Curators of the Agricultural Department visited these schools.[1] At Onitsha and Topo the Roman Catholic Mission established special Trade Schools for boys and girls.[2] The industrial and technical instruction given in the denominational and government schools supplemented the training given in the technical branches of the Civil Service. In 1910 alone, 200 apprentices attached to such government departments as the Railway, Public Works, Marine, Telegraphs, Printing, Forestry and Agriculture received technical instruction.[3]

Under the new Education Code introduced in 1910, the government made the teaching of hygiene a compulsory subject in all schools and for all Teachers' Certificates examinations.[4] Yet, in this and other respects, the government and denominational schools in the Eastern, Central and Western Provinces suffered from an acute shortage of qualified teachers. To meet this problem of under-staffing, the government, under the new Code, legalised the 'pupil-teacher' system.[5]

Except in its attitude towards the Koranic Schools, the government, through its educational policy, tried to fulfil part of its constitutional obligations to promote religion and education among the people. It remains to be seen how far it carried out the other major obligation of allowing the people 'free enjoyment of their possessions'.

LAND POLICY

Among the foremost of such possessions came land. Except in Lagos Colony, the major controversies over land arose less from its ownership than from its use. Until 1913, the land-use problems were those affecting the indigenous inhabitants, the government and private outsiders. In Lagos, the ownership and use of land constituted twin problems for a while.

[1] CO. 592/3, Annual report on the Eastern Province, 1906. CO. 592/5, Annual report on the Central Province, 1908. CO. 592/7, Annual report on the Education Department, 1909. CO. 592/9, Annual report on the Education Department, 1910.
[2] CO. 592/9, Annual report on the Education Department, 1910.
[3] Ibid.   [4] Ibid.   [5] Ibid.

In Lagos Colony, the long controversy over the status of land following the British annexation in 1861 and the pre-colonial claims of the White Cap chiefs to the ownership of land was settled in favour of the latter in July 1921.[1] In the judgment, on appeal, of the Apapa land case, the Judicial Committee of the Privy Council upheld the general principles of land tenure enunciated in 1898 and 1912. The Lords of the Judicial Committee agreed that in his report on 'Land tenure in West Africa' (1898), Chief Justice T. C. Rayner, a former Chief Justice of the Lagos Supreme Court, correctly maintained that the community, not the individual, owned land. They also upheld the decision given by Chief Justice A. W. Osborne in *Oduntan Onisiwo v. The Attorney-General of Southern Nigeria* (1912) on the effects of the 1861 annexation. Osborne then ruled that the annexation did not impair the rights of the White Cap Chiefs to the ownership of land in Lagos. Their Lordships therefore rejected Chief Justice E. A. Speed's decision, in the Apapa Land Case, that the 1861 annexation had the effect of transferring the rights of ownership to the British Crown.

Outside Lagos colony, the essential land issues crystallised over its use. The government had greater freedom there in settling such issues in the absence of a large number of European settlers. Egerton, in particular, considered that in the absence of direct taxation, the people's land should constitute the main basis of agricultural production and revenue for the government.[2] Moreover, so long as the basis of agriculture remained peasant farming, which, however, produced the necessary surpluses for export, the government discouraged any attempts at plantation-type production lest the masses be deprived of their land.

In asserting their rights to the use of their land, the people encountered serious threats from the government and private outsiders – Europeans and African. Frequently, for the use of the government and these private outsiders, the indigenous people lost large tracts of land on 99-year lease terms, particularly in the towns and commercial centres. Usually, the government exempted agricultural land from such alienation.[3] The government

[1] *Macaulay Papers:* The Apapa Land Case: *Amodu Tijani v. The Secretary, Southern Provinces,* Privy Council Appeal No. 30/1919, Judgment given on 11 July 1921.
[2] CO. 520/103, Egerton to C.O., conf. 30 May 1911.
[3] *Ibid.*

Social Obligations and Performance

needed land for its stations and for other public use. In Lagos Colony, the government acquired power to get it under the Public Lands Ordinance, 1876,[1] stipulating that land transferred under such circumstances should have reasonable compensation to be determined, when in dispute, by the Supreme Court.

In the Lagos Protectorate, the long-standing obstacle raised by the question of jurisdiction prevented the formulation of a clear land policy by MacGregor and Egerton. The position about land, particularly in the districts near Lagos, remained confused until 1914. In the Protectorate of Southern Nigeria, the government assumed power over land without serious jurisdictional difficulties. Satisfied that most of the hinterland districts of that protectorate were *de facto* 'conquered territories', the government there acquired greater freedom of action. Under the Public Lands Acquisition Proclamation, 1903,[2] Moor authorised the alienation of land for 'public purposes' subject to compensation. The revolutionary aspect of that law lay in the clause which provided:

> Where lands required for public purposes are the property of a native community, the Head Chief of such community may sell and convey the same for an estate in fee simple, notwithstanding any native law or custom to the contrary.[3]

Under this law, later extended to the rest of post-1906 Southern Nigeria, the government acquired the Apapa land, covering about 255 acres, claimed on behalf of his community by the White Cap Chief Oluwa (Amodu Tijani). After prolonged and costly litigation involving Chief Oluwa and the government over the basis of compensation, a solution came in 1921. The Judicial Committee of the Privy Council then favoured compensation along the lines of the pre-colonial principle of community ownership.

Through legislation and usage, the government further acquired the rights to the sub-soil and its exploitation for mineral prospecting.[4] The first mining law (Proclamation No. 18 of

---

[1] No. 8 of 1876, dated 19 April 1876.
[2] CO. 588/1, No. 5 of 1903, dated 10 January 1903 but came into operation on 1 March 1903. [3] *Ibid.*, clause 6.
[4] CO. 520/103, Egerton to C.O., conf. 30 May 1911. CSO. 1/21/11, James to C.O., conf. 14 August 1912, enclosure. CSO. 1/22/9, C.O. to Lugard, conf. 12 November 1912.

1902) of the Protectorate of Southern Nigeria proceeded on the theory 'that all lands in the Protectorate are vested either in the chiefs of native communities in trust for such communities, or in the Government'. Hence, the government assumed the sole right of granting prospecting licences, but allowed the holders to obtain the consent of the chiefs where their concessions covered community lands. Under the same law, the government exercised power to grant mining leases for land which it claimed as its own property. Subject to the High Commissioners' approval, the chiefs had the right to grant mining leases for community land. Where they objected, the Supreme Court could compel such a grant provided it considered their refusal 'detrimental to the interests of such community'. The treasury released one-fifth of the fees and rents and one-third of the taxes on the profits from such licences and leases to the chiefs for the benefit of their respective communities.[1]

Under Ordinance No. 6 of 1905 the government made similar provisions for prospecting licences and mining leases covering lands in the Lagos Colony and Protectorate. In this case, however, the treasury remitted half the fees and rents and one-third of the taxes on the profits from such licences and leases to the African authorities for expenditure according to customary law.[2] With the 1906 amalgamation, a new mining law[3] replaced Proclamation No. 18 of 1902. Later, in November 1912, the Colonial Office sanctioned the amendment of the Mining Ordinance recommended by Egerton since May 1911. Under the new arrangements, the government deprived the chiefs and people of the Central and Eastern Province of their share of the fees, rents and profits to which they were previously entitled. Simultaneously, it denied them the right of objecting to prospecting licences or mining leases being granted for their land. Thereafter, as 'legal occupiers', they were entitled to compensation only for damage done to surface land and buildings by mining operations. Because of the well-known jurisdictional problems, the Colonial Office exempted the Western Province from these radical changes in the mining law of the land.[4]

[1] CSO. 1/22/9, C.O. to Lugard, conf. 12 November 1912.
[2] *Ibid.*
[3] Ordinance No. 6 of 1905 which formerly applied only to Lagos Colony and Protectorate.
[4] CSO. 1/22/9, C.O. to Lugard, conf. 12 November 1912.

As overlord, the government further assumed the power of allocating the use and occupation of land not only for mineral prospecting but also for forest concessions, particularly in the cultivation of *para* rubber. John Holt severely criticised the assumption of such powers in September 1909 on the grounds that it would be subject to abuse.[1] For its part, the government feared that without exerting powers of control, European and African speculators would deprive the people of their land. Between 1900 and 1903, Moor had appreciated the magnitude of that danger and adopted measures to deal with it in the Protectorate of Southern Nigeria. By Proclamation No. 1 of 1900, persons other than the indigenous inhabitants could not acquire any interest or right over land from the latter without the High Commissioner's written consent.[2] The government had power to deal with defaulters under the Native Lands Acquisition Proclamation, 1903.[3] The 1903 law, as F. G. A. Butler explained, sought to 'catch the coloured alien as well as the European concession-hunter'.[4] Under the Lands Registry Proclamations of 1900 and 1901,[5] Moor provided another form of check through the compulsory registration of all instruments affecting the disposal of land in the Protectorate of Southern Nigeria.

Egerton also made it a cardinal aspect of his land policy to protect the indigenous inhabitants from the activities of European and African land-sharks. That policy he reaffirmed after 1909 when the British government desired to relate its land policy in Southern Nigeria to that already approved for Northern Nigeria in 1908.[6] The central issue in that attempt lay from 1909 in the exercise of British overlordship in land matters affecting post-1906 Southern Nigeria, the Yoruba part of which, at least, differed from the status of 'conquered territory' officially applied to Northern Nigeria after the capitulation in 1903 of Kano and Sokoto. Even in the non-Yoruba parts of Southern Nigeria where the concept of 'conquered territory' generally influenced the psychology of such administrators as C. W. Alexander, the

[1] *E.D.M.P.* F/8, Holt to Morel, 26 September 1909.
[2] CO. 588/1, No. 1 of 1900.
[3] CO. 588/1, No. 1 of 1903.
[4] CO. 520/18, Moor to C.O., 14 January 1903, minute by F.G.A.B.
[5] CO. 588/1, No. 16 of 1900 and No. 18 of 1901.
[6] *E.D.M.P.* F/8, Egerton to Morel, 5 December 1911. CO. 520/103, Egerton to C.O., conf. 30 May 1911.

Commissioner of Lands,[1] the government clearly recognised that there had been no public declaration of the confiscation of land immediately after conquest.[2] Legal, political and moral arguments therefore beset the path of the government's attempts after 1909 to reform its land policy in Southern Nigeria. During that controversy, the views of such African spokesmen as Obadiah Johnson and Herbert Macaulay clashed with those of E. D. Morel, one of the leaders of the 'Third Party' group of British humanitarians.

From 1912, Herbert Macaulay actively participated in the public agitation against the land reforms contemplated by the British government in Southern Nigeria and other parts of West Africa.[3] Acting with an African barrister, J. E. Shyngle, Macaulay toured parts of Yorubaland and the Itsekiri territory, raising funds for a delegation to Britain to protest against the projected land reforms. The agitation led by Macaulay and Shyngle, however, helped to split the Lagos Auxiliary of the A.P.S. Some of its members, including O. Obasa, alleged that the public funds so raised had been misappropriated by Macaulay and Shyngle.[4]

Over the land question, O. Johnson and E. D. Morel exchanged correspondence.[5] Morel believed that Johnson belonged to the group of Africans who did 'not wish the British government to have the slightest power in dealing with the matter of land tenure'. Morel, however, wanted that group checked to prevent a large-scale alienation of land which would have the effect of reducing the masses to the status of landless labourers working for wages. Morel had noticed, he said, that with a few exceptions the 'cocoa plantations' in the colony of Southern Nigeria (previously Lagos) were 'not run by cultivators in their own right but by labourers working for native landlords'. Though not an advocate of 'European-managed plantations' in West Africa, Morel wanted land leased for economic development under two safeguards. He advised that such leases should not cover 'too long a period' nor 'too large an area'. Morel

[1] CSO. 1/21/11, James to C.O., conf. 14 August 1912, enclosure – Memorandum by C. W. Alexander dated 16 September 1911.
[2] Ibid.
[3] Thomas I. B.: *Life History of Herbert Macaulay*, Lagos 1947, p. 46.
[4] E.D.M.P. F/9, O. Sapara to Morel, 29 May, 1913. E.D.M.P. F/9, O. Sapara to Morel, 19 June 1913.
[5] E.D.M.P. F/9, Morel to H. Strachan, 6 January 1913.

believed that the people of West Africa had the ability to cultivate their own land in their own way. He feared, however, that if not checked, 'the European system' would supplant the West African principles of land tenure. He considered the latter so important because 'the preservation of native tenure is . . . the indispensable safeguard to the maintenance of native economic independence, and of native polity'. He therefore demanded that the British government, as the 'overlord' of West African land, assume the power of protecting the people against the effects of 'human folly and human ignorance' in such matters.

In December 1912, Morel denied Johnson's main criticisms of his rôle in the post-1909 trend of British land policy for Southern Nigeria and the rest of West Africa. Johnson charged that the British government was then being advised to deprive the entire people of West Africa of their lands and that Morel had been involved in giving such advice.[1] Morel instead affirmed that he wanted security of tenure for West African cultivators and 'European planters' without prejudice to the customary land tenure. He therefore desired

> that the land of West Africa and its fruits shall be legally safeguarded from alienation – from passing out of the hands of the people into the hands of a restricted number of individuals whether European or Native: that unrestricted buying and selling of land between Natives and Natives, and alienation of extensive tracts of country to European companies, shall not be permitted . . .[2]

Clearly, E. D. Morel, O. Johnson, H. Macaulay, J. E. Shyngle and others who participated actively in the post-1909 land controversy in Southern Nigeria and elsewhere in British West Africa differed not in the goal but in the means proposed to achieve it. Both sides appreciated the desirability of maintaining security in land tenure for the masses whose interests in such matters had been threatened by African and European speculators. Whereas Johnson, Macaulay, Shyngle and others wanted the Africans to be left with the power of protecting themselves, Morel and others of his school urged the British government to assume that power legally and exercise it thoroughly. Once more, the meaning of a British protectorate in this part of West Africa

[1] *E.D.M.P.* F/9, Morel to Johnson, 13 December 1912.
[2] *Ibid.*

was severely tested during the land controversy. Morel wanted Britain's constitutionally-accepted social obligations to include the protection of land and no longer to be left at the previous level of *de facto* jurisdiction. The African critics of that policy sought to preclude such an expansion of the meaning of a protectorate.

Generally, the controversy over the basis of the government's land policy in Southern Nigeria could not alter the course of events. The government cared little about the actual basis of the exercise of its land policy there. In the non-Yoruba sections of Southern Nigeria, distinctions between *de jure* and *de facto* jurisdiction were abstract issues which did not stop the British authorities from making their control there real in every sense. The post-1913 inquiries into the basis of land tenure in British West Africa therefore did not radically alter government attitude to such matters in Southern Nigeria. The question of land policy raised the related issue of the government attitude to labour. There again, the government assumed and exercised considerable powers of interference in its general efforts to increase the degree of its control and advance the pace of Southern Nigeria's economic development.

11 Labour and Domestic Slavery

FACTORS IN THE REGULATION OF LABOUR

Certain major factors influenced government labour policies and measures in Southern Nigeria. Moor, MacGregor and Egerton undertook to discharge the imperial obligation, after 1833, of abolishing slavery and all forms of slave-dealing in the territories under their charge. They recognised, however, the practical difficulties in pushing reform measures about slavery too far too fast. The government encountered the problem of some chiefs in holding tenaciously to the pre-colonial institution of domestic slavery while most of the masses desired freedom. Consequently, the government at first tried compromise measures.

MacGregor and Egerton faced a second problem in the Yoruba part of the protectorate, where the long-standing jurisdictional issue made it extremely difficult for them to formulate and execute any clear-cut labour policy. Whereas the Protectorate of Southern Nigeria had its Native House Rule Proclamation of 1901, the Master and Servant Proclamations of 1901 and 1903, and the Roads and Creeks Proclamation of 1903, the Lagos Protectorate lacked any comparable legislation. Consequently, persons in the Protectorate of Southern Nigeria seeking to evade the provisions of these labour laws often found the Lagos Protectorate a convenient refuge. Others more daringly escaped to the neighbouring Spanish territory of Fernando Po.

Both Moor and Egerton found it more convenient to obtain forced labour through the chiefs, who usually also served as the members of the reorganised native courts. To ensure ready compliance, Moor, Egerton and their deputies upheld the authority of these chiefs upon whom devolved the unpleasant and unpopular task of recruiting forced labour whenever required by the government. This link gave the system of indirect administration a bad public image.

317

Despite its unpopularity, the system of forced labour gave the government a more convenient alternative to direct taxation, then detested by the people, as the liquor controversy revealed. At the same time, the government recognised that it could not excessively impose this other form of indirect taxation without considering its effect on agricultural production and the general satisfaction of the people under its charge. In excess, the system of forced labour could and did cause political unrest which in turn meant 'pacification' through coercion, at considerable cost and loss of valuable man-power.

The government also found in forced labour a convenient means of promoting limited economic development, particularly at village level. Through this approach and at little cost, it was able to clear village creeks and clean the bush-paths for the benefit of the public, troops and officers on tour. Forced labour also gave government officers relatively cheap labour for porterage, field operations and the like without adding unduly to the territory's annual expenditure. The amount saved went into the development of minor or major public works.

FORCED LABOUR PROBLEMS

Moor sought to conserve the available man-power in the Protectorate of Southern Nigeria for its use in intensive and extensive agricultural development. He therefore detested any organised and government-inspired schemes for exporting the protectorate's unskilled labour. Owing to his objections, the Colonial Office rejected[1] the 'experiment' proposed by the Transvaal Chamber of Mines in 1903 to recruit about 1,000 labourers in Nigeria on terms of repatriation after a two-year contract.[2]

In general, Moor and Egerton met the labour needs of their territories through special arrangements, of which the main one was forced labour. Under the carrier system, the government obtained labour for punitive expeditions, patrols and official tours. It adopted other means to obtain labour for work on public roads and creeks. The Roads and Creeks Proclamation, 1903,[3] empowered the chiefs, on the orders of the District Com-

[1] CO. 520/19, O.A.G. to C.O., tel. 8 May 1903, minutes by M.F.O. and J.C.
[2] *Ibid.*   [3] CO. 588/1, No. 15 of 1903.

missioner, to ask able-bodied men and women to clear roads, rivers and creeks on such days as the government required but 'not exceeding six days in each quarter of a year'.[1] In practice, the government failed to keep a strict check on the duration of the forced labour provided.

The government did not exempt women from forced labour. Speaking of the Roads and Creeks Proclamation, 1903, W. Asmis, the German Consul at Boma, remarked:

> This is the only example in English, French, or German native law on the West Coast [of Africa], of *women* [sic] being summoned to public work by a *special provision* [sic], although in German and French colonies women are often employed in helping to clear the roads.[2]

In practice, however, the government sought to prevent the employment of women for long-distance porterage so as to enable them to return to their respective villages 'without molestation'.

Under the carrier system and through usage, the government recruited men and women indiscriminately in the Western, Central and Eastern Provinces of post-1906 Southern Nigeria. At times, the system led to serious abuses, as, for instance, at Ijebu-Igbo in February 1910.[3] The 'forcible seizure' of carriers from churches at Iseri and Imuku brought sharp criticisms from Bishop I. Oluwole and the Lagos press.[4] Official investigations, ordered by Egerton, confirmed that with or without the explicit orders of H. B. Kent, the Medical Officer on probation at Epe, government messengers had seized carriers during divine service in both churches. The government strongly disapproved of Kent's action – he had already left the colony – censured him in writing and offered compensation of £5 each to the Churches concerned.[5] The Colonial Office approved the termination of Kent's probationary employment.[6] Oluwole felt satisfied with

---

[1] *Ibid.*, clause 5(a).
[2] W. Asmis, 'Law and policy relating to the natives of the Gold Coast and Nigeria', part 2, *J.A.S.*, vol. 12, 1912–13, London, p. 159.
[3] CO. 520/93, Egerton to C.O., 26 April 1910, enclosure.
[4] CO. 520/93, Egerton to C.O., 26 April 1910. *The Nigerian Chronicle*, 18 March, 1910.
[5] CO. 520/93, Egerton to C.O., 26 April, 1910, enclosures.
[6] CO. 520/93, Egerton to C.O., conf. 21 May 1910, minute by G. V. Fiddes.

the action taken by the government but declined the financial compensation.¹

About the same time, the A.S.-A.P.S. protested that the carrier system caused considerable inconvenience and hardship to the people who were thus compelled to be absent from their homes for several days and weeks. The system, it continued, was both degrading and dangerous when obtained for military operations. Even as a substitute for direct taxation, forced labour so utilised adversely affected agricultural production and the price of foodstuffs. The society considered forced labour for work on roads or waterways as a form of slavery which was subject to abuse by the government and called for its replacement by a 'more enlightened machinery of government'.²

Egerton defended both the carrier system and forced labour for work on roads and waterways on administrative, financial and economic grounds.³ He and F. S. James maintained that the carriers often received 'dashes' of 6d–1s which were equivalent to the daily wages then earned by workers in Southern Nigeria.⁴ But in its reply to the A.S.-A.P.S., the Colonial Office withheld the information supplied by Egerton on the special complaints made by the people of Ikom – that the carrier system had become so burdensome that in their attempts to evade it some people had died from drowning.⁵ Egerton admitted that the Ikom complaints arose from the large number of carriers needed for the transport of the stores and ammunition required by the Anglo-German Boundary Commission and their escort in 1908. More carriers had also been employed to supply provisions to the new government station at Obudu.⁶ Otherwise, argued Egerton, the carriers for the punitive expeditions and patrols usually came from the areas with well-known large populations. He also contended that the 'few hundreds' of carriers employed at any given time out of a total population of over seven million did not adversely affect the territory's agriculture and trade. Though Egerton admitted that the carrier system imposed 'a great tax' on the people, he expressed confidence that with the extension

¹ *Ibid.*, enclosure.
² CO. 520/87, A.S.-A.P.S. to C.O., 5 October 1909.
³ CO. 520/46, Egerton to C.O., conf. 28 May, 1907. CO. 520/92, Egerton to C.O., conf. 17 March 1910.
⁴ *Ibid.*, enclosures.
⁵ CO. 520/87, A.P.-A.P.S. to C.O., 5 October 1909, enclosure.
⁶ CO. 520/92, Egerton to C.O., conf. 17 March 1910.

of the railway and the construction of more roads the number of persons employed for compulsory porterage would decrease.[1]

In road-work, Egerton distinguished between thoroughfares and bush-paths. The former were built by paid labour, but the chiefs, acting as agents of the government, relied on forced labour to improve the bush-paths.[2]

The unrest in the newly established Agbor sub-district between 1906 and 1907 demonstrated the unpopularity of forced labour, and was intensified by the attitude of the political officers to the chiefs. In June 1906 Acting District Commissioner F. O. S. Crewe-Read, the Benin Chief Bamawo, his retinue and members of his family were all murdered.

Crewe-Read, the first political officer sent to open up the government station in the Agbor sub-district, had arrived there in April 1906. According to the reports based on official inquiries, his death was closely connected with requests for labour on roads and provisions for the government station.[3] Detailed inquiries disproved any link with the *Ekumeku* Society as the government at first feared.[4]

Crewe-Read had on several occasions mishandled the chiefs and people of the Agbor sub-district. P. C. Gilpin, the Native Court clerk at Agbor, testified to seeing Chief Binigie, the head chief of Ogan, flogged at Agbor in April 1906 for 'not sending his people to work on the roads'. Crewe-Read, Gilpin continued, ordered, and the police carried out, the flogging. Similarly, Chief Meri of Allesime was flogged in May 1906 for 'not attending the Native Court' of which he was a member. Furthermore, young men in Agbor sub-district were flogged on Crewe-Read's orders for 'not turning up to work on the roads as a rule'.[5] In sworn statements made at Agbor on 9 October 1906, Chiefs Binigie and Meri affirmed that they had been flogged,[6] and Chief Obinoba of Agbor and Vice-President of the native court confirmed that he had witnessed the floggings.[7] The Colonial Office agreed that

[1] *Ibid.* [2] *Ibid.*
[3] CO. 520/37, Egerton to C.O., conf. 7 October 1906, enclosure. CO. 520/46, Egerton to C.O., conf., 28 May 1907, enclosure.
[4] CO. 520/36, Fosbery to C.O., tel. 12 June 1906. CO. 520/36, Fosbery to C.O., conf. 16 June 1906. CO. 520/36, Fosbery to C.O., conf. 30 June 1906. CO. 520/36, Fosbery to C.O., conf. 28 July 1906.
[5] CO. 520/37, Egerton to C.O., conf. 7 October 1906, enclosure.
[6] CO. 520/37, Egerton to C.O., conf. 20 October 1906, enclosures.
[7] *Ibid.* CO. 520/38, Egerton to C.O., conf. 29 December 1906, enclosure.

Gilpin's testimony had been 'fully corroborated'.[1] Egerton did not deny it, though, according to him, the flogging of chiefs and other persons in such circumstances was 'unauthorised and illegal'.[2]

The circumstances of Crewe-Read's death evoked considerable comment outside Southern Nigeria. E. D. Morel considered the Agbor incident the result of 'administrative incompetence'.[3] The A.P.S. traced its roots to the Roads and Creeks Proclamation, 1903, and 'the employment of forced labour' generally in Southern Nigeria.[4] In the British House of Commons, J. C. Wason, the Liberal M.P. for Orkney and Shetland, attributed it to 'forced' labour in Southern Nigeria.[5]

John Holt did not miss the opportunity to drive home his own lessons on colonial administration. He resented the system of forced labour adopted in Southern Nigeria, which had a revenue large enough to pay its workers, and maintained that 'it leads to the same results as the abominable Congo system which we are so strongly condemning as being inhuman, and a disgrace to our Christianity and civilisation.'[6] Holt further considered the whole episode of Crewe-Read's activities a sad commentary on the indiscretion of government officials in general,[7] while the 'revenge expedition' which followed Crewe-Read's death showed the folly of such methods of coercion among the people.

> This is not the way to rule these people by attraction, nor the way to get the best out of them for the good of the country. We must get rid of the over-bearing ways of the white official – make him know his place – make him feel that there is law to punish him if he outrages the rights and liberties of other people – taking advantage of his colour and position to do things contrary to all justice and common sense.[8]

[1] CO. 520/38, C.O. to Egerton, conf. 15 March 1907.
[2] CO. 520/37, Egerton to C.O., conf. 3 November 1906, enclosure. CO. 520/37, Egerton to C.O., conf. 7 October 1906.
[3] E. D. Morel, 'The Crewe-Read tragedy and its sequel' in *The West African Mail*, 21 September 1906. This article was filed with CO. 520/36, Fosbery to C.O., conf. 28 July 1906, MP. No. 30466.
[4] CO. 520/40, Fox-Bourne to C.O., 19 September 1906.
[5] HC. Deb. 4s. 164, 5 November 1906, 119.
[6] *E.D.M.P.* F/8, Holt to Morel, 13 July 1906.
[7] *Ibid. E.D.M.P.* F/8, Holt to Morel, 12 September 1906.
[8] *E.D.M.P.* F/8, Holt to Morel, 12 September 1906.

Egerton attributed Crewe-Read's death to the 'indiscreet action on the part of officers sent to administer' the newly-established sub-district at Agbor.[1] The Colonial Office also regretted that Crewe-Read had demanded 'much unnecessary and even useless work' and so provoked very grave discontent among a population whose character was 'not peaceable'.[2] F. S. James, the Commissioner in whose province the Crewe-Read incident occurred, disagreed. In his memorandum of 2 May 1907, James rejected the view that Crewe-Read had 'brought his death upon himself'.[3] Nor did James find any close link between such incidents and punitive expeditions. James instead emphasised that the need for punitive expeditions and patrols was 'not due to any indiscretion in indiscriminate road making or in the treatment of the Native by the European Officer, but to the fact that these people are as they are, and will remain so until the country is properly opened up by railways and their feeder roads'.[4]

DOMESTIC SLAVERY

Besides facing a public outcry from the operation of the carrier system and the provisions of the 1903 Roads and Creeks Proclamation, the government had to defend its other labour measures which implied its sanction of domestic slavery on a permanent basis. It soon discovered that the imperial acts of 1807 and 1833 which forbade the slave trade and slavery in British territories needed special attention in the Protectorate of Southern Nigeria and the Colony of Lagos.

The government saw the need for improving upon the legal arrangements made in Lagos Colony since 1874 when it abolished slave-dealing and provided for its punishment.[5] It discovered, however, that till 1900 no corresponding action had been taken about slavery. Similarly, in the Oil Rivers (Niger Coast) Protectorate, the measures already adopted by MacDonald and Moor during the 1890s had not been put on a proper legal basis. In

[1] CO. 520/46, Egerton to C.O., conf. 28 May 1907.
[2] CO. 520/38, C.O. to Egerton, conf. 16 March 1907.
[3] CO. 520/46, Egerton to C.O., conf. 28 May, 1907, enclosure.
[4] *Ibid.*
[5] The Slave-dealing Ordinance, No. 1 of 1874, dated 17 December 1874.

1900, therefore, Moor sought new legal remedies to deal with slave-dealing and slavery.

After discussions with MacGregor for similar action in Lagos, Moor submitted a draft public notice on slavery, in January 1900, for the Colonial Office's consideration. The Colonial Office did not approve the draft until R. L. Antrobus had inserted in it 'the blessed words' – the 'abolition of the legal status of slavery' – which Joseph Chamberlain desired.[1]

Following that endorsement, MacGregor and Moor abolished the legal status of slavery in their territories. In Lagos this was done through a public notice, on 25 July 1900, by the government. Thereafter, it legally ceased to recognise property in slaves, debarred its law courts and officers from handing over fugitive slaves to their former 'owners', and declined to be a party to arbitration proceedings affecting domestic slaves and their emancipation.[2] In the Protectorate of Southern Nigeria the government issued the Slave Dealing Proclamation, 1901.[3] But in April 1901, when this proclamation came into operation in certain districts, much of the hinterland had not come under firm administrative control. Success there came on completion of the work of the Aro Field Force of 1901–2.

In anticipation of the successful termination of the Aro expedition, Moor abolished slave-dealing in all parts of the protectorate from 1 January 1902. He had to deal with two major problems as a result. In the first place, he had to keep a steady supply of labour, and secondly, he had to find a legal method by which the government could retain domestic slaves under improved conditions as members of the Houses so as not to disturb unduly the labour system in parts of the protectorate.

Moor dealt with the first problem under the provisions of the Master and Servant Proclamation, 1901.[4] He amended this law in 1903[5] to cover government contracts and enable the chiefs to obtain 'apprentices' in place of 'bought' domestic slaves. By this amendment, the government also extended the term for which children under 16 years old could be apprenticed to learn a trade

---

[1] CO. 520/1, Moor to C.O., conf. 28 January 1900, minute by R.L.A.
[2] CO. 147/150, Denton to C.O., conf. 28 July 1900, enclosure.
[3] CO. 520/1, C.O. to Moor, 24 May 1900, enclosure. CO. 588/1, Proclamation No. 5 of 1901.
[4] CO. 588/1, No. 3 of 1901.
[5] CO. 588/1, No. 12 of 1903.

Labour and Domestic Slavery

from five to twelve years in order to give the chiefs some security of tenure in their services. To safeguard the interests of such apprentices, the 1901 proclamation[1] stipulated that a contract of service should be confirmed before a British Commissioner to whom the apprentice must be brought four times every year. What happened then is not clear. But as far as apprentices were concerned, this law later became 'a dead letter'.[2]

To deal with the second problem, Moor enacted the Native House Rule Proclamation, 1901.[3] This proclamation, which in effect perpetuated the system of domestic slavery, was essentially an instrument for the commercial development of the protectorate pending the more intensive exploitation of its hinterland. Before the establishment of firm administrative control of the hinterland, Moor had relied on the economic resources of the coastal people among whom the Native House system had been a cherished pre-colonial institution.

Moor realised, however, that the Native House system showed signs of breaking down under the cumulative effects of the far-reaching political, economic and evangelical developments of the late nineteenth century. By 1898 he had noticed 'a revolution' in trade because the domestic slaves engaged in commerce independently of their respective Houses.[4] He had also witnessed the crippling effect on trade exercised by the old practice which allowed the House heads to demand and receive from trading members a percentage, about 25 per cent, of the turnover, known in the various districts as 'topping' or 'workbar'.[5]

Anxious to utilise some aspects of the House system for the commercial development of the protectorate, Moor nevertheless sought to improve the conditions of the domestic slaves, most of whom showed signs of restlessness. He wished to prevent 'a general uprising which would mean anarchy, crime, and a general stoppage of trade'.[6]

In the absence of any safety-valve of a poor law, Moor naturally felt alarmed at the prospect of a socio-economic revolution with

[1] CO. 588/1, No. 3 of 1901, clause 7 and the schedule.
[2] CO. 520/107, Egerton to C.O., conf. 19 October 1911, enclosures.
[3] CO. 588/1, No. 26 of 1901. Dated 21 November 1901.
[4] CO. 444/2, Moor to C.O., 1 October 1899, enclosure: Annual report on the Niger Coast Protectorate, 1898–9.
[5] *Ibid.* CO. 520/12, Moor to C.O., 7 July 1901. CO. 520/14, Moor to C.O., 24 April 1902, enclosure.
[6] CO. 520/12, Moor to C.O., 7 July 1901.

serious political consequences should he emancipate at once all the domestic slaves in the protectorate. Between 1901 and 1902 the government concentrated on the far more difficult Aro problem and did not wish its attention to be diverted. Until this problem was dealt with, Moor felt reluctant to undertake a major reform of the existing, but inadequate, corps of Civil Police who then lacked the means of handling widespread social unrest in the event of unrestricted emancipation.

Moor therefore approached the problem of domestic slavery cautiously. The Native House Rule Proclamation, 1901, which came into operation on 1 January 1902, simultaneously with the abolition of slave-dealing throughout the protectorate, provided a compromise between slavery and free labour. This law and the Master and Servant Proclamations, 1901 and 1903 gave the protectorate a much-needed transitional arrangement, a valuable breathing space, until the government felt able to bear the complex consequences of free labour.[1]

The Native House Rule Proclamation ratified the reciprocal duties and obligations the House head and members owed each other under native law and custom. It also endeavoured to mend the cracks which had appeared in the pre-colonial system through the evasions made by both parties to a solemn, though unwritten, contract of service. The House head or member who evaded his obligations was, on conviction, liable to a fine not exceeding £50, or to a term of imprisonment not over one year, or both. Where the House head convincingly ill-treated any member, 'the Court' – the District Commissioner sitting alone or at his discretion with a native council – had power to free such a member from all further obligations.

The proclamation further provided for offences committed by European and African employers in their business relations with members of Houses. Every employer had to obtain the prior consent of the House head before engaging any of the members under his control.

The proclamation also served as a vagrancy law and poor law. Any person caught 'wandering abroad or having no apparent means of subsistence' could be arrested, questioned and punished 'unless he proves that he has sufficient means of subsistence, or

[1] CO. 520/95, C.O. to Egerton, conf. 12 December 1910. CO. 520/110, A.S.-A.P.S. to C.O., 11 January 1911, minute by J.A. H.C. Deb. 5s. 28, 20 July 1911, 1347.

Labour and Domestic Slavery

that his want of such means is not the result of his own fault . . .'[1]

Critics of this law saw it merely as a one-sided enactment which favoured House heads and did little for the members. These failed to see that the law had its complement in the native trade tax arrangement which, Moor emphasised, served as the *sine qua non* for enjoying the benefits allowed House heads under the Native House Rule Proclamation, 1901.[2] After a series of meetings with the chiefs of the coastal areas, Moor enjoined upon them the passing of a model trade by-law in their native councils. The by-law sought to reduce the former 'topping' or 'workbar' of 25 per cent on the trade profits received from the trading members of the Houses to a maximum of 10 per cent. In some cases, the government kept it as low as 5 per cent. Moor allowed this reduced trade commission for the support of the House heads.[3]

The Colonial Office readily approved Moor's measures. Together with the system of apprenticeship, they impressed P. H. Ezechiel as establishing 'a most ingenious and . . . successful device for maintaining the practical and beneficial features of domestic slavery . . .'[4]

In his enthusiasm[5] for this measure, Moor mistakenly extended what was *par excellence* a coastal system to the hinterland, including the Aro territory brought under control after the Aro expedition.[6] The extent of the area which Moor originally had in mind could be inferred from the territories of the chiefs he had consulted. In July 1901, Moor claimed to have canvassed the wishes of 'representative chiefs' at Old Calabar, Opobo, Okrika, Bonny, Degema, Brass, Warri, Sapele, Benin River and Benin City before enacting the Native House Rule Proclamation in November 1901.[7]

Inheriting this law in 1904, Egerton also extended it beyond

---

[1] CO. 588/1, No. 26 of 1901, clause 8.
[2] CO. 520/14, Moor to C.O., 24 April 1902, enclosure. For the draft native trade by-law see: CO. 520/12, Moor to C.O., 7 July 1901, enclosure.
[3] *Ibid.*
[4] Memorandum by P.H.E.(zechiel) filed with CO. 520/95, Thorburn to C.O., conf. 15 October 1910, MP. No. 33875.
[5] CO. 520/14, Moor to C.O., 14 April 1902, enclosure. CO. 520/14, Moor to C.O., 25 June 1902.
[6] CO. 520/14, Moor to C.O., 28 May 1902, enclosure.
[7] CO. 520/12, Moor to C.O., 7 July 1901. Proclamation 26 of 1901 was dated 21 November 1901.

the coastal areas. Through mistaken zeal,[1] Moor, Egerton and their deputies conveniently ignored the qualifications attached to the definition of the word 'House' in section 2 of the 1901 proclamation. In their flexible interpretation of its provisions, these officers paid little regard to the restrictions imposed upon the definition of 'House' as 'a group of persons subject by Native Law and Custom to the control, authority and rule of a Chief, known as a Head of a House'.[2] By ignoring the last seven key words, the British officers applied the law loosely to any African under the authority of a chief in the Eastern and Central Provinces of post-1906 Southern Nigeria.

Public criticism of the Native House Rule Proclamation (later Ordinance) increased under Egerton's administration. Between 1906 and 1912 a combination of circumstances demonstrated, directly and indirectly, the need for re-examining the problems of operating the law. The Lagos press, Christian missionaries, Members of Parliament and the A.S.-A.P.S. joined in a chorus of protests against what seemed to them very close to legalised slavery. In its leader in August 1910, *The Nigerian Times* labelled this law the 'Southern Nigeria Slavery Ordinance'.[3]

To the Liberal government in Britain, such serious allegations proved challenging. It nevertheless exercised caution until the cumulative effects of successive complaints and reports forced its hand in favour of further reform. The Igbotu arrests (1906), the allegations of the separation of families (1906-11), the cases of Eyitoyoh and 'Joe of Lagos' (1910) and of Jabez Linette and others at Fernando Po (1911-12) dramatised the inadequacies of the Native House Rule Law as it operated in parts of post-1906 Southern Nigeria. In response to these formidable complaints, the government first amended the law and later abolished it.

The arrest in 1906 at Igbotu in the Western Province and trial at Warri in the Central Province of two deserters from Houses in the latter territory provided the critics of the Native House Rule law with a convenient test case. In the absence of the District Commissioner, the Native Council at Warri tried and imprisoned one of the deserters later brought back from Igbotu. When

[1] CSE. 5/1/5866, Minute on 'House Rule' by F. D. Lugard, 20 May 1912. CSE. 5/1/5866, Memorandum by F. S. James, 28 February 1913.
[2] CSE. 5/1/5866, Memorandum by F. S. James, 11 October 1913.
[3] *The Nigerian Times*, 16 August 1910. See also its issues of 22 November 1910, 17 January and 21 March 1911 for further criticisms.

Labour and Domestic Slavery

informed, Egerton ordered the release of the accused and allowed the second man who had not yet been tried to return to Igbotu.[1] The A.S.-A.P.S. later blamed Egerton's administration for its treatment of another fugitive, Eyitoyoh, *alias* Jimmy Johnson, from a House in the Central Province about 1909. The society expressed strong dissatisfaction when it learnt that, with the approval of the Acting District Commissioner at Forcados, Eyitoyoh had been required by Chief Magbemi, his House head, to pay monthly instalments from his wages on board the government dredger. After an inquiry, Egerton cancelled Eyitoyoh's payment of the instalments scheduled to begin from June 1910.[2]

In February 1911, J. King (M.P. for Knutsford) raised in the House of Commons the case of another deserter from a House at Warri.[3] The fugitive, 'Joe of Lagos', was arrested in Lagos in 1910 for desertion from his House head and for petty theft committed about 1908.[4] The Police Magistrate who tried Joe for larceny discharged him and refused to send him back to Warri for trial on the other charges. Egerton endorsed the Lagos Police Magistrate's decision.[5]

Deserters sometimes escaped to the neighbouring Spanish territory of Fernando Po. During his trip to the Congo in 1911, the Rev. (later Sir) H. J. Harris, the Organising Secretary of the A.S.-A.P.S. visited Fernando Po where he claimed to have found 'an unsuspected confirmation' of the 'evils' of Southern Nigeria's Native House Rule law in the presence of 100–200 fugitives from the Eastern and Central Provinces who had gone there to escape it.[6] Until 1911 the recruitment of labour in Southern Nigeria for use in Fernando Po was illegal.[7] Hence, these 100–200 persons, if their number had not been exaggerated,

[1] CO. 520/38, Egerton to C.O., conf. 7 December 1906. CO. 520/40, A.S.-A.P.S. to C.O., 10 October 1906, enclosure. *The Lagos Weekly Record*, 11 August 1906.
[2] CO. 520/95, Thorburn to C.O., conf. 15 October 1910, enclosure. CO. 520/99, J. H. Harris to C.O., 20 September 1910, enclosure. CO. 520/110, A.S.-A.P.S. to C.O., 11 January 1911. He was to pay 15s. every month to his House head. [3] HC. Deb. 5s. 21, 15 February 1911, 1037.
[4] CO. 520/108, J. King to Harcourt, private, 15 February 1911, enclosure. Joe was alleged to have stolen cloth valued at 16s., 2 handkerchiefs and a canoe.
[5] CO. 520/103, Egerton to C.O., conf. 17 May 1911.
[6] *Anti-Slavery Papers*, MSS. Brit. Emp. s. 19. D5/1, J. H. Harris to A.S.-A.P.S., 13 May 1911.
[7] CO. 520/106, Egerton to C.O., conf. 18 October 1911.

had gone there clandestinely. Subsequent inquiries, however, showed that Harris' estimates were grossly exaggerated. The government of Southern Nigeria did not feel perturbed over Harris' charge because it had regularly made on-the-spot inquiries through an *exequator* of July 1909 which made the Commissioner of the Eastern Province also the British Consul for the Spanish possessions in the Gulf of Guinea.[1] During his earlier visits to Fernando Po in 1909 and 1910,[2] Provincial Commissioner Bedwell had received no representations from the so-called fugitives there. Bedwell found in Fernando Po only 50–60 labourers from Southern Nigeria of whom 19 came from the Eastern and Central Provinces where the ordinance applied. These labourers, Bedwell stated, had gone to Fernando Po 'some twelve to fifteen years ago'. Concerning the fugitives from the Eastern and Central Provinces, Bedwell maintained that they 'were for the most part either escaped criminals or boys who were afraid of punishment by their houses for some misdemeanour committed'. If Bedwell is to be believed, these fugitives had left Southern Nigeria before 1901. In that case, they had sought to avoid the Native House system as distinct from the Native House Rule law.

Jabez Linette (*alias* Sampson Odok), the central figure in the A.S.-A.P.S. complaint, did not appear before Bedwell during the latter's inquiries at Fernando Po. In Southern Nigeria, Sampson Odok, as he was then known, had enjoyed the Primitive Methodist Mission's protection at Calabar on several occasions between 1900 and 1903 and after 1904 in Fernando Po. On reaching Fernando Po, about 1904, Sampson Odok assumed the alias 'Jabez Linette' to prevent detection.[3] However, as Sampson Odok he had been an insubordinate House member at Calabar. The Native Council's proceedings there on 11 February 1904 had shown that Ekanem Esin (*alias* Sampson Odok) had been guilty of disobeying his House head's 'lawful orders'.[4] At Fernando Po, the Primitive Methodist Mission informed Bedwell that Jabez Linette (*alias* Sampson Odok *alias* Ekanem Esin) had on previous occasions in Southern Nigeria been ill-treated by his 'masters'.[5]

[1] CO. 520/86, F.O. to C.O., 22 July 1909.
[2] CO. 520/114, James to C.O., conf. 28 April 1912, enclosure: Bedwell to the Colonial Secretary, Lagos, 23 March 1912.
[3] *Ibid.*, enclosures.   [4] *Ibid.*, enclosures.
[5] *Ibid.* His masters had been Ekanem Esin (Snr.) who died in 1897, the

Labour and Domestic Slavery

Bedwell, however, maintained that Linette's case was exceptional.¹

The government received further complaints against the Native House Rule law on moral and religious grounds. The A.S.-A.P.S. charged that families had been forcibly separated on the occurrence of deaths in Houses.² In Parliament, J. King contended that persons married with Christian rites had been separated against their will because of the ordinance.³

The conference of Anglican bishops and clergy in West Africa which met at Lagos in 1906 forwarded to Egerton a resolution against the Native House Rule law. They complained of injury to individual and public morality in the Niger Delta, because House heads forbade their members to contract marriages with persons from other Houses and urged Egerton's administration to give relief in such matters.⁴ Later, in April 1909, Bishop H. Tugwell repeated the charge he had made in October 1907 that the 'House System' checked, among other things, 'liberty to marry' except 'under grievous conditions'.⁵

The more specific complaint that persons married with Christian rites had been improperly separated as a result of this ordinance received the immediate attention of the District Commissioners at Calabar, Aba, Bonny, Brass, Bende, Degema, Eket, Opobo, Owerri and Uyo. For inexplicable reasons, the Commissioner of the Eastern Province considered these districts 'the most likely' from 'which such a report might emanate'.⁶ The District Commissioners, however, found no substance in the allegation.⁷ District Commissioners and judicial officers with more than seven years' experience in the Central and Eastern Provinces reported other difficulties in operating the Native House Rule law outside the Western Province. Egerton had ordered these inquiries after receiving Secretary of State Harcourt's direction in December 1910. Even though Harcourt admitted that the

---

deceased's elder brother, Archibong Ekanem Esin, and his son, C. E. Esin, who later became the Inspector of Police at Calabar.
¹ *Ibid.*
² CO. 520/110, A.S.-A.P.S. to C.O., 11 July 1911.
³ HC. Deb. 5s. 21, 13 February 1911, 671.
⁴ Cd. 4907, London 1909, Appendix C, 3. 446.
⁵ Cd. 4907, 1909, p. 446.
⁶ CSO. 12/23/1, Provincial Commissioner, Calabar, to the Colonial Secretary, Lagos, conf. 15 April 1911.
⁷ *Ibid.*, CO. 520/102, Egerton to C.O., conf. 20 April 1911, enclosure.

existing system had worked fairly well, he then raised the question 'whether the time has not come for taking a more decisive step in the direction of a system of free labour'.[1] The investigations showed that the administration of the ordinance had been 'lax' in the Central and Eastern Provinces. Secondly, it had been indiscriminately applied outside the coastal areas for which it was originally intended. Third, it had had but 'little effect' on the relative positions of the 'free-born' and 'servile' members of Houses.[2]

Egerton attributed the lax administration of the Native House Rule law to such general problems of West African administration as resulted from a short-handed staff, constant transfers and frequent leaves of absence and sickness. He further maintained that because of poor means of communications and transport and the futility of complaints when made, the chiefs had been reluctant to report cases of desertion by members of their Houses. House members had also been employed in government departments and private firms without fulfilling the undertaking to remit to the House heads about 5 per cent of their salaries. The libertarian influences of education in the mission and government schools and the absence of a similar law in the Western Province, the regular rendezvous of many deserters,[3] were additional obstacles to the law's success.

Though not mentioned by Egerton, the breakdown of traditional authority also had much bearing on the lax administration of the Native House Rule law. As British administrative control over Southern Nigeria increased, the chiefs who were also House heads could no longer impose the pre-colonial sanctions against defaulting members. Powerless to prevent the increase in fugitive members, the House heads became reluctant to recruit apprentices. This was one reason why the Masters and Servants law failed in its provisions for apprenticeship.

A further cause of the breakdown of traditional authority lay in the decreasing necessity to belong to the community for self-preservation. With the strengthening of government control over various districts people became more and more detached from the pre-colonial ties to their respective communities.

The government accepted both the charge of laxity in execut-

[1] CO. 520/95, C.O. to Egerton, conf. 12 December 1910.
[2] CO. 520/107, Egerton to C.O., conf. 19 October 1911, and minute by J.A.   [3] CO. 520/107, Egerton to C.O., conf. 19 October 1911.

Labour and Domestic Slavery

ing the Native House Rule law and that of applying it indiscriminately. In March 1913, the government admitted that Sapele, Warri, Brass, Degema, Opobo, Bonny and Calabar constituted the ideal districts for the operation of this law.[1] Two years earlier, Acting Colonial Secretary F. S. James had maintained that the indiscriminate application had resulted less from the 'mistaken zeal' of the officers than from the absence of central direction.[2] The confusion arising from the loose rendering of the definition of the expression 'House' in the law and the meaning of 'House Heads' persisted until 1912.[3] For the British indirect administrators, such a liberal interpretation had several advantages. For example, A. Norton Harper, the Acting District Commissioner among the Ishan in the hinterland of the Central Province, observed in December 1912:[4]

> The Native House Rule Para[graphs] 6 & 7 while in force was invaluable for the purpose of supporting the orders of [a] Chief. Instructions are sent to a Chief for R[oa]d labour, etc. the invariable reply 'Boys refuse my orders'. All a D[istrict] C[ommissioner] can do is to arrest 'Refusing to carry out the orders of the Chief in accordance with Native Custom' and punish the Ringleaders.

The government's demand for compulsory labour for small-scale public works made the free use of the Native House Rule law very attractive even outside the coastal parts of the Eastern and Central Provinces. Convinced that the period of transition from domestic slavery to a system of free labour had not ended by 1911, W. Fosbery, the Provincial Commissioner for the Eastern Province, opposed its repeal then. In his view,

> ... if so called [sic] free labour is to be instituted ... then where are carriers to come from? How is the development of the Province to be continued by construction of roads, etc. etc.? ... At the present time there is no difficulty in obtaining carriers, labourers, etc., in this Province and such work is

[1] CSE. 5/1/5850, Minute by F. D. Lugard, 15 March 1913.
[2] CO. 520/107, Egerton to C.O., conf. 19 October 1911, enclosure.
[3] CSE. 5/1/5866, Memorandum on the working of the Native House Rule Ordinance, 1901 and 1912, by Acting Police Magistrate E. D. Simpson, dated 30 October 1912.
[4] CSE. 5/1/5850, Minute by A. Norton Harper, dated 14 December 1912.

333

willingly performed which is mainly due to the maintenance of the Native Authority under the House Rule Ordinance.¹

The utilitarian aspects of the Native House Rule law, not merely the absence of central direction, encouraged zealous administrative officers to make maximum use of it.

The various officers who investigated the operation of the Native House Rule law gave conflicting accounts of its effects on the House members under it. Puisne Judge W. H. Stoker gave the most balanced account in his report of 30 March 1911.

> In many cases the existing system works hardship on members of houses. Instances have come to my notice in which clerks and others in the Government and other service [sic] have been summoned and . . . arrested at their places of duty and brought a considerable distance to answer charges . . . the neglect or disobedience being that they have not paid over [sic] proportion of their earnings to the head of their house or kept him posted of their whereabouts or complied with directions sent to them, sometimes after being away from their houses for many years. Members of house are looked upon as a source of Revenue [sic] by their heads. On the other hand, I have known instances of fines inflicted upon members of houses by courts paid for them by their head to save them from imprisonment and in one instance a Native Court Clerk who was tried before me, at Arochuku Assizes and convicted, was defended by counsel employed by his head resident as far as Bonny, who also sent a member of the house to watch the case and give evidence on the accused's behalf if necessary.²

During the government inquiry in 1911, the chiefs, who were almost invariably the House heads, of Bonny, Opobo, New Calabar (Kalabari), Brass and Okrika petitioned Egerton against the repeal of this ordinance.³ In July 1911, the Itsekiri chiefs protested against the repeal of the same law 'before another seven or ten years have elapsed'.⁴

The Calabar chiefs, however, raised no objection to its repeal if the government would allow the House heads adequate compensation. Most of them had been stopped by the establishment

¹ CO. 520/107, Egerton to C.O., conf. 19 October 1911, enclosure.
² Ibid., enclosure.
³ Ibid., enclosure 1(a) – Appendix D: petition dated 4 July 1911.
⁴ Ibid., enclosure 1 – petition dated 27 July 1911.

Labour and Domestic Slavery

of European 'factories' or trading stations up the Cross River and its tributaries from participation in trade as middlemen.¹ Consequently, the Native House Rule law no longer offered commercial attractions of much value to them. The protests of the Niger Delta chiefs failed to prevent the amendment of the ordinance, a step which made its subsequent repeal inevitable. In this and other matters, the views of the government counted most.

The reports on the working of the Native House Rule law convinced Harcourt of the need to reconsider it further. In December 1911, Harcourt observed:

> I am amazed to find that we have a condition existing in Southern Nigeria so little removed from slavery not only under our flag but under the authority of our own ordinance. It is quite clear that the House Rule Ordinance is valued and maintained by the Government officials there mainly as a thinly veiled system of forced labour which enables them to obtain porterage and canoe haulage free of cost and probably other services besides. The native chiefs naturally support it for the considerable advantages which it gives to them.²

In response to Harcourt's views, the government amended the discredited law in February 1912.

That the government preferred amendment to repeal partly lay in its fear of a violent disruption of trade channels if the ordinance were repealed suddenly.³ It also considered the question of trade debts. In the Opobo district alone the Houses owed the European traders about £100,000 given to them as credit.⁴ The government also believed that the repeal of the ordinance, say in 1911, would have amounted to a breach of faith with the chiefs whose authority, as a matter of policy, it desired to support.⁵

Shortly before the amendment, the government passed, in November 1911, the Vagrant Ordinance⁶ which provided for the

¹ *Ibid.*, enclosure 1(a).
² *Ibid.*, minute by L.H., 31 December 1911.
³ *Anti-Slavery Papers*, MSS. Brit. Emp. s.22. G.224, G. V. Fiddes to A.S.-A.P.S., 12 August 1911.
⁴ CO. 520/107, Egerton to C.O., conf. 19 October 1911, and enclosure 1(a).
⁵ *Ibid.*, CO. 520/103, A. G. Boyle to C.O., conf. 31 May 1911.
⁶ CO. 588/3, No. 29 of 1911. Amended by No. 13 of 1912 in CO. 588/4.

335

punishment of 'idle and disorderly persons and rogues and vagabonds'.

The amended law – the Native House Rule (amendment) Ordinance, 1912[1] – enabled House members to purchase their freedom from the obligations they owed their respective Houses. The government allowed payments in lump sums or instalments which had first to be made through the District Commissioners. It limited such payments to £15–£50 depending on the incomes of the members concerned.[2] As Governor-designate of Northern and Southern Nigeria, Lugard in May 1912 approved redemption money

> in order primarily to prevent too rapid a dissolution of the House, and the consequent addition to the community of a large number of 'masterless-men' who may increase the criminal classes, and on the other hand, to save the heads of Houses from sudden disorganisation.[3]

Passed with doubts and little enthusiasm, the amended law proved inadequate to protect the integrity of the Houses. Frequently, the enterprising House members were those most able and willing to secure their freedom through the process of redemption fees because of the added attraction of taking their own property with them when they legally ceased to belong to their respective Houses. Since most able-bodied and prosperous members thereby had the legal right to discontinue membership of their Houses at will, the remaining old, infirm and poor members had few chances of survival under changed circumstances. The amendment thus provided a legal means of securing freedom for the fortunate few without attempting to specify how the majority of the less able members could benefit from their past labours.

In practice, the amended law threatened the stability of the Houses by making splits more frequent. Women, for instance, found the 'freedom papers' allowed under the amendment convenient for obtaining divorce.[4] To combat these threats, the chiefs-*cum*-House heads used subtle means to prevent whole-

---

[1] CO. 588/4, No. 1 of 1912, dated 8 February 1912.
[2] *Ibid.*, clause 5.
[3] CSE. 5/1/5866, minutes on 'House Rule' by F. D. Lugard, dated 20 May 1912.
[4] CSE. 5/1/5850, F. D. Lugard to C.O., 19 March 1913.

Labour and Domestic Slavery

sale desertions by members. E. D. Simpson, the Acting Police Magistrate at Warri, reported in October 1912 that the chiefs in their Native Courts usually sued for 'imaginary debts' those who had been legally granted 'freedom papers' after making satisfactory financial arrangements for their redemption.[1]

In June 1913 the government attempted to stop the malpractices of such chiefs by ordering that the jurisdiction of the Native Courts no longer extend to the trial of 'causes and matters' under the Native House Rule law.[2]

Dissatisfied with the further operation of the amended law, Lugard in May 1913 sought to replace the Native House system with 'Native Trading Firms' of voluntary, registered members whose activities would have been subject to stricter government regulation and control.[3] Harcourt, however, rejected the proposal and recommended the repeal of the entire law after three years.[4] Lugard pressed for an earlier repeal, from 1 January 1915,[5] which was sanctioned by the Colonial Office.[6] Lugard's Native House Rule (Repeal) Ordinance was dated 31 December 1914.[7]

Neither before nor after its amendment in 1912, did, or could, the Native House Rule law strengthen the authority of the chiefs-*cum*-House heads. Generally, the authority of the chiefs in the territory where it had freely operated had shown signs of weakness even before its promulgation.[8] Again, in the face of the expanding export-import trade in Southern Nigeria between 1900 and 1913, it is difficult to surmise how far the Native House Rule law adversely affected commerce by preventing or delaying free individual enterprises. Even in its pre-colonial form, the Native House system had suited the economic needs of an area ill-equipped with modern transport facilities. But in the era of economic development through railways, harbours, roads and improved waterways, the 'motive power' previously provided by domestic slaves was no longer an impressive asset.

[1] CSE. 5/1/5866, E. D. Simpson's memorandum on the working of the Native House Rule Ordinance 1901 and 1912, dated 30 October 1912.
[2] CSE. 5/1/5866, Order No. 19 of 1913.
[3] CSO. 1/19/58, Lugard to C.O., 24 May 1913.
[4] CSO. 1/20/59, C.O. to Lugard, 21 July 1913.
[5] CSO. 1/19/59, Lugard to C.O., 28 July 1913.
[6] CSO. 1/20/59, C.O. to Lugard, 8 August 1913.
[7] CSE. 4/1/3945, Native House Rule (Repeal) Ordinance, No. 15 of 1914.
[8] CO. 442/2, Moor to C.O., 1 October 1899, enclosure.

However, the Native House Rule law made for social stability besides providing a reservoir of forced labour tapped at will by the government officers. Despite the obvious abuses which crept into its execution, the ordinance before the 1912 amendment had the merit of limiting the desertions from the Houses to a trickle. The government thereby avoided undertaking the heavy responsibility of providing an alternative machinery for handling the complex problems of a large number of helpless vagrants at a time when it had developed no organised social welfare services for such persons. In the districts already notorious for unrest, punitive expeditions and patrols, the delay in pouring out roving bands into areas sometimes inadequately controlled contributed considerably to stability, law and order. The amendment and subsequent repeal of this law indicated the government's increased confidence in its ability to deal firmly with the political, economic and social consequences of such action. By 1915, the era of firm administrative control in Southern Nigeria had already become quite conspicuous.

12 Conclusion

Two major related developments clearly emerge in Southern Nigerian history between 1898 and 1914. One of these – the evolution of the Nigerian state – proceeded through various stages which had serious diplomatic, constitutional, political, economic and social aspects and impacts. The other involved the establishment, expansion and consolidation of an administrative machinery designed to secure the firm control of the areas brought under British central authority. Special emphasis has been given in this book to an analysis of the operational difficulties of the machinery which British officials set up in Southern Nigeria until 1914.

The major issues arising from the evolution of the Nigerian state and the operation of the colonial machinery will be briefly reviewed in this chapter. In Southern Nigerian history, the period 1898–1914 was crucial but not necessarily cataclysmic. Politically, economically and socially the period was one of major changes and adjustments.

In the gradual adaptation of the old order to the requirements of the new, some of the chiefs and people rose whereas others fell. At the same time, some actively opposed the forces of the new order with relatively little success. The more discreet withdrew into such pre-colonial institutions as secret cults, which avoided direct confrontation with the agents of the new order.

Politically, it was significant that no mass revolt which cut across ethnic boundaries occurred. The Aro opposition, the *Ekumeku* unrest, the Benin scare and others of their kind were primarily ethnic-based protest movements. As the people's opposition to the expansion and consolidation of British administrative control over Southern Nigeria occurred in such small instalments, so the British found in the annual field operations a convenient device for dealing with pockets of unrest.

There were various reasons for absence of widespread mass revolts. The war-weary and cautious Yorubas served by intelligent chiefs, educated Africans inside and outside the Legislative Council and an alert press frowned upon the strategy and tactics of armed insurrection against British rule. Instead, they adopted such means as protests through pamphleteering, press criticism, mass meetings and 'monster' petitions. They also found in the perennial jurisdictional difficulty a temporary protective shield which, in such matters as judicial agreements, distinguished between them and the less fortunate people of the Protectorate of Southern Nigeria. In the public protests, Yorubas noticeably made the most concerted efforts. In spite of the variety of dialects, Yoruba provided a strong linguistic bond in the Lagos Colony and Protectorate. But in the Protectorate of Southern Nigeria, ethnic pluralism and cultural diversity precluded the development of a similar common bond as the basis of political action against British rule.

No commonly accepted leaders emerged from the several communities to organise and co-ordinate any prolonged armed struggle against the superior forces of the new régime.

Indeed, the conditions of the Protectorate of Southern Nigeria at the time did not encourage the emergence of multi-ethnic based political parties through which mass movements of a non-violent kind could be channelled. In their absence, some members of the traditional élite led the village and inter-village based armed conflicts against the new régime. Their failure indicated the need for another approach, the party political approach, by their more literate successors who appealed to wider audiences to adopt the tactics of non-violent agitation. The new leaders found it more convenient to address, and command the following of, more people at a time when the use of English had become more widespread and means of transportation and communications had improved, particularly in the major Nigerian towns.

In theory at least, the existence of secret cults raised the possibility of organisations which could transcend lineage feuds and ethnic differences. Yet not even the faceless leaders of these secret organisations then commanded the type of trans-ethnic support to sustain a serious mass revolt. It was much easier for the *Ekumeku* Society to command the support of its lodges in the Asaba hinterland. It could not claim as much success, say, among the Awka Ibos most of whom pledged their loyalty to the

Agballa oracle. Neither could it obtain the support of the Aros, who looked to their Long Juju; not that of the other ethnic groups with their own cults and jujus. Among other difficulties, a secret cult attempting to spread its wings in the Southern Nigeria of 1898–1913 would have found its principal obstacles in language and local confidence. The conditions in Yorubaland offered more theoretical advantages to the *Ogboni* and other cultists if they wished to use their pre-colonial secret societies as political weapons against the new order. The more diplomatic Yorubas, however, avoided such tactics. Again, the very presence of secret cults at the village or other more convenient level provided safety-valves for the masses who did not wish to revolt openly against the new order either in village-based or wider movements. Protecting themselves with their secret paraphernalia and local confidence, some of these cults successfully defied such legislation as the Ordeal, Witchcraft and Juju Proclamation (No. 13 of 1903) and the Unlawful Societies Proclamation (No. 16 of 1905). For such devoted cultists, discretion, as in other things, constituted the better part of valour.

Difficulties of transport and communications also operated against mass revolts or movements which needed an organisation as well as freedom and facility of movement or contact. The facilities in the Yoruba section of the protectorate were decidedly better than those in other parts of Southern Nigeria.

For financial reasons, the British government did not encourage Moor's plans for simultaneous multi-railway development. His repeated enthusiasm for the construction of a Cross River-based railway failed to win the Colonial Office's approval. Until Lugard's choice in late 1912 of Port Harcourt as the terminus of the eastern branch of the Nigerian Railway, the south-eastern part of the protectorate had no railway development which in turn could have attracted feeder roads and harbour improvements. But since 1896 the Yoruba part of the protectorate had the Lagos Railway and later the services of such feeder roads as the motorable Oyo-Ibadan road.

Concerted mass revolts, even if they had occurred, then had fewer chances of success so long as local feuds survived and loyal chiefs emerged to serve as the agents of the new régime. Nearly every community in the Protectorate of Southern Nigeria had a loyalist warrant-chief who commanded some support, no matter how small, in his own village. The Benin scare of 1906 dramatised the tensions which the phenomenon of the co-operative native council chiefs brought to some communities. In the frequent power struggles among the loyalists and the unofficial opposition, personal rivalries and village feuds seriously compromised the solidarity and integrity of several communities. The cumulative effects of government, commercial and Christian missionary enterprise increased, but did not necessarily originate, the divisive strands in African society. The effects of their various activities gave a new focus to the pre-colonial sources of conflict in several communities. In some of these areas, the new polarisation of conflict developed around two major groups – the supporters and opponents of the new order. In others, a third group occupied the middle ground.

Among those who supported the new régime and the fence-sitters were the Africans who succeeded in making the necessary adjustments. Most of these found several employment opportunities in the native courts, the police and military establishments and the lower sectors of the Civil Service. Moreover, under British protection, several Africans left their villages to seek their fortunes elsewhere. Others benefited from the agricultural prosperity which typified post-1906 Southern Nigeria's development. The rôle of the other loyal Africans – the traditional élite – through whom British officials in Southern Nigeria practised indirect administration deserves closer examination. They were more the agents or executives of the new régime rather than its major policy-makers. So long as they remained loyal, these Africans continued to constitute the élite of power but at a lower level in the administrative hierarchy dominated by British officials.

Other members of the traditional élite discovered that they could not cope with the arduous and unpopular tasks required of the African loyalists. Since they received no recognition from the government, those who refused to co-operate with the new régime confined their activities, wherever possible, to the colonially non-apparent sector of society. Among such members of the traditional élite were those who felt embittered about losing to the new régime the policy-making power in the external and internal affairs of their communities.

At the provincial, divisional, district and sub-district levels of the administration, the prime-movers, the major decision-makers, were the British officers, and not Africans. Such chiefs of Yorubaland as the Owa of Ilesha, the Akarigbo of Ijebu-Remo and the

Conclusion

Bales of Ibadan realised how their freedom of choice, even in local matters, had been compromised by the mandatory 'advice' given by the British District Commissioners and similar officers in their midst. Deportation, arrests, and death (as claimed by W. A. Ross in 1912), these chiefs saw, awaited those of their number who declined to be puppets. That some members of the traditional élite did not always resent their puppet rôle was amply indicated by the activities of W. A. Ross in favour of the Alafins of Oyo.

The new major policy-makers in Southern Nigeria included dedicated British officials, and others who were plain adventurers seeking medals, knighthoods and other material rewards for services rendered to their own country. Some of these officials died at the hands of Africans, some during the punitive expeditions and patrols, and others from disease and adverse climatal conditions. Nonetheless, several of them benefited from the increased employment opportunities and pensions provided for them in Southern Nigeria. Under the patronage system adopted by Joseph Chamberlain and his successors, the career posts in Southern Nigeria, as elsewhere in the British Empire, brought political advantages to the United Kingdom government.

In an analysis of the major political developments which occurred between 1898 and 1914 sufficient attention must be given to the double standards applied by the government in the administration of the Yoruba section of the protectorate on one hand and the non-Yoruba parts on the other. This book has provided some explanations for that phenomenon. By far the most important factor arose from the jurisdictional difficulty which resulted from the nineteenth century treaties, agreements and pledges. Of these compacts, the government gave the most serious consideration to the Egba treaty of 1893. There also, the developments in this era showed the gradual loss of the E.U.G.'s claim to complete autonomy within the meaning of the 1893 treaty. By their more tolerant attitude, MacGregor and Egerton postponed the evil day – the abrogation of the 1893 treaty in 1914 – for the Egbas. In Egbaland as in the other parts of the protectorate, the diplomatic revolution emphasised in Chapter 1 continued between 1898 and 1914. After losing power over their external affairs through the nineteenth-century treaties and agreements of protection, commerce and friendship, the various chiefs and people of Southern Nigeria steadily lost control over their internal affairs as well. Even in the hinterland of the Protectorate of Southern Nigeria where no such compacts had been made, coercion through punitive expeditions, patrols and the like achieved similar changes, as did diplomacy and usage in Yorubaland.

The constitutional developments throughout Southern Nigeria until 1914 showed the abstract nature of any division in responsibilities for external and internal affairs in a British Protectorate in this part of tropical Africa. In practice, there developed a steady erosion of power at the cost of the protected territory. Southern Nigeria thus provided a valuable field for the study of developments in the nature of a protectorate administration. After 1895, if not much earlier, the British government no longer contented itself with assuming power only for the external relations of a protectorate in this part of Africa. In Southern Nigeria, Britain exercised as well the right of control over the internal affairs of the people and appointed chiefs and other Africans with proven loyalty and ability to assist her in the administration.

Considering the frequency of punitive expeditions and patrols and the force which in the final analysis backed Britain's exercise of authority in the external and internal affairs of the people, the Protectorate of Southern Nigeria differed very little from a 'conquered territory'. Yet the government continued to make a few technical distinctions getween a protectorate and a colony or conquered territory. In the first place, though the concept of 'conquered territory' influenced the psychology of some of the British administrators there, the government, nevertheless, attempted to ensure the retention of modified African law and custom and the principle of African ownership of land – distinctions which would have been more difficult to make and enforce in a typical Crown colony.

The second distinction arose from the special recognition given to domestic slavery in the Protectorate of Southern Nigeria. Even though in the Protectorates of Lagos and Southern Nigeria, the government had in 1900 and 1901 abolished the legal status of slavery, the institution of domestic slavery did not immediately disappear. In the Protectorate of Southern Nigeria, the government openly allowed domestic slavery under the Native House Rule law from 1901 until 1914.

A third technical difficulty over the status of a protectorate *vis-à-vis* a colony was, however, removed by the 1906 amalgama-

Conclusion

tion. In the Protectorate of Southern Nigeria, the legal difficulty over the question of appeals from a protectorate court to the Judicial Committee of the Privy Council, which Moor had pointed out in 1902, ceased after the 1906 amalgamation. The amalgamation of the Supreme Courts of the combined territories in 1908 enabled the British government to correct the above technical difficulty by the Order in Council of 1909. The fourth distinction, however, survived much longer. The government clung to the technical differences in the status of persons born in British colonies and protectorates. For example, in December 1911, it did not allow the inhabitants of the protectorate of post-1906 Southern Nigeria to be styled 'His Majesty's subjects'.[1]

By far the most remarkable of the political developments covered in this work were the 1906 and 1914 amalgamations. Though neither of them settled the most controversial internal boundary questions which affected Ilorin, Otun and others, the amalgamations provided major political means of promoting the intensive and extensive economic development of parts of Nigeria. They further demonstrated the close links between administration and development in general.

The symbiotic relationship between administration and economic development arose from the link provided by the need for revenue. Even without industrialisation before 1914, the government showed remarkable eagerness for economic development through reliance on increased agricultural production and major public works. Basically, the government geared the economy to export needs. Although the government also tried to diversify the basis of Southern Nigeria's export trade by encouraging the cultivation of cotton, rubber, maize, cocoa and other crops, its efforts did not alter the continued primacy of palm produce. Nature and human efforts combined to increase Southern Nigeria's palm produce exports without correspondingly remarkable improvements through plantation methods and extraction techniques based on machinery. Even without any rigorous planned development schemes, Southern Nigeria, particularly after 1906, enjoyed remarkable economic prosperity as indicated by its increasing import-export trade figures. By 1913, Southern Nigeria had been exposed to price fluctuations in world markets and other foreign influences as a result of her increasingly heavy

[1] CO. 520/107, Egerton to Harcourt, 20 November 1911, minute by C.S. dated 13 December 1911.

dependence on international markets for her export-import trade. The people of Southern Nigeria then had also ceased to exercise any serious control over their economic and fiscal affairs. Above all, they had lost their political power to protect their general economic interests whenever necessary.

In the social sphere, the people had greater chances of freedom. The government railway, launches and steam vessels provided faster means of transportation; but for the masses these continued to be expensive luxuries reserved for the officials and a few private citizens. Similarly, the government's posts and telegraphs services covered a few towns but left the village sector untouched. The government, which hesitated to impose direct taxation, also avoided any schemes for compulsory education and vaccination against such endemic diseases as smallpox and yellow fever. In several rural areas, the village herbalists' homes, and not the crowded hospitals established by Christian missionaries and the government in a few towns, provided the basic health centres for millions of people. In the communities not adequately covered by Christian missionary and government schools, the family-unit continued its pre-colonial rôle as the primary educational institution which enforced its own moral standards and not those made conventional by the new régime. Although in terms of social welfare programmes, the government made negligible contributions, the right of intervention it claimed in this sphere was in itself remarkable. Through the few hospitals and schools it had established, and the new sanitation regulations and public health laws it imposed, the government undertook social obligations whose scope increased in time. Moreover, the power which the government claimed to reform African institutions so as to excise aspects abhorrent to tender Western European consciences meant increasing interference with such pre-colonial practices as ordeals, human sacrifice, infanticide, accusations of witchcraft, reparation in certain cases of homicide, mutilation and other harsh punishments for theft and so on. Hence, the Ordeal, Witchcraft and Juju Proclamation, 1903 and the Unlawful Societies Proclamation, 1905, at least in theory, had a significance which exceeded their actual effectiveness.

To spread Western European concepts of 'civilisation', the government relied partly on its own efforts and partly on the cooperation of humanitarian organisations and Christian missionaries for whose activities it again offered protection. In assessing

Conclusion

the value of these efforts, it must, however, be recognised that the goal of Britain's 'civilising mission' in this part of Africa was not explicitly stated. But if properly executed as John Holt cherished, it would have resulted in the creation of 'black Englishmen'[1] in Southern Nigeria. On the other hand, Chamberlain found in punitive expeditions and patrols a 'civilising' purpose, particularly when aimed at destroying African institutions which the government considered barbarous. The difficulties which beset the path of British officials and Christian missionaries in spreading Western European ideas of 'civilisation' in Southern Nigeria before 1914 were considerable. There was no doubt that the government's discouragement of infanticide, human sacrifices, ordeals and the like saved precious lives from needless death. Yet the moral aspects of these practices left some issues unresolved. For example, could the moral standard applied to condemn infanticide be used to condone some modern forms of family planning? Moreover, some Africans, particularly the priestly class and the corps of diviners, found in the government's proscription of practices considered 'uncivilised' a veritable threat to their professions.

The liquor controversy demonstrated the absence of any sure 'standard' Western European conscience or code over the morally charged debate on the merits and demerits of raising much government revenue from the spirits consumed in Southern Nigeria. Over this controversy, the standards of 'civilisation' imposed by the C.M.S. clergymen and the leaders of temperance societies in the United Kingdom differed from those of the government.

Elsewhere, the land policies of the government left a heritage of basic contradictions. In Lagos Colony, the government allowed the sale of lands, but in parts of the protectorate acquired land from the people even where contrary to pre-colonial practice. By 1913, the government denied the people of the Protectorate of Southern Nigeria any claims to the sub-soil and the fees and rents which accrued from prospecting licences and mining leases. Again, the idea of parting with land on 99-year lease terms for private use, allowed under the land laws of Southern Nigeria, had no pre-colonial basis. On balance, the government's land policy prevented the emergence of a landless proletariat in Southern Nigeria.

[1] *E.D.M.P.* F/8, Holt to Morel, 23 April 1901.

The Evolution of the Nigerian State

Generally, the major political, economic and social developments until 1914 contributed considerably to the foundations of the Nigerian state. Such institutions as the Executive and Legislative Councils, the Law Courts, the Civil Service as well as the police and military establishments set up then, have been carried through, in a modified form, to the immediate post-independence period.

In economic terms, the Nigerian railway, the improvement of the Lagos harbour and the Apapa wharf as well as the construction and maintenance of modern roads and telegraphs have been permanent assets in Nigeria's development from the colonial era to independence. The phenomenal progress made in intensive and extensive agricultural production throughout Nigeria has, for the last seven decades or more, served as a steady boost to the country's economy. In more recent times, Nigeria's abundant agricultural capacity has been encouragingly utilised as the handmaiden of industrialisation. The pioneering work undertaken by the B.C.G.A. in Nigeria, though in the short term a failure, in the long run helped to sustain interest in cotton cultivation which provided the raw material for Nigeria's nascent textile industry in the immediate post-independence period. Above all, the factor of economic interdependence in a large and very promising domestic market, a major source of strength to the Nigerian economy from early colonialism to independence, has continued to provide one of the enduring pillars of the developing Nigerian state. Despite the objectionable aspects of the alien rule which predominantly catered for Britain's self-interest, the early colonial emphasis on commerce succeeded, directly and indirectly, in underpinning the economic basis of the territories amalgamated in 1914.

There were other developments of moment relating especially to the long and difficult process of state formation and consolidation in Nigeria. The joint contributions of British officials and Nigerians to the establishment and development of a new state must be seen in proper focus and without emotional overtones. Despite some negative aspects of British colonialism in Southern and Northern Nigeria in this era, Britain made a positive contribution to the evolution of the Nigerian state. Between 1898 and 1914, British officials in both parts of Nigeria aimed at amalgamating these territories so as to centralise their control and pool their economic resources. To secure both objectives, the British

Conclusion

government in Northern and Southern Nigeria used coercion and diplomacy to remove all African opposition to the emergence and consolidation of a central authority under its direction. The punitive expeditions and patrols in parts of the Protectorate of Southern Nigeria and the diplomatic exchanges with the Yoruba provinces as well as similar operations and activities in Northern Nigeria were steps in that direction.

By 1914, there had emerged a single political entity (Nigeria), a central authority (British), a capital (Lagos), and a common domestic market with free access to British and Nigerian traders. In the competition for a single capital, Calabar gave way to Lagos after the 1906 amalgamation, and Kaduna after the 1914 amalgamation.

The 1914 amalgamation left unanswered the important question whether Nigeria should become a unitary or federal state. As a beginning, there developed a quasi-federation of two groups of provinces – one in the north and the other in the south. Changes in 1939, 1954, 1963 and 1967 elaborated the 1914 arrangements and sought to maintain the integrity of the Nigerian state. In 1939, the Nigerian state comprised three groups of Provinces – the Northern, Western and Eastern. Under the 1954 Constitution, Nigeria formally became a federal state consisting of the Northern, Western and Eastern Regions as well as the Federal Territory of Lagos. The 1963 Republican Constitution provided for a fourth Region, the Mid-West. On 27 May 1967, the Federal Military Government, by a decree, created twelve autonomous states.

In at least two ways Nigeria's experience between January 1966 and January 1970 was relevant to the 1914 amalgamation. The secessionist threats then, though not for the first time in Nigerian history since 1914, raised the question of whether any breakaway movement was the answer to Nigeria's long-standing problem of unity in diversity. If secession were allowed in the Nigeria of more than 250 ethnic groups, the degree of provocation notwithstanding, what would be the basis of the new political entities – a return to the pre-colonial caliphate, empires, kingdoms, city-states, republics, village-groups and such compound-loving communities as those of the Tiv?

The civil war experience between July 1967 and January 1970 further showed the effects of the two rival forces which either rejected or accepted the 1914 amalgamation as modified on

27 May 1967. Without having to elaborate the merits and demerits of the secessionist attempt in Nigeria between 30 May 1967 and January 1970, it is sufficient to emphasise here that the end of the civil war saved the Nigerian state from breaking into its pre-colonial units, a process which in the 1960s would have resulted in bloodier consequences. The durability, so far, of the Nigerian state can be explained in more than military terms. It owes a lot to the memories of pre-colonial commercial and cultural contacts, inter-marriages, a common political experience during and after colonialism, and a growing awareness of the need for economic interdependence in a large and attractive domestic market.

Was the Nigeria saved from disintegration between 1966 and 1970 a British creation? In a discussion of this politically and emotionally charged question, due consideration must be given to the fact that before the establishment and consolidation of British rule, no Nigerian ruler or rulers had successfully brought about the political merger of all the pre-colonial units which came under central authority from 1914. Of all these units, only the caliphate embraced by far the largest political entity in pre-colonial times. The jihadists, themselves, had limited success in expanding the territory under their control. Bornu and parts of Adamawa, Bauchi and the Benue valley were not included in the caliphate under the direction of the rulers of Sokoto-Gwandu. The other pre-colonial empires, kingdoms and republics in the rest of the territory which later became Nigeria had limited objectives concerning expansion. Even before their decline and collapse, such empires and kingdoms as those of old Oyo and Benin realised the danger of over-expansion without corresponding resources in men and material to consolidate new conquests.

These pre-colonial empires, kingdoms, city-states, republics and other communities lacked the resources which enabled Britain, from 1898, to embark upon the creation and consolidation of a colonial state in Nigeria. Britain had such advantages as mobility following the remarkable improvements in transportation and communications, besides financial and human resources including able administrators and well trained and properly equipped troops and police. Above all, in her encounters with several opposition groups in Nigeria, Britain demonstrated her will, power and ability to enforce her authority on a scale not attempted in pre-colonial times. For example, Britain did not hesitate to shed the blood of her own citizens, as well as that of

Conclusion

Nigerians, in the attempts to secure her objectives during the process of state formation in the pursuit of her already recognised interests.

To secure wider approval and legitimacy during the evolution of the Nigerian state, Britain attempted the techniques of participation and performance in meeting some ascertainable needs. In the first place, Britain tried to involve the people of Northern and Southern Nigeria in some aspects of administration. In Southern Nigeria, British officials made token gestures in securing unofficial representation on the Legislative Council based in Lagos. The technique of participation was further tried in the system of indirect administration through the several Native Courts and Councils set up in Northern and Southern Nigeria. But neither the rôle of the Legislative Council nor that of the native courts and native councils in Southern Nigeria altered the fact that British rule during the period 1898–1914 was substantially a mild autocracy. The other test of performance had some relevance to the British efforts at meeting the needs of the people in such matters as security, stability and welfare. The preceding chapters have shown how limited were the government-sponsored welfare measures carried out before 1914. Besides, the British policies and practices designed to promote the security and stability needed by the new authorities in the emergent state clashed with the interests of the Africans who opposed the legitimacy of any colonial set-up, no matter how well-meaning.

The series of secessionist threats which threatened the solidarity and territorial integrity of the Nigerian state since 1914 sometimes hung on the theory that, before British rule began, there had been no realisation of the concept of 'one country' in the territory later called Nigeria. Despite the validity of that viewpoint, assessed in political terms, most Nigerians later endeavoured to work within the framework of the state formally established in January 1914. That trend was more noticeable during the period of dyarchy in the 1950s. As responsible office-holders in the regional and federal governments in Nigeria in the era of dyarchy, many Nigerian leaders associated themselves with maintaining the territorial integrity of the Nigerian state. During the same period, they and the Nigerian masses interested themselves in the consolidation and independence of the state which had emerged under British auspices. If therefore the credit of creating the Nigerian state rightly belonged to

The Evolution of the Nigerian State

Britain, that of its further consolidation rests squarely with British personnel as well as Nigerians before and after independence. In these respects, therefore, the steps taken during the crucial period 1898–1914 to create and consolidate the Nigerian state continued to influence major developments afterwards.

Appendix A

THE EGBA TREATY 1893

Treaty of Friendship and Commerce made at Abeokuta in the Egba country, this 18th (eigtheenth) day of January, in the year 1893

BETWEEN His Excellency Gilbert Thomas Carter, Esquire, Companion of the Most Distinguished Order of Saint Michael and Saint George, Governor and Commander-in-Chief of the Colony of Lagos, for, and on behalf of Her Majesty the Queen of Great Britain and Ireland, Empress of India, &c., Her Heirs and Successors on the one part, and the undersigned King (Alake) and Authorities of Abeokuta representing the Egba Kingdom, for and on behalf of their Heirs and Successors on the other part. We the undersigned King and Authorities do, in the presence of the Elders, Headmen and people assembled at this place hereby promise:

1st. That there shall be peace and friendship between the subjects of the Queen and Egba subjects, and should any difference or dispute accidentally arise between us and the said subjects of the Queen, it shall be referred to the Governor of Lagos for settlement as may be deemed expedient.

2nd. That there shall be complete freedom of Trade between the Egba Country and Lagos, and in view of the injury to commerce arising from the arbitrary closing of roads, we the said King and Authorities, hereby declare that no roads shall in future be closed without the consent and approval of the Governor of Lagos.

3rd. That we the said King and Authorities pledge ourselves to use every means in our power to foster and promote trade with the Countries adjoining Egba and with Lagos.

4th. That we the said King and Authorities will as heretofore, afford complete protection, and every assistance and encouragement to all Ministers of the Christian religion.

5th. It is further agreed and stipulated by the said Gilbert Thomas Carter on behalf of Her Majesty the Queen of England, that so long as the provisions of this Treaty are strictly kept, no annexation of any portion of the Egba Country shall be made by Her Majesty's Government without the consent of the lawful Authorities of the Country, no aggressive action shall be taken against the said Country, and its independence shall be fully recognised.

6th. The said King and Authorities having promised that the practice of offering human sacrifices shall be abolished in the one township where it at present exists and having explained that British Subjects have already freedom to occupy land, build houses, and carry on trade and manufacture in any part of the Egba Country, and likewise that there is no possibility of a cession of any portion of the Egba Country to a Foreign Power without the consent of Her Majesty's Government, it is desired that no special provision be made in regard to these subjects in this Treaty.

Done at Abeokuta this Eighteenth day of January, 1893.

(Signed) Osokalu [his mark] King Alake ⎫
      "   Osundare Onlade [his mark]   Representatives of
      "   Sorunke Jaguna [his mark]   King Alake and
      "   Ogundeyi Magaji [his mark]   Egba United Kingdom ⎭

(Signed) G. T. Carter
          Governor and Commander-in-Chief,
          Colony of Lagos.

Appendix B

THE OYO TREATY, 1893

TREATY made at Oyo in the Yoruba Country this third day of February, in the year 1893, between His Excellency Gilbert Thomas Carter, Esquire, Companion of the Most Distinguished Order of Saint Michael and Saint George, Governor and Commander-in-Chief of Lagos, for and on behalf of Her Majesty the Queen of Great Britain and Ireland, Empress of India, &c., Her Heirs and Successors, on the one part, and the undersigned King Alafin of Oyo and Head of Yoruba land for and on behalf of His Heirs and Successors on the other part.

I the undersigned Alafin of Oyo do hereby promise:

1st. That there shall be peace between the subjects of the Queen of England and Yoruba subjects, and should any difference or dispute accidentally arise between us and the said subjects of the Queen, it shall be referred to the Governor of Lagos for the time being whose decision shall be final and binding upon us all.

2nd. That British subjects shall have free access in all parts of Yoruba land and shall have the right to build houses and possess property according to the laws in force in this country. They shall further have full liberty to carry on such trade and manufacture as may be approved by the Governor of Lagos.

3rd. That I the said Alafin of Oyo agree to allow a right of way to Lagos to all persons wishing to go there.

4th. That I the said Alafin of Oyo pledge myself to use every means in my power to foster and promote trade with the countries adjoining Yoruba land and with Lagos.

5th. That I the said Alafin of Oyo will afford complete protection and every assistance and encouragement to all ministers of the Christian Religion.

6th. That I the said Alafin of Oyo solemnly promise to abolish the practice of offering human sacrifices and to prohibit it throughout the country under my control.

7th. That I the said Alafin of Oyo will not enter into any war or commit any act of aggression on any of the Chiefs bordering on Lagos by which the trade of the country with Lagos shall be interrupted or the safety of the persons and property of the subjects of the Queen of England shall be lost, compromised or endangered.

8th. That I the said Alafin of Oyo will at no time whatever cede any of my territory to any other power, or enter into any agreement, treaty, or arrangement with any Foreign Government, except through and with the consent of the Government of Her Majesty the Queen of England, &c.

9th. It is hereby agreed that all disputes that may arise between the parties to this Treaty shall be enquired into and adjusted by two arbitrators, the one appointed by the Governor of Lagos, the other by the Alafin of Oyo, and in any case when the arbitrators so appointed shall not agree the matter in dispute shall be referred to the Governor of Lagos, whose decision shall be final.

10th. In consideration of the faithful observance of all the foregoing articles of this Treaty the Governor of Lagos will make from 1st January next ensuing into the King of Oyo a yearly present of one hundred pounds but such present may upon breach of all or any one or more of the provisions of this agreement, and at the discretion of the Governor of Lagos for the time being, be altogether withdrawn or suspended.

11th. I likewise pledge myself to obtain the consent and co-operation of all the subordinate Kings and Authorities of representative Towns in Yorubaland to the provisions of this Treaty.

ADEYEMI his mark | Alafin of Oyo and Head of Yorubaland.

(Signed), G. T. CARTER,
        Governor and Commander-in-Chief, Colony of Lagos.

Appendix C

THE IBADAN AGREEMENT, 1893

AGREEMENT made at Ibadan this 15th day of August, 1893, between His Excellency, George Chardin Denton, Esquire, Companion of the Most Distinguished Order of Saint Michael and Saint George, Acting Governor and Commander-in-Chief of the Colony of Lagos for and on behalf of Her Majesty the Queen of Great Britain and Ireland, Empress of India, Her Heirs and Successors of the one part and the undersigned Bale and Authorities of Ibadan for and on behalf of their heirs and of the people of Ibadan on the other part.

We the undersigned Bale and Authorities of Ibadan on behalf of ourselves and of the people of Ibadan, do hereby agree and declare as follows:

1. That the general administration of the internal affairs of the following Yoruba towns viz: Iwo, Ede, Oshogbo, Ikirun, Ogbomosho, Ejigbo and Iseyin and in all countries in the socalled Ekun Otun Ekun Osi, is vested in the general Government of Ibadan and the local Authorities of the said towns act in harmony with and are subject to Ibadan notwithstanding that the Alafin is recognised as the King and Head of Yorubaland.

2. That we fully recognise all the provisions of the Treaty dated the 3rd February, 1893, made at Oyo between His Excellency Sir Gilbert Thomas Carter, Knight Commander of the Most Distinguished Order of Saint Michael and Saint George, then Companion of the said Most Distinguished Order on behalf of Her Majesty the Queen of Great Britain and Ireland and the Alafin of Oyo as Head of Yorubaland.

3. That we fully agree to carry out within the territory of Ibadan all the provisions of the said Treaty.

4. That we further agree in amplification of the said Treaty on our own behalf to the following terms and conditions:

First. That we will use every effort to secure the free passage of all persons coming through Ibadan either from the Interior to Lagos or from Lagos to the Interior and we promise to afford protection to persons and property so passing.

Second. That for the purpose of better securing the performance of the said Treaty of the 3rd February, 1893, and of this Agreement we do hereby agree to receive at Ibadan such European Officers and such a force of the Lagos Constabulary as the Governor shall from time to time deem necessary for the said purpose and for securing to us the benefits of the said Treaty and Agreement: and we also agree to provide land for the occupation of such Officers and Force.

Third. We further agree upon the request of the Government of Lagos, to provide land for the construction and maintenance of a Railway through our territory, should the construction of such a Railway be determined upon, and to accept for such land such compensation, if any, as shall be agreed upon between the parties hereto or between the Authorities of Ibadan and the persons undertaking the construction of such a Railway.

5. And we do finally agree that all disputes which may arise under or in reference to this Agreement shall be enquired into and adjusted by two Arbitrators, the one to be appointed by the Governor of Lagos for the time being, the other by the Bale and Authorities of Ibadan and in any case where the Arbitrators so appointed shall not agree, the matter in dispute shall be referred to the Governor of Lagos whose decision shall be final.

Done at Ibadan this fifteenth day of August one thousand eight hundred and ninety-three.

GEORGE C. DENTON
Acting Governor

Fijabi the Bale	his x mark
Osuntoki the Otun Bale	his x mark
Fajinmi the Osi Bale	his x mark
Akintola the Balogun by his representative Oyeniye	his x mark
Babalola the Otun Balogun	his x mark
Kongi the Osi Balogun	his x mark

Appendix C

Sumani Apanpa the Asipa	his x mark
Ogundipo the Seriki	his x mark

....

Participators in and witnesses to the Agreement.

Lanlatu the Iyalode	her x mark
Mosaderin the Ekerin	his x mark
Ogungbesan the Ekarun	his x mark
Obisesan the Agbakin	his x mark
Tanipe the Maye	his x mark
Akitunde the Ekefa	his x mark
Salako the Are Alasa	his x mark
Bamgbegbin the Are Ogo	his x mark
Enimowu the Abese	his x mark
Olafa the Asagi	his x mark
Omosanya the Otun Seriki	his x mark
Aina Fagbemi the Osi Seriki	his x mark
Eweje the Sarumi by his representative Alawo	his x mark
Dada Ojo the Ekerin Seriki	his x mark

Appendix D

MOOR'S SPEECH AT BENIN CITY, 1897

Meeting with King Overami and Chiefs of Benin City held at the Consular Court at 9 a.m. 7th September 1897

Consul-General:
When the palaver is settled as regards Ologbosheri I will tell you what Overami's position will be. But the first thing is I will caution Overami and all his Chiefs and people to make up their minds to one thing that is – what the white man says is true – when the white man says a thing will be that is what will be. Now this is the white man's country. There is only one King in the country and that is white man; the only person therefore to whom service need be shown is the white man and all the Chiefs should come here independently of one another to give their service at the proper time. There is no necessity for them to give their service to Overami before coming here – they are in the habit of going and giving their service to Overami before they come here which delays the work of this Court. Overami is no longer the King of this country – the white man is the only man who is King in this country and to him only service is due. The white man being the King of this country is the only person who can demand from the villages in the form of chop,[1] produce, service anything ... In the large villages we will put village Councils to settle the palavers in the same way as we have the big Council here; but the village Council will of course be under the Council of Benin City. This has been explained to the Native Council before and they know all about it. I am telling it now again in order that Overami and all the other Chiefs here may understand. Next thing we come to the position which Overami is to occupy in Benin City and also the position which the Chiefs who have

[1] Pidgin English for food.

Appendix D

come in with him should occupy. With regard to the Chiefs who have come in with him, their position is easily settled. Those of them who are found to be good men and men with good head will be put in the Native Council – those of them who are not suitable will be allowed to carry on their ordinary life in the same way as any other Chief in the country but they will have no voice in the settlement of affairs – at the same time they will be recognised as Chiefs and it will be their duty to report to the Native Council any difficulties or troubles which they may hear in the country that they may be settled at once. This means that no Chief who was formerly a Chief of the Benin Country will have his chieftainship taken from him – but the best of them will be selected to assist in governing the country. These Chiefs who are not in the Native Council will be minor Chiefs – no matter what their positions were before.

Appendix E

THE LAGOS PROTECTORATE

Order in Council 1901

WHEREAS His Majesty hath acquired power and jurisdiction within divers countries on the West Coast of Africa, near or adjacent to His Majesty's Colony of Lagos:

And whereas by an Order in Council of Her late Majesty Queen Victoria bearing date the 29th day of December 1887, it was provided that it should be lawful for the legislative Council for the time being of the Colony of Lagos, by Ordinance or Ordinances, to exercise and provide for giving effect to all such powers and jurisdiction as Her Majesty might, at any time before or after the passing of the said Order in Council, have acquired in the said territories adjacent to the Colony of Lagos, subject to such provisions as are in the said Order in Council described and set forth:

And whereas by a further Order of Her late Majesty in Council, bearing date the 27th December 1899, provision was made for the exercise of Her Majesty's jurisdiction within the territories therein described and set forth:

And whereas the said last recited Order has never been brought into operation within the said territories, and it is expedient that the said Order should be revoked:

And whereas it is expedient to define the limits within which the powers and jurisdiction of His Majesty in the said territories under the provisions of the Order in Council of the 29th December 1887 shall in future be exercised:

NOW, THEREFORE, His Majesty, in pursuance of the powers by the Foreign Jurisdiction Act, 1890, or otherwise in His Majesty vested, by and with the advice of His Privy Council, is pleased to order, and it is hereby ordered, as follows:

Appendix E

I. This Order may be cited as the 'Lagos Protectorate Order in Council, 1901'.

II. Subject to the provisions of the said Order in Council of the 29th December 1887, the Legislative Council for the time being of the Colony of Lagos may, by Ordinance or Ordinances, exercise and provide for giving effect to all such powers and jurisdiction as His Majesty may, at any time either before or after the passing of this Order, have acquired or may acquire within such of the territories of the West Coast of Africa near or adjacent to the Colony of Lagos as are within the limits of this Order.

Provided that nothing in any such Ordinance or Ordinances contained shall take away or affect any rights secured to any natives in the said territories by any treaties or agreements made on behalf or with the sanction of His Majesty, and that all such treaties and agreements shall be and remain operative and in force, and that all pledges and undertakings therein contained shall remain mutually binding on all parties to the same.

III. The limits of this Order are the territories of Africa which are bounded on the south by the Atlantic Ocean, on the west by the line of the frontier between the British and French possessions on the north and south-east by the British Protectorate of Northern Nigeria, and on the east by the British Protectorate of Southern Nigeria.

Provided always, that such parts of the territories so bounded as are within that portion of His Majesty's Dominions which is known as the Colony of Lagos, shall not be included within the limits of this Order. The territories within the limits of this Order shall be known and described as the Lagos Protectorate.

IV. The Order of Her late Majesty Queen Victoria in Council of the 27th December 1899 is hereby revoked.

V. This Order shall be published in the Gazette of the Colony of Lagos, and shall thereupon commence and come into operation; and the Governor shall give directions for the publication of this Order at such places, and in such manner, and for such time or times as he thinks proper for giving due publicity thereto within the Lagos Protectorate.

And the Right Honourable Joseph Chamberlain, one of His Majesty's Principal Secretaries of State is to give the necessary direction herein accordingly.

A. W. FITZROY.

Appendix F

MACGREGOR'S VIEWS ON ADMINISTRATIVE
AFFAIRS, 1902

Extracts from the report on an interview between Sir William MacGregor and a deputation from the A.P.S. on 20 June 1902

Mr Martin Wood: I think I may say that Mr Pease and all of us were anxious to see and talk with you, Sir William, because of our strong impression of your just dealing in former times. We have come to regard you almost as a model colonial officer.

Sir W. MacGregor: It is very good of you to say that. Of course, there were many things new to me in Africa. I do my best there to ascertain native customs, usages, and prejudices; to respect them, and to administer justice accordingly; more particularly in regard to questions of land tenure, in which your Society cannot but be greatly interested. I have collected notes of land tenure in every province I have visited, and find the subject not a simple one. In some provinces all the land is divided up into family blocks. A family who own a block of land cannot sell or alienate it, but may lease with the sanction of the provincial chief or council. In other districts there is no permanent individual ownership. As to the determination of what is private property, the solution I suggested was to leave the question of the definition of private, tribal, and family property in each province entirely in the hands of the native authorities. And this for the best of all reasons; it would be most inadvisable to place the solution in the hands of the Supreme Court or of any European.

The importance of preserving native land tenure

Mr Martin Wood: Do you regard it as a general principle through-

Appendix F

out West Africa that these tribal rights are maintained in the sense of public property?

Sir W. MacGregor: In dealing with the natives one must never touch their rights of land, or compromise the authority of the chiefs. If one wished to stir up trouble in West Africa, all one would have to do would be to suggest that the land of the natives is about to be taken away from them. Unfortunately, their credulity is in this respect sometimes practised on.

Mr Pease: It has been the trouble in every country.

Sir W. MacGregor: I think I have provided against that as far as it is possible for man to do so, in the Native Councils and Forest Ordinances.

Mr Fox Bourne: Coming to the Native Councils question, the first part of the ordinance seems to us admirable, so far as it establishes a central Native Council in Lagos as an advisory body for the colony.

Sir W. MacGregor: It is in full operation, and the natives already regard it as a great honour to serve on the Councils, and take a deep and intelligent interest in its work.

Mr Fox Bourne: Then, as regards the Provincial and Town Councils, the idea of encouraging and helping natives to manage their own affairs in their own provinces appears to us no less admirable. But as regards these Provincial Councils, difficulties present themselves with reference to the administrative powers assigned to them.

Sir W. MacGregor: There is no administrative Native Council in Lagos. As an advisory body it is valuable.

Mr Fox Bourne: The Central Council is only advisory for Lagos colony. But the Provincial Councils are to be administrative, and your scheme proposes that the old Native Councils shall continue to sit as the agents or representatives of the Government in association with the European Residents.

Sir W. MacGregor: They are in no way whatever representative of the Government – that is an erroneous idea of them.

Mr Fox Bourne: But you propose to keep the old machinery in working order in the provinces?

Sir W. MacGregor: The Provincial Councils are, as expressed in the ordinance, entirely responsible for the administration of justice in the provinces, for the maintenance of peace and order, and entirely responsible also for carrying out the general administrative business of the province, not as representatives of the

Governor, but as the natural heads of the people, and under the usages of the country.

Mr Fox Bourne: As empowered by you.

Sir W. MacGregor: Not exactly as empowered by me. Their position is now defined and safeguarded by law, and the law is the embodiment of usage and custom.

Mr Martin Wood: But they look to you as the superior who sanctions them and can overrule their work.

Sir W. MacGregor: If I told them they were only my representatives they would not trust me. They would feel that their status was being compromised.

Mr Fox Bourne: May I offer an illustration? It would be the duty of a Provincial Council to find out and punish an offender. If it refused to do so –

Sir W. MacGregor: I don't know what might happen in such a case. Quite recently a murder was committed in a certain province. The native authorities proceeded to deal with it in their own way. Certain accused persons were brought then; but the real murderer was not identified. Then the Provincial Council dealt with the quarter of the town in which the murder took place. As they could not discover who the murderers were, they imposed a fine upon that quarter of the town. It was, I believe, £200. They then reduced it to £100. Upon this I made representations to the chief concerned, saying that in the case of a brutal murder such as had occurred it was not right to allow the case to be disposed of on payment of £100, but they must make further efforts to discover who the murderers were. In that case I still continue to exercise pressure, and will do so probably till the culprit is discovered. That is an example from actual practice.

Mr Fox Bourne: That is a case in which you doubtless enforced, and will continue to enforce, pressure by judicious and quite justifiable methods. In many cases likely to arise the local Residents would go to work in a different way; they would promptly take the law into their own hands and use force in asserting it.

The Yoruba states not independent

Sir W. MacGregor: Generally speaking, one can manage without proceeding to extremities. That just reminds me there is a phrase here in paragraph 10 of Mr Fox Bourne's letter in answer to my

Appendix F

despatch of 7 February which requires correction. It speaks of 'a meeting of the Egba Independent State Council'. It would be a most dangerous idea to put into the heads of a Protected State that they are an Independent Sovereign Power. They are simply the rulers of their own province, and it is best to leave the matter there.

Mr Fox Bourne: What did Sir Gilbert Carter mean when, in negotiating the Egba Treaty of 1893, he undertook that 'the independence of the country should be fully recognised?'.

Sir W. MacGregor: They are not independent as a State, although they are held responsible for the maintenance of peace and order in their provinces, for the administration of justice, and responsible for seeing that there is no impediment to business being duly carried on. They are responsible authorities, but certainly not an Independent State.

Mr Fox Bourne: In accordance with the terms of Sir Gilbert Carter's treaty they called themselves and considered themselves 'independent'.

Sir W. MacGregor: That was a mere phrase; they are deprived of the position of an Independent State in the same article.

Mr Fox Bourne: Of your Bill?

Sir W. MacGregor: No; of the treaty. The treaty is not a treaty entered into between two Independent States. The native authorities are bound to do certain things that you could not ask an Independent State to do.

Mr Fox Bourne: But the treaty provided that there shall be no annexation of any portion of the country and no aggressive action.

Sir W. MacGregor: There has been no aggressive action and no annexation. The phrase about independence, if read without the context, might of course mislead.

Mr Fox Bourne: Sir Gilbert Carter promised it, and it is one of the treaties covered by last year's Order in Council.

Sir W. MacGregor: You see how I interpret the treaty. The Provincial Council is responsible for the maintenance of peace and order in its province. The Government does not charge itself with that duty. I hold them responsible for the administration of justice, and for the discharge of public duties in the province. It would be impossible to do that in the case of an independent State. If our neighbours were only led to think that the provinces are independent of the Government of the King, the provinces would speedily lose their independence. Will you show me where any treaty is violated by the Native Councils Ordinance?

Mr Fox Bourne: By the assumption that you can interfere with and control the native Governments.

Sir W. MacGregor: How long would you maintain even a semblance of British authority, or exercise protection; or how could you remonstrate or maintain peace without that? How long do you think we should be able to remain in the country without exercising some control? You should know that we have already expended over a million and before long we shall have spent a million and a quarter upon a railway that goes through two provinces. Unless we had control how could this be done?

Mr Fox Bourne: By agreement with them.

Sir W. MacGregor: By agreement with them! What would be the good of having an agreement with them if you cannot exercise some control? They might say, 'We are an independent State; let us see if we cannot send our ambassador to the Court of St James, or enter into a treaty with a Continental power.' Before the Native Councils Ordinance there was no law on the subject whatever, each European officer sent out to a province had his own ideas as to his position. But now that the Native Councils Ordinance is passed these European officers know perfectly well what their duties are. They never knew what they were before.

Mr Fox Bourne: The ordinance requires the Governor to sanction and approve the constitution of the Council.

Sir W. MacGregor: Most essential. That is absolutely necessary.

Sir William went on to say that safety might require the Governor to exercise his veto, but as yet he had not found it necessary to do so. He had had no reason to bring any pressure to bear upon any appointment so far. The ordinance was framed in accordance with native usage and custom.

Mr Fox Bourne: What we do object to is that the machinery which the Government employ must tend more and more to the exercise of autocratic power on the part of the European authority. It must break down –

Sir W. MacGregor: Break down what?

Mr Fox Bourne: The local institutions.

Sir W. MacGregor: On the contrary, it is setting up local institutions. The local institutions were fast becoming extinct.

Sir William then explained how a district that was recently

Appendix F

rebellious through the autocratic doings of a chief had been quieted down, and now has a Native Council. The object aimed at was to have a regularly constituted native authority in each district, which is in accordance with tradition and custom.

Appendix G

THE EGBA JURISDICTION ORDINANCE,
1904 (NO. 14 OF 1904)

An Ordinance to make provision for the exercise of the Powers and Jurisdiction acquired by HIS MAJESTY in Egbaland.

Whereas by an Order in Council of Her late Majesty Queen Victoria bearing date the 29th day of December 1887, and made in pursuance of the powers by the Foreign Jurisdiction Act 1843 or otherwise in Her Majesty vested, it was provided that it should be lawful for the Legislative Council for the time being of the Colony of Lagos, by Ordinance or Ordinances to exercise and provide for giving effect to all such powers and jurisdiction as Her Majesty might at any time before or after the passing of the said Order in Council have acquired in the territories adjacent to the Colony of Lagos, subject to such provisions as are in the said Order in Council described and set forth:

And whereas by an Order in Council bearing date the 24th day of July 1901, and made in pursuance of the powers by the Foreign Jurisdiction Act 1890 or otherwise in His Majesty vested, His Majesty has been pleased to order, subject nevertheless to the conditions and reservations in the Order in Council now under recital have acquired or may acquire, within such of the territories of the West Coast of Africa near or adjacent to the Colony of Lagos as are within certain limits, thereinafter described as the 'Lagos Protectorate';

And whereas by an Agreement dated the 13th day of January 1904 entered into between Sir William MacGregor, K.C.M.G., C.B., Governor of the Colony of Lagos, on behalf of His Most Excellent Majesty King Edward VII and the Alake and Authorities of Egba land on behalf of the Egba people, His Majesty has acquired certain powers and jurisdiction in the territory of the Egba people;

Appendix G

And whereas the territory of the Egba people lies within the limits of the Lagos Protectorate as defined by the aforesaid Order of His Majesty in Council of the 24th day of July 1901;

And whereas it is expedient to provide by Ordinance for the exercise of and for giving effect to the aforesaid powers and jurisdiction acquired by His Majesty;

Be it therefore enacted by the Governor of the Colony of Lagos with the advice and consent of the Legislative Council thereof, as follows:

1. This Ordinance may be cited as the 'Egba Jurisdiction Ordinance 1904'.

2. In this Ordinance except where the context requires some other interpretation 'Agreement' means the Agreement entered into between the Governor of Lagos and the Alake and Authorities of Egba land on the 13th day of January 1904 and set out in the Schedule hereto;

'Mixed Court' means the Mixed Court mentioned in the Agreement.

3. The jurisdiction acquired by His Majesty under the Agreement shall be vested in the Supreme Court of the Colony of Lagos (hereinafter called 'the Court') and the Court is hereby empowered to carry the said jurisdiction into effect.

4. The jurisdiction by this Ordinance vested in the Court shall, except as hereinafter mentioned, be exercised under and according to the provisions of the Supreme Court Ordinance 1876 including the Rules and Orders of Courts made thereunder, and the Criminal Procedure Ordinance 1876, and any Ordinance which may be passed supplementary thereto or in substitution therefore.

5. The laws relating to indictable crimes and offences, for the time being in force in the Colony of Lagos shall extend to and be in force within and under the jurisdiction by this Ordinance vested in the Court. The laws relating to Civil matters for the time being in force in the Colony of Lagos shall extend to and be in force within and under the jurisdiction by this Ordinance vested in the Court, but shall be deemed to extend thereto and be in force so far only as the jurisdiction of the Court and local circumstances reasonably permit and render such extension and enforcement suitable and appropriate.

6. The Court in the exercise and administration of the jurisdiction vested in it by this Ordinance shall have the right to

observe and enforce the observance of the laws and customs existing in Egba land, such laws or customs not being repugnant to natural justice, equity and good conscience. Such laws and customs shall be deemed applicable in causes and matters between Egbas and persons not being natives of Egba land only when it may appear to the Court that substantial injustice would be done to either party by a strict adherence to the rules of English law, and in such other causes and matters as the Court may deem just and equitable.

7. All laws of the Colony of Lagos relating to any powers given to or exercised by the Governor shall be in force within the jurisdiction by this Ordinance vested in the Court in so far as they are necessary to carry into effect the jurisdiction acquired by His Majesty.

8. Whenever any person is charged with any crime or offence within the jurisdiction by this Ordinance vested in the Court, the trial shall be held with the aid of Assessors not being ordinarily less than four.

9. Sections 118 to Section 134 (both inclusive) of the Criminal Procedure Ordinance 1876 shall not apply to the jurisdiction by this Ordinance vested in the Court.

10. Order fifty-two of Schedule II of the Rules of Court made under the provisions of the Supreme Court Ordinance 1876 shall not apply to appeals from the Mixed Court.

11. The Chief Justice may at any time make any Rules of Court for carrying this Ordinance into effect, and in particular for regulating the practice and procedure to be observed in Appeals from the Mixed Court both in civil and criminal matters, including all matters connected with the forms to be used and the fees to be payable, and may from time to time alter, amend and revoke all or any of such Rules, provided that no such Rules, or any alteration, amendment or revocation thereof shall be deemed binding until the same shall have been approved by the Legislative Council, and shall have been published in the Gazette; but all such Rules, and such alterations, amendments and revocations thereof, when so approved and published as aforesaid, shall have the same force and effect for all purposes as if the same had been made by Ordinance, and shall in like manner come into operation, either immediately or on such day as shall be provided in such Rules, subject to disallowance by His Majesty.

Appendix G

Schedule

AGREEMENT made this 13th day of January, 1904, between His Excellency Sir William MacGregor, Knight Commander of the Most Distinguished Order of Saint Michael and Saint George, Companion of the Most Honourable Order of the Bath, Governor and Commander-in-Chief in and over the Colony of Lagos, for and on behalf of His Most Excellent Majesty Edward the Seventh of the United Kingdom of Great Britain and Ireland and of all the British Dominions beyond the Seas, King, Emperor of India, his heirs and successors of the one part, and the Alake and Authorities of the Egba Nation for and on behalf of themselves their heirs and successors, and the Egba Nation, of the other part;

Whereas the Territory of the Egba Nation is adjacent to the Colony of Lagos; and Trade and Commerce have vastly increased in Egba land in recent years; and large numbers of British subjects and others have settled there.

Now therefore, the Alake and Authorities of the Egba Nation for and on behalf of themselves their heirs and successors and the Egba Nation hereby Cede and Grant to His Most Excellent Majesty Edward the Seventh of the United Kingdom of Great Britain and Ireland and of all the British Dominions beyond the Seas, King, Emperor of India, his heirs and successors, for a period of twenty years from the date hereof the following Powers and Jurisdictions in the Territory of the Egba Nation:

1. Power and Jurisdiction over all persons not being natives of Egba land for the repression and punishment of all crimes and offences which are denominated Indictable Crimes and Offences in the law of England.

2. Power and Jurisdiction over all persons whatsoever for the repression and punishment of the crimes of Murder and Manslaughter.

3. Power and Jurisdiction for the Judicial hearing and determination of matters in difference whereone or both of the parties to the suit is not a native of Egba land and the subject matter in dispute is of the value or amount of Fifty pounds or upwards.

4. Power and Jurisdiction for the administration and control of the property and persons of all persons not being natives of Egba land.

5. Power and Authority to appoint the President of the 'Mixed Court' hereinafter mentioned.

6. Power and Jurisdiction for the Judicial hearing and determination of appeals from decisions of the aftermentioned 'Mixed Court' in criminal cases both on questions of fact and on questions of law.

7. Power and Jurisdiction for the Judicial hearing and determination of appeals from decisions of the aftermentioned 'Mixed Court' where the decision of such court is given in respect of a sum of Five pounds or upwards, or determines directly or indirectly a claim or question respecting money goods land or other property or any civil right or other matter of the amount of value of Five pounds or upwards.

8. Power and Jurisdiction to execute and carry into effect the powers and jurisdiction hereinbefore ceded and granted.

And the Alake and Authorities of the Egba Nation for and on behalf of themselves their heirs and successors and the Egba Nation hereby undertake and bind themselves to His Most Excellent Majesty to pass the Resolutions in the Egba Council necessary for the formation of a Court to be called 'The Mixed Court' giving to it the Constitution, Powers and Jurisdiction following that is to say:

(a) 'The Mixed Court' shall consist of a President and two other Members, which members shall be appointed by the Egba Council. The decision of the Majority of the members shall prevail. A quorum shall consist of two members of whom the President shall be one.

(b) 'The Mixed Court' shall have jurisdiction for the summary trial and punishment of persons not being natives of Egba land committing offences which are not indictable.

(c) The penalties and punishments which may be imposed by 'The Mixed Court' shall not exceed those which can be imposed for similar offences by District Commissioners of the Colony of Lagos.

(d) 'The Mixed Court' shall have a civil jurisdiction over matters in difference where one or both of the parties to the suit are not natives of Egba land and the subject matter in dispute is less than Fifty pounds in value or amount.

(e) 'The Mixed Court' shall be guided in its decisions so far as practicable by the laws in force in the Colony of Lagos.

Appendix G

And the Alake and Authorities of the Egba Nation for and on behalf of themselves their heirs and successors and the Egba Nation hereby further undertake and bind themselves to His Most Excellent Majesty

(a) to pass the Resolutions in the Egba Council necessary to give the right of appeal on question of fact as well as of law from the decisions of the 'Mixed Court'. (It being understood that such appeal in criminal cases shall only lie if one of the members of the 'Mixed Court' has dissented from the decision of the Court.)
(b) to render all possible assistance for the carrying into effect of the above mentioned ceded Powers and Jurisdictions.
(c) to provide proper prisons for the detention of prisoners.

And the Alake and Authorities of the Egba Nation for and on behalf of themselves their heirs and successors and the Egba Nation hereby declare that it is their strong desire that barristers and solicitors shall not be allowed to practise in the courts exercising the civil jurisdiction hereinbefore ceded.

And His Excellency the said Sir William MacGregor for and on behalf of His Most Excellent Majesty Edward the Seventh of the United Kingdom of Great Britain and Ireland and of all the British Dominions beyond the Seas, King, Emperor of India, hereby accepts the before mentioned ceded Powers and Jurisdictions.

And it is hereby understood and agreed between the Parties hereto that nothing in this treaty shall be deemed to take away the powers and jurisdictions of the Native Courts of Egba land over matters between and affecting natives of Egba land only, except as regards the power and jurisdiction hereinbefore ceded for the repression and punishment of the crimes of murder and manslaughter.

And it is further understood and agreed between the Parties hereto that all persons charged with committing indictable crimes or offences – the jurisdiction over which has been ceded by this treaty – shall be tried by a judge of the Supreme Court of the Colony of Lagos with the aid of Assessors the number of which shall not ordinarily be less than four and such assessors may be judges, magistrates or councillors of the Native Courts or other fit and suitable persons.

In witness whereof the said parties have hereunto set their hands and seals the day and year first above written.

Wm. MacGregor

	their	
Gbadebo	×	Alake
Adepegba	×	Olowu
Olubunmi	×	Agura
Alli	×	Seriki
Yesufu	×	Osi of the Egbas
Sule	×	Moslem Chief
C. Shoruntan	×	Head of the Parakoyis
Oga	×	Apena of Iporo
Shofoluwe	×	Apena of Itoku
Egunjobi	×	Otun of the Egbas
Ogunsholu	×	Jaguna of Ijeja
Kilasho	×	Jaguna of Kemta
Dagi	×	Odofin of Ikija
Shobulo	×	Jaguna of Itoko
	marks	

J. H. Samuel – Government Secretary.
C. B. Moore – Treasurer, E.U.G.
D. O. Williams.

Signed and sealed at Lagos by the said Sir William MacGregor in the presence of
W. Nicoll – Chief Justice of Lagos.
C. H. Harley Moseley – Colonial Secretary.

Signed and sealed at Abeokuta by the said Alake and Authorities of the Egba Nation in the presence of
Cyril Punch – Commissioner, Aro.
Ladapo Ademola.

Appendix H

THE YORUBA JURISDICTION ORDINANCE,
1904 (NO. 17 OF 1904)

An Ordinance to make provision for the exercise of the Powers and Jurisdiction acquired by His Majesty in the Province of Ibadan and the territory of the Alafin of Oyo.

Whereas by an Order in Council of Her late Majesty Queen Victoria bearing date the 29th day of December 1887, and made in pursuance of the powers by the Foreign Jurisdiction Act 1843 or otherwise in Her Majesty vested, it was provided that it should be lawful for the Legislative Council for the time being of the Colony of Lagos, by Ordinance or Ordinances to exercise and provide for giving effect to all such powers and jurisdiction as Her Majesty might at any time before or after the passing of the said Order in Council have acquired in the territories adjacent to the Colony of Lagos, subject to such provisions as are in the said Order in Council described and set forth;

And whereas by an Order in Council bearing date the 24th day of July 1901, and made in pursuance of the powers by the Foreign Jurisdiction Act 1890 or otherwise in His Majesty vested, His Majesty has been pleased to order, subject nevertheless to the conditions and reservations in the Order in Council now under recital contained, that subject to the provisions of the hereinbefore recited Order in Council of the 29th day of December, 1887, the Legislative Council of the Colony of Lagos may by Ordinance or Ordinances exercise and provide for giving effect to all such powers and jurisdiction as His Majesty may at any time either before or after the passing of the Order now under recital have acquired or may acquire, within such of the territories of the West Coast of Africa near or adjacent to the Colony of Lagos as are within certain limits, thereinafter described as the 'Lagos Protectorate';

And whereas by an Agreement dated the 8th day of August, 1904, entered into between C. H. Harley Moseley, C.M.G., Acting Governor of the Colony of Lagos, on behalf of His Most Excellent Majesty King Edward VII, and the Bale and Authorities of the Province of Ibadan, His Majesty has acquired certain powers and jurisdiction in the Province of Ibadan;

And whereas by an Agreement dated the 16th day of August, 1904, entered into between C. H. Harley Moseley, C.M.G., Acting Governor of the Colony of Lagos, on behalf of His Most Excellent Majesty King Edward VII, and the Alafin of Oyo, His Majesty has acquired certain powers and jurisdiction in the territory of the Alafin of Oyo;

And whereas the Province of Ibadan and the territory of the Alafin of Oyo are within the limits of the Lagos Protectorate as defined by the aforesaid Order of His Majesty in Council of the 24th day of July, 1901;

And whereas it is expedient to provide by Ordinance for the exercise of and for giving effect to the aforesaid powers and jurisdiction acquired by His Majesty;

Be it therefore enacted by the Governor of the Colony of Lagos with the advice and consent of the Legislative Council thereof as follows:

1. This Ordinance may be cited as the 'Yorubaland Jurisdiction Ordinance 1904'.

2. In this Ordinance 'Agreements' means the Agreements set out in Schedules 1 and 2 annexed hereto and 'Yorubaland' includes the Province of Ibadan and the territory of the Alafin of Oyo.

3. The jurisdiction acquired by His Majesty under the Agreements shall be vested in the Supreme Court of the Colony of Lagos (hereinafter called 'the Court') and the Court is hereby empowered to carry the said jurisdiction into effect.

4. The jurisdiction by this Ordinance vested in the Court shall except as hereinafter mentioned be exercised under and according to the provisions of the Supreme Court Ordinance 1876 including the Rules and Orders of Court made thereunder and the Criminal Procedure Ordinance 1876, and any Ordinance which may be passed supplementary thereto or in substitution therefor.

5. The laws relating to crimes and offences for the time being in force in the Colony of Lagos shall extend to and be in force within and under the jurisdiction by this Ordinance vested in the

Appendix H

Court. The laws relating to Civil matters for the time being in force in the Colony of Lagos shall extend to and be in force within and under the jurisdiction by this Ordinance vested in the Court, but shall be deemed to extend thereto and be in force so far only as the jurisdiction of the Court and local circumstances reasonably permit and render such extension and enforcement suitable and appropriate.

6. The Court in the exercise and administration of the jurisdiction vested in it by this Ordinance shall have the right to observe and enforce the observance of the laws and customs existing in Yorubaland, such laws or customs not being repugnant to natural justice equity and good conscience. Such laws and customs shall be deemed applicable in causes and matters between natives and persons not being natives of Yorubaland only when it may appear to the Court that substantial injustice would be done to either party by a strict adherence to the rules of English law, and in such causes and matters as the Court may deem just and equitable.

7. All laws of the Colony of Lagos relating to any powers given to or exercised by the Governor shall be in force within the jurisdiction by this Ordinance vested in the Court in so far as they are necessary to carry into effect the jurisdiction acquired by His Majesty.

8. Whenever any person is charged with any indictable crime or offence within the jurisdiction by this Ordinance vested in the Court the trial shall be held with the aid of Assessors not being ordinarily less than four.

9. Sections 118 to Section 134 (both inclusive) of the Criminal Procedure Ordinance 1876 shall not apply to the jurisdiction by this Ordinance vested in the Court.

10. The Chief Justice may at any time make any Rules of Court for carrying this Ordinance into effect, and in particular for regulating all matters connected with the forms to be used and the fees to be payable and may from time to time alter, amend and revoke all or any of such Rules, provided that no such Rules, or any alteration, amendment or revocation thereof shall be deemed binding until the same shall have been approved by the Legislative Council, and shall have been published in the Gazette; but all such Rules, and such alterations, amendments and revocations thereof, when so approved and published as aforesaid, shall have the same force and effect for all purposes as if the same had

been made by Ordinance, and shall in like manner come into operation either immediately or on such day as shall be provided in such Rules, subject to disallowance by His Majesty.

Schedule 1

Agreement made this 8th day of August, 1904, between His Excellency Charles Herbert Harley Moseley, Esquire, Companion of the Most Distinguished Order of Saint Michael and Saint George, Acting Governor and Commander-in-Chief in and over the Colony of Lagos, for and on behalf of His Most Excellent Majesty Edward the Seventh, of the United Kingdom of Great Britain and Ireland, and of all the British Dominions beyond the Seas, King, Emperor of India, his heirs and Successors of the one part and the Bale and Authorities of the Province of Ibadan, for and on behalf of themselves their heirs and Successors and the people of the Province of Ibadan on the other part:

Whereas the Province of Ibadan is under the Protection of His Most Excellent Majesty King Edward the Seventh, and trade and commerce have vastly increased in Ibadan in recent years, and large numbers of British subjects and others have settled there:

Now therefore the Bale and Authorities of the Province of Ibadan for and on behalf of themselves their heirs and Successors and of the people of the Province of Ibadan do hereby agree and acknowledge that the hereinafter mentioned powers and Jurisdiction in the Province of Ibadan are vested in His Most Excellent Majesty Edward the Seventh of the United Kingdom of Great Britain and Ireland and of all British Dominions beyond the Seas, King, Emperor of India, his heirs and Successors, that is to say:

1. Power and Jurisdiction over all persons not being natives of the Province of Ibadan for the repression and punishment of all crimes and offences.

2. Power and Jurisdiction for the Judicial hearing and determination of matters in difference where one or both of the parties to the suit is not a native of the Province of Ibadan.

3. Power and Jurisdiction for the administration and control of the property and persons of all persons not being natives of the Province of Ibadan.

4. Power and Jurisdiction over all persons whomsoever for the

Appendix H

repression and punishment of the crimes of murder and manslaughter.

5. Power and Jurisdiction to execute and carry into effect the aforesaid powers and Jurisdiction.

And the Bale and Council of the Ibadan Province for and on behalf of themselves their heirs and Successors and the natives of the Ibadan Province hereby declare that it is their strong desire that Barristers and Solicitors shall not be allowed to practise in the Courts exercising the civil jurisdiction hereinbefore acknowledged.

And it is hereby understood and agreed between the parties hereto that all persons charged with committing indictable crimes and offences – the jurisdiction over which has been acknowledged by the treaty – shall be tried by a Judge of the Supreme Court of the Colony of Lagos with the aid of Assessors, the number of which shall not ordinarily be less than four, and such Assessors may be Judges, Magistrates or Councillors of the Native Courts or other fit and suitable persons.

In witness whereof the said parties have hereunto set their hands and seals the day and year first above written.

C. H. HARLEY MOSELEY.

Mosaderin	his × mark	Bale Ibadan	(L.S.)
Dada	his × mark	Otun Bale	(L.S.)
Olafa	his × mark	Osi ,,	(L.S.)
Oyebode	his × mark	Ashipa ,,	(L.S.)
Irefin	his × mark	Ekerin ,,	(L.S.)
Akinale	his × mark	Maye ,,	(L.S.)

Obalano	his × mark	Abese	,,	(L.S.)
Apampa	his × mark	Balogun		(L.S.)
Bamgbegbin	his × mark	Otun Balogun		(L.S.)
Akintayo	his × mark	Osi	,,	(L.S.)
Shitu	his × mark	Ashipa	,,	(L.S.)
Suberu	his × mark	Ekerin	,,	(L.S.)
Ola	his × mark	Maye	,,	(L.S.)

Signed and sealed at Lagos by the said Charles Herbert Harley Moseley in the presence of
W. Nicoll – Chief Justice of Lagos.
R. J. B. Ross – Acting Attorney General.
Signed and sealed at Ibadan by the said Bale and Authorities of Ibadan in the presence of
C. H. Elgee – Capt.
　　Resident.

Schedule 2

Agreement made this 16th day of August, 1904, between His Excellency Charles Harley Herbert Moseley, Esquire, Companion of the Most Distinguished Order of Saint Michael and Saint George, Acting Governor and Commander-in-Chief in and over the Colony of Lagos for and on behalf of His Most Excellent Majesty Edward the Seventh of the United Kingdom of Great Britain and Ireland and of all the British Dominions beyond the

Appendix H

Seas, King, Emperor of India, his heirs and Successors of the one part, and the King Alafin of Oyo, and Head of Yorubaland for and on behalf of himself his heirs and Successors and the people of Yorubaland on the other part:

Whereas Yorubaland lies adjacent to the Colony of Lagos and is under the protection of His Most Excellent Majesty King Edward the Seventh and trade and commerce have vastly increased in Yorubaland in recent years, and large numbers of British subjects and others have settled there;

And whereas the Alafin of Oyo is King and Head of Yorubaland;

And whereas the Bale and Authorities of the Province of Ibadan have entered into an Agreement with the Governor of the Colony of Lagos dated the 8th day of August 1904, acknowledging that certain powers and jurisdictions in the Province of Ibadan are vested in His Most Excellent Majesty King Edward the Seventh;

Now therefore the King Alafin of Oyo and Head of Yorubaland for and on behalf of himself his heirs and Successors hereby confirms and approves of the Agreement dated the 8th day of August, 1904, entered into and concluded between His Excellency Charles Herbert Harley Moseley, Acting Governor of the Colony of Lagos for and on behalf of His Most Excellent Majesty King Edward the Seventh and the Bale and Authorities of the Province of Ibadan for and on behalf of themselves their Heirs and Successors, and the people of the Province of Ibadan a copy of which Agreement is annexed and signed as relative hereto;

And further the King Alafin of Oyo and Head of Yorubaland for and on behalf of himself his heirs and Successors and of the people of Yorubaland does hereby agree and acknowledge that the hereinafter mentioned powers and jurisdictions in Yorubaland are vested in His Most Excellent Majesty Edward the Seventh of the United Kingdom of Great Britain and Ireland and of all the British Dominions beyond the Seas, King, Emperor of India, his heirs and Successors, that is to say:

1. Power and Jurisdiction over all persons not being natives of Yorubaland for the repression and punishment of all crimes and offences.

2. Power and Jurisdiction for the Judicial hearing and determination of matters in difference where one or both of the parties to the suit is not a native of Yorubaland.

3. Power and Jurisdiction for the administration and control of the property and persons of all persons not being natives of Yorubaland.

4. Power and Jurisdiction over all persons whomsoever for the repression and punishment of the crimes of murder and manslaughter.

5. Power and Jurisdiction to execute and carry into effect the aforesaid powers and Jurisdiction.

In witness whereof the said parties have hereinto set their hands and seals the day and year first above written.

C. H. HARLEY MOSELEY,

ADEYEMI   his x mark   Alafin of Oyo

Appendix I

AMALGAMATION DAY SPEECHES, 1906

The Ceremony observed at the Promulgation of the Royal Instructions amalgamating the Colony and Protectorate of Lagos and the Protectorate of Southern Nigeria under the title of the Colony and Protectorate of Southern Nigeria, and the speeches delivered in The Law Courts, Lagos, on Tuesday, the 1st day of May, 1906, at 9 a.m.

The Governor having taken the Oaths, the Honourable Mr C. S. Williams rose and addressed His Excellency as follows:

Your Excellency,

Allow me to congratulate you on behalf of the Unofficial members of the Legislative Council and the community at large on this auspicious occasion when a vast territory larger than England has been amalgamated under one Government. This is not the first time in the history of Lagos that she has formed part of a Colony; during her infancy she was under what was known as the West African Settlements, subsequently in 1874 she was made to form part of the Gold Coast Colony when her progress unfortunately was greatly retarded. Consequent on the petition of the community Lagos was in 1886 erected into an independent Colony and a vast Protectorate added on from time to time up to 1901. She then continued her progress by leaps and bounds – today she is again by the Letters Patent just read united and become the capital and the centre of the Colony and Protectorate of Southern Nigeria.

On you, Sir, His Majesty's Government has been pleased to confer the privilege of formulating the scheme for the Government of this vast territory. The weal and woe of the various peoples composing this territory must necessarily depend on the way and manner the territory will be administered, and the community therefore views this scheme with the greatest concern. It cannot be denied that if the administration of the Government is carried on in a manner beneficial to the governed, this Colony and Protectorate will in a few years hence develop to such an extent that it will become one of the priceless gems of His Majesty's dominions on the West Coast of Africa.

There are great possibilities commercially and otherwise for this Colony and Protectorate which you must have noticed during your travels throughout its entire extent and which only require a guiding hand to foster and develop them, and we trust that this guiding hand will not be found wanting consequent on the extended territory.

By this amalgamation the administration is called upon to deal with the idiosyncrasies, manners and customs of various peoples entirely different from each other, and we fervently trust that by a judicious studying of their welfare the whole may form one solid compact of a contented people.

It cannot be denied that the criterion of the goodness of a Government is the degree in which it tends to increase the sum of good qualities in the governed collectively and individually – and the Government which you have this day formed will be judged by its action upon men and by its action upon things, and by what it makes of us its citizens and what it does with us, its tendency to improve or deteriorate the people themselves, the goodness or the badness of the work it performs for us and by means of us.

The citizens of this great Colony and Protectorate believe in and desire its future progress, and your name, Sir, will be handed down to posterity as the originator of what we hope will tend beneficially to their interest.

We further trust that this Colony and Protectorate will be saved from punitive expeditions and the destruction of lives consequent thereon, and that no act of the administration will impair the authority of the Native Kings and Chiefs of the Protectorate, or in any way interfere with their undoubted rights to govern their countries under the judicious guidance of His Majesty's Representatives. We also trust that in the administration of this vast territory of native peoples, the advancement of the natives will be the dominant idea. England has taken under her protection the Government of native races and the promotion of their interests; she can only fulfil this noble mission with the

Appendix I

good will of the natives themselves in the administration of their affairs; and it is the prayer of all the natives of this community that Your Excellency may illustrate by your administration the benevolence, consideration and humanitarian principles which have become historical in connection with the name of Great Britain.

We must again congratulate Your Excellency as the first Governor and Commander-in-Chief over this vast territory. We all know that a Governor has never an easy task of it, but the knowledge you have gained within the last two years in this part of His Majesty's dominions will, we hope, aid you in all your endeavours. We wish Lady Egerton during her stay amongst us good health, and we earnestly hope that in the social circle of this Colony we will have in her another Lady Denton who has left behind her an imperishable name among all classes of the community.

Firmly believing that the All Wise Providence who rules and guides the destinies [sic] of nations will protect with His Almighty power this barque which has this day been launched to sail amidst storms and shoals into a safe haven of prosperity, we wish the Colony of Southern Nigeria abundant peace and prosperity.

His Excellency, the Governor, replied as follows:

Mr Sapara Williams, My Lord Chief Justice, Mr Thorburn, Ladies and Gentlemen,

I thank you for the congratulations which you have just offered me by your spokesman Mr Williams on my appointment as Governor of Southern Nigeria and you may be sure I shall do my best to carry out efficiently the great trust His Most Gracious Majesty the King has reposed in me so as to secure the greatest good to the greatest number of the inhabitants of these lands whether they are natives of the soil or temporary residents. But my appointment is a very small incident in the proceedings of this memorable day. We are met together to hear the promulgation of the Royal Letters Patent constituting this Colony and the Order in Council making its Governor the King's Representative in the Protectorate. (This is being read today at the chief towns throughout this extensive territory). We have met as Loyal Subjects of our King to celebrate the welding together of two of His

Majesty's Protectorates with this Colony, and to celebrate the assumption by the Governor and Council of this Colony of responsibility for the welfare of the peoples of these lands.

I must necessarily talk principally of Lagos but I do not wish to belittle the capable and energetic chiefs of the Coast towns of Southern Nigeria, of the chiefs of Benin, Brass, Bonny, Opobo and Calabar. Hitherto the trade of the Country and its development have been in their hands and they have done yeoman service. There is plenty of room for them and they should not lose by the advent of Lagos traders who can never supplant but only supplement their efforts, and, I hope, introduce new industries. You cannot stand still in the twentieth century; you must either go forward or be overwhelmed by those who do. There is no doubt that we shall go forward: We do not mean to be left behind.

As Mr Williams has said, Lagos has seen many changes. In 1861 the Island first became a British possession. In 1866 it was placed under a Governor in Chief resident in Sierra Leone. In 1874 it became a part of the Gold Coast Colony. In 1886 it was made a separate Colony. Now 20 years later it becomes the capital of the largest and most important British Administration on the West Coast of Africa, an administration possessing a population which cannot be less than six millions, an import and export trade of over five millions sterling, and a revenue exceeding a million sterling a year – raised almost exclusively by taxation of imports. West Africans, like other communities all over the world, strongly object to direct taxation and, more fortunate than most, the inhabitants of the new Southern Nigeria are still free from all direct taxes.

The Old Colony and Protectorate of Lagos is a little more than half the area of Southern Nigeria. The two together form a dominion exceeding eighty thousand square miles in extent. The development of this populous and fertile country only commenced in earnest some ten years ago. The revenue was then only £300,000, and little attempt was made to preserve law and order or to ensure the proper administration of justice except at, and in the vicinity of, the coast ports. The interior was almost unknown. Now we can say, at any rate of the Lagos Province, which is synonymous with the former Colony and Protectorate of Lagos, that it is thoroughly peaceful, that law and order are maintained and the rights of private ownership respected, while the great

Appendix I

chiefs of the Interior have been preserved in their former positions. In the late Protectorate of Southern Nigeria a large extent of the Country is still unknown and unsettled; but much has been done, and in the Settlement and Civilisation of that territory Lagos men have played and are playing a considerable part.

Throughout the territory West of the Niger law and order is established and the same may be said of nearly two-thirds of the territory lying to the east of the river. In a few years more I feel sure that throughout the Protectorate the people will be able to cultivate their village lands without fear of raids by more powerful neighbours, and in the certainty of being left in quiet enjoyment of their farms and homesteads.

Lagos traders will then be able to traverse the whole country in the same way as they now do the portion under settled government, and I wish here to emphasise the fact that the Niger and Calabar Provinces owe very much to Lagos – the Civil Serivce, the Police, the Military Forces are largely recruited from Lagos. Lagos traders are to be met with in all settled districts and, influenced no doubt by the knowledge that they now have their own Governor to appeal to in case of their meeting with difficulties in a strange country, the influx recently into Calabar has been very great. Each successful trader brings back wealth to his native land of Lagos. This is in a small way a reflection of what happens in the United Kingdom. England, Scotland and Ireland are daily sending out their sons to help in the development of the outlying possessions of the British Empire. We have many of them here in the Government service and in the Commercial community. They come to benefit themselves as well as the Empire, and British prosperity is maintained in great part by the trade and wealth brought to the motherland from the British possessions abroad.

In the same way you natives of Lagos send out your sons into the interior parts of the Protectorate and into what was Southern Nigeria, both to West and East of the Niger and into the rich valley of the Cross River, and the growth and prosperity of Lagos must be much increased by the trade secured and the wealth sent home by the emigrants. You have a noble task before you. There should be a great development in the territories to the North and East between here and the Kamerun boundary. I look to you of Lagos to help in its exploitation. I look to you to help me in spreading the blessings of civilisation, of peace, of security of property amongst its people and in providing teachers for the constantly increasing number of schools which are being established throughout this wide and populous territory.

Now Mr Williams mentioned punitive expeditions. There is no one who hates punitive expeditions more than I do. I am sorry to say that they are sometimes necessary. They have been necessary in the past in the interior of the Lagos Protectorate but that time has passed and I hope it will never come back again. Do you think that I, as a Governor, like punitive expeditions? Do you know how expensive they are – how many thousands of pounds they cost which I could expend in making roads or railways or in otherwise increasing the prosperity and the development of the country?

I hate punitive expeditions, but when I hear that slave trade has been rife, that human sacrifices are carried on, when I find that villages that are quietly cultivating their farms are being raided by their neighbours I am compelled to send my Military forces to prevent these occurrences. I hope in a few years they will not be necessary. I should be delighted if the change came in my time, but if it does not I know it must come in the time of my successor.

Mr Williams also spoke of the maintenance of the position of the native chiefs. I wish to maintain their position. I wish to strengthen their powers; but native chiefs are very much like great men in Europe, America and in other parts of the world who often make mistakes or worse. When they do not rule their people for the benefit of the whole population, then I am compelled to interfere and punish them by either temporarily removing them or even deposing them. This is not a new thing. It was done long before the British had possession of the country. You may be sure that I sympathise with the native chiefs and that I will do all I can to help them in the development of their country.

One disadvantage Lagos suffers from is that large ocean steamers cannot enter its harbour. We have all suffered from this disability, some much more seriously than others. Most of you have read the late Miss Kingsley's book about the West Coast and what she, who loved West Africa and its peoples and saw their faults and virtues more clearly than any of us, says of the Lagos Bar. I fear that she fell a victim to several of that numerous class of West Coasters who spin marvellous yarns for the benefit of their fellow passengers. Be that as it may the terrors of our Bar prevented her visiting Lagos, and her not doing so was a very

Appendix I

serious loss for she would have written an account of Lagos and its people better than any yet written and – this is the important point – an account that would have been read wherever English is spoken.

With the large revenues possessed by the new government there will be ample security for any loans that may be required for harbour works and for railway extension.

I was only last week informed by the Secretary of State that tenders have been received for a large Dredger to be employed in attempting to remove the Bar – that barrier which cuts off Lagos from free intercourse with other countries.

If dredging is ineffectual then the scheme prepared long ago by Messrs Coode Son and Matthews of moles to ensure a deep channel to the sea will be taken in hand without further delay.

You all know the efforts that have been made during the last two or three years to establish a large cotton-growing industry in West Africa. Nowhere have these efforts met with such success as in Lagos hinterland.

There is now little doubt that, given the establishment of sufficient Ginneries in the Cotton growing districts, the cultivation of cotton can be developed to almost any extent. It is the absence of ginning and transport facilities that has hitherto prevented this development and there shall be no reason to fear that we cannot grow cotton here and place it on the Liverpool market as cheaply as can be done in America. The growers of cotton in America are chiefly descendants of West Africans – you must show them that you on this side of the Atlantic are not inferior agriculturists to those of your race in America.

Perhaps I may add here that we have met today to celebrate a purely Colonial function. I have not invited any of the chiefs of the hinterland. This is because I have directed my officers in the interior to proclaim today, in the presence of the Chiefs, His Most Gracious Majesty's Order in Council constituting the new Protectorate and making the Governor of this Colony His Majesty's Representative in that Protectorate.

I trust that the native Chiefs will appreciate the benefits that should result from the whole Protectorate being administered from Lagos.

Lagos has been successively placed under Sierra Leone and under the Gold Coast, now it is not placed under any outside administration but becomes the Capital of the important one that we have just assisted to inaugurate.

Some people have said that Lagos is to disappear, that it is swallowed up in Southern Nigeria – I hope that you will not believe this. In calling this Province the Western or Lagos Province it is my intention to preserve the old name which is naturally loved by the natives of the Land. Lagos will become better known than ever. There is little doubt that in twenty years' time the population of this town will exceed 100,000. By that time the railway we are now extending to Oshogbo on the way to the Niger will have reached that river and probably will have been continued into the heart of Northern Nigeria. Lagos will then become the entrepôt and distributing centre for all the trade of the hinterland. Lagos Merchants both European and Native are amongst the most enterprising on the Coast and I have every faith that you will rise to the occasion and that you will see the necessity for increased energy and enterprise.

These countries are developing rapidly. Education and religion are spreading among their peoples. Commerce is increasing. For this progress I have to thank my officers – both Europeans and Natives of West Africa and also the large and increasing body of enterprising European traders. Let there be less jealousy between European and Native. One cannot get on without the other and the more cordially they work together the better for both.

Lagos in her time has owed much to the older settlements of Sierra Leone and the Gold Coast. Now in turn she is assisting in the Civilisation of less advanced communities of the Niger Delta.

I wish most fervently prosperity to the new Administration and I hope you will help me in making it prosperous.

Appendix J

STATISTICAL RECORD OF THE PROGRESS OF SOUTHERN NIGERIA TRADE AND COMMERCE

Summary of the Trade of Southern Nigeria

	IMPORTS						EXPORTS						
	Merchandise						Merchandise						
Year	Coml. £	Govt. £	Total £	Coin and Bullion £	Total £		Produce of S. Nigeria £	Foreign Goods £	Total £	Coin and Bullion £	Total £	Total Trade £	Customs Duties £
1900	1,735,244	—*	1,735,244	210,809	1,946,053		1,858,091	28,792	1,886,883	131,834	2,087,717	4,033,770	516,847
1901	1,452,668	359,464	1,812,132	222,269	2,034,401		1,986,192	32,583	2,018,775	144,163	2,162,938	4,197,339	563,065
1902	1,706,944	270,671	1,977,615	199,611	2,177,226		2,416,345	96,034	2,512,379	80,182	2,592,561	4,769,797	692,168
1903	1,892,025	236,121	2,128,146	228,746	2,356,892		2,201,916	154,701	2,356,617	221,691	2,578,308	4,935,200	660,963
1904	2,210,859	211,856	2,422,715	289,577	2,712,292		2,604,760	176,353	2,781,113	148,825	2,929,438	5,641,730	766,744
1905	2,349,046	243,359	2,592,405	266,612	2,859,017		2,386,212	166,499	2,552,711	178,026	2,730,737	5,589,754	793,168
1906	2,537,750	309,566	2,847,316	300,951	3,148,267		2,773,386	177,006	2,950,392	201,026	3,151,418	6,299,685	885,585
1907	3,540,723	298,617	3,839,340	599,566	4,438,906		3,611,567	251,764	3,863,331	339,372	4,202,708	8,641,609	1,182,781
1908	3,262,309	784,263	4,046,572	238,258	4,284,830		3,102,143	233,768	3,335,911	73,377	3,409,288	7,694,118	1,016,657
1909	3,514,011	1,015,593	4,529,604	432,940	4,962,544		3,829,315	284,922	4,114,237	54,924	4,169,161	9,131,705	991,401
1910	4,578,989	543,381	5,122,370	734,965	5,857,335		4,963,749	294,703	5,258,452	45,734	5,304,186	11,161,521	1,441,305
1911	4,727,472	510,102	5,234,874	446,106	5,680,980		5,072,418	281,683	5,354,101	37,367	5,391,468	11,072,147	1,441,775

Imports and Exports in transit to and from Porto Novo were included in the trade figures up to 1904.
* Commercial and Government Imports not shown separately in 1900.

Appendix K

SOUTHERN NIGERIAN CENSUS, 1911

(i) Distribution

Area in square miles	Province	Total population	Natives of West Africa	Europeans	Asiatics	Other non-West Africans	Density of natives per square mile	Remarks
28,600	Western	2,152,848	2,151,483	862*	63	440	75.23	*Including 72 Europeans on ocean boats.
22,670	Central	2,408,594	2,407,664	906†	3	21	106.20	†Including 476 Europeans on ocean boats.
28,610	Eastern	3,297,247	3,296,602	586‡	33	26	115.22	‡Including 158 Europeans on ocean boats.
79,880		7,858,689	7,855,749	2,354**	99	487	98.34	**Including 706 Europeans on ocean boats.

(ii) *Western Province*

Area in square miles	District	Total population	Natives of West Africa	Europeans	Asiatics	Other non-West Africans	Average density of natives per square mile	Remarks
1,167	Badagri	91,113	91,134	21	—	—	78.07	
1,869	Egba (Abeokuta)	264,814	264,723	80	—	11	141.63	
1,720	Epe	45,276	45,255	21	—	—	26.31	
3,192	Ibadan	341,968	341,875	66	20	7	107.10	
572	Ikorodu	75,742	75,784	3	—	5	132.40	
2,964	Ilesha	339,290	339,289	1	—	—	114.46	
1,467	Ijebu-Ode	131,331	131,326	5	—	—	89.52	
547	Lagos	108,266	102,190	621*	43	412	186.82	*Including 72 Europeans on ocean boats
1,390	Meko	6,964	6,950	1	—	4	5.00	
3,121	Ondo	164,562	164,558	4	—	—	55.72	
2,568	Oshogbo	370,898	370,878	20	—	—	144.42	
8,023	Oyo	217,603	217,583	19	—	1	27.11	
28,600		2,152,848	2,151,483	862†	63	440	75.23	†Including 72 Europeans on ocean boats

(iii) *Central Province*

Area in square miles	District	Total population	Natives of West Africa	Europeans	Asiatics	Other non-West Africans	Average density of native population per square mile	Remarks
1,584	Abo (Aboh)	101,673	101,647	25	—	1	64.17	
465	Agbor	75,008	74,997	6	—	—	161.28	
822	Asaba	200,280	200,262	16	—	2	243.63	
678	Awka	252,070	252,057	7	—	6	371.77	
3,752	Benin	84,377	84,340	37	—	—	22.48	
925	Forcados	37,657	37,171	480*	1	5	40.18	*Including 396 on ocean boats
1,727	Idah	49,273	49,259	14	—	—	28.52	
1,761	Ifon	78,683	78,680	3	—	—	44.68	
1,629	Ishan (Ubiaja)	125,849	125,840	9	—	—	76.94	
657	Kwale	135,004	135,000	4	—	—	205.48	
1,441	Onitsha	400,000	399,916	79	—	5	277.53	
2,576	Okwoga	183,365	183,359	6	—	—	71.18	
1,840	Sapele	85,743	85,654	87†	2	—	46.55	†Including 31 on ocean boats
1,537	Udi	458,377	458,368	9	—	—	298.22	
1,276	Warri	141,740	141,614	124‡	—	2	110.98	‡Including 49 on ocean boats
22,670		2,408,594	2,407,664	906**	3	21	106.21	**Including 476 Europeans on ocean boats

(iv) *Eastern Province*

Area in square miles	District	Total population	Natives of West Africa	Europeans	Asiatics	Other non-West Africans	Average density of natives per square miles	Remarks
827	Aba	157,642	157,641	1	—	—	190.61	
263	Abak	27,278	27,275	3	—	—	103.70	
1,774	Abakaliki	400,000	399,995	5	—	—	225.47	
1,159	Afikpo	181,521	181,512	9	—	—	156.61	
697	Ahoada	98,346	98,339	7	—	—	141.08	
421	Aro-Chuku	18,091	18,088	3	—	—	42.96	
1,045	Bende	350,000	349,997	3	—	—	334.92	
301	Bonny	14,393	14,268	118*	6	1	47.40	*Including 88 on ocean boats
3,790	Brass	90,221	90,171	50†	—	—	23.79	†Including 33 on ocean boats
1,217	Calabar	57,742	57,544	150	27	21	47.28	
2,263	Degema	127,276	127,287	89	—	—	56.22	
690	Eket	184,016	183,987	29	—	—	266.64	
1,776	Ikom	68,714	68,172	2	—	—	38.38	
455	Ikot-Ekpene	198,796	198,787	8	—	1	436.89	
124	Itu	27,361	27,341	20	—	—	220.49	
1,710	Oban	5,361	5,837	2	—	—	3.41	
960	Obubra	96,173	96,168	5	—	—	100.17	
3,211	Obudu	84,666	84,661	5	—	—	26.36	
2,430	Ogoja	230,583	230,572	11	—	—	94.88	
919	Okigwi	123,601	123,594	7	—	—	134.48	
945	Opobo	199,519	199,432	84‡	—	3	211.03	‡Including 37 on ocean boats
1,085	Owerri	400,000	399,984	16	—	—	368.64	
548	Uyo	156,009	156,000	9	—	—	284.67	
23,610		3,297,247	3,296,602	536**	33	26	115.22	**Including 158 Europeans on ocean boats

Appendix L

STATEMENT BY THE SECRETARY OF STATE FOR THE COLONIES ON THE TREATIES BETWEEN THE CROWN AND THE OIL RIVERS CHIEFS, SEPTEMBER–OCTOBER, 1958

These Treaties have been made from 1884 onwards with the Chiefs in areas which now form part of the Eastern Region.

Dr Udoma and Mr Biriye have spoken earnestly about these Treaties and I have given very careful consideration to what they said.

The Minorities Commission said that they did not feel called upon, nor indeed, they added, were they qualified, to form conclusions on any legal or moral obligations of Her Majesty's Government which might arise from these Treaties.

It is for me, as Secretary of State, to deal with these legal and moral obligations, and if I do so at some length you will, I know, forgive me. Matters arising from Treaties entered into by Her Majesty's predecessors demand careful and detailed consideration.

There were many of these Treaties, and they all followed one or other of two forms, a shorter version and a longer version. In each case the Chief concerned placed his people and his territory under the protection of the British Crown and undertook to refrain from entering into relations with foreign powers except with the sanction of Her Majesty's Government. Under the longer version the Chiefs concerned entered into a number of specific obligations, and in particular agreed to assist British officers in the execution of their duties and to act on their advice in matters relating to the administration of justice, the development of the resources of the country, the interests of commerce and in other matters relating to peace, order and good government and what was called the general progress of civilisation.

There has of course been a great alteration in the circumstances

Appendix L

of Nigeria since these Treaties were entered into some seventy years ago. As I think we all know, the British Crown has for a great many years exercised without question full jurisdiction over all the areas comprised in the Protectorate of Nigeria, including the particular areas to which the various Treaties relate, and has made provision by various orders in Council for the government of the whole country. At the time when the Treaties were made, the Chiefs concerned constituted the only form of government in their respective territories, but they have long since ceased to exercise the functions of government, and it is no longer possible to say that there now exist authorities who can be regarded as effective successors to the Nigerian parties to the Treaties. I do not think it is necessary for me to point out that the material and cultural circumstances of the inhabitants of what is now the Eastern Region have undergone enormous changes during these seventy years; indeed it would be no exaggeration to say that these circumstances have been transformed beyond recognition. With the march of time new institutions have come into being to replace the old authorities that entered into the Treaties, and the descendants of those who formerly were under their rule now look to the various legislatures and governments established by Her Majesty in Council as the source of their laws and as the authority responsible (subject to the ultimate authority of the United Kingdom Government) for the peace, order and good government of the various parts of Nigeria.

Various arguments have been advanced, and advanced very strongly and capably, to the effect that, notwithstanding the radical changes in the circumstances of Nigeria between the eighties of the last century and the present day, and the fact that the tribal authorities that made them have long ceased to exist as such, the Treaties oblige the Crown, as a matter of law, to accord special treatment to the inhabitants of the areas concerned which the Crown is not obliged to accord to other inhabitants of Nigeria.

I ought at this stage to refer to the strict legal position. I am advised that Treaties of this kind have no standing in international law and it follows from this that it would be quite inappropriate to adopt the suggestion that the question of the proper interpretation of the Treaties should be referred to the International Court. I am also advised on the highest authority that such Treaties confer no rights that are enforceable in our Courts, and it seems clear therefore that the question of the interpretation of the Treaties is not one which could appropriately be referred (as had been suggested) to the Judicial Committee of the Privy Council.

In stating, gentlemen, as I must, that in the view of Her Majesty's Government these Treaties did not create obligations that could be enforced either under international law or municipal law, I do not of course wish to imply for one moment that these Treaties were merely worthless scraps of paper that created no obligations whatever. Her Majesty's Government has in fact both accepted and I think faithfully discharged the obligation to extend the protection of the Crown over the territories affected by the Treaties and their inhabitants and it is still discharging that obligation at the present moment. It should be remembered however, that the inhabitants of the areas affected by the Treaties are not the only persons in Nigeria who are entitled to Her Majesty's protection. The people of the Colony of Lagos, who are British subjects, and the people of all the rest of Nigeria (whether Protectorate or Trust Territory), who are British protected persons, are all entitled to receive, and do in fact receive, the same degree of protection and consideration as do the inhabitants of those particular areas affected by the Treaties. I could not therefore accept the proposition that because under Treaties entered into many years ago the inhabitants of particular areas were given a right to protection, they are entitled to special treatment at the present day, when the circumstances are radically different, and when every inhabitant of Nigeria is entitled to Her Majesty's protection.

So in view of what I have said, it may be asked what obligations Her Majesty's Government regards the Treaties as creating at the present time. In my view there are moral obligations on Her Majesty's Government to secure justice and fair dealing on the matters mentioned in the Treaties. We have always sought to carry out these obligations and I certainly do not propose to repudiate them now. As I have said, under many of the Treaties the Chiefs agreed to accept the advice of the British authorities in matters relating to 'peace, order and good government and the general progress of civilisation'. This progress necessarily involves progress in constitutional development such as that on which we have for so long been engaged together and the inhabitants of the areas affected by the Treaties have of course participated in the various steps that have been taken towards

Appendix L

self-government. They are, and have for long been, represented on the Federal and Regional legislatures.

The progress towards self-government has been a continuous process that leads logically to the position where Her Majesty's Government in the United Kingdom will soon be relinquishing its special responsibilities as the protecting Power. We intend therefore to pursue this policy to its logical conclusion, namely, the grant of full self-government, in the confident belief that there is nothing in the Treaties inconsistent with this course.

Bibliography

1. ARCHIVES

At the Public Record Office, London

(i) CO. series: 96, 147, 148, 149, 150, 151, 267, 380, 444, 446, 464, 473, 520, 554, 583, 588, 591, 592, 657, 659.
(ii) FO. series: 2, 84, 97.

At the National Archives, Enugu and Ibadan

Series of dispatches, reports and constitutional instruments:
Ben. Dist.
Cal. prof.
CSE.
CSO.
Riv. prof.

2. INTELLIGENCE REPORTS

Blair, J. *Intelligence report on Abeokuta,* 1937.
Jackson, J. *Ngwa clan intelligence report with a supplementary memorandum by E. J. G. Kelly,* 1930.
Newns, A. F. F. P. *Epie-Atissa group intelligence report,* 1935.
Newns, A. F. F. P. *Re-organization report on the Kalabari clan,* 1947.
Porter, J. C. *Okrika intelligence report,* 1933.

3. PARLIAMENTARY SOURCES

Hansard

(i) House of Commons Debates.
(ii) House of Lords Debates.

Bibliography

Command Papers

C. 6048: *General Act of the Brussels conference, 1889–90 with annexed declaration*, 1890.
C. 7596: *Africa. No. 1. (1895). Report on the administration of the Niger Coast Protectorate, August 1891 – August 1894*, 1895.
Cd. 2325: *Papers relating to the construction of railways in Sierra Leone, Lagos, and the Gold Coast*, 1904.
Cd. 4523: *Further correspondence relating to railway construction in Nigeria*, 1909.
Cd. 4589: *Papers relating to mechanical transport in the colonies*, 1909.
Cd. 4906: *Report of the committee of inquiry into the liquor trade in Southern Nigeria, 1909*, 1909.
Cd. 4907: *Inquiry into the liquor trade in Southern Nigeria – Minutes of evidence and appendices, 1909*, 1909.
Cmd. 468: *Sir F. D. Lugard's report on the amalgamation of Northern and Southern Nigeria, and administration, 1912–1919*, 1920.
Cmd. 2744: *Report by the Hon. W. G. A. Ormsby-Gore, M.P., on his visit to West Africa during the year 1926*, 1926.
Cmd. 3784: *Dispatch from the Secretary of State for the Colonies (Lord Passfield) to the Officer Administering the Government of Nigeria regarding the report of the Commission of Inquiry into the disturbances at Aba and other places in South-Eastern Nigeria in November and December 1929*, 1931.

4. SOURCES AT THE COLONIAL OFFICE LIBRARY

(i) African (West), No. 591. CO., September 1899, Nigeria – financial arrangements.
(ii) African (West), No. 1005. Confidential – Correspondence (May 15th, 1913 to Jan. 27th, 1914) relating to the amalgamation of Northern and Southern Nigeria.
(iii) West African Pamphlets.

5. SOURCES AT THE AFRICANA SECTION OF THE UNIVERSITY OF IBADAN LIBRARY

(i) Minutes of the Central Native Council.

(ii) The Macaulay Papers.
(iii) Judgment of the Lords of the Judicial Committee of the Privy Council (Privy Council Appeal No. 30 of 1919) delivered on 11 July 1921.

6. THESES AND DISSERTATIONS

Adeleye, R. A. *The overthrow of the Sokoto Caliphate, 1890–1903* (Ph.D. Thesis), Ibadan 1967.
Aderibigde, A. A. B. *The expansion of the Lagos Protectorate, 1863–1900* (Ph.D. Thesis), London 1959.
Adewoye, O. *The legal profession in Southern Nigeria, 1863–1943* (Ph.D. Dissertation), Columbia, New York, 1968.
Afigbo, A. E. *The warrant chief system in Eastern Nigeria, 1900–1929* (Ph.D. Thesis), Ibadan 1964.
Agiri, B. A. *Development of local government in Ogbomoso, 1850–1950* (M.A. Dissertation), Ibadan 1966.
Akintoye, S. A. *The Ekiti-parapo and the Kiriji war* (Ph.D. Thesis), Ibadan 1966.
Atanda, J. A. *The new Oyo Empire: a study of British indirect rule in Oyo Province, 1894–1934* (Ph.D. Thesis), Ibadan 1967.
Awe, B. A. *The rise of Ibadan as a Yoruba power in the nineteenth century* (D.Phil Thesis), Oxford 1964.
Ayantuga, O. O. *Ijebu and its neighbours, 1851–1914* (Ph.D. Thesis), London 1965.
Folayan, K. *Egbado and Yoruba-Aja power politics, 1832–1894* (M.A. Dissertation), Ibadan 1967.
Gbadamosi, G. O. *The growth of Islam among the Yoruba, 1841–1908* (Ph.D. Thesis), Ibadan 1968.
Hopkins, A. G. *An economic history of Lagos, 1880–1914* (Ph.D. Thesis), London 1964.
Ifemesia, C. C. *British enterprise on the Niger, 1830–1869* (Ph.D Thesis), London 1959.
Igbafe, P. A. *Benin under British Administration, 1897–1938* (Ph.D. Thesis), Ibadan 1967.
Jenkins, G. D. *Politics in Ibadan* (Ph.D. Dissertation), Evanston (Ill.) 1965.
Nair, K. K. *Politics and society in Old Calabar, 1841–1906* (Ph.D. Thesis), Ibadan, 1967.

Nworah, K. K. D. *Humanitarian pressure groups and British attitudes to West Africa, 1895–1915* (Ph.D. Thesis), London 1966.
Omu, F. I. A. *The Nigerian newspaper press, 1859–1937: a study in origins, growth and influence* (Ph.D. Thesis), Ibadan, 1965.
Smith, S. R. *The Ibo people. (A study of the religion and customs of a tribe in the Southern provinces of Nigeria)* (vol. 1, Ph.D. Thesis), Cambridge 1929.

7. ARTICLES, PAPERS AND ADDRESSES

Atanda, J. A. 'The Iseyin-Okeiho rising of 1916: an example of socio-political conflict in colonial Nigeria'. *JHSN.*, vol. 4, no. 4, June 1969.
Asmis, W. 'Law and policy relating to the natives of the Gold Coast and Nigeria', parts 1 and 2. *JAS.*, vol. 12, 1912–13.
Birtwistle, C. A. 'Cotton growing and Nigeria', *PRCI.*, vol. 39, 1907–8.
Bruce, C. 'The Crown colonies and places', *PRCI.*, vol. 36, 1904–5.
Chamberlain, J. Annual Dinner Speech at the Royal Colonial Institute, 31 Mar. 1897, *PRCI.*, vol. 28, 1896–7.
Churchill, W. S. 'The development of Africa', *JAS.*, vol. 6, 1906–7.
Cowan, A. A. 'Sir Walter Egerton's pioneer adventure: cycling across Nigeria in 1905', *West African Pamphlets*, vol. 3, 9346, No. 71, Sept. 1933.
Dorward, D. C. 'The development of the British colonial administration among the Tiv, 1900–1949,' *African Affairs*, vol. 68, no. 273, Oct. 1969.
Dumett, R. E. 'The campaign against malaria and the expansion of scientific, medical and sanitary services in British West Africa, 1898–1910', *African Historical Studies*, vol. 1, no. 2, 1968.
Johnston, H. H., 'British West Africa and the trade of the interior', *PRCI.*, vol. 20, 1888–9.
Marlborough, Duke of, Presidential address given on 5 July 1906, *JAS.*, vol. 6, 1906–7.
Morel, E. D. (E.D.M.) 'The Crewe-Read tragedy and its sequel', *The West African Mail*, 21 Sept. 1906.
Onslow, Earl of, Speech given on 8 March 1907, *JAS.*, vol. 6, Lond., 1906–7.

Ottenberg, S. 'Ibo oracles and intergroup', relations *South Western Journal of Anthropology*, vol. 14, 1958.
Porter, A. T. 'The social background of decision-makers in Sierra Leone', *Sierra Leone Studies*, New Series, no. 13, June 1960.
Sampson, M. J. 'George Ekem Ferguson of Anomabu', *Transactions of the Gold Coast and Togoland Historical Society*, vol. 2, 1956.
Thompson, H. N. 'The forests of Southern Nigeria', *JAS.*, vol. 10, 1910–11.
Ryder, A. F. C. 'Missionary activities in the kingdom of Warri to the early nineteenth century', *JHSN.*, vol. 2, no. 1, Dec. 1960.
— 'The Benin Missions', *JHSN.*, vol. 2, no. 2, Dec. 1961.

8. NEWSPAPERS AND MAGAZINES

The African Mail.
The Lagos Standard.
The Lagos Weekly Record.
The Nigerian Chronicle.
The Nigerian Daily Times.
The Nigerian Times.
The West African Mail.
The Westminster Gazette.
West Africa.

9. BOOKS

Ajayi, J. F. A. *Christian Missions in Nigeria, 1841–1891.* London 1965.
Ajayi, J. F. A. and **Smith, R. S.** *Yoruba warfare in the nineteenth century*, Cambridge 1964.
Ajisafe, A. K. *History of Abeokuta*, Bungay 1924.
Akinyele, I. B. *The outlines of Ibadan History*, Lagos 1946.
Alagoa, E. J. *The small brave city-state*, Ibadan 1964.
Anene, J. C. *Southern Nigeria in transition, 1885–1906*, Cambridge 1966.
Ayandele, E. A. *The Missionary Impact on Modern Nigeria, 1842–1914*, London 1966.

Bibliography

Biobaku, S. O. *The Egba and their neighbours, 1842–72*, Oxford 1957.
Blyden, E. W. *West Africa before Europe*, London 1905.
Boyle, A. *Trenchard*, London 1962.
Bruce, C. *The broad stone of Empire*, vol. 1, London 1910.
Burns A. *History of Nigeria*, London 1958.
Dike, K. O. *Trade and politics in the Niger Delta, 1830–1885*, Oxford 1956.
Egharevba, J. *A short history of Benin*, Ibadan 1960.
Elias, T. O. *Groundwork of Nigerian law*, London 1954.
Flint, J. E. *Sir George Goldie and the making of Nigeria*, London 1960.
Folarin, A. *The demise of the independence of Egbaland. (The Ijemo trouble)*, Parts 1 and 2, Lagos 1916 and 1919.
Fyfe, C. *A history of Sierra Leone*, London 1962.
Ikime, O. *Merchant prince of the Niger Delta (The rise and fall of Nana Olomu last governor of the Benin River)*. London 1968.
— *Niger Delta Rivalry: Itsekiri-Urhobo relations and the European presence, 1884–1936*, London 1969.
Johnson, S. (ed. O. Johnson), *The history of the Yorubas*, London 1921.
Jones, G. I. *The trading states of the Oil Rivers*, London 1963.
Kimble, D. *A political history of Ghana*, Oxford 1963.
Kirk-Greene, A. H. M. (ed.) *The principles of native administration in Nigeria: selected documents, 1900–1947*, London 1965.
Kopytoff, J. H. *A preface to modern Nigeria*, Madison 1965.
Losi, J. B. *History of Lagos*, Lagos 1967.
Loynes, J. B. *The West African Currency Board, 1912–1962*, London 1962.
Morel, E. D. *Affairs of West Africa*, London 1902.
— *Nigeria: its peoples and its problems*, London 1911.
Newbury, C. W. *The western slave coast and its rulers*, Oxford 1961.
Newlyn, W. T. and **Rowan, D. C.** *Money and banking in British Colonial Africa*, Oxford 1954.
Nicolson, I. F. *The administration of Nigeria, 1900–1960*, London 1969.
O'Brien, B. *She had a magic*, London 1958.
Partridge, C. *Cross river natives*, London 1905.
Perham, M. *Lugard: the years of authority, 1898–1945*, London 1960.

Perham, M. *Native administration in Nigeria*, London 1937.
— *The colonial reckoning*, London 1961.
Speed, E. A. *Lagos revised edition of ordinances and orders and rules with appendix*, London 1902.
Stallard, G. and **Richards, E. H.** *Laws of the Colony of Lagos, 1865–93*, London 1894.
Symonds, R. *The British and their successors*, London 1966.
Szereszewski, R. *Structural changes in the economy of Ghana, 1891–1911*, London 1965.
Tamuno, T. N. *Nigeria and elective representation, 1923–1947*, London 1966.
— *The police in modern Nigeria*, Ibadan 1970.
Thomas, I. B. *Life history of Herbert Macaulay*, Lagos 1947.
— *The House of Docemo: full proceedings of an inquiry into the method of selection of a Head to the House of Docemo before H. L. Ward-Price, Commissioner*, Lagos 1933.
Wight, M. *The development of the legislative council, 1606–1945*, London 1946.

10 MISCELLANEOUS

Proceedings of the General Conference on review of the Constitution, January, 1950, Lagos 1950.
Report by the Resumed Nigeria Constitutional Conference, 1958, Lagos 1958.
Who was who, 1929–40, London 1947.

Index

Aba, 43, 44, 166, 193, 331
Abak, 43, 44
Abakiliki, 43, 44, 168
Abaku, 26
Abeokuta, 64–6, 68–72, 77–81, 82–5, 88–91, 98, 170, 173, 175, 261, 269–72, 273, 296, 307
Abeokuta, Alake of, 72–3, 76, 80–1, 86–92, 186, 216: *see* Gbadebo I
Abinis, 155
Aboh, 10, 43, 168, 223, 227
Abonnema, 5
Aborigines' Protection Society (APS), 36, 51–2, 70, 97, 107, 171, 173, 177, 179, 205, 256, 322: *see* Lagos APS
Accra, 145, 191
Adamawa, 60, 350
Addo, 25–6, 31
Ademola, Prince (later Alake), 81–2
Adeniyi-Jones, C. C., 196
Adeyemi, Alafin, 81
Afenmai (formerly Kukuurku), 224, 231–2
Afikpo, 43, 44
African Association, 260
Africans, economic and social changes among, 13ff., 191ff., 222–3, 269ff., 287ff., 309ff., 342–352; European attitude to, 2ff., 17ff., 32ff., 55–63, 95ff., 103, 184ff., 195, 339–52; internal dissension among, 1ff., 222ff., 349–352; political developments among, 24ff., 122, 154–5, 342ff.; traders among, 13ff., 256, 265–7

Agbala, 39–40, 341
Agbebi, G. D., 197, 199
Agbebi, M., 99
Agbor, 4, 43, 54, 162, 165, 219, 321–3
Agiri, B. A., 215
agriculture, 13ff., 59, 101, 146, 243, 246, 249, 252ff., 263, 277, 309, 310, 318, 345, 348
Aguobasimi (later Eweka II of Benin), 23
Ahoada, 43, 44
Ajasa, Kitoyi, 90, 123, 131, 134, 136, 137, 140, 142, 230
Ajiliti, 25
Ajimoko, Owa, 177
Ajose, 203ff.
Akassa, 43, 224–5, 227, 306
Ake, 88
Akiode, 175
Akitoye, Oba of Lagos, 3–4
Akunakunas, 155
Akure, 4, 68, 224
Alakes, 2
Alexander, C. W., 313–14
Allesime, Chief, 321
Amakiri dynasty, 5, 22–3
amalgamation project, 125, 142, 152, 158, 173, 188, 221–2, 344–345, 348–9
Amassoma, 294
Ambrose, W. G., 177–80, 229
Anambra river, 293
Anderson, J. (later Lord Waverley), 68–9, 101
Anglicans, 308, 331
Anglo-French frontier problems, 170

409

Index

Anglo-German Boundary Commission, 320
annexations, 18ff.
Annie Pepple House, 4–5
anthropology, 33, 56, 58–9, 109, 163, 199
Anti-Slavery Society (A.P.S.), 97
Anti-Slavery and Aborigines Protection Society (A.S.–A.P.S.), 97, 101, 103, 104, 320, 328–31
Antrobus, R. L., 36, 66, 70, 84–5, 108, 126, 152, 172, 194, 232–3, 234, 236–8, 274, 293, 324
Apapa, 281, 285, 305, 348
Apapa Land Case, 206, 310–11
Apetu, head chief of Ipetu, 211
Aro, 74, 84, 86, 89
Aro-Chuku, 38, 39, 43, 44, 306, 334
Aro expedition, 34ff., 43, 271
Aro Field Force, 37ff., 53, 59, 324
Aro Hinterland Expedition, 43
Aro Long JuJu, 36–8, 39, 56, 59, 164, 341
Aromire, Chief, 216
Aros, 10–11, 14–16, 36ff., 50, 52, 54, 56, 58, 59, 65, 237, 326–7, 339, 341
Asaba, 12, 25, 40–1, 43, 56, 155, 227, 340
Asani, Bale, 26
Aseh, 10
Ashantis, 36, 105, 18
Ashanti War, 37, 38
Ashogbon, Chief, 134
Asmis, W., 319
Asquith, H. H., 119–20, 290
Atanda, J. A., 215
Ataiyero, Owa, 177–8
Auchi, 162
autocracy, 95ff., 122ff., 147, 164, 191, 244, 351
Awe, B. A., 31
Awka, 39, 44, 155, 165
Awopa, Asada, 25–6
Awujale, of Ijebu Ode, 29–30
Azumini, 166, 306

Badagry, 25, 176, 305
Bakana, 5
Balogun, Ali, 134
Bamawo, Chief, 321
banks, 15, 268
Bank of British West Africa, 269
Barboy House, 5
Baro, 285
Baro–Kano Railway, 240, 285
barter system, 14
Bassambiri, 12, 23
Bassey, J. Coco, 193
Bauchi, 60, 350
Bedwell, Horace, 42–3, 45–6, 53, 55, 56, 166, 330–1
Beecroft, John, 3
Bellamy, C. V., 197
Bende, 39, 43, 44, 163, 331
Benin, Bight of, 2, 7, 11
Benin City, 21, 23, 43, 96, 116, 161, 219, 253, 304, 327; Benin City Native Council, 116
Benin, kingdom of, 4, 10, 14, 21, 22–3, 25, 43, 218, 224, 321, 339, 350; Benin Native Council, 161–162
Benin River, 15, 225, 327; Benin River Native Council, 237
Benue River, 14, 224, 227, 276
Benue Valley, 60, 350
Berlin West Africa Conference, 17, 224
Beverley, Major W. H., 43
Biafra, Bight of, 2, 7, 11
Bida, 60
Binigie, Chief, 321
Binis, 50
Birtwistle, C. A., 250, 260, 267, 279
Blyden, E. W., 48–9, 170, 193, 195
Bob-Manuel, Chief, 5
Boma, 319
Bonny, 4–5, 43, 164, 267, 305, 306, 327, 331, 333, 334
Bornu, 14, 60, 350
botanical stations, 252–3
boundary problems, 222ff.
Boyle, A. G., 54, 91, 109
Braide, Chief Will, 5
Bramston, J., 125
Brass, 43, 224–5, 227, 294, 303, 305, 327, 331, 333–4

Index

Brass-Akassa people, 224
British, Administration, 1ff., 16ff., 28–32, 33ff., 45ff., 64ff., 84ff., 95ff., 127ff., 148ff., 184ff., 222ff., 246ff., 317ff., 339–52; annexations, 2, 18ff.; concept of civilisation, 12, 58; conquests, 42ff.; courts, 148ff.; humanitarians, 5–7, 97, 103, 314; Parliament, 97, 99, 104ff.; public opinion, 97ff.; Railway Commissioner, 74; Treasury, 225–6: *see* Colonial Office, Foreign Office, House of Commons
British Cotton Growing Association (B.C.G.A.), 261ff., 309, 348
British East Africa Protectorate, 296
British Somaliland, 296
bronze, 14
Brown, H. Buowari, 24–5, 28
Brussels Conference, 17, 26, 225, 289, 290
Brussels Liquor Conference, 301
Buchanan, A. M., 93
Buckingham, Duke of, 136
Buguma, 5
Butler, F. G. A., 195, 232, 250, 284, 313
Butler-Wright, H., 117
Buxton, C. R., 119

Calabar, 5, 9–10, 24, 28, 39, 43, 55, 110, 151, 161, 191, 193, 238, 248, 253, 276, 305, 327, 331–5, 349; New Calabar, 334
Calabar, Obongs of, 186
Calabar Observer, 110
Campbell-Bannerman, H., 290
Cameron, D., 208
Cameroons, 293, 297
canoes, 16
Canterbury, Archbishop of, 290–1
Carter, G. T., 26, 137
Carter-Denton bridges, 285, 294
Carr, Henry, 193–5, 199
Central Native Council, 116–19, 132ff., 171, 173, 183, 205, 208ff.
Central Province, 42, 45, 59, 102, 120, 129, 135, 149, 154–5, 156, 159, 162, 168, 188, 200, 222, 238, 260, 280, 305, 307–8, 312, 319, 328–33
Chad, 65
Chad, Lake, 236, 277, 282
Chamberlain, Joseph, 27, 37, 48–9, 52, 100, 104, 107, 111, 234, 237, 247, 256ff., 272, 277–8, 282–3, 324, 343, 346
Chambers of Commerce, 51, 99, 100, 103, 173: *see* Liverpool Chamber of Commerce, Manchester Chamber of Commerce
Christianity, 4, 5, 7, 11, 16ff., 40–2, 49, 56, 58, 144, 176, 191, 212–13, 218, 297, 301, 305ff., 308–9, 328, 331, 342, 346
Church issue, 132, 143ff.
Church Mission Society, 11, 145, 213, 295, 301, 347
Churchill, W. S., 240, 247, 262
civil war, 349–50
coastal communities, 1, 17
cocoa, 260, 265, 314, 345
coercive legislation, 45ff., 109, 120, 135
Cole, W. A., 196, 199
Collective Punishment Ordinance, 45ff.
Colonial Audit Department, 87, 93
colonial chaplaincy, 132, 143ff.
Colonial Office attitude to African affairs, 28, 95ff., 105ff., 123ff., 139, 150, 153–4, 160, 174, 195–202, 211, 220, 231–3, 233–45, 249–50, 268, 276, 290ff., 318, 319–23, 324, 337; relations with Egerton, 45, 118, 181, 196, 232, 238, 249–50, 284, 312; relations with MacGregor, 27, 66–7, 69, 73ff., 83–5, 179, 204, 216–17, 236–7, 255, 262, 271–5; statements by Colonial Secretaries, 21, 48, 96–7, 105, 106, 109–10, 202, 235, 240, 256, 262, 272, 278; views on punitive expeditions, 36–9, 52; views on railways, 65, 276ff., 341

411

Index

colonialism, 108, 120, 123, 269, 348
colour bar, 195-7
Companies Ordinance of Southern Nigeria, 139
Conakry, 277
Congo, 322
constitutional developments, 123-4, 344
Coode, Son, and Matthews, 251-2
Copland-Crawford, W. E. B., 40-1
cotton, 100, 105, 216, 243, 247, 249, 260ff., 266, 272-3, 279, 297, 309, 345, 348
court system, 148ff.
Cowan, A. A., 300
cowries, 14-15, 267, 269, 270
Cox, H. B., 39, 153-4
Creek Town, 5, 11
Crewe, Lord, 118, 233, 301
Crewe-Read, F. O. S., 54, 321-3
Crocodile JuJu, 165
Cross River, 14, 15, 37, 238, 276, 293, 335, 241
Crown Agents, 93, 278
Crown Colony system, 95ff., 106
crowns, wearing of, 208-9
cultural pluralism, 222ff., 245, 306, 340
currency, 37, 267ff., 303
customs duties, 266, 271, 273, 282, 291-2
Customs Union, 234-5

Dada, Bale of Ibadan, 220-1
Dahomey, 3, 273, 277, 293, 297; Railway, 279
Da Roche, C. A., 99
Davidson, Most Rev. R. T., 290-1
Dawson, E., 166
death penalty, 174-5
decolonisation, 123
Degema, 5, 23, 43, 167, 305, 327, 331, 333
Demerara, 106, 112
Denton, G. C., 26, 31, 52, 69, 109
Deportation of Prisoners (Amendment) Ordinance, 213

deportations, 21-2, 25, 27, 46, 49, 109, 149, 206, 211-13, 220, 343
disease, 293, 304, 343, 346
District Commissioners' Courts, 148ff.
District Councils, 172
Divisional Courts, 148ff.
Dogho, 4 (see Numa)
Dosunmu, 3-4, 202ff.
Dosunmu-Oyekan House, 145, 203ff.
Dove, S., 155
Dudgeon, G. C., 249-50
Duke, King, 5, 23
Duke Town, 5, 11, 23
Duncombe, H. F., 211-12
dyarchy, 124, 351
Dyer, W. T., 253, 258

East Africa, 247
Eastern Province, 35, 42, 45, 59, 102, 120, 129, 135, 149, 154-6, 159, 164, 166, 168, 188, 200, 222, 238, 260, 280, 305, 307-8, 312, 319, 328-9, 331, 333
Ebem (Edem) Native Court, 163, 167
Ebute Metta, 304, 305
economic developments, 5-6, 13ff., 185, 188, 242, 246ff., 283, 318, 345ff.
Ede, 218, 275
Edo, 4, 11, 224
education, 129, 288, 303, 306ff., 332, 346
Edun, A., 63, 72, 75, 79, 81-2, 91-2: *see* Samuel, Rev. J. H.
Efiks, 9, 102, 223
Egbado, 3, 25
Egba Financial Advisory Board, 89, 93
Egba Jurisdiction Ordinance, 71, 73, 77, 82, 86-8
Egba Mixed Court, 73-4
Egba Police Force, 92
Egbas, 2-3, 11, 15, 29, 30, 52, 57, 64ff., 86ff., 150, 152, 156, 175, 272, 273, 275
Egba State Council, 82

Index

Egba treaty, 343
Egba United Government (E.U.G.), 29, 66, 71–5, 76, 80, 81–6, 89, 90–1, 156, 175, 197, 263, 272, 343
Egerton, Walter, African policies of, 125–6, 133–5, 141–5, 152ff., 161, 172, 173ff., 184ff., 200–1, 205–6, 208–11, 213, 215ff., 227, 230–1, 235, 287ff., 331ff.; justification for punitive expeditions, 35–6, 54–5, 59–60, 63; legislation, 41, 45ff., 113ff., 120–1, 133–5, 138ff., 159–60, 184ff.; record as Governor, 64ff., 76–7, 86ff., 104–5, 144–5, 198, 248ff., 268, 275ff., 283–6, 311–13, 317ff., 343
Ejirin market, 26
Eket, 43, 44, 223, 267, 306, 331
Ekiti, 65, 68, 79, 213, 218, 224, 228, 230, 231, 261, 302
Ekitiparapo, 218, 224, 229, 274
Ekoi, 163, 223
Ekpe lodge, 7
Ekowe, 294
Ekumeku, 12, 40ff., 56, 64, 155, 165, 321, 339, 340–1
Elder, Dempster and Company Limited, 48, 50, 261–2, 282
Eleko, Prince Eshugbayi, 99, 145, 148–9, 203ff.
Eleme, 161
Elem Kalabari, 5
Eletu, Chief, 118–19
Elgee, C. H., 180–1, 220, 300
Elgin, Lord, 191, 240, 249, 252
emirates, 60, 62–3
English language, 56, 58, 306, 240
Epe, 3, 26, 305, 319
Epe, Elepe of, 209
Epie-Atissas, 162
Episcopal Native Church, 296
Ereko, 304
Erunwon, Ashipa of, 88
Esin, Ekanem, 328: *see* Linette, Jabez
Etche, 165, 223
ethnic boundaries, 161, 222, 245, 339

European attitude to Africans, 2, 5, 17, 40ff., 53, 89, 102, 125, 130–1, 171, 310, 346; commercial interests, 4, 5, 6, 16, 48, 50–1, 64, 71–2, 82, 98, 101–2, 130–1, 217, 256, 267, 271, 273, 275, 279, 291, 313–15, 335; education, 11, 306–9; lawyers, 76–6
Executive Council, 117, 121, 122, 348
exports, 246, 260ff., 281, 310, 345
Eyitoyoh, 328–9: *see* Johnson, Jimmy
Eyo, King, 5, 11
Ezechiel, P. H., 48, 74, 80–1, 85, 86, 172, 274–5, 327
Ezi, 40
Ezimoha, 167
Ezza Patrol, 43
Ezzas, 168, 223

Fabumi, Chief, 218
Faulkner, E., 192
Ferguson, G. E., 192, 195
Fernando Po, 317, 328, 329ff.
Fiddes, G. V., 240
Fiddian, A., 196, 200
fishing, 7, 13–14, 210, 282
Forcados, 43, 251, 276, 281, 305, 329
Foreign Jurisdiction Ordinance, 67, 139–40
Foreign Office, 9, 10, 19ff., 27, 233, 276
forestry, 98–9, 146, 249, 252ff., 277, 309, 313
Forestry Ordinance, 107, 110, 131, 187, 253ff.
Forsythe, C., 192
Fosbery, W., 333
Fox-Bourne, H. R., 51–2, 70, 179
Freetown, 191
French colonies, 277, 279, 293–4, 319
Fulani, 3, 62, 223, 229

Gallway, Lieutenant-Colonel H. L., 53, 55–6
Gambia, 252
Gando, 229: *see* Sokoto-Gwandu

413

Index

Gbadebo I. Alake, 72, 75–6, 80–4, 86–9, 90–3, 186, 275
Geary, W. H., 114
George, C. J., 25, 111, 131, 137, 141, 142, 143
General Board of Health, 304
German Boundary Expedition, 43
German colonies, 293, 319
Germany, 89, 266–7, 319
Gilpin, P. C., 321–2
Girouard, P., 231
Giwa, Sule, 134
Glasier, F. B., 280
gold, 268
Gold Coast, 36, 37, 46, 70, 101, 106, 114, 124, 127, 145, 150, 152, 154, 250, 252, 253, 296
Gold Coast Supreme Court, 150
Goldie, G. T., 52, 233
Gordon, Arthur (later Lord Stanmore), 27
Government Gazette, 139, 171
groundnuts, 260, 265, 279

Halliday, J., 166–7
Hamburg, 289
harbours, 251–2, 280ff., 303, 341
Harcourt, A. G. B., 220
Harcourt, L., 93, 96–7, 101, 105, 109–10, 139, 198–9, 242–3, 301, 331ff.
Harding, A. J., 129, 135–6, 140, 141, 146, 197
Harper, A. Norton, 333
Harris, Reverend (later Sir), H. J., 329–30
Hausa, 14, 60
Hausa Force, 33–4, 115
Hausa Lands Ordinance, 114
Hausa Lines, 113–15
Henshaw, R., 193
Henshaw Town, 5
heathens, 10, 231–3, 234, 273
Hewett, E., 20, 22, 27
hides and skins, 265
Hill, C., 233
Hives, F., 163, 200
Hogg, Captain Ian, 40

Holt, John, 49–50, 97–9, 101, 119, 144, 184–5, 187–8, 191, 199, 236, 256–7, 263–4, 271, 282ff., 291ff., 297ff., 322, 347
Hopkins, A. G., 269
Hopwood, F. J. S., 301
House of Commons, 48, 119, 120, 178, 240, 242, 262, 290–1, 322
House system, 6–9, 325ff., 344
Hughes, W., 192
human sacrifice, 7, 12, 31, 52, 58, 149, 346–7
Humbert, Father, 40
Hutton, J. A., 263

Ibadan, 2, 24, 30–1, 64–5, 66, 68–9, 70–1, 77–8, 80, 89, 93, 98, 150, 170, 173, 175–6, 180–2, 197, 213, 214, 217, 218–20, 221, 261, 263, 269–72, 273, 277, 279, 281, 300, 305, 341
Ibadan, Bale of, 180, 214, 220, 273, 343
Ibadan, Bashorun of, 175, 217, 219–20
Ibadan Native Council, 170, 180–2, 220
Ibadan Native Court, 181
Ibanichuka, King, 22, 23–4, 25
Ibibio-Efik, 5, 7, 8, 11, 22, 24, 25, 163
Ibibios, 223
Ibos, 10, 12, 15, 39–40, 42, 54, 102, 163, 222, 340–1
Ibun, 36
Ibusa, 12, 305
Idah, 14, 43, 224, 227–8, 258
Idah, Attah of, 227–8
Idanre, 68
Iddo, 87, 279, 280–1, 305
Idimo-boro, 42
Idimugi-Unu, 42
Idoma, 60, 224
Idumaje-Ugboko, 40
Ife, 14, 28, 31, 71, 77–8, 175
Ife, Oni of, 78, 209, 210, 216
Ifon, 43

Igala, 224
Igbessa, 31
Igbodo Native Court, 165
Igbotu, 328–9
Ijaiye, 2
Ijebu, 2, 14, 15, 29–30, 64, 176
Ijebu-Ode, 25, 29, 71, 77–8, 175, 211, 319
Ijebu-Ode, Awajale of, 176–7
Ijebu-Ode Native Council, 176
Ijebu-Remo, 31, 211–12, 342
Ijemo disturbance, 79–80, 83, 91, 94, 137
Ijos, 8, 9, 14, 163, 223, 225
Ika, 162, 223
Ikija, 92
Ikirun, 275, 277, 280, 192, 293
Ikom (Okuni), 43, 44, 320
Ikorodu, 2
Ikot-Ekpene, 43, 44
Ikwes, 10, 37
Ilaro, 3
Ilawo, Oluwo of, 82, 175
Ilbert, C.P., 19
Ilesha, 65, 68, 79, 131, 174, 177, 178, 218, 274–5, 277
Ilesha Native Council, 177, 178, 211
Ilesha, Owa of, 174, 177, 211, 218, 342
Ilesha Provincial Council, 177
Illa, 79
Ilorin, 3, 170, 218, 223–4, 227–30, 231, 265, 290, 345
Imperial Institute, 249, 257
Imuku, 319
India, 117, 118, 128–9, 160, 200
indirect administration, 127, 202ff., 270, 317
infanticide, 149, 346
Inokun, 37
interpreters, 108–9
Ipetu, 211
Iporo, 87
Iporo, Base of, 88
Irefin, Bale of Ibadan, 221
Irish Coercion Acts, 46, 106
Iseri, 319
Iseyin-Okeiho disturbance, 57

Ishan (Ubiaja), 43, 219, 223, 265, 333
Isheri, 83
Isiokpo, 43
Islam, 62, 204, 301
Isoko, 165
Issele-Uku, 12, 42
Itoku, 87–8
Itori disturbances, 83, 86, 91, 186
Itsekiri, 4, 9, 10, 11, 15, 21, 23, 223, 314, 334
Itu, 43, 166, 193
ivory, 14
Iwo, 218, 220, 275, 277
Iyedi, 162

Jackson, J., 163–4
JaJa, later King of Opobo, 4–5, 8, 17, 21–2, 25, 57
James, F. S., 93, 109, 174, 188–9, 199, 201, 320, 322, 333
Jebba, 230, 279, 280, 290
Jenkyns, H., 18–19, 25
jihadists, 3, 62, 223, 250
'Joe of Lagos', 328–9
Johnson, Dr. Obadiah, 111–12, 130, 131, 134, 135–7, 140, 142, 143, 144–6, 230, 263, 314
Johnson, Rev. James, 25, 26, 99, 137, 138, 194–5, 273, 295–6, 300
Johnson, Jimmy, 329: see Eyitoyoh
Johnson, Rev. Samuel, 126
Johnson, W. H., 250
Johnston, A., 117
Johnston, Harry H., 20, 22, 57, 199–200
Jones, Alfred L., 51, 184
Jones, J. E. A., 193
Judicial Department, 160
jujus, 35, 58, 109, 160, 163, 165, 167, 305, 341

Kabba, 224, 227
Kaduna, 349
Kalabari, 5, 22, 23, 223
Kano, 14, 60, 236–7, 265, 280, 290, 313
Katsina, 60

Index

Kelly, Chief Justice H. G., 151, 152, 153
Kemta disturbance, 83–6, 91, 186
Kennaway, J., 291
Kent, H. B., 319
Kew Gardens, 255, 257, 258
Kiji-Mesi battlefield, 31
King, J., M.P., 120, 329, 331
King's College, 307
Kingsley, Mary, 97
Koko, King, 22
Kongi, 219–20
Konka freemasonry, 22
Koranic Schools, 308–9
Kosoko, 3
Kuku, 211
Kukuruku, 223–4
Kwa Ibo, 43, 223
Kwale, 41, 168, 223

Laborde, A. L. C., 162
labour, forced, 6, 46, 55, 79, 105, 109, 167, 168, 214, 276, 316ff., 333, 335, 338
Ladies League, 304
Lagos (town), 2, 3, 15, 25–8, 46, 49, 51, 67, 80–1, 84, 87, 93, 100, 102, 104, 110, 111–12, 121, 154, 156, 173, 179, 209, 233, 238ff., 242, 248, 251ff., 262, 265, 270ff., 303, 305, 307, 309, 329, 331, 349
Lagos Anti-Slavery Society, 99; Auxiliary A.P.S., 99–100, 179, 314
Lagos Battalion WAFF, 34, 37
Lagos Chamber of Commerce, 117, 141, 272
Lagos Colony and Protectorate, 26, 27, 31–2, 33, 52, 64ff., 103, 107, 123ff., 148, 170–1, 174, 185, 192–3, 197, 202ff., 224–5, 236, 270, 280
Lagos Constabulary, 33, 115
Lagos Government, 25, 82, 84, 150
Lagos harbour, 280ff., 348
Lagos Institute, 63, 295
Lagos Native Advisory Board, 49
Lagos Railway, 64–6, 71, 77, 82, 89, 230, 235–6, 238, 240, 265, 276ff., 290ff., 341
Lagos Standard, 170, 173, 177, 191–2
Lagos Supreme Court, 71–2, 74–5, 115, 150ff., 175, 310–1
Lagos Times, 191
land policy, 114, 132, 149, 155, 206, 288, 309ff., 347
Lander brothers, 16
Lands Registry Proclamations, 313
language problems, 103, 108–9, 118, 162, 184, 340
law courts, 148ff.
legal system, 74ff., 148ff.
Legislative Council, 25–6, 28, 55, 64, 67, 69, 70, 73, 86, 90, 95, 101, 102, 111, 112, 115, 118, 121, 171, 204, 210, 215, 243, 254, 340, 348, 351
Lennox-Boyd, A. (later Lord Boyd), 21
libel, 111ff.
Liberal Party, 144, 290, 328
Linette, Jabez, 328–9: *see* Esin, Ekanem
Liverpool, 48, 49, 101, 189, 297, 300
Liverpool Chamber of Commerce, 48, 100, 103, 139, 258, 261, 270, 272, 299
Liverpool Peace Society, 51
liquor traffic controversy, 105, 109, 132, 286, 288, 289ff., 318, 347
Lokoja, 145, 227
London, 82, 93, 94
London Chamber of Commerce, 103, 184
Loro, Chief of Ilesha, 178–9
Loynes, J. B., 269
Lugard, Sir Frederick (later Lord), African policy of, 52, 62, 63, 70–1, 78, 79–80, 90, 91, 94, 95–6, 135, 173–4, 176, 181–3, 184ff., 201, 227ff., 233, 242–4, 278, 336–7; officer with WAFF, 37; opinions on, 51, 236, 242–3
Lugard, Lady, 278
Lumpkin, C. J., 196, 199

Index

Lyttelton, A., 106–7, 179, 247

Macaulay, Herbert, 113–17, 126, 127, 143, 179, 206, 314–15
MacDonald, Claude, 9, 19ff., 32, 151, 323
MacGregor, Sir William, African policy of, 26ff., 63, 64ff., 86, 95, 98, 100, 103, 106–7, 110–11, 120–1, 125, 131, 133, 170ff., 198, 203ff., 210–11, 227ff., 248ff., 261, 270–5, 275ff., 287ff., 295, 303ff., 311, 317ff., 324, 343; opinions on, 49, 51, 98, 171, 275; personality of, 26, 27, 109, 198, 293, 295, 303
MacGregor Canal, 114, 304
Magbemi, Chief, 329
mahogany, 265
maize, 260, 265, 345
malaria, 198, 293, 304
Malaysia, 248, 260
Manchester Chamber of Commerce, 100–1, 102, 103, 171, 258, 261, 270, 272
Manilla Pepple House, 4–5
manillas, 267–8
Manson, P., 198
Maritime Provinces, 234ff.
Marlborough, Duke of, 247
Master and Servant Proclamations, 317, 324–5, 332
Matheson, Angus, 138
McCallum, Herny E., 26, 32, 66, 170, 185, 233ff.
McLeod, N. C., 251, 260, 265
Mechanical Transport Committee, 249
Medical Department, 304ff.
Mediterranean Sea, 14
Meko, 79, 261
Menendez, M. R., 151, 161
Mercer, W. H., 63
Meri, Chief, 321
military operations, 33ff., 49, 105, 232, 320, 348
Miller Brothers and Company Limited, 260, 300
Mills, J. H., 193

minerals, 243, 257, 311ff.
mining, 311ff., 347
Mining Ordinance, 312
Minna, 279–80, 290
missionaries, 4, 5, 6, 7, 11, 16ff., 40–2, 56, 58, 101, 110, 166, 191, 212, 218, 273, 297, 301, 305ff., 328, 342, 346
Moloney, Alfred, 125, 150, 203
Montanaro, Lieutenant-Colonel A. F., 34, 37
Moor, Sir Ralph, African policy of, 9–11, 20ff., 32, 34, 53, 63, 70, 95–6, 102–4, 110, 121, 135, 151–2, 156, 157, 160–1, 164, 172–3, 184ff., 198, 225, 227–8, 233ff., 248ff., 261, 275ff., 291, 294, 303, 317–18, 323–8, 341, 345; Aro expedition, 10–11, 37ff., 52ff., 164; opinions on, 49–50, 51, 52, 102; personality of, 27–8, 109, 184, 198, 253; retirement, 35
Moorhouse, Lieutenant-Colonel H. C., 34–5, 43–4, 134, 155, 211, 219
Moor's Plantation, 263
Morel, E. D., 47–8, 49, 51, 97ff., 187, 191, 221, 236, 283, 298, 314–16, 322
Morley-Minto reforms, 128
Moseley, C. H., 81, 109, 145, 176, 211, 216–17, 220
Mozambique, 250
municipal government, 116
Mushin, 26
Muslims, 62, 143–4, 170, 176, 204, 208, 211, 213, 308

Nana, 4, 10, 21–3, 25, 219, 225
Nathan, M., 70
Native Advisory Board, 170, 173
Native Councils, 20, 22, 24, 39, 47, 69–70, 102, 107, 109, 110, 131, 132, 149, 157ff., 173–4, 175, 176, 182, 187, 220, 351
Native Courts, 40, 79, 87–8, 132, 149, 157ff., 185, 317, 337, 351,
Native House Rule Proclamation,

417

Index

39, 159, 237, 317, 325ff.; amendment, 336
Native Lands Acquisition Proclamation, 313
Native Races and Liquor Traffic United Committee (N.R.L.T.U.C.), 97, 104, 290ff.
Native Trading Firms, 337
Nembe, 22, 43, 225
Nembe-Brass people, 22
Nembe-Ijos, 12
Newbury, C. W., 176
Newspaper Ordinance, 106, 110ff., 120, 129, 131, 187
newspapers, 28, 55, 110ff., 242, 340
Ngwa Ibos, 163–4
nickel, 268–9
Nicoll, Chief Justice W., 72, 74, 76, 112, 152–3
Niger Coast Protectorate, 10, 17, 19, 20–1, 23, 192, 218, 233, 252, 323; constabulary, 34; court messengers, 34: *see* Oil Rivers Protectorate
Niger Committee, 233ff., 243
Niger-Cross River Expedition, 44
Niger River, 14, 16, 43–4, 65, 224, 227, 285, 293; Delta, 5, 7, 10, 14, 15, 22, 25, 185, 269, 275, 335; Delta States, 7–8, 13
Nigerian Constitutional Conference, 21, 24
Nigerian Executive Council, 127
Nigerian Legislative Council, 164
Nigerian Railway, 240
Nigerian state, evolution of, 1, 148, 185, 238, 339, 348
Nigerian Times, 328
Nkarhia, 306
N'Kissi, 261
North Africa, 14
Northern Hinterland Expedition, 44
Northern Nigeria, 3, 37, 60, 62, 70, 142, 145, 150, 164, 186–7, 224, 227, 230ff., 240, 243, 253, 271ff., 281–3, 289, 291, 293, 296, 313, 349ff.

Numa, Chief Omadoghoghone, 4: *see* Dogho
Nupe, 14
Nzekwe, Chief, 42
Nzekwe-Okonjor dispute, 155

Oban, 306
Obasa, O., 116, 314
Obaseki, Chief, 23, 219
Obayagbon, Chief, 219
Obegu massacre, 38–9
Obinoba, Chief, 321
Obubra, 43, 44, 306
Obubra Hill, 161
Obudu, 44, 320
Ockiya, King, 23
Odo, Oba, 178
Odok, Sampson, 328–9: *see* Linette, Jabez
Oduntan, 203–4
Ogan, 321
Ogbeyan, 294
Ogbolomabiri, 12, 23
Ogbomosho, 176, 218, 261, 275, 277
Ogbonis, 77, 82, 84, 87, 175, 229, 341
Ogoja, 44
Ogoni, 43, 165, 223
Oguara, King, 23
Ogun River, 14, 83
Oguta, 45–6
Ogwa, Chief, 162
Ohumbella, 22
Oil Rivers Protectorate, 4, 8, 9, 15, 17, 19, 20, 24, 26, 27, 31–2, 151, 224, 323–4
Ojora, Chief, 118
Oke-Messi-Ipoli, 218
Okigwi, 44, 45, 165, 167
Oko, Aselegbe of, 87
Oko Jumbo, 4–5
Okonjor, Chief, 42, 155
Okpoto, 231, 232
Okrika, 22, 23, 161, 327, 334
Okumoku, 167
Okuni, 44
Okwoga, 44
Oldham Chamber of Commerce, 261

418

Olivier, S., 231
Oloko Minor Court, 163
Oluwa, White Cap Chief, 206, 311
Oluwole, Bishop I., 99, 213-14, 295, 296, 301, 319-20
Ommanney, M. F., 85, 186
Ondo, 65, 68, 79, 174
Onitori, 83
Onitsha, 25, 42, 302, 305, 306, 309
Onitsha-Olona, 40-1
Onitsha-Uku, 40, 42
Onslow, Lord, 107, 262
Onye-eke, 163
opium trade, 290
Opobo, 5, 8, 43, 57, 161, 267, 305, 306, 327, 331, 333, 334-5
Opobo, King of, 17
oracles, 10, 38, 39, 56, 58, 164, 165, 288, 341
ordeal, trials by, 165, 169, 346
Ordeal, Witchcraft and JuJu Proclamation, 165, 341, 346
Order of Bloodmen, 7
Orlu, 44
Ormsby-Gore, W. G. A. (later Lord Harlech), 201
Oron Expedition, 43
Osborne, Chief Justice A. W., 67, 79, 152-4, 174, 310
Oshogbo, 230, 275, 277, 279
Otonba-Payne, J. A., 192
Otta, 277
Otuchichi, 40
Otun, 228-32, 345
Otun, Disu, 119, 133
Otun, Ore of, 229
Overami, 10, 21-3, 25, 219, 224
Ovonramwen, Oba, 4, 10: *see* Overami
Owerri, 39, 43, 44, 45, 165, 306, 331
Owo, 224, 232
Owu, Molasin of, 87
Oyekan, Prince, 203
Oyo, 1, 25, 30, 65, 68, 71, 77, 78, 131, 170, 173, 175, 176, 181, 206, 212, 213-15, 217, 223, 261, 275, 277, 281, 341, 350

Oyo, Alafin of, 2, 29, 64-5, 78, 81, 175, 181-2, 212, 215ff., 220-1, 343
Oyo Native Council, 170
Oyo, New, 2-3
Oyo-Yoruba, 57

pagans, 10, 231-3, 234, 273
Palmer, F. C., 180
Palmer, H. R., 164
palm produce, 6-7, 10, 13ff., 255, 257, 260ff., 277, 280, 345
Pan-Anglican Congress, 297
Parkes, J. C. E., 192
Partridge, C., 200
Passfield, Lord, 202
Pax Britannica, 47ff., 54, 169, 222
Peace Preservation Ordinance, 45ff., 106
Pearse, S. H., 99, 126
Pennington, A. R. P., 45-7, 68, 78, 92, 135-6, 140, 174
People's Union, 116
Pepple, Prince William Dappa, 164
Perham, Margery, 190
petitions, 132
Pinnock, Rev. S. G., 212-13, 302
Podevin, G. S., 200
police, 33ff., 89, 92, 145, 168, 288, 303, 326, 348
polygamy, 214
Ponlade, 79
Port Harcourt, 267, 341
pottery, 13
Pratt, A., 192
pre-colonial institutions and customs, 12, 19, 30, 41, 48, 52, 56-9, 62, 75, 109, 148-9, 159, 160, 167-8, 171, 199ff., 209ff., 221, 222, 224, 288, 303, 317, 326, 339, 342, 346, 349-50
Presbyterians, 110
Primitive Methodist Mission, 330
Privy Council, 149, 150-1, 206, 310-11, 345
Probyn, L., 109, 237
protectorate treaties, 17ff., 106, 344
Provincial Councils, 172

419

Index

public health, 198, 234–5, 243, 288, 303ff., 346; Public Health Ordinance, 304
Public Lands Acquisition Proclamation, 311
Public Lands Ordinance, 115, 311
Public Works and Roads Department, 249–51, 284, 309, 318
Punch, C., 77, 84
punitive expeditions and patrols, 35ff., 42ff., 50, 51, 106, 109, 120, 155–6, 164, 165, 169, 170, 185, 202, 219, 224, 246, 288, 318ff., 323, 338, 343, 344, 349

Qua Ibo, 308
Quas, 10, 163

racial prejudice, 127, 195–7
railways, 16, 59, 64–6, 71, 89, 105, 127, 142, 143, 150, 234, 239–40, 244, 247–8, 250–1, 265, 274, 276ff., 288, 290, 302, 303, 309, 323, 337, 341–6; Railway Commissioner, 74–6, 84; Railway Department, 117, 143
Rayner, Chief Justice T. C., 310
Reeve-Tucker, W. R., 177
Rhodesia, 296
Risley, J. S., 39
roads, 248, 281, 303, 317ff., 323, 333, 337, 348
Roads and Creeks Proclamation, 276, 317, 318–19, 322–3
Roman Catholic Mission, 301, 308–9
Rosebery, Lord, 17
Ross, R., 198
Ross, W. A., 81, 181–2, 199, 200, 212, 214–15, 217, 221, 343
Rotterdam, 289
Rowden, E. G., 195
Royal Anthropological Institute, 200
Royal Garrison Artillery, 34
Royal Niger Company, 9, 12, 22, 34, 37, 43, 52, 218, 224–5, 227, 233, 252
rubber, 236, 253ff., 265, 313, 345

Sabagreia, 43, 162, 294
Sahara desert, 14
Samuel, Herbert (later Lord), 178
Samuel, Rev. J. H., 63: *see* Edun, A.
Sapara, O., 196, 199
Sapara-Williams, C. A., 59, 90, 99, 111–12, 114, 125–6, 131, 134, 136–8, 140, 141, 142, 143–5, 146, 179, 204–5, 230, 256
Sapele, 9, 43, 161, 305, 327, 333
Satiru, 60
schools, 306ff.
Scramble for Africa, 31–2
secession, 349–50
secret cults, 8, 12, 35, 40ff., 58, 62, 109, 160, 164, 165, 229, 274, 288, 339ff.
Seditious Offences Ordinance, 106, 113ff., 129, 131, 132–3, 139, 210
Seely, J. E. B. (later Lord Mottistone), 114–15, 119, 144, 195, 296, 299, 301
Selborne, Lord Chancellor, 18, 233, 236
Shagamu, 31, 211
Shagamu, Akarigbo, of 186, 209
Shyngle, J. E., 314–15
Sierra Leone, 38, 154–5, 186, 192, 247, 252, 262
silver, 268–9
Simpson, E. D., 337
Situ, Balogun, 221
slavery, 6–9, 14, 19, 31, 37, 39, 48, 52, 58, 104, 105, 109, 177, 289, 317, 323ff., 335, 344
Slessor, Mary, 166
S.M.A. (Catholic Society of African Missions), 11, 12
smallpox, 283, 304–5, 346
Smith, Chief Justice S., 150
smuggling, 292–3
social welfare, 287ff., 351
Sokoto, 60, 62, 96, 236–7, 302, 313
Sokoto, Sultan of, 62
Sokoto-Gwandu, 3, 350
Soudan, 234
South Africa, 37, 119, 290, 296
South African War, 278

420

Southern Baptists of the United States of America, 11
Southern Nigeria, Protectorate of, 33, 37, 42, 45, 52, 55, 57–8, 60, 62–3, 66, 70, 93–4, 95ff., 101, 102–5, 110, 116ff., 129, 142, 148ff., 164, 172–3, 184ff., 192, 197–8, 200, 215, 218, 222, 224, 227, 230ff., 254ff., 262ff., 275, 281, 282, 289, 306ff., 313, 317ff., 323ff., 336, 339, 344ff.
Southern Nigeria Regiment WAFF, 34, 54
Spanish colonies, 330
Spanish dollars, 15
Speed, Chief Justice E. A., 92–3, 112–13, 117, 152, 283, 310
spirits, 266, 272, 291, 347
Sprotson, S. W., 200
Statute Laws Revision Ordinance, 175
steamship companies, 16
Stoker, Puisne Judge W. H., 334
stone, 280
Strachey, C., 38, 76, 85, 88–9, 101, 144, 195–6, 199, 200, 216, 293

Talbot, P. A., 200
taxation, 116, 131, 202, 205, 290ff., 302, 310, 318, 346
Tchaourou, 279
temperance societies, 294ff., 347
textiles, 14
Third Party, 97, 103, 314
Thomas, J. J., 137
Thomas, N., 200–1
Thompson, H. N., 253, 258
Thorburn, J. J., 109, 137, 179
Tijani, Amodu, 206, 311
timber, 277
Tiv, 60, 223, 231, 232, 349
tolls, 98, 100, 107, 109, 110, 132, 171, 187, 208, 216–17, 270ff.
Tomlinson, G. J. F., 302
Topo, 309
Torti, Okori, 38
Trade Credit Proclamation, 159
transportation, 6, 16, 103, 108, 188, 234, 239, 243, 248ff., 275ff., 332, 337, 340, 350
Transvaal Chamber of Mines, 318
treaty rights, 69ff., 173, 184
Trenchard, Brevet-Major H. M. (later Lord), 35, 53–4, 232
Tugwell, Bishop H., 295–8, 331
Turton, C. D., 192

Udi, 44
Uganda, 278, 296
Ugbodo, 42
Ugwashi-Uku, 40, 42
United Free Church of Scotland mission, 55, 165, 308
United Native African Church, 308
United Presbyterians of Scotland, 11, 166
United States of America, 261
Unlawful Societies Proclamation, 41, 106, 341, 346
Unsettled Districts Ordinance, 45ff
Urhobo, 43, 261
Uwet, 306
Uyo, 43, 44, 331
Uzairue, 162
Uzere, 165

vaccination, 305, 346
Vagrant Ordinance, 335ff.

Warrant Chiefs, 46, 132, 149
Warri, 9, 43, 168, 238, 260, 305, 327, 328, 329, 333
Warri Native Council, 328
Wason, J. C., 322
water rate scheme, 113, 115–16, 133, 205, 210, 304
Waverley, Lord, 68–9
weaving, 13
Welsh, T., 292, 300
Wesleyans, 11, 144–5, 301, 308
West Africa, 48, 50, 51, 52, 124, 126, 289, 314
West Africa, 50
West African Frontier Force (WAFF), 33–4

Index

West African Medical Service, 196
West African Trade Association, 103, 189
Western Province, 113, 120, 140, 174, 176, 188, 200, 222, 238, 260, 280, 305, 307–8, 312, 319
West Indies, 105, 106, 112
White Cap Chiefs, 25, 116, 131, 132, 145–6, 202ff, 310, 311
Wight, M., 122–4, 127
Williams, G. A., 99
Willoughby, A. C., 192
Willoughby, I. H., 192
Winkfield, J., 151, 220
witchcraft 58, 109, 149, 165, 169, 346

Women's Riots, 42, 164, 201
World War I, 116, 122
World War II, 124

Yaba, 306
Yellow Isaiah, 167
Yorubas, 1–3, 15, 25ff., 31, 59, 63, 65ff., 110, 118, 133, 135, 150, 156, 170ff., 185, 194, 209, 218–219, 222ff., 228, 230, 234, 254, 261, 265, 269, 273, 305, 313ff.
Young, P. V., 86–9, 90

Zaria, 60, 280